FINE FRENCH
DESSERTS
Essential Recipes and Techniques

Key to symbols & handy page references

Level of difficulty	★ to ★ ★ ★
See video sequence	
See recipes	
See techniques	
Useful information and general advice	>> p. 466
Glossary	>> p. 469
Index	>> p. 473

Translated from the French by Carmella Moreau
Design: Alice Leroy
Copyediting: Penelope Isaac
Typesetting: Thierry Renard and Gravemaker+Scott
Proofreading: Nicole Foster
QR codes: BookBeo
Color Separation: IGS, L'Isle d'Espagnac, France
Printed in China by Toppan Leefung

Originally published in French as *Encyclopédie des desserts*
© Flammarion, S.A., Paris, 2012

English-language edition
© Flammarion, S.A., Paris, 2013

editions.flammarion.com

13 14 15   3 2 1

ISBN: 978-2-08-020157-7

Dépôt légal: 10/2013

Vincent Boué • Hubert Delorme • Didier Stéphan
Photographs by Clay McLachlan

FINE FRENCH
DESSERTS
Essential Recipes and Techniques

Flammarion

How to use this book

Techniques (pp. 12–219)

All the basic techniques, with specialist step-by-step explanations

Easily visible
page numbering

Step-by-step photographs
referring to the text

Level of difficulty

76

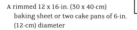

Genoese Sponge ⋆

This simple, light sponge is a fundamental in French pastry making. Spread it thinly to use as a base for a layered dessert or bake it as a cake, slice it into layers, and fill it with a cream or ganache of your choice.

Ingredients (Makes 1 lb. (450 g)
of sponge; each sponge serves 4)
4 eggs
⅔ cup (4 oz./125 g) sugar
1 cup (4 oz./125 g) flour

A rimmed 12 x 16-in. (30 x 40-cm)
baking sheet or two cake pans of 6-in.
(12-cm) diameter

http://flamm.fr/ffd06

Preheat the oven to 350°F (180°C). Butter and flour the cake pan or line the baking sheet with parchment paper. Place the eggs and sugar in a round-bottom mixing bowl and set it over a bain-marie heated to 140°F (60°C) **(1)**. Whip until the mixture reaches the ribbon stage. Sift the flour and carefully fold in half of it with a flexible spatula **(2)**. When it is incorporated, fold in the remaining half, taking care not to deflate the mixture. Do not overmix. Pour onto the baking sheet to a thickness of no more than ¼ inch (6-7 mm), or into the cake pans, and even the mixture with a spatula or palette knife.
Bake for 15 minutes (baking sheet) to 20 minutes (for cake). The sponge should stay moist and should not color. Slide it onto a rack and let cool.

● **Chef's note**
To make a chocolate Genoese sponge, replace 2 ½ tablespoons (25 g) of the flour with 3 ½ tablespoons (25 g) unsweetened cocoa powder, sifted.

❗ **Recipe ideas**
Black Forest Cake >> p. 346
Strawberry and Mousseline Cream Layer Cake (*Fraisier*) >> p. 349
Mocha Cake >> p. 353
Baked Alaska >> p. 450

Access to
the video sequence

Scan the QR codes with the BookBeo app, free for iPhone and Android. When you have read the explanation, watch the sequence and/or download it to view as convenient. Use Wi-Fi for faster viewing and downloads.

You can also:
• use another QR code reader compatible with your smartphone;
• copy the URL next to the codes to browse on your PC/Mac or smartphone.

Chef's notes

Cross-references to the recipes that use this technique

Recipes (pp. 250–465)

One hundred basic recipes, with seven additional recipes
created and tested by renowned pastry chefs

Ingredients

Level of difficulty

Easily visible
page numbering

Ingredients
Garnish
Fresh fruit
7 oz. (200 g) assorted red berries

Dough (can be prepared a day ahead)
½ cup (3 oz./80 g) raisins
3 tablespoons (50 ml) rum
1 cake (0.6 oz./20 g) fresh yeast
1¼ cups (300 ml) water, divided
4 cups (1 lb./500 g) flour
2 teaspoons (10 g) salt
2 ½ teaspoons (10 g) sugar
4 eggs, room temperature
1 ¾ sticks (7 oz./200 g) butter

Syrup
1 ¼ cups (9 oz./250 g) sugar
2 cups (500 ml) water
Flavoring of your choice (star anise,
citrus zest, cinnamon stick, etc)

Glaze
2 oz. (60 g) light glaze
3 tablespoons (40 ml) water

Chantilly cream
⅔ cup (150 ml) heavy cream
2 ½ tablespoons (⅔ oz./20 g) confectioners' sugar
1 teaspoon vanilla extract or the seeds
of 1 vanilla bean

Techniques
Baba or Savarin Dough >> p. 43
Chantilly Cream >> p. 94
Moistening sponge layers >> p.133

Rum Babas ★ ★

Serves 8
Preparation time: 2 hours
Cooking time: 25 minutes

8 individual baba molds or one 10-inch (25-cm) baba mold

A day, or at least 2 hours ahead. prepare the dough.
Rinse the raisins under cold water and soak them in the rum.
Dilute the yeast in 3 tablespoons (50 ml) tepid water. Sift the flour and make a well in the center. Sprinkle the salt at the outer edge of the flour so that it does not come into direct contact with the yeast. Add the sugar. Lightly beat the eggs. Pour the diluted yeast and eggs into the well. Mix with a spatula or by hand. Work the dough energetically until it becomes elastic, gradually incorporating the remaining water. You can also use a stand mixer fitted with a dough hook, starting at low speed and then increasing to medium, about 25 minutes altogether.
Stop kneading when the dough no longer sticks to your fingers or the sides of the bowl. It should now be smooth, shiny, and very elastic. Melt the butter until just warm and mix it into the dough. Knead energetically (or at medium to fast speed, 8-10 minutes), again until the butter is thoroughly combined in the dough. Cover with plastic wrap and let rise for 30 to 40 minutes at 77°to 83°F (25°to 30°C), until doubled in volume.
Flatten the dough to expel any air bubbles (punching down).
Drain the raisins and lightly knead them into the dough until just evenly distributed. Butter the molds and half-fill them with the dough, either by hand or with a piping bag. Let rise again until the dough reaches the top of the molds. Preheat the oven to 400°F (200°C) for individual babas and 350°F (180°C) for a large one. (The larger size needs to be baked more slowly.) Bake the individual babas for about 25 minutes, and the large size for up to 40 minutes, until a cake tester comes out dry.
Immediately turn them out onto a cooling rack so that no condensation forms on the crust. Let cool completely.

Make the syrup.
Combine all the ingredients and bring to a boil. Simmer for 2 to 3 minutes, remove from the heat, and let infuse until a thermometer registers about 105°F (40°C). Place the babas in the syrup and with a ladle, drench them with it. To test that they are sufficiently soaked, prick with a long needle, which should slide in without any resistance at all. Set them on a rack to drain and transfer to a plate. Heat the glaze with the water and brush the babas.

Prepare the Chantilly cream.
Whip the cream and confectioners' sugar until it forms firm peaks. Stir in the vanilla. Spoon the whipped cream into a piping bag fitted with a star tip and pipe the cream into the center of the babas. Garnish with the fruit.

● **Chef's note**
You can drench your babas with rum or any other alcoholic beverage when they have been soaked in syrup

361

Cross-references to
the techniques used
in this recipe

Contents

Recipes

France's finest pastry chefs introduce the chapters while revealing the secrets of one of their creations.

Appendixes

Foreword

Joël Bellouet

Meilleur Ouvrier de France (Best Craftsman of France)
Member of the French Academy of Chocolate and Confectionery

I am immensely pleased to have been asked to write the foreword for an encyclopedic work on desserts. For many years I have taught French pastry recipes all over the world and know how highly French pastry making is esteemed. The French gastronomic meal has been inscribed on UNESCO's Representative List of the Intangible Cultural Heritage of Humanity; pastry making is of course an integral part.

This book contains an impressive number of recipes, and the outstanding work done by the authors is sure to satisfy readers with its precision and explanatory detail. In our new century, it is stunning to see how pastries, chocolates, plated desserts, iced desserts, and candies are gaining in popularity, not to mention the classics, as well as all the basic recipes and techniques indispensable for new creations.

It is a great pleasure to make desserts for the joy of both children and adults, and a privilege to enhance a good meal or celebrate a special event with a delicious homemade sweet creation. What satisfaction when everyone finds it not only wonderful to look at, but also delicious. The aromas of baking and the smells of the ingredients foreshadow the tastes to come when we eat. Pastries for breakfast, to end a meal, at teatime: you'll find all the recipes for the appropriate time of day. A delicious pastry will transform any time of day into a memorable moment.

The transmission of one's expertise and passion to ensure that skills are passed on to the next generation is an important responsibility.

The more I turn the pages and read the delectable recipes, the more I believe that this work is a veritable encyclopedia of pâtisserie. I am certain that true gourmets will put this significant book to good use.

Foreword

Christophe Michalak

Pastry chef, World Pastry Cup Champion, 2005

As a child, I wanted to be a superhero, and when I was a teenager, I dreamed of becoming a rock star. I didn't manage either; instead I became a pastry chef. As soon as I entered the unique world of pastry making, I was enthralled. My passion knew no limits. I had to put up with the teasing of my high school friends, who simply couldn't understand why I would want to land up in a store, spending every Sunday filling choux puffs with whipped cream. Today I can tell them that it was worth every effort, because I am a happy man, having learned the importance of meticulousness, determination, and, most importantly, the love of a job well done.

I would like to give special thanks to the people who have made such significant contributions to the craft I practice: Gaston Lenôtre, Pierre Hermé, Philippe Conticini, and so many others. Every day it gives me great pleasure to discover young talents, chefs who use our recipes and advice to take the craft even further and make the light of French pâtisserie shine even more brightly. Yes, gentlemen, today pastry chefs are recognized for what they are worth, even though we had to wait until the turn of the twenty-first century for the media to acknowledge the profession.

I am proud to write a foreword for this magnificent book and to say loud and clear that the world envies and copies the excellence of French pastry.

It is hard to say that any particular cuisine is better than another, whether we are talking about French, Middle Eastern, Italian, or Chinese cuisine, all of which are remarkable. But, in my opinion, there is only one country whose pastry making beats that of the rest of the world, and we are lucky to have it here in France. Paris-Brest, Traou Mad, macarons, choux puffs, tarte Tatin, floating islands, Kouign Amman, and mille-feuille, to mention just a few—what other country can boast of so many regional specialties? Desserts have never been as good in France as they are today, and exceptional artisans are producing creations of exponentially improving quality. This is in large part due to the Internet, where foodie blogs have brought pâtisserie within the reach of everyone. And this is just the beginning.

I am certain that this work will help to spread French pastry making worldwide. For a long time, we jealously kept our techniques to ourselves, like state secrets. Fortunately, many artisans and chefs have decided to reveal their best recipes, and thanks to this trend, our profession has widened and the level is continually improving.

I wish you much enjoyment as you discover the treasures on these pages, the intricacies of the crème de la crème of professions: pâtisserie.

Techniques

Doughs and batters

Flour

Flour, when it is not preceded by a qualifier, refers to wheat flour. Milling wheat involves successive grinding processes, with each stage grinding the product of the previous one. These long, complicated procedures are carried out by sophisticated machines—crushers, sifters, and purifiers—to make the refined white flour we use in our cakes and breads. It is white because of the meticulous way in which the outer layers of the wheat kernel are removed. These outer layers give us bran, which makes a slightly gray flour that cannot be used to make bread but is high in fiber.

Good quality flours contain, on average, 12 percent proteins, the most important of which is the gluten, a veritable water guzzler. In the USA, the different types of flour contain varying amounts of gluten: 6–7 percent in cake flour, 7.5–9.5 percent in pastry flour, 9.5–11.5 percent in all-purpose flour, 11.5–13.5 percent in bread flour; high-gluten flour has at least 13.5 percent. It's the gluten that gives elasticity to your doughs, which is why intensive kneading makes them as elastic as chewing gum. That's exactly what you want your brioche dough to be like—in fact, it's essential. However, if your shortcrust pastry has this texture, it means you've kneaded or worked it too much. You need to work these pastries quickly, not to overmix, and to stop when the ingredients are combined. The gluten network, as it is called, traps the carbon dioxide produced by the raising agent (yeast or baking powder), and this is what causes the dough to swell. So if you don't need the strength provided by gluten, you don't need professional-grade flour—it's not necessary for making crêpe batter or a sponge layer, for example. However, if you're making rum babas, bread, or croissants, try to use a flour that has a higher gluten content. Depending on your area, different types of flour are available and you may have to experiment with them. But to simplify matters, generally speaking all-purpose (plain) flour will work for practically all recipes here, and cup conversions have been provided for this type.

You will see that all recipes for tart crusts involve a chilling period. This is to allow the gluten network to relax. It improves the final texture of the pastry and reduces shrinkage. It's an important stage in the baking process, so do allow sufficient time for it. When a dough is placed to chill in the refrigerator, it is always covered completely in plastic wrap so that it doesn't absorb the odors of other foods.

● Chef's note
For a smoother texture, it's advisable to sift your flour, particularly if the recipe calls for baking powder.

● Did you know?
Flour can be milled from a large variety of grains. Chestnut and corn flour both give excellent baking results.

Margarine and butter

It may come as a surprise to learn that margarine was invented by a Frenchman, Hyppolite Mège-Mouriès, a research scientist who entered a competition in 1867 to find a substitute for butter for the poor. Margarine takes its name from the Greek word *margaron*, which means "pearl." The naturally white compound was called margaric acid because of the pearly sheen of its crystals. Mège-Mouriès originally used beef fat, but vegetable oils soon replaced it. Margarine was introduced into the USA in 1873, and was the object of laws to restrict its consumption. In fact, the state of New York banned it outright in 1884, but the law was repealed by the courts soon after.

The taste of margarine does not compare to that of butter, but it does have advantages for the baker, being more affordable and longer lasting. When hydrogenated, the texture of oil can be made firmer. Margarine is an emulsion and, like butter, contains 82 percent fat and 16 percent water, with the remaining 2 percent including flavorings, salt, preservatives, and coloring. Professionals use special

margarines for creamy fillings and others to incorporate into their doughs and puff pastries. With growing health concerns about the consumption of trans fats, it is advisable to check labels carefully when selecting margarine.

For home consumption, however, it is just as easy to use butter. If using butter for pastries and doughs (puff pastry and brioche dough, for example), select butter with the highest possible butterfat content, so that it will be more malleable and easier to incorporate into the mix.

France is the largest butter producer in Europe, and has the highest per capita consumption worldwide. Normandy and Brittany, two particularly fertile regions renowned for their dairy farming, produce particularly fine butter, as does the Poitou-Charentes region. This is reflected in the vast range of buttery regional cakes, some of which you will discover in this chapter.

Yeast

Yeast is a living substance that allows dough to rise. This is because of the carbon dioxide emitted when the cells of the microscopic organisms that make up yeast "breathe." In each gram of yeast, there are about twelve billion such organisms, living creatures that, like all others, breathe, drink, eat, eliminate, reproduce, and then die. Their favorite form of nourishment is sugar, and this is why their Latin name alludes to sucrose: *saccharomyces cerevisiae*. They create what we call "holes" in bread, the holes being air pockets containing the CO_2 emitted during fermentation. For a brioche, for example, a particularly elastic dough should be produced after the kneading process. It is the gluten that creates the smooth texture, the shine, and softness, retaining the gas emitted when the organisms breathe.

This is actually an interrupted alcoholic fermentation. The dough rises when it has been well kneaded and is left in a warm, humid environment. When risen, it is very fragile and should be carefully handled when transferred to the oven for baking.

Yeast naturally consumes sugar and breaks down starches during its life cycle. It gives off carbon dioxide but can survive without

oxygen. The process is thus both aerobic and anaerobic. Each cell divides into two every three hours, thereby increasing very rapidly. The fermentation process is a delicate one as it involves living organisms. Professionals have to work meticulously if they want quality products on a daily basis.

● **Chef's notes**
Fresh, active dry, and instant yeast are all available in the stores. We strongly recommend fresh (compressed) yeast: it is more forgiving and the final result is more satisfactory.

Baking powder

Baking powder makes cakes rise, ensuring they are lighter to eat. It is composed of bicarbonate of sodium and tartaric or citric acid. Unlike fresh yeast, which leads to a highly complex alcoholic fermentation, baking powder induces a chemical reaction that, when all is said and done, is relatively simple. When it comes into contact with moisture, the powder becomes effervescent and emits carbon dioxide. You can easily test this: put a few drops of water into a spoonful of baking powder and see what happens. The reaction is even more pronounced if the temperature is high.

If your recipe calls for baking powder, always sift it with the flour so that it is evenly distributed. Baking powder also contains starch, which protects its active agents, but it nevertheless should be kept in an airtight container. It is used in doughs and batters that contain eggs, which work in conjunction with this raising agent to ensure rising. The heat of the oven and the water in the dough (from the flour, butter, and eggs) react with the bicarbonate, which in turn produces carbon dioxide. The air bubbles rise through the dough. The eggs, also because of the heat, coagulate and gradually enclose the air bubbles, thereby entrapping them. This chemical reaction takes place only once, during the first minutes of baking. Take a look through your oven window—just don't open the door—and see chemistry at work. During the second stage, when the initial reaction is finished, the other ingredients continue to bake, ensuring that your cake remains as high as possible.

Note that French baking recipes generally do not call for baking soda.

● **Chef's note**
One of the methods used to manufacture soap involves soda with fatty products (animal or vegetable). If you use too much baking powder, it can cause a reaction known as saponification (the process of making soap), and this feels very unpleasant in the mouth. A normal dose of baking powder is 1 teaspoon per cup of flour (5 g for 125 g flour) or 4 teaspoons of baking powder per pound of flour (20 g for 500 g flour).

Firm doughs

Short pastry is one of the family of crumbly (or friable) pastries. There are two methods to make it, either rubbing in with your hands, or using an electric beater. This recipe is suitable for tarts, tartlets, and cookies, and has been traced back to the 1850s, when it was apparently created in Lisieux, Normandy.

Sweetened Short Pastry (crumbled) ★

Ingredients (makes a tart shell for 4 [9 oz./250 g of pastry])
5 tablespoons (2 ½ oz./65 g) butter, room temperature
1 cup (4 oz./125 g) flour
⅓ cup (2 oz./60 g) sugar (if making cookies)
  or scant ½ cup (60 g) confectioners' sugar
  (if making tart crusts)
½ teaspoon (2 g) salt
1 egg

Dice the butter. Sift the flour onto a work surface or into a mixing bowl. Make a well in the center (1) and place the butter in it. Working with your fingers, quickly crush the butter into the flour until the texture is like sand (2). For an optimal crumbly texture, stop when just combined. Sprinkle in the sugar and salt and combine. Lightly beat the egg with a fork. Incorporate the egg with a pastry scraper and the palm of one hand (3). Stop as soon as the dough is smooth: it should not become elastic. Shape the dough into a thick disk and cover in plastic wrap. Chill for 20 minutes. (If making ahead, store for up to 48 hours in the refrigerator, covered in plastic wrap or in an airtight container.)

Place on a lightly floured surface and roll to the desired shapes. If baking blind, prick with a fork to allow any air to escape. This ensures that the dough won't swell as it bakes. However, if the dough is filled with a moist filling, do not prick it before baking.
Bake according to instructions. Transfer immediately to a cooling rack so that the moisture is not reabsorbed into the crusts, which would make them soggy. Baked tart crusts must be kept in an airtight container until filled.

● Chef's notes
If you are making individual cookies, use granulated sugar. This will result in a nice crunchy texture. If you are going to be lining a tart pan with the dough, it's preferable to use confectioners' sugar.
You can replace one-third of the flour with ground almonds to make a softer, tastier crust.
If you are making baked petits fours, add ¾ teaspoon (3 g) baking powder to the recipe.
And of course, feel free to add any of your favorite flavors: vanilla, other spices, citrus zest, and more, depending on your filling.
Freezing instructions: let cool completely, cover in plastic wrap or store in an airtight container for up to 1 month.

❚ Recipe ideas
Gourmet Breton Traou Mad >> p. 277
Chocolate Tart with Chocolate Mousse >> p. 421
Lemon Meringue Tart >> p. 425
Cream Cheese Tartlets >> p. 426
Seasonal Fruit Tartlets >> p. 429
Tarte Tatin >> p. 433

Firm doughs

Sweetened Short Pastry (creamed) ★

Sweetened short pastry is mainly used for tart and tartlet crusts. It may either be filled before baking or blind baked.

Ingredients (makes a tart shell for 4 [9 oz./250 g of pastry])

5 tablespoons (2 ½ oz./65 g) butter, room temperature
½ cup (2 ½ oz./65 g) confectioners' sugar
1 egg
¼ teaspoon (1 g) salt
1 cup (4 oz./125 g) flour

http://flamm.fr/ffd01

In a mixing bowl, combine the butter with the sugar using your fingers, or a whisk if the butter is very malleable. It will become creamy, which is why we call this process creaming the butter. Whisk in the egg and salt. When combined, incorporate the flour with a flexible spatula or even with your hands. Work until just combined.
Shape into a thick disk, cover in plastic wrap, and chill for 20 minutes.
Roll out on a lightly floured surface according to the recipe. If blind baking, prick with a fork.

● Chef's notes

This method, which involves combining the butter with the sugar, gives the grains of sugar a coating that protects them from moisture. Some of it melts during baking, but the rest creates a nice crunchy, slightly sandy texture when eaten.
Here is an excellent technique for making perfectly shaped tartlet crusts. Fit the dough over upside-down aluminum tartlet pans, trim, and bake according to instructions. (See photograph p. 23.)

Shortbread Cookies

Almond Shortbread

Ingredients (makes twelve 1 ½-in./4-cm cookies)

1 cup (4 oz./125 g) flour
Generous ⅓ cup (1 oz./30 g) ground almonds
½ teaspoon (2 g) salt
5 tablespoons (3 oz./75 g) butter, room temperature
⅓ cup (1 ½ oz./40 g) confectioners' sugar
1 ½ teaspoons (½ sachet/7.5 g) vanilla sugar (or ½ teaspoon vanilla extract)
1 egg yolk

Combine the flour with the almonds and the salt. Dice the butter and cream it with the confectioners' sugar and vanilla sugar. Work in the flour mixture. Incorporate the egg yolk with a pastry scraper and the palm of one hand until just combined. Shape the dough into a thick disk and cover in plastic wrap. Chill for 20 minutes. Place on a lightly floured surface, roll out, and cut into rounds. Bake at 350°F (180°C) for about 10 minutes, until lightly golden. Transfer to a cooling rack.

Breton Shortbread

Ingredients (makes about ten 1 ½-in./4-cm cookies)

1 cup plus 2 tablespoons (5 oz./150 g) flour
2 teaspoons (8 g) baking powder
6 tbsp. (3 oz./90 g) salted butter
⅓ cup (2 ½ oz./75 g) sugar
2 egg yolks
1 large egg for the egg wash

Sift the flour and baking powder together. Dice the butter. Make a well in the center of the flour and place the butter in it. Working with your fingers, quickly crush the butter into the flour until the texture is like sand. For an optimal crumbly texture, stop when just combined. Sprinkle in the sugar and combine. Slightly beat the egg yolks and incorporate with a pastry scraper and the palm of one hand. Stop when just combined. Shape the dough into a thick disk and cover with plastic wrap. Chill for 20 minutes. On a lightly floured surface, roll out the dough to just under ½ inch (1 cm) thick and cut into rounds. Brush with lightly beaten egg. Press the tines of a fork lightly into each cookie, making a crisscross shape. Bake at 350°F (180°C) for about 10 minutes, until slightly risen and lightly golden. Transfer to a cooling rack.

Chocolate Shortbread

Ingredients (makes about twelve 1 ½-in./4-cm cookies)

1 cup (4 oz./125 g) flour
¼ cup (20 g) ground almonds
2 tablespoons (15 g) unsweetened cocoa powder, sifted
5 tablespoons (2 ½ oz./75 g) butter
1 egg yolk
¼ cup (2 oz./50 g) sugar
½ teaspoon (3 g) salt

Combine the flour, ground almonds, and cocoa powder. Follow the instructions for sweetened short pastry (p. 18). Bake at 350°F (180°C) for about 10 minutes, until firm. You can also use this recipe to make tartlet crusts.

Sparkling Shortbread

Ingredients (makes about twelve 1 ½-in. /4-cm cookies)
1 cup (4 oz./125 g) flour
6 tablespoons (3 oz./90 g) butter, softened
⅓ cup (2 oz./50 g) confectioners' sugar
½ teaspoon (3 g) salt
1 tablespoon (1 sachet/15 g) vanilla sugar
  or ½ teaspoon vanilla extract
Granulated or flavored sugar to coat the dough
1 egg, lightly beaten, for the egg wash

Follow the instructions for sweetened short pastry (p. 18), omitting the egg. Alternatively, place all the ingredients (excluding the egg and granulated sugar) in the bowl of a food processor and pulse with the blade knife until just combined into a ball of dough.
On a lightly floured surface, shape the dough into a 1 ¼-inch (3-cm) diameter log. Cover with plastic wrap and chill for 10 minutes. Sprinkle sugar generously on the work surface and roll the log in it until coated. Cut into slices just under ½ inch (1 cm) thick. Brush with the egg and dip the top and bottom into the sugar. Transfer carefully to a silicone baking sheet and bake at 350°F (180°C) for about 10 minutes, until firm but not too colored. Transfer to a cooling rack.

Speculoos Cookies

Ingredients (makes about twelve 2 ¼ x 1 ¼-in./
  6 x 3-cm cookies)
4 tablespoons (2 oz./50 g) salted butter
¼ cup (2 oz./50 g) light brown sugar
1 heaping tablespoon (15 g) sugar
¾ teaspoon (2 g) ground cinnamon
½ teaspoon (2 g) baking powder
¼ teaspoon (1 g) salt
1 teaspoon (5 ml) milk
1 egg yolk
¾ cup plus 2 tablespoons (3 ½ oz./100 g) flour
¼ teaspoon (1 ml) vanilla extract

Cream the butter with the sugars. Add the cinnamon, baking powder, and salt. Stir in the milk and the egg yolk. Sift the flour and pour it all in at once. Beat it in and stir in the vanilla. Shape into a ball, cover with plastic wrap, and chill for 10 to 20 minutes. Roll the chilled dough to just under ⅛ inch (3 mm) thick and cut rectangles. Bake at 350°F (180°C) on a silicone baking sheet for 7 to 8 minutes, until firm and nicely browned. Transfer to a cooling rack.

Chocolate and Vanilla Shortbread

Ingredients (makes about 20 cookies)
Chocolate Shortbread
5 tablespoons (2 ½ oz./75 g) butter
1 cup (4 oz./125 g) flour
2 tablespoons (15 g) unsweetened cocoa powder
¼ cup (20 g) ground almonds
¼ cup (50 g) sugar
½ teaspoon (3 g) salt
1 egg yolk

Vanilla Shortbread
4 tablespoons (2 oz./65 g) butter
1 cup (4 oz./125 g) flour
Scant ⅓ cup (2 oz./65 g) sugar
½ teaspoon (3 g) salt
1 egg
½ teaspoon (3 ml) vanilla extract

For the chocolate shortbread, follow the method for sweetened short pastry (p. 18), sifting the cocoa powder and ground almonds with the flour. On a lightly floured surface, shape the dough into a log shape measuring 8 inches (20 cm) long and 1 ¼ inches (3 cm) in diameter. Cover with plastic wrap and chill for 10 minutes.
For the vanilla shortbread, follow the method for sweetened short pastry (p. 18), diluting the vanilla extract in the egg before incorporating into the crumbled mixture. Cover with plastic wrap and chill for 10 minutes. Roll it into a rectangle 8 x 6 inches (20 x 15 cm) that is 2 inches (5 cm) thick. Wrap the chocolate log in the vanilla dough, ensuring the chocolate dough is neatly centered and that the two ends meet neatly. Trim any excess so that the vanilla dough is the same thickness all around. Cover in plastic wrap and chill again for 10 minutes. Cut into slices just under ½ inch (1 cm) thick. Transfer carefully to a silicone baking sheet and bake at 350°F (180°C) for about 10 minutes, until firm and the vanilla part is a nice golden color. Transfer to a cooling rack.

Linzer Cookies

Ingredients (makes about 12 cookies)
1 cup (4 oz./125 g) flour
1 cup (4 ½ oz./125 g) sugar
1 stick (4 oz./125 g) butter
3 eggs
½ teaspoon (3 g) salt
1 teaspoon (4 g) baking powder
Generous ½ cup (1 ½ oz./45 g) ground hazelnuts
Scant ½ teaspoon (1 g) ground cinnamon
Finely grated zest of ¼ unsprayed or organic lemon

You can either make this recipe with your hands or using a stand mixer fitted with a paddle beater at average speed for 2 to 3 minutes maximum. Combine all the ingredients. Spoon into a piping bag and pipe onto a silicone baking sheet. Bake at 375°C (190°C) for small cookies for about 10 minutes until golden.

Basque Cake

Ingredients (serves 6)
7 tablespoons (3 ½ oz./95 g) butter
1 cup (4 oz./125 g) flour
Scant ½ teaspoon (1.5 g) baking powder
Scant ½ cup (3 oz./85 g) sugar
1 egg
1 or 2 drops bitter almond extract

Follow the method for sweetened short pastry (p. 18), sifting the baking powder with the flour, omitting the salt and adding the almond extract. Roll the dough to a thickness of just under ½ inch (1 cm) and cut out two disks, one slightly larger than the other. Over the smaller disk, spread a ½-inch (1-cm) layer of frangipane cream (see recipe p. 101) to just over ½ inch (1.5 cm) from the rim. Alternatively, use black cherry jam, a Basque specialty, as a filling. Carefully set the larger disk over it and seal the edges, pressing down carefully. Bake at 375°F (190°C) for about 25 minutes, until a lovely golden color.

Broyé (from the Poitou region)

Ingredients (serves 6 [about 9 oz./250 g])
4 tablespoons (2 oz./60 g) butter
1 cup (4 oz./125 g) flour
⅓ cup (2 oz./60 g) sugar
Scant ½ teaspoon (2 g) salt
1 tablespoon (15 ml) cognac or other brandy
1 egg, lightly beaten, for the egg wash

Follow the method for sweetened short pastry (p. 18), adding the cognac after the sugar and salt (instead of the egg used in the recipe on p. 18) and incorporating with a pastry scraper to make a smooth dough. Roll the dough into a disk just under ½ inch (1 cm) thick. Brush with the egg wash and use the tines of a fork to make a striped or cross-hatched pattern on the top. Transfer to a silicone baking sheet and bake at 375°F (190°C) for 20 minutes, until golden.

● Did you know?
Traditionally, someone punches this pastry with a fist to make servings for guests to help themselves.

Streusel Topping

Ingredients (makes topping for a crumble or cake for 6)
1 cup (4 oz./125 g) flour
⅔ cup (4 oz./125 g) sugar
1 stick (4 oz./125 g) butter
1 ½ cups (4 oz./125 g) ground almonds
1 small pinch ground cinnamon

Rub all the ingredients together with your hands until the mixture resembles coarse crumbs. Use to top crumbles and for streusel toppings for coffee cakes and tarts.

Spritz Cookies

Ingredients (makes 8 cookies)
5 tablespoons (2 ½ oz./75 g) butter, room temperature
⅓ cup (2 oz./50 g) confectioners' sugar
1 egg yolk
1 tablespoon (15 ml) heavy cream
¾ cup plus 2 tablespoons (3 ½ oz./100 g) flour
1 tablespoon (10 g) cornstarch
Scant ½ teaspoon (2 g) table salt
¼ teaspoon (1 ml) vanilla extract

In a mixing bowl, beat the butter with the confectioners' sugar until the texture is light and creamy. Beat in the egg yolk and cream. Working with a flexible spatula, beat in the flour, cornstarch, salt, and vanilla until the batter is smooth. Spoon into a piping bag fitted with a star tip and pipe onto a silicone baking sheet, making S-shapes if you wish. Bake at 320°F (160°C) for 15 minutes, until lightly colored. Cool on a rack.

Piped Cookies

Ingredients (makes 8 cookies)
6 tablespoons (3 oz./90 g) butter, room temperature
Scant ¼ cup (1 oz./30 g) confectioners' sugar
½ teaspoon (3 g) salt
1 tablespoon egg white (15 g)
¾ cup plus 2 tablespoons (3 ½ oz./100 g) flour, sifted
Candied fruit or nuts for garnish

Beat or whisk the butter with the confectioners' sugar and salt until creamy. Beat in the egg white. Mix in the flour. Spoon into a piping bag and pipe small mounds on a silicone baking sheet. Garnish with candied fruit or nuts. Let stand for at least 1 hour, uncovered, at room temperature, until a crust forms. Bake at 350°F (180°C) for 15 minutes, until golden.

Puff Pastry ★★★

Classic Puff Pastry

Ingredients (makes a base for
  a tart for 4 [1 lb./450 g of pastry])
1 ⅔ cups (7 oz./200 g) flour
Scant 1 teaspoon (4 g) salt
Scant ½ cup (100 ml) water
1 ¼ sticks (5 oz./150 g) butter
  (or margarine), room temperature

http://flamm.fr/ffd02

On a work surface or in a mixing bowl, sift the flour and incorporate the salt. Make a well and pour in the water (1). Working rapidly with your hands, mix the ingredients together until fully blended. At this stage, you have a smooth paste, known in French as the *détrempe* (water dough) (2). Shape it into a disk and chill for 20 minutes. Ensure that the butter has the same consistency as that of the water dough. If not, you may have to bash it (still wrapped) with a rolling pin. Roll the dough into a rough cross shape, leaving the center thicker than the rest. Place the butter between two sheets of parchment paper and soften it further with the rolling pin, at the same time shaping it into a square so that it fits into the center of the dough. Set the butter in the center and fold over each of the four parts of the cross. It will look like the back of an envelope (3). Lightly flour the work surface and roll the dough to form a rectangle three times longer than its width. Place it lengthwise in front of you. Fold the upper third downwards and then fold the lower third over this to make three layers (4). This is called a simple turn. Rotate the folded dough a quarter-turn and repeat the procedure, rolling it out to make a rectangle with the same proportions and folding it in three in the same way. Each time, be careful to make neat angles and to roll out evenly and not too thinly, as this would crush the butter-dough structure and be detrimental to the end result. Cover well with plastic wrap and chill for 30 minutes. Repeat the procedure: roll out, fold in three, and make a quarter-turn; roll out, fold in three, cover with plastic wrap, and chill for 30 minutes. Repeat once more to make the fifth and sixth turns. Once again, wrap and chill for at least 30 minutes. Roll out the dough to the desired shape and cut according to the recipe. Cover with plastic wrap and chill for 1 hour before baking. Sufficient chilling time to relax the dough, neat folds and corners, and even rolling are the keys to successful puff pastry.

● Did you know?
Not all puff pastry undergoes six folding procedures. The fewer times it is folded the more it rises, but it does not bake as evenly as this particular pastry. Whatever folding procedure you follow, the amount of fat to incorporate must be half the weight of the détrempe *(water dough), the flour plus the water.*

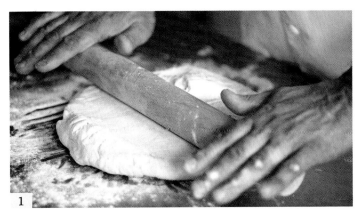

A double turn actually involves making four layers, whereas a simple turn involves making three layers.

● Does a mille-feuille really have one thousand leaves?

We can calculate the number of leaves (feuilles) created by layering the dough and fat using the folding process. Let's take a puff pastry with six turns. After the first time it is folded into three, there are three layers of butter and six layers of dough. However, two layers of dough are in direct contact and so in fact form one layer only. Here's the calculation:
- 1st turn: $3 \times 3 = 9 - 2 = 7$ • 2nd turn: $7 \times 3 = 21 - 2 = 19$
- 3rd turn: $19 \times 3 = 57 - 2 = 55$ • 4th turn: $55 \times 3 = 165 - 2 = 163$
- 5th turn: $163 \times 3 = 489 - 2 = 487$ • 6th turn: $487 \times 3 = 1461 - 2 = 1459$

Given that a classic mille-feuille (or napoleon) is made with three layers of puff pastry, it has altogether $1,459 \times 3 = 4,377$ leaves. Note that when puff pastry has undergone five turns, it rises to form an extra-light pastry, and, if very finely rolled, it may have certain advantages, rising less but more regularly.

The water dough takes its name from the fact that the flour is wetted with half its weight in water. But depending on the quality of the flour and how much water it absorbs, it may require a little more than this.

It's important for the butter and the water dough to be the same consistency: this facilitates the rolling and folding, and ensures that the butter slips properly between the leaves of the water dough.

Inside-Out Puff Pastry

This is known as inside-out puff pastry because the butter (or other fat) surrounds the water dough, just the opposite of the classic method for puff pastry.

Ingredients (makes a dessert for 8 [1 lb. 14 oz./850 g of pastry])

Butter and flour paste (*beurre manié*)
2 ¼ sticks (9 oz./260 g) butter, room temperature
¾ cup plus 2 tablespoons (3 ½ oz./100 g) flour

Water dough (*détrempe*)
2 ½ cups (10 ½ oz./300 g) flour
1 ¾ teaspoons (8 g) salt
2 tablespoons (1 ½ oz./40 g) butter, room temperature
⅔ cup (150 ml) water

Make the butter and flour paste: knead the butter and flour together to form a smooth paste. Shape into a rectangle and cover with plastic wrap. Chill for 30 minutes, until the butter has become firm.

Make the water dough: sift the flour with the salt on a work surface. Soften the butter. Make a well in the center and place the water and butter in it. Working quickly, incorporate the flour into the water and butter until they form a smooth dough. Shape the dough into a rectangle half the size of the butter-and-flour paste. Cover it in plastic wrap and chill for 20 minutes.

Place the butter and flour paste on a lightly floured surface. Set the water dough over the lower half **(1)**. Fold the other half of the butter and flour paste over the water dough to enclose it completely. Roll the resulting dough out to form a rectangle three times longer than its width **(2)**.

Fold the lower third upward and then fold the top third over the other two layers **(3)**. Rotate the dough a quarter-turn **(4)**. Roll out again, but this time shape a rectangle four times as long as it is wide. Fold the two extremities together so that they meet in the center of the rectangle.

Cover in plastic wrap and chill for 30 minutes. Repeat the last folding procedure.

Lastly, fold in three as you did at the beginning. Cover and chill again for 30 minutes before rolling out according to the recipe.

Quick Puff Pastry

Ingredients (makes 1 lb./450 g of pastry)
1 ¼ sticks. (5 oz./150 g) butter (or margarine), chilled
1 ⅔ cups (7 oz./200 g) flour
Scant ½ cup (100 ml) water
Scant 1 teaspoon (4 g) salt

Dice the butter. Prepare the water dough with the flour and water. Mix the diced butter with the water dough, without mixing all of it in and leaving some pieces whole. Roll the dough out to form a rectangle three times longer than its width and make four or five simple turns (folding it in three), with 20 minutes chilling time between every two turns.

Viennese Puff Pastry

Ingredients (makes 1 lb./450 g of pastry)
⅓ cup (80 ml) milk
Scant 1 teaspoon (4 g) salt
4 tablespoons (2 oz./50 g) butter, room temperature
1 teaspoon (4 g) sugar
1 ⅔ cups (7 oz./200 g) flour
1 egg yolk
1 teaspoon (5 ml) rum
1 stick (4 oz./120 g) butter to incorporate into the folding process

Heat the milk, salt, butter, and sugar to about 85°F (30°C). Sift the flour and make a well in the center. Lightly beat the egg yolk and rum together and pour into the well with the heated ingredients. Working as rapidly as possible, combine the ingredients until you have a smooth dough. Cover with plastic wrap and chill for 30 minutes. Soften the butter as instructed for the classic puff pastry recipe (p. 24) and proceed according to the folding instructions, making six turns.

Chocolate Puff Pastry

This makes a delicious puff pastry, but there is a risk of its becoming dry. It is a recipe that works well with creamy toppings.

Ingredients (makes 1 lb./450 g of pastry)
Water dough
5 tablespoons (2 ½ oz./75 g) butter
2 cups (9 oz./250 g) flour
1 slightly heaping teaspoon (5 g) salt
½ cup (125 ml) water

Butter and cocoa paste
2 sticks (8 oz./225 g) butter, room temperature, diced
7 tablespoons (1 ¾ oz./50 g) unsweetened cocoa powder

Make the water dough: soften the butter (use the method described in the classic puff pastry recipe, p. 24). Sift the flour with the salt onto a work surface or into a mixing bowl and make a well in the center. Place the water and butter in the well and, working as rapidly as possible, combine the ingredients until they form a smooth dough. Cover with plastic wrap and chill for 30 minutes.

Make the butter and cocoa paste: working with your fingers, combine the butter with the cocoa powder.
Follow the instructions for classic puff pastry (p. 24).

Alternatively, when you make the water dough, replace ½ cup minus 1 tablespoon (2 oz./50 g) flour with the cocoa and use the same amount of butter indicated above. Proceed as for classic puff pastry (p. 24).

● Did you know?
A very basic form of puff pastry was used in ancient times by the Greeks and Arabs, who made it with oil. The inventor of the puff pastry that resembles what we use today was a Frenchman, Claude Gelée (also known as Le Lorrain) who, in the eighteenth century, worked for the Condé nobility. He improved the recipe, and then Antonin Carême, one of the major figures of French gastronomy, developed it further several decades later.

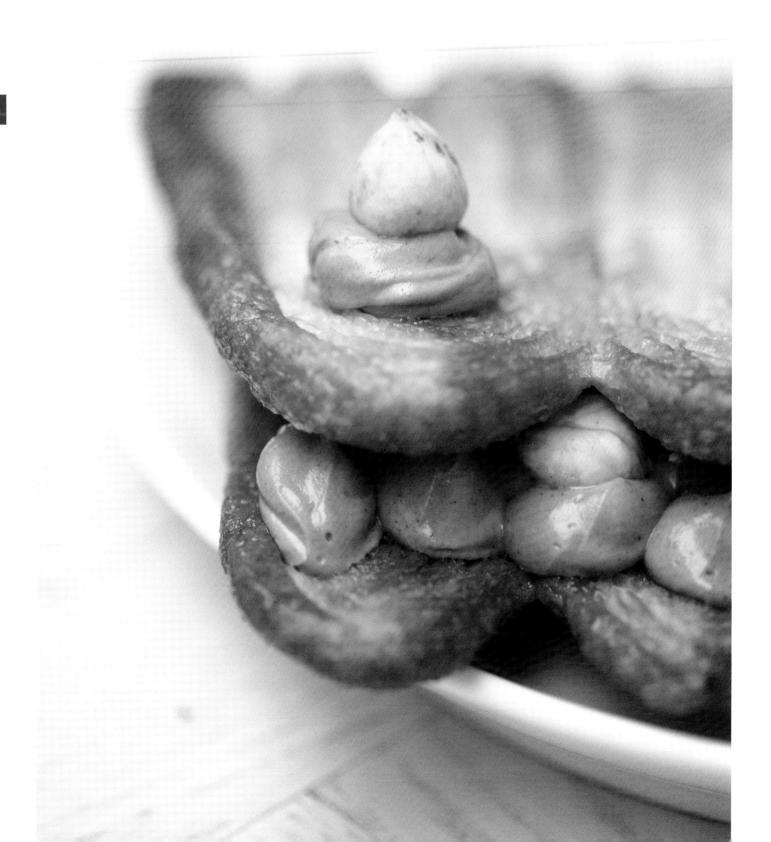

Puff pastries: advantages, disadvantages, and uses

	Advantages	Disadvantages	Used for
Classic	• Rises well and evenly • Turns can be simple or double (with an extra fold)	• Takes time to make, with many different stages • Requires careful organization	• Layered cakes served in wide strips • *Pithiviers* • Dartois
Inside-Out	• Lighter pieces of pastry that break pleasantly when eaten • Shrinks relatively little • Rises evenly • Barely forms a crust	• Needs to be handled with dexterity • Requires controlled working temperature: 60°F–68°F (15°C–18°C)	• Mille-feuilles • Vol-au-vents • Croustades
Quick	• Quick to make, so good for emergencies! • Does not need to be aerated	• Rises unevenly • Does not rise much	• Decorative pieces (usually savory) • Cheese straws • *Palmiers* • Tart bases • Base for tarte Tatins
Viennese	• Delicate texture • Delicious for *viennoiserie* pastries	• Can only be used for certain pastries and *viennoiseries*	• Turnovers • Breakfast pastries • *Éventails* • Apricot croissants

When making tart crusts or dry cookies, it is important not to knead the dough too much. Overmixing makes the dough elastic, and elasticity often means shrinkage during rolling out and, more seriously, during baking. Shrinkage is particularly unfortunate if you are finishing your tart with a liquid filling, such as a set cream for a quiche or fruit tart.

Shortcrust Pastry ★

Sweet Version

Ingredients (makes a tart base to serve 4-6)
5 tablespoons (2 ½ oz./65 g) butter, room temperature
1 cup (4 oz./125 g) flour
2 ½ teaspoons (10 g) sugar
Generous ½ teaspoon (3 g) salt
3 tablespoons (40 ml) water
1 egg

Dice the butter. Sift the flour onto a work surface. Working with your fingertips, crush the butter into the flour (1). Work as quickly as possible until the butter is incorporated into the flour; it should look like pale sand (2).
It is this procedure that gives this pastry its distinctive texture; what's more, it neutralizes the gluten in the flour, thereby preventing it from becoming elastic.
Dissolve the sugar and salt in the water.
Make a well in the center and pour in the water and egg (3).
Still working with your fingers, incorporate the sand-like flour into the liquid ingredients (4).
Use the heel and palm of your hand (5) to knead lightly, just until the dough is smooth.
Shape it into a ball (6), cover with plastic wrap, and chill for 20 minutes.
On a lightly floured surface, roll it out according to the recipe (7).

❙ Recipe ideas
❙ Alsace-Style Plum Tart >> p. 417
❙ Pear and Almond Cream Tart >> p. 418

1

2

Savory Version

Ingredients (makes a savory crust for a quiche or tart for 4)
1 cup (4 oz./125 g) flour
½ teaspoon (1 g) salt
5 tablespoons (2 ½ oz./65 g) butter, room temperature
1 egg
1 tablespoon plus 1 teaspoon (20 ml) water

In a stand mixer fitted with a paddle beater at low speed combine the flour, salt, and butter, for just a few seconds. Lightly beat the egg with a fork and add the water. Pour the liquid ingredients into the bowl and continue at low speed for 1 or 2 minutes, until the dough forms a smooth ball. Shape into a thick disk, cover with plastic wrap, and chill for 20 minutes before proceeding according to your recipe.

● Did you know?
This is probably one of the oldest known pastry doughs. Formerly, it contained no egg at all. It is called pâte brisée *in French because* briser *means "to break": all the dry ingredients were simply "broken" with water. Shortcrust pastry is used to line tart rings, for quiches and pies, and tartlets. It can be used to hold savory stuffings and pâtés.*

Pasta Dough ★

Pasta and various kinds of noodles have been known for many centuries and hold an important place in daily diets in many countries in the world. Marco Polo, on his return from China in 1295, reported on the widespread consumption of noodles there. In Europe, it is in Italy that the most pasta is eaten, and it is thanks to Italian cuisine that we enjoy spaghetti, cannelloni, ravioli, tortellini, and many, many more varieties. Some French regions have their own pasta specialties too: *spätzle* from Alsace in the east; *crozets*, tiny squares made of either buckwheat or durum wheat from the mountainous Savoie region; and in the nearby Dauphiné region, *raviole de Royans*, small, delicate, cheese-filled ravioli.
The name *raviole* is now found frequently on menus, even though they are often larger with different fillings. Filled forms of pasta such as ravioli are increasingly part of dessert menus.

● Chef's notes
If you are making ravioli, use the laminator to make the dough as fine as possible to avoid an overly floury taste. Make this dough ahead of time so that it relaxes and loses elasticity. Of course, it must be tightly covered with plastic wrap so that it doesn't absorb other flavors and odors. For an original touch, add a flavored oil or other flavoring to your dough. You can also color it. To blacken it, use cuttlefish ink. For red pasta, add a little tomato paste. A pinch of turmeric will color the dough yellow and a little saffron will make it orange. For green, add parsley.

Basic Savory Pasta Dough

Ingredients (makes ravioli [filled] for 6-8)
2 eggs
1 tablespoon plus 1 teaspoon (20 ml) sunflower seed oil
1 teaspoon (5 g) salt
1 ¾ cups (8 oz./220 g) flour

Lightly beat the eggs, oil, and salt. Sift the flour and make a well in the center. Pour the egg mixture in and, working as quickly as possible, combine the ingredients. Stop as soon as the dough is smooth; if you overmix, it will become elastic. Shape it into a ball, cover with plastic wrap, and chill for 30 to 45 minutes. Roll out the dough with a rolling pin, just enough for it to be processed in a laminator. Cut it into the desired shapes, using a cookie cutter if you are making ravioli, for example. Let the shapes dry for several hours (3 hours indoors, less if outside), until dry and almost brittle, before using.

Basic Sweet Pasta Dough

Ingredients (makes ravioli [filled] for 8)
2 eggs plus 3 egg yolks
2 tablespoons (1 oz./25 g) sugar
2 cups (9 oz./250 g) flour

Lightly beat the eggs, egg yolks, and sugar. Sift the flour and make a well in the center. Pour in the egg mixture and, working as quickly as possible, combine the ingredients. Stop as soon as the dough is smooth; if you overmix, it will become elastic. Shape it into a ball, cover with plastic wrap, and chill for 30 to 45 minutes. Roll out the dough with a rolling pin, just enough for it to be processed in a laminator. Cut it into the desired shapes, using a cookie cutter if you are making ravioli, for example. Let the shapes dry for several hours (3 hours indoors, less if outside), until dry and almost brittle, before using. You could make sweet ravioli filled with Nutella, for example.

Semolina Pasta Dough

Ingredients (makes 1 lb./450 g of pasta dough, to serve 8-10)
9 oz. (250 g) fine durum semolina
9 egg yolks (6 oz./180 g)
2 teaspoons (10 g) butter or oil
1 teaspoon (5 g) salt

Sift the semolina into a mixing bowl and make a well in the center. Lightly beat the egg yolks, oil, and salt together and pour them into the well. Working quickly with your hands, combine the wet ingredients with the semolina. Stop when just combined so that it does not gain any elasticity. Form into a ball, cover with plastic wrap, and chill for 30 to 45 minutes. Roll out roughly and then process through a laminator. Cut to the desired shapes and let dry for several hours before using according to your recipe.

Galette Charentaise ★★

This simple, buttery cake, typical of the Charentes region, is excellent with tea.

Ingredients (makes 2 large cakes, each serving 6)
2 sticks plus 6 tablespoons (12 oz./325 g) butter, room temperature
2 cups (14 oz./400 g) sugar
1 teaspoon (5 g) salt
4 eggs
1 teaspoon (5 ml) vanilla extract
2 teaspoons (10 ml) lemon extract
3 oz. (80 g) candied angelica, chopped
3 ⅔ cups (1 lb./460 g) flour
1 egg, lightly beaten for the egg wash

Beat the butter, sugar, and salt until light and creamy.
Beat in the eggs, one by one, making sure each one is fully incorporated before continuing. Stop when smooth.
Stir in the vanilla and lemon extract and candied angelica.
With a flexible spatula, fold in the flour until just incorporated.
Shape into two disks, cover with plastic wrap, and chill for 30 minutes.
Preheat the oven to 350°F (180°C).
Roll into rounds just under ½ inch (1 cm) thick. Brush with the lightly beaten egg, decorate with a fork, and bake on a baking sheet for 20 minutes, until firm and nicely golden.
Transfer to a cooling rack.

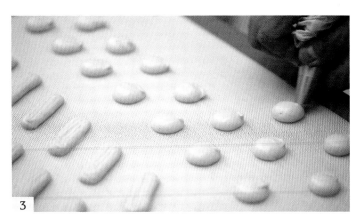

Soft pastries & batters

Basic Choux Pastry ★★

Ingredients (makes 9-10 choux puffs or éclairs)
7 tablespoons (3 ½ oz./100 g) butter, room temperature
1 cup (4 oz./125 g) flour
1 cup (250 ml) water
1 teaspoon (5 g) salt
1 teaspoon (5 g) sugar
3 eggs, plus 1 egg for the egg wash

For helpful hints on obtaining best results, see chef's notes p. 37.
Dice the butter. Sift the flour.
In a large saucepan, bring the water, salt, sugar, and butter
to a boil. When all the butter has melted, remove from the
heat and stir in all the flour. Return the saucepan to the heat.
With a wooden spoon or spatula, beat briskly to dry out the
mixture (1). (At this stage, it is known in French as a *panade*,
a panada.) Continue beating until it pulls away from the sides
of the saucepan (2). Transfer to a mixing bowl and let cool
to 122°F (50°C) or a little less, when it can be touched. (Any
hotter and the eggs that are added will be cooked.)
Continue working with a wooden spoon and beat in the eggs,
one by one, only adding an egg when the previous one is
fully incorporated. The mixture must be smooth and shiny.
It is ready when a large scoop, lifted up, falls from the spoon
within 10 seconds. The texture of the batter is important—it
must not be too soft or too hard.
Preheat the oven to 400 °F (200 °C) if you are baking choux
puffs or éclairs or 350°F (180°C) for a large size (which needs
to bake more slowly). Spoon the batter into a piping bag and
pipe onto a baking sheet in the desired shape (choux puffs,
éclairs, or profiteroles, for example) (3). Brush with the beaten
egg (4). For choux puffs, dip a fork into water and score the
top with the tines to ensure the puffs are evenly shaped (5).

Transfer immediately to the oven so that the dough does not form a crust. Bake for 25 to 30 minutes, until golden brown and nicely puffed. Lower the heat to 340°F (170°C) and bake for an additional 20 minutes to dry out the choux pastry, if possible with the oven door ajar. Let cool on a rack so that the pastry does not absorb any moisture.

Recipe ideas
Croquembouche ›› p. 368
Gâteau Saint-Honoré ›› p. 386
Profiteroles ›› p. 457

Choux Pastry with Crumbled Topping

Ingredients (makes 20 choux puffs)

Topping
¾ cup plus 2 tablespoons
   (3 ½ oz./100 g) flour
½ cup (3 ½ oz./100 g) sugar
7 tablespoons (3 ½ oz./100 g) butter

http://flamm.fr/ffd03

Choux pastry
2 sticks (8 oz./220 g) butter, room temperature
2 ⅓ cups (10 oz./290 g) flour
1 cup (250 ml) water
1 cup (250 ml) milk
1 teaspoon (5 g) salt
1 tablespoon (12 g) sugar
10 eggs

Prepare the topping: working with your fingers, rub the flour, sugar, and butter together just until they form a smooth dough. Alternatively, combine them briefly in a food processor with the blade knife. Shape the dough into a disk and roll out very thinly, less than ⅛ inch (1-2 mm), between two sheets of parchment paper. Place it, flat, in the freezer, for about 30 minutes, and cut out disks ½ inch (1 cm) larger than the choux puffs you will be making.

Make the choux pastry: dice the butter. Sift the flour. In a large saucepan, bring the water, milk, salt, sugar, and butter to a boil. When all the butter has melted, remove from the heat and stir in all the flour. Return the saucepan to the heat. With a wooden spoon or spatula, beat briskly to dry out the mixture.

Continue until it pulls away from the sides of the saucepan. Transfer to a mixing bowl and let cool to 122°F (50°C) or a little less, when it can be touched. (Any hotter and the eggs that are added will be cooked.) Continue working with a wooden spoon and beat in the eggs, one by one, only adding an egg when the previous one is fully incorporated. The mixture must be smooth and shiny. It is ready when a large scoop lifted up falls from the spoon within 10 seconds. The texture of the batter is important—it must not be too soft or too hard.

Preheat the oven to 400°F (200°C). Spoon the batter into a piping bag and pipe rounds onto a baking sheet. Carefully place a disk of crumble topping on top of each one. (It does not need to be brushed with egg wash.) Bake for 25 to 30 minutes, until nicely puffed and golden brown. Lower the heat to 340°F (170°C) and bake for an additional 20 minutes to dry out the choux pastry, if possible with the oven door ajar. Let cool on a rack so that the pastry does not absorb any moisture.

● Chef's notes

For best results when making choux pastry, ensure that the diced butter is melted when the water boils. Only add the flour when the water is at a full boil.

The panada (the batter before eggs are incorporated) must not be too hot when you add the eggs, or they will coagulate.

The texture of the batter is all-important. If it is too soft, it will spread in the oven, and if it is too hard, it will rise unevenly and unsightly cracks will form. It is ready when a large scoop lifted up falls from the spoon within 10 seconds.

Bake as soon as possible, otherwise the pastry will dry and form a crust. If you are baking different sizes for the same dessert (for example, Choux Puff Religeuses, p. 382), a tray of piped choux puffs can safely stay at room temperature while a first batch bakes, but no longer.

There are two stages to baking: First stage: rising and browning, at 400°F (200°C) for small sizes, and 375°F (190°C) for larger sizes, like the Paris-Brest (see p. 376).

Second stage: drying out, at 340°F (170°C), with the oven door ajar to evacuate the moisture. Don't succumb to curiosity and open the oven door during the first stage: the choux puffs will deflate. When you remove the choux puffs from the oven, transfer them immediately to a cooling rack so that they do not reabsorb any moisture. Let them cool completely before garnishing them.

Uses of choux pastry: Choux pastry can be used for sweet or savory dishes, on its own or combined with mashed potatoes, béchamel sauce, pastry cream, and more. They may be fried, poached, or baked.

Some examples: Choux pastry + mashed potatoes = dauphine potatoes; Choux pastry + pastry cream = garnish for Pastry Cream Turnovers (see p. 365); Choux pastry + rum and raisins = Pont-Neuf pastry; Choux pastry, flavored and fried = Pets-de-Nonne Soufflé Fritters (see p. 41); Choux pastry poached in water then baked = gnocchi; Choux pastry + diced Gruyère cheese = gougère.

● Did you know?

An Italian pastry chef named Popelini, who worked for Catherine de' Medici, is said to have invented choux pastry. Jean Avice, an early nineteenth-century pastry chef who trained Antonin Carême, perfected the recipe. Carême developed the choux puff as we know it.

Choux Pastry-Based Recipes

Sweet Gnocchi

Gnocchi are of Italian origin, but also found in the region of Alsace, where they take the form of little dumplings or quenelles.

Ingredients (makes about 50 gnocchi, to serve 8-10)
1 cup (250 ml) milk
1 cup minus 1 tablespoon (2 ½ oz./75 g) ground almonds, hazelnuts, or walnuts
1 stick (4 oz./125 g) butter
⅓ cup (2 ½ oz./75 g) sugar
1 cup (4 oz./125 g) flour
4 eggs

Syrup

4 cups (1 liter) water
2 ⅔ cups (1 lb. 2 oz./500 g) sugar
Flavoring of your choice (vanilla bean, cinnamon stick, star anise, etc.)

Heat the milk to lukewarm. Soak the ground nuts in the milk for 15 minutes. Strain the milk, discarding the ground nuts (they will have imparted all of their flavor to the milk), and then proceed according to the recipe for basic choux pastry (p. 34), substituting the flavored milk for the water. Pipe or spoon out small, oblong gnocchi.
In a large pot, bring the ingredients for the syrup to a boil. Place the gnocchi in the boiling syrup and cook for about 3 to 4 minutes. Remove them with a slotted spoon as they rise to the surface and drain.

⬤ Chef's notes
Serve the gnocchi with custard or a fruit coulis. Alternatively, make them au gratin with a sabayon (see p. 123).

Chocolate Choux Pastry

Ingredients (makes about 9 large choux puffs or éclairs)
1 cup plus 1 tablespoon (5 oz./140 g) flour
1 tablespoon (8 g) unsweetened cocoa powder
1 stick (4 oz./125 g) butter, room temperature
½ cup (125 ml) water
1 cup (250 ml) milk
1 teaspoon (5 g) salt
1 tablespoon (12 g) sugar
4 eggs plus 1 egg, lightly beaten, for the egg wash

Sift the flour and cocoa powder together. Follow the directions for basic choux pastry (see p. 34).

Delicate Choux Pastry

Ingredients (makes about 10 choux puffs or éclairs)
1 stick (4 oz./125 g) butter
1 cup (4 oz./125 g) flour
½ cup (125 ml) water
½ cup (125 ml) milk
1 teaspoon (5 g) salt
2 teaspoons (10 g) sugar
3 eggs, plus 1 egg, lightly beaten for the egg wash

Follow the directions for basic choux pastry (see p. 34), combining the water with the milk.

Orange-Scented Dauphine Fritters

Ingredients (makes 18-20 fritters)
7 tablespoons (3 ½ oz./100 g) butter
1 cup plus 2 tablespoons (5 oz./150 g) flour
½ cup (125 ml) water
½ cup (125 ml) orange juice
Finely grated zest of ½ orange
½ teaspoon (3 g) salt
2 tablespoons (1 oz./25 g) sugar
4 eggs
2 tablespoons (30 ml) crème fraîche or heavy cream

For frying

½ cup minus 1 tablespoon (2 oz./50 g) flour
⅓ cup (2 oz./50 g) confectioners' sugar
2 eggs
3 ½ oz. (100 g) dried brioche crumbs

Follow the directions for basic choux pastry (see p. 34), combining the water with the orange juice and adding the orange zest to the liquid. Stir in the cream once the eggs have been incorporated. Pipe 1 ¼-inch (3-cm) balls on a baking sheet and place in the freezer for 1 hour. Heat an oil bath to 340°F (170°C).
Combine the flour with the confectioners' sugar. Lightly beat the eggs. Roll the frozen choux puffs in the flour and confectioners' sugar mixture and then coat them in the beaten egg. Roll them in the crumbs and fry for 2 to 3 minutes, until golden brown. Remove as soon as they rise to the surface and drain on paper towel.

⬤ Chef's notes
These fritters may be served on their own or with a fruit coulis. Change the fruit juice, using whatever takes your fancy. Our suggestions: lemon, mango, or passion fruit.

Crêpe Batter ★

Ingredients (makes sixteen 6-in./15-cm crêpes)
2 cups (9 oz./250 g) flour
½ teaspoon (2 g) salt
3 ½ tablespoons (1 ½ oz./40 g) sugar
3 eggs
2 cups (500 ml) milk, room temperature
½ teaspoon (2 ml) vanilla extract, orange blossom water,
   or rum
3 tablespoons (1 ½ oz./40 g) unsalted butter, melted until brown
A little oil for frying

Sift the flour and salt into a mixing bowl and combine
with the sugar. Make a well in the center and crack the eggs
into the mixture one by one, adding the next one when the
previous one is incorporated. Whisk briskly with a little of the
milk. Incorporate the remaining milk, beating or whisking
energetically until the batter is smooth and fluid. Add the
flavor of your choice and strain through a fine-mesh sieve.
(This will remove any lumps.) Stir in the melted brown butter
and chill for about 30 minutes. Heat a skillet or crêpe pan
over high heat. Stir the crêpe batter. Drizzle a few drops of oil
in and cook the crêpes one by one, turning them when they
are golden-brown at the edges.

● **Chef's notes**
*For variation, replace some or all of the milk with beer or hard cider;
you may also substitute wheat flour with other types of flour, such
as buckwheat or spelt. For savory crêpes, add finely chopped herbs,
spices, or even finely grated vegetables to the batter.*

● **Did you know?**
*Simple pancakes were made as early as 7000 BCE. Crêpes like
these were made considerably later, in the thirteenth century.
Blinis, which come to us from Russia, are thick, leavened crêpes
made with wheat and buckwheat. What are called galettes in
France—savory crêpes—are of Celtic origin. They are a specialty
of Brittany and are made with buckwheat and water.*

Recipe ideas
Crêpes Suzette-Style ›› p. 264
Exotic Fruit Pouches ›› p. 287

● **Crêpe batter is used for:** *Aumonières (almoner's purse),
a crêpe filled with a sweet or savory garnish tied up to look like
a little pouch; Crêpe Suzette, batter flavored with curaçao and
caramelized with mandarin-scented sugar; Crêpe cake, a pile
of crêpes interspersed with a filling, such as jam, pastry cream,
almond cream, and ganache, which has the height of a cake;
Pannequet, a sweet or savory filling spread over a crêpe that
is folded in four.*

Blini Batter ★

Ingredients (makes about 30 small blinis)
2 cups (9 oz./250 g) flour
Small pinch salt
2 eggs, separated, plus 2 egg whites
2 cups (500 ml) milk, room temperature
3 ½ tablespoons (1 ½ oz./40 g) sugar
3 tablespoons (1 ½ oz./40 g) butter, melted until lightly browned
2 teaspoons (10 ml) orange flower water
A little oil for frying

Sift the flour into a mixing bowl and stir in the salt. Add the egg yolks and whisk energetically with a little of the milk. Pour in the remaining milk, whisking energetically until the batter is smooth and fluid. Strain through a fine-mesh sieve. Whip the egg whites until they form soft peaks. Stir in the sugar with the whisk until firm and shiny. Fold carefully into the batter, taking care not to deflate the mixture. Stir in the browned butter.
Add a drop of oil to a blini pan over high heat and cook the blinis. Alternatively, use a pastry ring placed in a pan. Check the bottom and turn over as soon as they are lightly browned. When they are lightly colored on both sides, transfer to a rack to cool.
If necessary, trim them with a cookie cutter so that they are nicely shaped.

Recipe idea
Layered Blinis with Mulberries >> p. 295

Pets-de-Nonne Soufflé Fritters ★★

Ingredients (makes 15 fritters)
3 tablespoons (1 ½ oz./40 g) butter, room temperature
⅔ cup (2 ½ oz./75 g) flour
1 cup (125 ml) milk
½ teaspoon (2 g) salt
¾ teaspoon (3 g) sugar
2 eggs
Orange flower water for flavoring
Sugar to coat

Dice the butter. Sift the flour. In a large saucepan, bring the milk, salt, sugar, and butter to a boil. The butter should melt as the water comes to a boil. When all the butter has melted, remove from the heat and stir in all the flour. Return the saucepan to the heat. With a wooden spoon or spatula, beat briskly to dry out the mixture. Continue until the batter pulls away from the sides of the saucepan. Remove from the heat and let cool slightly until you can touch it with a finger. Still using a wooden spoon or spatula, beat in the eggs, one by one (if the batter is too hot, the eggs will coagulate). Make sure each egg is fully incorporated before adding the next one. Stir in the orange flower water (the amount you need depends on its strength).
Heat an oil bath to 350°F (180°C).
Spoon the batter into a piping bag fitted with a plain tip, pipe enough to make a small ball, and cut it off with a pair of scissors, letting it fall directly into the oil but taking care not to splatter yourself. Let the batter swell and brown, about 10 minutes. Remove and drain on paper towel. Immediately roll them in sugar to coat and serve.

● Did you know?
This delicacy was already known in Roman times, and is recorded in archives at the Abbey of Marmoutier, at the time well known for its cuisine.

Yeast doughs

Baba or Savarin Dough ★★

Before you begin, keep in mind that:
· Whenever possible, use flour with a high gluten content (strong flour). Otherwise, use all-purpose (plain) flour.
· To encourage the rise of yeast dough, all the ingredients should be at room temperature.
· Never place yeast in direct contact with salt, which destroys this living organism.
· For yeast dough to rise, the ideal temperature ranges between 68°F-77°F (20°C-25°C). It will rise at a lower temperature but take more time. Just ensure that it doubles in volume.
· Carefully weigh the butter. Excess fat slows the fermentation process, weighs down the dough, and makes it difficult to moisten evenly.
· Cover the dough with a clean, damp cloth or plastic wrap while it rises. If you leave it uncovered, it tends to form a crust, spoiling the texture.
· To moisten the cakes, let them cool completely and use the syrup while it is still very hot (you can use a candying rack).
· The center of a savarin is traditionally filled with Chantilly cream, pastry cream, or poached fruit.

Doughs and batters

Rum Babas (basic recipe)

Ingredients (serves 6)
Generous ¾ cup (4 oz./125 g) raisins or currants
3 tablespoons (50 ml) rum
½ cake (0.3 oz./10 g) fresh yeast
Scant ½ cup (125 ml) water or milk, room temperature
2 cups (9 oz./250 g) flour
1 teaspoon (4 g) salt
2 tablespoons (1 oz./25 g) sugar
3 eggs, room temperature
7 tablespoons (3 ½ oz./100 g) butter

Special equipment: six individual baba/savarin molds
  or a 9-inch (22-24-cm) baba/savarin mold

A day, or at least 2 hours ahead: rinse the raisins under cold water and soak them in the rum.
Dilute the yeast in the water or milk. Sift the flour and make a well in the center. Sprinkle the salt outside the well so that it does not come into direct contact with the yeast. With a scraper, incorporate the liquid into the flour. Add the sugar. Lightly beat the eggs and gradually add them to the mixture. Knead the dough well until it becomes elastic, either by hand or using a stand mixer fitted with a dough hook, starting at low speed and then increasing to medium, about 25 minutes altogether (longer by hand). Stop kneading as soon as the dough is smooth and pulls away from the sides of the bowl or no longer sticks to your fingers. It will be smooth, shiny, and very elastic. Melt the butter until it is just warm and knead it into the dough. Stop when incorporated. Cover the dough with plastic wrap and let rise at 77°F-82°F (25°C-28°C) for 30 to 40 minutes, until doubled in volume. Break it up and fold it over itself to remove any air. Drain the raisins and lightly knead them in, until just evenly distributed.
Butter the baba molds and half-fill them with the dough. Let rise again until the dough reaches the top of the molds. Preheat the oven to 400°F (200°C) for individual babas and 350°F (180°C) for a large one. (The larger size must bake more slowly.) Bake the individual babas for about 25 minutes, and the large size for up to 40 minutes, until a cake tester comes out dry and the crust is a nice golden color. Immediately turn them out onto a cooling rack so that no condensation forms on the crust. Let cool completely and follow your recipe for instructions on how to drench in syrup and garnish.

● Chef's note
You can soak the raisins in water instead of rum.

Chocolate Savarin

Ingredients (serves 6)
½ cake (0.3 oz./10 g) fresh yeast
Scant ½ cup (100 ml) milk
2 cups (9 oz./250 g) flour
1 teaspoon (4 g) salt
1 ½ tablespoons (20 g) sugar
3 eggs, room temperature
3 tablespoons (50 g) melted butter, browned if you wish,
  and cooled to lukewarm
2 tablespoons (15 g) unsweetened cocoa powder, sifted

Special equipment: six individual savarin molds

Follow the recipe for the rum babas, incorporating the cocoa powder when the butter is mixed into the dough. Moisten with syrup: vanilla and kirsch are two flavors that complement the chocolate savarin particularly well.

● Did you know?
We use two names for the cakes made from this batter, depending on the mold used. Savarin molds are rings (that is, they have a hollow in the center, see photo on facing page), while baba molds are full.
The baba was supposed to have originated when, around 1725, King Stanislas Leszczynski of Poland, exiled in the Lorraine, poured rum over the traditional kugelhopf *as he thought it tasted too dry. His favorite book being* The Thousand and One Nights, *the new cake was named after one of its heroes, Ali Baba. Over one hundred years later, in 1836, a pastry chef by the name of Stohrer set up shop on the rue Montorgeuil in Paris. There he further improved the recipe by soaking the cake in rum-flavored syrup. The savarin was created by the French pastry chef Auguste Julien, as a tribute to Jean Anthelme Brillat-Savarin: lawyer, politician, gastronome, and author of* La Physiologie du goût *(The Physiology of Taste), published in 1825.*

This dough is also used for other forms of cake:
• Marignans are baked in oblong molds, slit open horizontally, and garnished with cream.
• Pomponettes are baba cakes baked in individual brioche molds and shaped like a Parisian brioche, with a little head. They are then soaked in a rum-scented syrup and can also be garnished and decorated with candied fruit.

Brioche Dough ★★

http://flamm.fr/ffd04

Basic Brioche

Ingredients (makes 1 brioche loaf
   [10 x 4 in./25 x 10 cm], or
   8 individual brioches)
⅓ cake (0.2 oz./7 g) fresh yeast
3 tablespoons (50 ml) tepid water
2 cups (9 oz./250 g) flour (preferably a strong, or high-gluten, flour)
2 tablespoons (1 oz./25 g) sugar
1 teaspoon (5 g) salt
3 eggs, room temperature
1 stick (4 oz./125 g) butter, room temperature

Dilute the yeast in the water. Sift the flour into a large bowl
or onto a work surface. Make a well in the center. Sprinkle
the sugar and salt at a distance from the well so that they do
not come into direct contact with the yeast. When the yeast
mixture is foaming, pour it into the well. With your hands
or a scraper, incorporate the liquid into the flour mixture.
Lightly beat the eggs and, working either by hand or with
a stand mixer fitted with a dough hook, knead them into the
dough (1) until it is elastic (2) (about 25 minutes at medium

speed in a mixer). Knead in the butter. Transfer the dough to a lightly greased mixing bowl and smooth it over. At this stage, it is shiny and stretchy (3). Cover with plastic wrap or a clean cloth and let rise at 68°F-77°F (20°C-25°C) for 30 to 40 minutes, until doubled in volume. (If the temperature is lower, the dough will take longer to rise.) Do not leave the dough uncovered or it will form a crust. Turn the dough onto a lightly floured surface, flatten it, and fold it in three to remove any air bubbles. Shape it into a ball and place in the mold, if using. (Otherwise, shape as desired.) Let rise until it reaches the rim. Bake small brioches at 400°F (200°C) for 25 minutes, or at 350°F (180°C) for a large brioche for about 40 minutes, until nicely browned on top and a cake tester comes out dry.

● Did you know?

Brioche dough has been made for a very long time; there are many regional variations of the basic recipe. Here are some, but far from all, of the shapes and garnishes: the Nanterre brioche, two parallel rows of balls of dough baked in a rectangular pan; the braided brioche, made with two, three, or four strands; the Swiss brioche, a type of raisin loaf (they are rolled into the dough) that includes pastry cream; the Parisian brioche, which has a little "head," probably the best known and popular for breakfast; the crown-shaped Bordelaise brioche with candied fruit and an incision on the top; the IGP (protected geographical status) Vendée brioche, flavored with eau-de-vie and orange flower water, braided, and baked in rectangles, rounds, or ovals (it also goes by the name of galette pacaude or Easter bread) sugar brioche, lightly sprinkled with sanding sugar (a large-grained decorative sugar); Tropezienne brioche, made by rolling the dough into a ½-inch (1-cm) thick disk, brushed with egg wash, and generously sprinkled with sugar. It is left to rise and, when baked, cut horizontally and filled with diplomat cream (see recipe p. 103).

Kugelhopf Dough

Ingredients (makes a 2-lb./950-g loaf, to serve 8)
3 cups (13 oz./375 g) flour
¾ cake (0.5 oz./15 g) fresh yeast
⅔ cup (180 ml) milk, room temperature
⅓ cup (2 ½ oz./75 g) sugar
1 egg plus 1 egg yolk, room temperature
7 tablespoons (4 oz./110 g) butter,
   room temperature, plus some for the mold
¾ cup (4 oz./125 g) raisins
3 ½ oz. (100 g) sliced or whole almonds

Special equipment: 9-inch. (23-24-cm) *Kugelhopf* mold
   (alternatively, use a Bundt pan of the same size)

Follow the basic recipe for brioche dough (see pp. 44-45), with a 1-hour initial rise, until the dough has increased to one and half times its volume. Incorporate the raisins after punching down, working as quickly as possible. Butter the mold and scatter with almonds. Transfer the dough to the mold, let rise for 1 hour, until doubled in volume, and bake at 400°F (200°C) for 35 to 40 minutes, until golden. Turn out immediately onto a cooling rack.

Syrup-Coated Brioche (a specialty of the Bordeaux region)

Ingredients (makes 1 brioche for 10)
½ cake (0.3 oz./10 g) fresh yeast
2 ¾ cups (12 ½ oz./350 g) flour
2 eggs, room temperature
⅓ cup (2 oz./60 g) sugar
⅓ cup (75 ml) tepid water
1 stick (4 oz./120 g) butter, room temperature
2 teaspoons (10 ml) orange flower water
1 ¾ teaspoons (7 g) salt
1 egg, lightly beaten, for the egg wash
Sanding sugar for sprinkling
Assorted candied fruit for garnish

Syrup to finish
⅓ cup (80 ml) water
Scant ½ cup (3 oz./80 g) sugar

Crumble the yeast and place it with the flour in the bowl of a stand mixer fitted with a dough hook. Break the eggs in a separate bowl. Prepare a bain-marie heated to 95°F-104°F (35°C-40°C) and place the sugar, water, butter, orange flower water, and salt in a bowl set over the heated water. Let them melt to form a syrup, stirring to combine. Pour the eggs into the flour and yeast mixture and begin kneading at low speed. Continue for about 25 minutes, gradually adding the syrup until the dough is elastic and pulls away from the sides of the bowl. You may not need it all. Shape the dough into a ball, cover with plastic wrap, and chill for 2 hours. Roll the dough into a long log shape and join the two ends to form a circle. Let rise at 77°F-82°F (25°C-28°C) for 40 minutes to 1 hour, depending on the temperature, until doubled in volume. Carefully brush with the beaten egg. With a pair of scissors, make V-shaped incisions round the top. Sprinkle with sugar and bake at 350°F (180°C) for about 40 minutes, until a nice golden color and a cake tester comes out dry. Transfer immediately to a cooling rack. When cool, combine the water and sugar over high heat until the sugar is dissolved. Brush the brioche with this syrup and, before it dries, top with pieces of candied fruit.

Croissant Dough ★★★

Ingredients (makes 15 croissants)
4 cups (1 ¼ lb./500 g) flour
¼ cup (2 oz./50 g) sugar
¾ tablespoon (15 g) invert sugar
2 tablespoons (15 g) powdered milk
¾ cake (0.5 oz./15 g) fresh (compressed) yeast
Scant 1 cup (225 ml) water
2 teaspoons (10 g) salt
1 ¾ sticks (7 oz./200 g) butter to fold in
1 egg, lightly beaten, for the egg wash

Knead all the ingredients, with the exception of the butter,
lightly in a stand mixer fitted with a dough hook. When
they form a dough, cover in plastic wrap and chill for 1 hour.
Follow the method of classic puff pastry (see p. 24) for folding
to incorporate the butter, making two simple turns, with a
chilling period of 20 minutes between, and then a third simple
turn. After chilling, roll to ⅛ inch (4 mm), cut into triangles
with a base of about 4 inches (10 cm) and sides 6 inches (15 cm)
starting from the base, roll up the dough and tuck the tip
underneath. Bend to form a crescent. Let rise again for at least
40 minutes. Brush with egg wash and bake at 350°F (180°C)
for 20 minutes, until risen and golden on top.

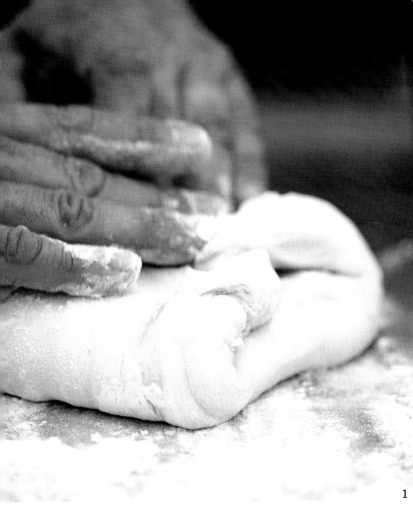

Bread doughs

Sandwich Loaf Dough ★

Ingredients (makes a 1-lb./450-g sandwich loaf)
2 teaspoons (5 g) powdered milk
½ cup (120 ml) water, room temperature
½ cake (0.3 oz./10 g) fresh yeast
2 cups (9 oz./250 g) flour
1 ¼ teaspoons (5 g) sugar
1 egg
2 tablespoons (1 oz./25 g) butter, room temperature
1 teaspoon (5 g) salt

8-inch (20-cm) sandwich loaf pan

This dough is best made with a stand mixer fitted with
a dough hook. Dissolve the powdered milk in the water.
Add the yeast and dissolve, allowing it to foam. Sift the flour
and combine it with the sugar. Make a well in the center and
pour in the milk mixture. Knead at low speed to combine the
ingredients. Add the egg and continue kneading, increasing
the speed slightly, until the dough is smooth (1) and slightly
elastic, about 15 minutes. Add the butter and salt. Knead for
an additional 5 minutes. Shape into a ball and cover the bowl
with plastic wrap, making sure it does not touch the dough.
Heat the oven to 77°F-82°F (25°C-28°C) and place a bowl
of water at the bottom. Let the dough rise in the oven for
1 ¼ to 1 ½ hours. Butter the loaf pan. Break the dough to
punch it down and shape it to fit the pan (2). Make one loaf or
several adjacent rolls (3). Cover the pan partially with plastic
wrap, and let the dough rise until doubled in volume, about
1 hour. If you wish, make shallow incisions on the top.

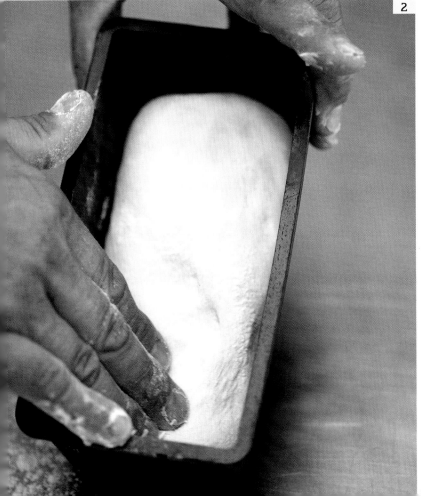

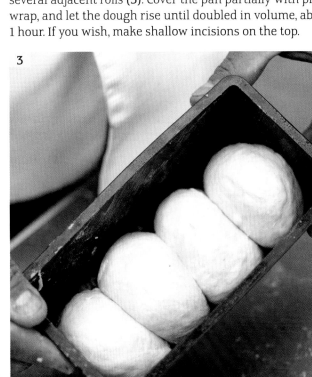

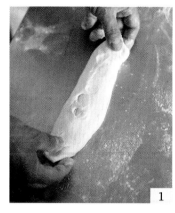

Preheat the oven to 425°F (220°C). Spray the bottom of the oven with water and immediately place the pan inside. Bake for 40 minutes. To test for doneness, rap the bottom of the loaf with your knuckle. If it sounds hollow, it is baked. Immediately transfer the loaf to a cooling rack so that it does not reabsorb any moisture.

Basic French Bread ★

Ingredients (makes 1 ¾ lb./800 g total weight)
4 cups (1 ¼ lb./500 g) flour, unbleached if possible (see chef's note)
1 ¼ cups (300 ml) water (more may be necessary)
½ cake (0.3 oz./10 g) fresh yeast, crumbled
2 teaspoons (10 g) salt

In a stand mixer fitted with a dough hook, place the flour, water, and yeast. Knead at low speed for 2 minutes and let rest for 30 minutes. (This phase is known as autolysis.) Begin kneading again at medium speed until the dough is smooth and elastic, about 25 minutes. You may need to add some water to adjust the consistency. Be careful to add just a little at a time. The dough must not stick to your fingers and should pull away from the sides of the bowl. Add the salt and knead at the same speed for 5 minutes more. Shape the dough into a ball and transfer to a lightly greased bowl. Cover with a clean, damp cloth and let rise for 35 to 40 minutes, depending on the room temperature, until doubled in volume. This is the first rise.
Divide the dough by the weight of the baguettes or bread rolls (average weight 2-2 ½ oz./60-70 g) you intend to make. To punch them down (knock them back), fold them over lengthwise (1, 2). Shape them (3) and let rise again (this is the proofing, or final fermentation). If you wish, make incisions on the top with a razor blade, cutter, or pair of scissors (4, 5). For bread rolls, preheat the oven to 465°F (240°C). If making loaves, preheat the oven to 450°F (230°C). Just before you put the bread in to bake, spray the bottom of the oven with water. This enhances the rise of the bread and helps develop a thin, crisp crust. Place the bread on a baking sheet in the oven and immediately lower the temperature to 400°F (200°C) for bread rolls or 350°F (180°C) for larger loaves. Bake bread rolls for 20 minutes, until a nice crust forms, and bake loaves for 40 minutes.

● **Chef's note**
The choice of flour is all-important. Try to use a high-gluten flour that will develop well.

1

2

3

Walnut Bread ★

Ingredients (makes 2 lb./900 g bread rolls)
3 ¼ cups (14 oz./400 g) flour, unbleached if possible
   (see chef's note p. 50)
1 cup plus 1 tablespoon (3 ½ oz./100 g) rye flour
1 ½ cups (270 ml) water
½ cake (0.3 oz./10 g) fresh yeast, crumbled
5 oz. (150 g) walnuts, chopped
1 ½ teaspoons (8 g) salt

Follow the recipe for basic French bread (p. 50) up until
and including the first rise. Punch the dough down and
incorporate the walnuts when you fold it over lengthwise (1).
Divide the dough and shape it into bread rolls (average
weight 2-2 ½ oz. /60-70 g) (2-3). Let rise again until doubled
in volume.
Preheat the oven to 465°F (240°C). Just before you place
the bread in the oven, spray the bottom with water. Place
the bread in the oven and immediately lower the temperature
to 400°F (200°C). Bake for about 20 minutes, until a nice
crust forms.

 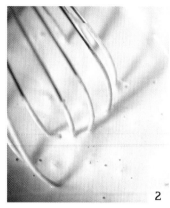

1 2

Poolish Bread ★★

Ingredients (makes 1 ¾ lb./800 g total weight)
4 cups (1 ¼ lb./500 g) flour, unbleached if possible, divided
½ cake (0.3 oz./10 g) fresh yeast, crumbled
1 ¼ cups (300 ml) water (more may be necessary),
   room temperature, divided
2 teaspoons (10 g) salt, divided

In a mixing bowl, place 1 scant cup (3 ½ oz./100 g) flour,
all the yeast, and 1 scant cup (100 ml) water (1). Whisk until
smooth and fluid (2). Cover the bowl with plastic wrap.
Let ferment at room temperature for 6 to 12 hours, until very
foamy and liquid. This is called the poolish. In a stand mixer
fitted with a dough hook, place the remaining flour and water.
Mix at low speed for 2 minutes. Increase the speed to medium
and continue kneading until a smooth, elastic dough forms,
about 20 minutes. Incorporate the poolish and half the salt
and knead until smooth. The dough should not stick to your
fingers and should pull away from the sides of the bowl. Add
the remaining salt and knead for an additional 5 minutes.
Shape the dough into a ball and transfer to a lightly
oiled bowl. Cover with a damp cloth and let rise at room
temperature for 35 to 40 minutes, until doubled in volume.
Weigh out 2-2 ½-oz. (60-70-g) pieces of dough and punch
them down by folding them in half lengthwise. Shape them
into the form of your choice and let rise again until doubled
in volume. The bread is now ready for baking.
Preheat the oven to 425°F (220°C). If you wish, make incisions
on the top with a razor blade, cutter, or pair of scissors
(see p. 50, illustrations 4, 5). Just before putting the bread
in to bake, spray the bottom of the oven with water. This
enhances the rise of the bread and helps develop a thin,
crisp crust. As soon as the bread is in the oven, lower
the temperature to 400°F (200°C). Bake for 20 minutes,
until nice and crusty.

Baguette with *Pâte Fermentée* (fermented starter dough) ★★

Ingredients (makes about 3 baguettes)
4 cups (1 ¼ lb./500 g) all-purpose flour, unbleached
   or French style (relatively high ash content)
1 ½ cups (350 ml) water
½ cake (0.3 oz./10 g) fresh yeast, crumbled
7 oz. (200 g) raw, fermented dough (from previous day's batch)
2 teaspoons (10 g) salt

In a stand mixer fitted with a dough hook, place the flour,
water, yeast, and fermented dough. Knead at low speed for
2 minutes. Increase the speed to medium and knead until
the dough is smooth and elastic (5-6 minutes). You may
need to add some tepid water; add it little by little until the
dough no longer sticks to your fingers and pulls away from
the sides of the bowl. Add the salt and knead for a further
5 to 6 minutes. Shape the dough into a ball and transfer to a
lightly oiled bowl. Cover with a damp cloth and let rise at room
temperature for 35 to 40 minutes, until doubled in volume.
Weigh 12-oz. (350-g) pieces and punch them down by folding
them in half lengthwise. Shape them into baguettes, tucking
the edge underneath, and let rise again until doubled in
volume. The bread is now ready for baking. If you wish,
make incisions on the top with a razor blade, cutter,
or pair of scissors (see p. 50, illustrations 4, 5).
Preheat the oven to 425°F (220°C). Just before putting the
bread in to bake, spray the bottom of the oven with water.
This enhances the rise of the bread and helps develop a thin,
crisp crust. As soon as the bread is in the oven, lower the
temperature to 400°F (200°C). Bake for about 20 minutes,
until nice and crusty. When you rap the bottom, it should
sound hollow.

● **Did you know?**
*As far as fermentation is concerned, temperature plays an
all-important role. Bakers use an empirical formula that takes
into account room temperature and flour temperature.
The ideal starting temperature for the dough is usually
considered to be 130°F (54°C). Room temperature, which influences
the temperature of the flour, cannot be changed, but the
temperature of the water can be adjusted relatively easily.
To make the calculation, add the room temperature to the
temperature of the flour. For example: the temperature in your
kitchen (68°F/20°C) plus the temperature of the flour (64°F/18°C)
equals 132°F (38°C). To reach the optimal temperature of 130°F
(54°C), ensure that your water is at 61°F (16°C).
In short: Water temperature = 130°F (54°C) – (Room temperature
+ Flour temperature).*

Raisin Bread Swirls ★★

Ingredients (makes about 18 swirls)

Dough
4 cups (1 lb. 2 oz./500 g) flour
2 teaspoons (10 g) salt
¼ cup (2 oz./50 g) sugar
Scant 1 tablespoon (15 g) invert sugar
1 ½ tablespoons (10 g) powdered milk
¾ cake (½ oz./15 g) fresh yeast
Scant 1 cup (225 ml) water
1 ¾ sticks (7 oz./200 g) butter, room temperature

Pastry cream
½ vanilla bean
1 cup (250 ml) milk
2 egg yolks
¼ cup (2 oz./50 g) sugar
2 tablespoons (20 g) custard powder
½ cup (3 oz./80 g) raisins

1 egg, lightly beaten, for the egg wash

Prepare the dough: combine all the ingredients except the
butter in the bowl of a stand mixer fitted with a dough hook
and knead at low speed just until a smooth dough forms.
Increase to medium speed and knead for no more than
3-4 minutes. Cover in plastic wrap and chill for 1 hour. Proceed
as for puff pastry (see p. 24) to incorporate the butter, making
three simple turns with 20 minutes' chilling between each one.
Make the pastry cream: slit the vanilla bean lengthwise and
scrape the seeds into the milk. Pour the milk into a saucepan,
add the vanilla bean, and begin heating. In a mixing bowl,
whisk the egg yolks, sugar, and custard powder at medium
speed for 25 minutes or until thick. When the milk is
simmering, pour half of it over the egg yolk mixture, beating
continuously. Return the mixture to the saucepan with the
remaining milk and bring to a boil, stirring continuously.
Let simmer for 2 to 3 minutes, still stirring. Transfer to a
mixing bowl, cover with plastic wrap flush with the surface,
and immediately place in the refrigerator to chill.
Roll the dough into a rectangle $\frac{1}{8}$ inch (4 mm) thick. Spread
the chilled pastry cream over it to just about ½ inch (1 cm)
from the far edge (1). Scatter with raisins and roll up (2).
Cut the roll into slices about 1 ½ inches (3-4 cm) thick and
transfer to a lined baking sheet (3). Flatten slightly with the
palm of your hand and make sure they are nicely rounded.
Brush with the lightly beaten egg. Let rise in a warm place
until almost doubled in volume, about 1 hour.
Bake in a 400°F (200°C) oven until nicely golden,
about 15 minutes. Transfer to a cooling rack.

Chocolate Croissants ★★

Ingredients (makes about 15 croissants)
Basic dough

4 cups (1 lb. 2 oz./500 g) flour

2 teaspoons (10 g) salt

¼ cup (2 oz./50 g) sugar

Scant ½ tablespoon (15 g)
  invert sugar

1 ½ tablespoons (10 g)
  powdered milk

¾ cake (0.45 oz./15 g) fresh yeast

Scant 1 cup (225 ml) water

1 ¾ sticks (7 oz./200 g) butter,
  room temperature,
  to fold into the dough

1 egg for the egg wash

½ cup (2 ¾ oz./80 g) bittersweet
  chocolate chips or small bars

Combine all the ingredients for the basic dough in the bowl of a stand mixer fitted with a dough hook at medium speed for 25 minutes and knead just until a smooth dough forms. Cover in plastic wrap and chill for 1 hour.

Now proceed as for puff pastry to incorporate the butter (see p. 24), making three simple turns with 20 minutes' chilling period between each one. Roll the dough into a rectangle ⅛ inch (4 mm) thick. Cut into 4 x 6-inch (10 x 15-cm) rectangles (1). Place a chocolate stick (or chopped chocolate the same length) near the smaller side and start rolling up. Place the second chocolate stick a little further along and finish rolling (2, 3). Place on a lined baking sheet and brush with the egg wash. Let rise (4) until puffy, about 1 hour.

Bake in a 400°F (200°C) oven until nicely golden, about 15 minutes. Transfer to a cooling rack.

Doughs and batters

Apricot Pastries ★★

Ingredients (makes about 20 pastries)

Basic dough
4 cups (1 lb. 2 oz./500 g) flour
2 teaspoons (10 g) salt
¼ cup (2 oz./50 g) sugar
Scant ½ tablespoon (15 g)
  invert sugar
1 ½ tablespoons (10 g)
  powdered milk
¾ cake (0.45 oz./15 g) fresh yeast
Scant 1 cup (225 ml) water
1 ¾ sticks (7 oz./200 g) butter,
  room temperature, to fold
  into the dough

Pastry cream
½ vanilla bean
1 cup (250 ml) milk
2 egg yolks (1 ½ oz./40 g)
¼ cup (2 oz./50 g) sugar
2 tablespoons (20 g) custard
  powder
10 canned apricot halves
1 egg, lightly beaten,
  for the egg wash
3 ½ oz. (100 g) clear glaze

Prepare the basic dough: except the butter combine all the
ingredients in the bowl of a stand mixer fitted with a dough
hook and knead just until a smooth dough forms. Cover in
plastic wrap and chill for 1 hour. Now proceed as for puff pastry
to incorporate the butter (see p. 24), making three simple
turns with 20 minutes' chilling period between each one.
Make the pastry cream: slit the vanilla bean lengthwise and
scrape the seeds into the milk. Pour the milk into a heavy-
bottom saucepan, add the vanilla bean, and begin heating.
In a mixing bowl, briskly whisk the egg yolks, sugar, and
custard powder at medium speed for 25 minutes or until
thick. When the milk is simmering, pour half of it over the
egg yolk mixture, beating continuously. Return the mixture
to the saucepan with the remaining milk and bring to a
boil, stirring continuously. Let simmer for 2 to 3 minutes,
still stirring. Transfer to a mixing bowl, cover with plastic
wrap flush with the surface, and immediately place in the
refrigerator to chill.
Assemble the pastries: roll the dough into a rectangle ⅛ inch
(4 mm) thick. Cut it into 6-inch (15-cm) squares. Spoon the
pastry cream into a piping bag and pipe a diagonal line from
one corner to the other. At each end, place an apricot half
(1). Fold the two ungarnished corners toward the center (2),
ensuring that one corner is neatly tucked at the bottom of
the pastry so that it does not unroll during baking. Place on a
lined baking sheet and brush with the egg wash. Let rise until
puffy, about 1 hour. Bake in a 400°F (200°C) oven until nicely
golden, about 15 minutes. Transfer to a cooling rack and let
cool. Heat the clear glaze and brush the cooled pastries with it.

Batters with chemical raising agents

Madeleines ★★

Ingredients (makes about 10 madeleines)
2 eggs
⅔ cup (4 oz./125 g) sugar
1 ⅓ cups (5 ½ oz./165 g) flour
1 teaspoon (4 g) baking powder
Flavoring, such as 1 teaspoon (5 ml) vanilla extract
   or finely grated lemon zest
4 tablespoons (2 oz./60 g) butter, plus a little extra for greasing
3 tablespoons (50 ml) milk

Special equipment: 3-inch. (7-cm) long madeleine molds

Butter the madeleine molds. Whip the eggs and sugar together until pale and thick. Sift the flour and baking powder together. Fold the dry ingredients into the egg mixture and stir in the flavoring.
Melt the butter and milk together and stir it into the batter. Center a baking pan large enough to hold the madeleine pan in the oven. If you have two pans, place one on top of the other. This increases the heat that the raw batter comes into contact with and enhances the formation of the characteristic little bump. Preheat the oven to 400°F (200°C). Spoon or pipe the mixture into the molds two-thirds full and place on the heated pans.
Bake for about 10 minutes, the time for standard-sized madeleines, until golden and a cake tester inserted into the center comes out clean. Immediately turn onto a cooling rack so that they do not absorb any moisture from condensation.

● Did you know?
There are many stories around the creation of these small cakes. The recipe is generally attributed to a certain Madeleine Paumier at the Château de Commercy in Lorraine around 1730, when she made them for the king of Poland, Stanislas Leszczynski, the father-in-law of Louis XV. The Polish king later made them famous.

Traou Mad ★★

Ingredients (makes about 20 cookies)
1 ½ sticks (6 oz./170 g) salted butter,
   room temperature
¾ cup (5 oz./150 g) sugar
5 egg yolks (3 oz./100 g)
2 cups (9 oz./250 g) flour
2 teaspoons (8 g) baking powder

Special equipment: tartlet rings the same diameter
   (about 3 inches/8 cm) as the cookie cutter

Preheat the oven to 350°F (180°C). Line a baking sheet with parchment paper.
In a stand mixer fitted with the paddle beater, or with an electric beater or whisk, cream the butter with the sugar at medium speed for about 10 minutes until very soft. Stir in the egg yolks, scraping down the sides, until fully incorporated. Sift the flour and baking powder together and work in with your fingertips. The dough will now have a grainy texture.
Roll the dough to a thickness of ⅕ inch (5 mm). (Try to ensure that it is as smooth as possible.) With a 3-inch (8-cm) cookie cutter, cut out circles. Transfer the disks of dough to the prepared baking sheet and enclose them in the tartlet rings. Bake for 17 minutes, until golden. Transfer to a rack and let cool.

● Did you know?
Traou mad, a traditional buttery cookie, is a Breton specialty from Pont-Aven. The name means "good thing."

Citrus Loaf ★

Ingredients (serves 6)
5 eggs
1 cup plus scant 1 cup (¾ lb./350 g) sugar
1 teaspoon (4 g) salt
Finely grated zest of 1 orange (unsprayed or organic)
   or other citrus fruit
⅔ cup (150 ml) heavy cream
2 teaspoons (10 ml) orange brandy (or rum, or other liqueur)
2 ¼ cups (9 ½ oz./270 g) flour
1 ¼ teaspoons (5 g) baking powder
7 tablespoons (3 ½ oz./100 g) butter, melted and cooled,
   plus extra for greasing

10-inch (25-cm) loaf pan

Preheat the oven to 350°F (180°C). Butter the loaf pan and dust it lightly with flour. If you wish, line the base with parchment paper. Whip the eggs, sugar, and salt until pale and thick.

Incorporate the citrus zest, cream, and orange brandy. Sift in the flour and baking powder and mix until just incorporated. Stir in the cooled melted butter. Pour into the prepared pan. Bake for 35 to 40 minutes, until nicely browned and a cake tester comes out clean. Immediately turn onto a cooling rack. Let cool completely before cutting.

● **Chef's note**
If you wrap this cake in plastic wrap as soon as it cools, it keeps well for several days.

❢ **Recipe idea**
Lemon Loaf Cake ›› p. 406

Savory Loaf ★

If you're invited for drinks in France, you may be served small pieces of a *cake salé*, a savory loaf, to nibble on.

Ingredients (makes a 1-lb./500-g loaf, to serve 12)
1 ¼ sticks. (5 oz./150 g) butter, room temperature
Scant ½ cup (5 oz./150 g) glucose syrup or atomized glucose
2 eggs
¾ cup plus 2 tablespoons (3 ½ oz./100 g) flour
3 tablespoons (2 oz./50 g) cornstarch
½ teaspoon (3 g) baking powder
4 oz. (120 g) savory garnish, such as chopped olives, diced hard cheese, bacon bits, chopped sun-dried tomatoes
A little flour to dust the garnish

10-inch (25-cm) loaf pan

Preheat the oven to 350°F (180°C).
Cream the butter with the glucose syrup. Beat in the eggs, one by one. Sift the flour with the cornstarch and baking powder. Fold in the dry ingredients until just combined. Lightly roll the savory garnishes in some flour to prevent them from sinking during baking, and stir in. Pour into the loaf pan. Bake for 15 minutes, until golden on top and a cake tester comes out dry (allowing for the type of garnish used).

● **Chef's note**
Use your imagination for this recipe, but be careful to balance the savory garnish. If you are using Roquefort or other blue cheese, for example, reduce the amount of butter by half.

Marbled Pound Cake ★

This particular recipe uses beaten egg whites as its principal raising agent.

Ingredients (makes a 1 ½-lb./
   700-g cake, to serve 12)
1 ¾ sticks (7 oz./200 g) butter,
   room temperature
¾ cup (5 oz./150 g) light
   brown sugar
4 eggs, separated
½ teaspoon salt
⅓ cup (2 oz./60 g) sugar
1 cup plus 2 tablespoons (5 oz./150 g) flour
3 tablespoons (2 oz./50 g) cornstarch
½ teaspoon (2 g) baking powder
3 tablespoons (20 g) unsweetened cocoa powder

http://flamm.fr/fj105

10-inch (25-cm) loaf pan

Line the loaf pan with parchment paper, or butter and flour it. Cream the butter with the light brown sugar. Whisk in the egg yolks, one by one, until completely incorporated. Beat the egg whites lightly to liquefy them. Then whisk energetically, lifting the whisk high to incorporate as much air as possible, until the egg whites hold soft peaks. Stir in the sugar with the whisk, using a circular movement, until firm and shiny. Fold it into the butter and egg yolk mixture, taking care not to deflate the mixture.
Sift the salt and flour with the cornstarch and baking powder and fold in carefully. Stop when just combined.
Divide the batter into two equal parts. Sift the cocoa powder into one and fold it in.
Preheat the oven to 340°F (170°C).
Fill the loaf pan three-quarters full, alternating spoonfuls of chocolate batter with spoonfuls of plain batter. Rap the pan on a cloth set over the work surface to even out the batter. Immediately place in the oven for about 40 minutes, until well risen and a cake tester inserted into the loaf comes out clean. (A slightly alternative method can be seen on the video above.)

● **Chef's note**
For a more marked marbled effect, pipe the two batters with two piping bags.

Fruit Loaf ★

Ingredients (makes a 1 ¾-lb./800-g cake, to serve 12)

1 ¼ sticks. (5 oz./150 g) butter, plus 1 tablespoon (20 g) softened
butter for the top of the loaf

¾ cup (5 oz./150 g) sugar

2 large eggs

Or, if using a liquid egg product: ½ cup (4 oz./120 g)

½ teaspoon (2.5 ml) rum

½ teaspoon (2.5 ml) vanilla extract

1 ⅔ cups (7 oz./200 g) flour

2 teaspoons (8 g) baking powder

5 oz. (150 g) assorted candied fruits (orange, cherries, raisins,
etc.), chopped

10-inch (25-cm) loaf pan

Line the loaf pan with parchment paper, or butter and
flour it. Preheat the oven to 325°F (165°C). In a mixing bowl,
cream the butter and sugar. Beat in the eggs, one by one, until
fully incorporated. Stir in the rum and vanilla extract.
Sift the flour with the baking powder and lightly roll the
candied fruit pieces in it (this prevents them from all falling
to the bottom of the cake during baking). Fold the dry
ingredients into the batter and stir in the pieces of fruit.
Pour into the prepared pan. Spoon the softened butter into
a paper decorating cone and draw out a line over the top.
This will ensure the cake cracks evenly and attractively.

Bake for 35 to 40 minutes, until golden brown on top and
a cake tester comes out clean. Turn onto a cooling rack.

● **Chef's note**

Because this cake is dense, it keeps and travels well.

Charentes Butter Cake ★ ★

Ingredients (makes two 7-in./18-cm diameter cakes,
to serve 8-10)

2 sticks (9 oz./250 g) salted butter, softened

1 ½ cups (10 oz./300 g) sugar

3 eggs, separated

3 ¼ cups (14 oz./400 g) flour

1 teaspoon (5 g) baking powder

½ cup (3 ½ oz./100 g) superfine sugar

Finely grated zest of ½ lemon

1 egg for the egg wash, lightly beaten with a pinch of salt

With a whisk, beat the butter and sugar together until soft
and creamy. Whip in the egg yolks, one by one, until fully
incorporated. Sift the flour and baking powder together
and stir in. Beat the egg whites lightly to liquefy them.
Then whisk them energetically, lifting the whisk high
to incorporate as much air as possible, until the egg whites
hold soft peaks. Stir in the superfine sugar with the whisk,
using a circular movement. Fold it into the butter-egg yolk
mixture, taking care not to deflate the mixture. Stir in the
lemon zest. Cover the mixing bowl with plastic wrap and
chill for 20 to 25 minutes, until firm.
Preheat the oven to 375°F (190°C). On a lightly floured
surface, roll the dough out to a thickness of about ¾ inch
(1-2 cm). Lightly beat the egg with a pinch of salt and brush
the top of the dough with it. With the tines of a fork and
the back of a knife, make a cross-hatch pattern on the top.
Bake on a baking sheet for 25 to 30 minutes, until golden
and firm to the touch.

● **Did you know?**

*This butter cake, which used to be called a galette de première
communion (cake for the first communion) or galette charentaise
(cake of Charentes), was served by children taking their first
communion and their parents when they welcomed their guests.
Nowadays it is still considered a ceremonial cake and set
on tables for important family ceremonies and festivities,
like weddings.*

Fritters ★★

Carnival Fritters (*Bugnes*)

Ingredients (makes about 12 fritters)
5 tablespoons (2 ½ oz./70 g) butter
2 tablespoons (1 oz./25 g) sugar
2 tablespoons (1 oz./25 g) vanilla sugar
  (see pp. 195 and 468)
1 egg
1 teaspoon (5 g) salt
2 cups (9 oz./250 g) flour
1 teaspoon (5 g) baking powder
¼ cup (60 ml) milk
3 tablespoons (50 ml) rum
Finely grated zest of 1 unsprayed lemon
Confectioners' sugar for dusting

Cream the butter, sugar, and vanilla sugar together. Beat
in the egg and the salt. Sift the flour and baking powder
together and stir in. Pour in the milk and rum and stir until
combined. Stir in the lemon zest. Beat the batter until it is
smooth, thick, and elastic. Shape it into a ball, cover in plastic
wrap, and chill for 2 hours. On a lightly floured surface, roll it
out very finely, about ⅛ inch (3-4 mm) thick. Cut it into 4 x
1 ½-inch (10 x 4-cm) rectangles. Make a hole in the center. Heat
an oil bath to 350°F (180°C) and drop the fritters in. When
they rise to the surface, turn them over to color them evenly.
When they are nicely browned, remove them from the oil
with a slotted spoon and drain on paper towel. Immediately
dust with confectioners' sugar and serve warm. These are
best eaten on the day they are made.

Fritters with Orange Flower Water

Ingredients (makes about 12 fritters)
4 tablespoons (2 oz./60 g) butter
2 ½ tablespoons (1 oz./30 g) sugar
2 eggs
Or, if using a liquid egg product: ½ cup (4 oz./125 g)
1 teaspoon (5 g) salt
2 cups (9 oz./250 g) flour
1 tablespoon plus 1 teaspoon (20 ml) orange
  flower water
Confectioners' sugar for dusting

Cream the butter and sugar together. Beat in the eggs and
salt. Sift the flour and stir in. Stir in the orange flower water.
Beat the batter until it is smooth, thick, and elastic. Shape
it into a ball, cover in plastic wrap, and chill for 1 hour.
On a lightly floured surface, roll it out very finely, about
⅛ inch (3-4 mm) thick. Cut it into 4 x 1 ½-inch (10 x 4-cm)
rectangles. Make a hole in the center. Heat an oil bath to
350°F (180°C) and drop the fritters in. When they rise to
the surface, turn them over to color them evenly. When they
are nicely browned, remove them from the oil with a slotted
spoon and drain on paper towel. Immediately dust with
confectioners' sugar and serve warm. These are best eaten
on the day they are made.

Donuts

Ingredients (makes about 10 donuts)
½ cake (0.3 oz./10 g) fresh (compressed) yeast
⅓ cup (80 ml) milk or water, room temperature
2 ½ cups (10 ½ oz./300 g) flour
1 pinch ground cinnamon
1 ½ tablespoons (20 g) sugar
1 teaspoon (4 g) salt
1 egg plus 3 egg yolks
5 tablespoons (75 g) butter
Confectioners' sugar for dusting or fondant icing
  for the topping

Dilute the yeast in the milk or water. Sift the flour and
cinnamon into a large bowl or on a work surface. Make
a well in the center. Sprinkle the sugar and salt at a distance
from the well so that they do not come into direct contact
with the yeast. When the yeast mixture is foaming, pour
it into the well. With your hands or a scraper, incorporate
the liquid into the flour mixture. Lightly beat the eggs and,
working either by hand or with a stand mixer fitted with a
dough hook, knead them into the dough until it is elastic.
Knead in the butter. Transfer the dough to a lightly oiled
mixing bowl and smooth it over. At this stage, it is shiny and
stretches. Cover with plastic wrap and let rise at 68°F-77°F
(20°C-25°C) for 30 to 40 minutes, until doubled in volume.
Cut pieces and shape them into rings. Heat an oil bath to
350°F (180°C) and drop the donuts in for about 2 minutes,
until nicely browned all over and risen to the surface. Remove
them from the oil with a slotted spoon and drain on paper
towel. Immediately dust with confectioners' sugar or spread
with fondant icing and serve warm. These are best eaten on
the day they are made.

Fritters with Cognac (*Merveilles*)

Ingredients (makes about 12 fritters)
2 cups (9 oz./250 g) flour
⅓ cup (2 oz./60 g) sugar
4 tablespoons (2 oz./60 g) butter
2 eggs
¾ teaspoon (3 g) baking powder
½ teaspoon (2 g) salt
2-3 teaspoons (10-15 ml) cognac
Confectioners' sugar for dusting

Combine all the ingredients except the cognac and confectioners' sugar in a large mixing bowl until the batter is smooth. Stir in the cognac, cover with plastic wrap, and chill until firm, about 30 minutes.
On a lightly floured surface, roll the dough to a thickness of just under ½ inch (1 cm). Cut it into triangles or diamond shapes with a sharp knife.
Heat an oil bath to 350°F (180°C) and drop the fritters in. When they rise to the surface, turn them over to color them evenly. Remove from the oil with a slotted spoon and drain on paper towel. Dust with confectioners' sugar and serve warm. These are best eaten on the day they are made.

● **Did you know?**
Behind a range of fritters with interesting names in French (merveilles or "marvels"; oreillettes or "little ears"; mensonges or "lies") is a widespread, ancient recipe for fried dough. It is thick, rich in flour, and rolled out. Some are cut into strips and braided, others made into diamond shapes, hearts, animals, etc., with cookie cutters. Fried in a hot oil bath, fritters are served hot, warm, or cool, dusted with sugar. They are traditionally served at carnival time and Mardi Gras (literally, Fat Tuesday), the last day before Lent.

Moist Chestnut Cake ★

Ingredients (makes a 1 lb. 14-oz./850-g cake)
9 oz. (250 g) chestnut cream (*crème de marron*, see chef's note)
1 cup (3 ½ oz./200 g) sugar
1 stick plus 2 tablespoons (5 oz./150 g) butter, softened
2 eggs
Or, if using a liquid egg product: ½ cup (4 oz./125 g)
1 tablespoon (15 ml) brown rum
1 cup (4 oz./125 g) flour
½ teaspoon (2 g) baking powder

9-10-inch (22-25-cm) diameter cake pan

Preheat the oven to 350°F (180°C). Butter and flour
the cake pan.
In the bowl of a stand mixer fitted with the paddle
attachment, beat the chestnut cream and sugar at
medium speed until smooth.
With the paddle still turning, add the butter and then
the eggs until fully incorporated. Stir in the rum.
Sift the flour with the baking powder and fold or whisk
it into the batter. Stop as soon as it is fully incorporated.
Pour into prepared pan. Bake for 18 to 20 minutes,
just until the top is dry. Do not overbake or the cake
will dry out; it must remain moist inside.

⬤ **Chef's note**
*Crème de marron, also known as chestnut spread, is made
of chestnuts, sugar, and vanilla, and sometimes glucose and
candied chestnuts.*

🥄 **Recipe idea**
Chestnut Sponge with Chestnut Cream Panna Cotta >> p. 299

Gingerbread ★

Ingredients (makes 2 lb./900 g of gingerbread,
 to serve about 20)
1 cup plus 1 tablespoon (4 oz./125 g) rye flour
1 cup (4 oz./125 g) flour
1 tablespoon plus 1 teaspoon (15 g) baking powder
1 teaspoon gingerbread spice mix (see chef's note)
⅔ cup (150 ml) heavy cream
⅔ cup (250 g) honey
2 tablespoons (oz. 30 g) butter
½ cup (3 ½ oz./100 g) sugar
3 eggs

10-inch (25-cm) loaf pan

Preheat the oven to 340°F (170°C).
Sift together the rye flour, white flour, baking powder,
and spices.
In a bain-marie, warm the cream, honey, butter,
and sugar until liquid.
Pour the mixture into the dry ingredients and mix together
with an electric beater. Incorporate the eggs one by one.
Pour into a buttered loaf pan and bake for 35 to 45 minutes,
until a cake tester comes out dry. Turn onto a cooling rack.

⬤ **Chef's note**
*Gingerbread spice mix usually includes cinnamon, star anise,
nutmeg, ginger, cloves, cardamom, and vanilla in varying
numbers and proportions. If you don't have a readymade mix,
you can compose your own. The type of honey you choose will
determine the taste of the gingerbread.*

Sponges, bases, and petits fours

Eggs

Whether eggs come from battery-raised chickens or hens that run freely in a farm yard, their composition is identical. An "egg," unless otherwise specified, always refers to a hen's egg.

All eggs that hens lay, whether for reproduction or our consumption, are initially made up of the same elements: about 75 percent water, 12 percent lipids (fat), 13 percent proteins, as well as many trace elements and vitamins. What differs are the color of the yolk and the flavor, which are dependent on the hen's feed. A bright yellow yolk is the result of feed that is rich in crushed corn, whose carotene lends colorant. The color of the shell has no effect on the quality of the egg and is simply dependent on the breed of the hens.

An egg can weigh between 1 ½ oz. (45 g) and 2 ⅔ oz. (75 g). The yolk of an average egg weighs about ¾ oz. (18 g) and the white around 1 ¼ oz. (33–36 g). In this book, unless otherwise specified, the recipes call for "large" eggs (USA and Canada) and "medium" for the UK.

If you break an egg and examine it carefully, you will be able to see exactly how fresh it is. A very fresh egg has a tiny air pocket with a well-rounded yolk and a white that clings closely to it. As it ages, it liquefies, the yolk flattens and the white spreads. Pasteurized egg products are also available—eggs sold whole, or separated in liquid form—which greatly reduce the dangers of contamination from salmonella or listeria. These products are also useful for weighing out precise quantities.

Without eggs, there could be no pastry as we know it. Or such a variety of cakes. The yolk is the richest part of the egg. It contains lecithin, an emulsifier that binds sauces with its fats. It also imparts color—just look at the delicate yellow of brioche dough or choux pastry, for example. In the recipes that follow, we rely on beaten egg for leavening. No baking powder is used, so for optimal airiness and best texture, carefully follow directions for beating.

Sponge layers (*biscuits*)

Most of the recipes presented in this chapter are used as components of layered cakes. Because French layered cakes tend to be modestly low, sometimes belying their luscious interiors, the sponges and other bases do not rise high. They are generally spread thinly on baking sheets and baked to just the right degree of moistness. Historically, however, they were served dry: they were baked twice (hence their name, *bis-cuit*, literally "cooked twice") so they would keep well, and eaten dipped into wine or milk.

You can use them interchangeably, for the most part, as bases and layers for the creamy fillings in the following chapter, and of course you can experiment with alternatives to our classics.

All the recipes here can be made up to one day ahead. If you need to make sponge or other layers earlier, let them cool completely (to avoid condensation), wrap very well, and place them, perfectly flat, in the freezer, where they will keep for up to one week. Yields will often exceed the requirements for a particular cake. This is because it is generally easier to make larger quantities than smaller ones, but if you have leftovers, your family and friends are unlikely to complain.

Soft Coconut Sponge ★

Ingredients (makes 2 lb. 1 oz./950 g of sponge,
  around 25 slices for the bottom of a dessert)
1 cup plus 2 tablespoons (5 oz./150 g) flour
1 tablespoon (12 g) baking powder
¾ cup (175 ml) low-fat milk (2 percent)
¾ cup (5 oz./150 g) sugar
Scant ⅓ cup (3 ½ oz./100 g) invert sugar
1 ¼ sticks (5 oz./150 g) butter, room temperature
3 eggs plus 1 white (or 6 oz./175 g eggs if using pasteurized
  egg products)
2 ⅓ cups (6 oz./180 g) unsweetened shredded coconut

Two rimmed 12 x 16-inch (30 x 40-cm) baking sheets

Preheat the oven to 350°F (180°C). Line the baking sheets
with silicone baking mats. Sift the flour with the baking
powder. Pour the milk into a bain-marie heated to 86°F-104°F
(30°C-40°C) and stir in the sugar and invert sugar. Let the
sugar dissolve gently (1). Soften the butter (2). Beat the eggs
lightly and whisk them into the butter (3). Incorporate the
shredded coconut. Fold the flour and baking powder into
the batter. Pour onto the prepared baking sheets and bake
for 15 minutes, until golden brown on top and still soft
to the touch. Immediately turn onto a cooling rack.

● Chef's note
*Use this sponge as a substitute for any of the other flat sponges
in your desserts.*

● Did you know?
*In the past, the Genoese sponge was the most frequently used in
pastry. These days, recipes for sponges are more varied. They may
be more or less soft, and considerably improve the texture
of the desserts of which they are a component. They are used
in most layered desserts and small cakes as both a base or to
line the sides, and sometimes as one of the inner layers.*

Chocolate Sacher Sponge ★★

Ingredients (makes enough for the base and inner
  layer of a 7-in./16-cm cake)
7 oz. (200 g) almond paste, 50 percent almonds
1 very large (USA) or large (UK) egg (2 ½ oz./70 g)
4 egg yolks (3 ½ oz./95 g)
⅔ cup (4 oz./125 g) sugar, divided
3 egg whites (4 oz./110 g)
½ cup minus 1 tablespoon (2 oz./50 g) flour
3 tablespoons (⅔ oz./20 g) unsweetened cocoa powder
3 tablespoons (2 oz./50 g) butter, melted and cooled to lukewarm
2 oz. (50 g) cocoa paste, melted and cooled to lukewarm

A rimmed 12 x 16-inch (30 x 40-cm) baking sheet

Preheat the oven to 350°F (180°C). Line the baking sheet
with a silicone baking mat. If the almond paste is not at
room temperature, place it for 2 seconds in the microwave
oven at low to medium power. Place the almond paste in a
mixing bowl and gradually mix in the egg, egg yolks, and half
the sugar to soften it (1, 2). Whip the egg whites until they
form soft peaks. Add the remaining sugar and whip until the
mixture is firm and shiny. With a flexible spatula, carefully
fold the egg whites into the almond paste and egg mixture
in several additions. Sift the flour and cocoa powder together
and fold in carefully. Stir in the melted butter and cocoa paste.
Stop when completely incorporated. Pour the batter into
the prepared baking sheet and spread into the corners with
a spatula (3). Bake for 10 minutes, until dry to the touch but
still springy. Transfer carefully to a cooling rack.

Joconde Sponge ★★

Ingredients (makes 2 lb./900 g of sponge,
  around 25 slices for the bottom of a dessert)
1 cup (3 oz./80 g) ground almonds
Scant ⅔ cup (3 oz./80 g) confectioners' sugar
2 ½ tablespoons (oz./25 g) flour
2 eggs
5 egg whites
3 ½ tablespoons (1½ oz./40 g) sugar
1 tablespoon (20 g) butter, melted until brown and cooled

Two rimmed 12 x 16-inch (30 x 40-cm) baking sheets

(Continued overleaf)

Sponges, bases, and petits fours

Preheat the oven to 350°F (180°C). Line the baking sheets with silicone baking mats or parchment paper.
Combine the ground almonds and confectioners' sugar and sift in the flour. In the bowl of a stand mixer, beat the eggs and 1 of the egg whites with the sifted dry ingredients at medium speed for 10 minutes. Meanwhile, whip the remaining 4 egg whites until they form soft peaks. Add the sugar and whip until incorporated. The meringue should not be too firm (1). Pour the browned melted butter into the egg mixture. Carefully fold in the meringue. Spread very thinly over the baking sheets (2). Bake for about 15 minutes, until dry on top, springy to the touch, and very light golden

● **Did you know?**
This sponge layer is characteristically used in classic layered desserts. It is an integral component of the Opéra (Coffee and Chocolate Layer Cake), made famous by the great pastry chef, Gaston Lenôtre.

❚ **Recipe ideas**
Creamy Peach and Orange Log Dessert ›› p. 330
Opéra Coffee and Chocolate Layer Cake ›› p. 354

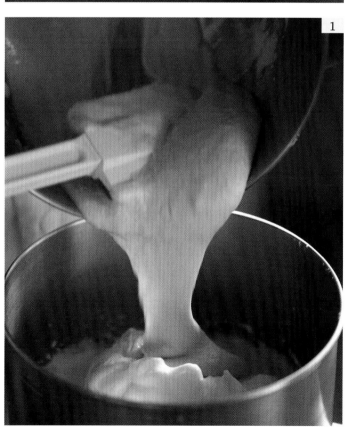

1

2

Genoa Loaf Cake ★

Ingredients (makes 2 lb. 14 oz./1.3 kg of sponge,
  around 25 slices for the bottom of a dessert)
5 eggs plus 2 egg yolks
1 cup plus 6 tablespoons (10 oz./275 g) sugar, divided
3 ½ cups (10 ½ oz./300 g) ground almonds
1 cup minus 2 ½ tablespoons (4 oz./125 g) cornstarch
3 tablespoons (1 oz./25 g) confectioners' sugar
1 ½ sticks (6 oz./175 g) butter, melted and cooled to lukewarm
3 egg whites (3 ½ oz./100 g)

Two rimmed 12 x 16-inch (30 x 40-cm) baking sheets
  or two 10-inch (25-cm) loaf pans

Preheat the oven to 350°F (180°C) if making thin layers,
or 340°F (170°C) for loaves. Line the baking sheets or loaf
pans. With an electric beater, whip the eggs, egg yolks, and
1 cup plus 3 tablespoons (8 oz./225g) sugar together for 6
minutes at a high speed until the ribbon stage. Combine
dry ingredients with a flexible spatula, fold into the egg
mixture. Stir in the melted butter. Whip the egg whites. Add
the remaining sugar and whip briefly until the mixture is
shiny. Carefully fold the meringue mixture into the batter.
Fill the prepared cake pans or spread the batter over the
baking sheets and bake until golden brown on top and a cake
tester comes out dry, about 15 to 20 minutes for thin layers

and 40 minutes for loaves. This sponge should remain very soft:
remove it from the oven while it still springs back to the touch.

❢ Recipe idea
Iced Layered Coffee Dessert >> p. 444

Flour-Free Chocolate Sponge ★

Ingredients (makes 1 lb. 5 oz./600 g of sponge,
  around 15 slices for the bottom of a dessert)
5–6 egg whites (6 ½ oz./190 g)
1 ¼ cups (8 ½ oz./240 g) sugar
7–8 egg yolks (5 oz./150 g)
⅔ cup (2 ½ oz./75 g) unsweetened cocoa powder

Two rimmed 12 x 16-inch (30 x 40-cm) baking sheets

Preheat the oven to 340°F (170°C). Line the baking sheets with
parchment paper. Whip the egg whites until they form soft peaks.
Stir in the sugar with the whisk until the mixture is firm and shiny.
Beat the egg yolks well. Carefully fold the egg whites into the egg
yolks. Sift in the cocoa powder and, with a flexible spatula, stir it
in until just combined. Spread it out on the baking sheets to about
¼ inch (5 mm) and bake for 15 to 20 minutes, until it springs back
to the touch; the inside should remain moist. Carefully transfer
it to a cooling rack (it is very fragile). Vary this recipe by adding
ground almonds or hazelnuts, potato starch, or cornstarch.

Hazelnut *Dacquoise* Sponge ★

Ingredients (makes 3 lb. 1 oz./1.4 kg of sponge,
  around 28 slices)
Scant cup (4 oz./115 g) confectioners' sugar
1 ⅓ cups (4 oz./115 g) ground hazelnuts
2 ½ tablespoons (1 oz./25 g) flour
5 egg whites (5 ½ oz./165 g)
Scant ½ cup (3 oz./85 g) sugar

Preheat the oven to 350°F (180°C). Line baking sheets
with parchment paper.
Combine the dry ingredients.
Make a French meringue: whip the egg whites until
they form soft peaks. Add the sugar and whip briefly
until the mixture is shiny but not too firm.
With a flexible spatula, carefully fold the dry ingredients
into the meringue until just incorporated (1).
Spoon the mixture into a piping bag and pipe spirals on
prepared baking sheets to use as bases for your desserts (2).
Bake for 10 minutes, until nicely golden but still soft.
Use very quickly or freeze as soon as cooled.

● **Did you know?**
*This sponge takes its name from the town of Dax in the Basque
region of France. It is very similar to the Succès Almond Meringue
(see p. 77) and remains soft when baked. The two recipes may be
used interchangeably.*

🥄 **Recipe idea**
Creamy Pistachio Log Dessert >> p. 334

1

2

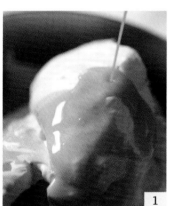

Ladyfingers ★

Ingredients (makes
sufficient for a charlotte
to serve 8)
5 eggs, separated
1 pinch salt
⅔ cup (4 ½ oz./125 g) sugar

¾ cup plus 2 tablespoons
(3 ½ oz./100 g) flour
2 ½ tablespoons (1 oz./25 g)
cornstarch
About 3 tablespoons (1 oz./
25 g) confectioners' sugar

Preheat the oven to 400°F (200°C). In a perfectly clean, dry,
round-bottom mixing bowl, liquefy the egg whites with a
pinch of salt. Then whisk energetically until the egg whites
hold soft peaks. Stir in the sugar with the whisk, using a
circular movement. The French meringue will be compact,
smooth, and hold small peaks when the whisk is held up.
Lightly beat the egg yolks and carefully fold them into the
French meringue with a flexible spatula (1). Sift the flour
and cornstarch together and fold in carefully (2). Spoon
the mixture into a piping bag and pipe lengths, separately
(for a charlotte) or in one strip (for a base) (3, 4). Individual
fingers should be about 3 x ⅔ inch (7.5 x 1.5 cm). Dust lightly
with confectioners' sugar twice at 5-minute intervals.
Bake for 10 to 15 minutes; they should barely color.

Recipe ideas
Tiramisu >> p. 317
Strawberry-Raspberry Charlotte >> p. 337

Sponges, bases, and petits fours

Progrès Sponge ★ ★

This is a very dry sponge base made with nuts that requires long baking at low heat. It is similar to the *Dacquoise* and the *Succès*.

Ingredients (makes 2 lb./900 g of sponge, around 20 slices)
3-4 egg whites (4 oz./120 g)
½ cup (2 oz./50 g) sugar
Generous ½ cup (2 oz./50 g) ground almonds
Generous ½ cup (2 oz./50 g) ground hazelnuts
⅓ cup (2 oz./50 g) confectioners' sugar

One rimmed 12 x 16-inch (30 x 40-cm) baking sheet

Preheat the oven to 250°F (120°C). Line the baking sheet with parchment paper. In a perfectly clean, dry, round-bottom mixing bowl, liquefy the egg whites. Then whisk energetically, lifting the whisk high to incorporate as much air as possible, until the egg whites hold soft peaks. Stir in the sugar with the whisk, using a circular movement. The French meringue will be compact, smooth, and hold small peaks when the whisk is held up. Combine the remaining ingredients and, with a flexible spatula, carefully fold them into the meringue. Spoon the mixture into a piping bag and pipe spirals to make bases for your recipe. Bake for 1 ½ to 2 hours. The meringue should be dry to the touch and should not color.

Cookies ★

Ingredients (makes about 2 dozen cookies)
2 sticks (9 oz./250 g) butter, room temperature
⅓ cup (3 oz./80 g) dark brown sugar
1 teaspoon (6 g) salt
2 eggs plus 1 egg yolk
2 ½ cups (10 ½ oz./300 g) flour
1 cup plus 3 tablespoons (3 ½ oz./100 g) ground hazelnuts
1 ½ teaspoons (6 g) baking powder
½ teaspoon (1 g) ground cinnamon
1 teaspoon (5 ml) vanilla extract
12 oz. (350 g) chocolate chips, or 6 oz. (175 g) chocolate chips and 6 oz. (175 g) nougatine bits (see recipe p. 166)

Whip the butter energetically with the sugar and salt until it is very creamy. Beat in the eggs one by one, making sure each is fully incorporated before adding the next one. Beat in the egg yolk. Sift the flour, and mix together with the ground hazelnuts and baking powder, then stir into the mixture. Stir in the cinnamon and vanilla extract. Incorporate the chocolate chips (and the nougatine bits, if using). Stop when evenly distributed. Gather the dough together and, on a sheet of parchment paper, shape it into a log. Ensure it is tightly rolled. Chill until firm, about 1 hour. Preheat the oven to 350°F (180°C). Cut the log into ½-inch (1-cm) slices and place them on a silicone baking mat. Bake for 20 minutes, until golden. Immediately transfer to a cooling rack so that they don't reabsorb any moisture.

Brownies ★

Ingredients (makes about 3 dozen brownies)
2 sticks (8 oz./225 g) butter
4 oz. (120 g) bittersweet chocolate, 70 percent cocoa
4 eggs
1 cup (7 oz./200 g) sugar
1 cup (4 ½ oz./130 g) flour
⅔ cup (2 oz./50 g) ground almonds
2 teaspoons (10 ml) vanilla extract
1 small pinch ground cinnamon
5 oz. (150 g) walnuts, chopped

Thirty-six 1-inch (2-3-cm) deep silicone molds

Preheat the oven to 340°F (170°C). Melt the butter and chocolate in a bain-marie. Whisk the eggs and sugar until pale and thick. Whisk in the melted butter and chocolate mixture. Sift the flour and ground almonds together and fold into the batter. Stir until just combined. Stir in the vanilla, cinnamon, and walnuts. Pour the batter into individual silicone molds, about 1 inch (2 to 3 cm) deep. Bake for about 10 minutes, until a cake tester comes out dry.

● Chef's notes
Use cashew nuts, pecans, or hazelnuts as alternatives to walnuts.

Pistachio Sponge ★

Ingredients (makes 2 lb. 9 oz./1.15 kg of sponge, around 20 slices)
4 eggs
5 egg yolks
1 cup plus 1 scant cup (12 oz./350 g) sugar
2 ¼ cups (10 oz./270 g) flour
1 teaspoon (5 g) baking powder
4 tablespoons (2 oz./60 g) butter
5 oz. (140 g) good-quality pistachio paste
Scant ½ cup (100 ml) heavy cream
1 teaspoon (4 g) salt

Two rimmed 12 x 16-inch (30 x 40-cm) baking sheets

Preheat the oven to 375°F (190°C). Line two 12 x 16-inch (30 x 40-cm) baking sheets with a silicone baking mat or parchment paper. Whisk the eggs, egg yolks, and sugar together until the mixture reaches the ribbon stage. Sift the flour and baking powder together and fold into the egg mixture until just combined. In a small saucepan, soften the butter, pistachio paste, cream, and salt. Whisk together and incorporate into the egg and flour mixture. Stop when combined. Bake for 6 to 8 minutes. It should remain soft to the touch and must not be overbaked, so that it retains its moistness.

🍴 **Recipe idea**
Pistachio and Raspberry Layer Cake >> p. 393

Financiers ★

Ingredients (makes 8 *financiers*)
1 stick (4 ½ oz./125 g) butter
¾ cup (5 oz./150 g) sugar
1 cup minus 1 tablespoon (2 ½ oz./75 g) ground almonds
4 egg whites
½ cup (2 oz./60 g) flour

Special equipment: 8 *financier* molds or other shallow molds

Preheat the oven to 340°F (170°C). Melt the butter in a small saucepan until browned. Let cool to lukewarm. In a bain-marie set over water at 120°F (50°C), combine the sugar, ground almonds, and egg whites. Mix well to dissolve the sugar and enhance the flavor of the almonds. Watch the temperature carefully so that the whites do not cook. Remove from the heat and in a slow, steady stream, beat in the browned butter. Beat in the flour until the mixture is smooth. Pour into molds and bake for about 10 minutes, until lightly browned. They must remain moist, so do not overbake.

⬤ **Chef's notes**
Financier batter can be used to make other recipes than the small cakes eaten on their own. Spread it onto a prepared baking sheet to use as a base for layered desserts, or, for petits fours, bake in small molds and let cool in the molds so that they retain even more of their characteristic moistness.

⬤ **Did you know?**
This recipe goes back to the Middle Ages, but gradually lost its popularity during the Renaissance due to its aroma of bitter almonds, which suggested the arsenic used to poison members of the nobility. It was revisited and improved by the pastry chef Lasne in about 1890. His pastry shop was located near the Paris stock exchange. According to him, the original oval form meant that eaters got their fingers dirty, and so he shaped them like small bars of gold—to the delight of his financier clients.

🍴 **Recipe idea**
Financiers (alternative method) >> p. 394

Coconut Macaroons ★

Ingredients (makes about 15 macaroons)
5 egg whites
1 small pinch salt
1 ¼ cups (9 oz./250 g) sugar
3 ½ cups (9 oz./250 g) unsweetened shredded coconut
2 ½ tablespoons (1 oz./25 g) flour

In a perfectly clean, dry, round-bottom mixing bowl, liquefy the egg whites with the salt. Pour in the sugar and whisk, lifting the whisk up high to incorporate as much air as possible. When the whites form soft peaks, set the bowl over a large saucepan half-filled with water heated to 120°F-130°F (50°C-55°C). Continue whipping until the mixture whitens, increases in volume, and becomes shiny, no hotter than 115°F (45°C). Remove from the heat and continue whipping until the meringue has cooled completely. With a flexible spatula, carefully fold in the shredded coconut and flour. Preheat the oven to 285°F (140°C). On a lined baking sheet, form small pyramids or rock shapes with a spoon. Bake for 12 minutes, until the macaroons are dry to the touch. Leave them soft in the center if you prefer them like this. Turn onto a cooling rack immediately. Let cool and store in an airtight container.

⬤ **Chef's notes**
Replace some or all of the shredded coconut with ground almonds, hazelnuts, or walnuts. You may also use very finely chopped candied fruit. Reduce the amount of sugar accordingly for this addition. Add an additional flavor note by dipping the cakes wholly or partially in melted dark chocolate. This recipe can also be made using the Italian meringue technique (see p. 177).

🍴 **Recipe idea**
Coconut Macaroons (alternative method) >> p. 385

Genoese Sponge ★

This simple, light sponge is a fundamental in French pastry making. Spread it thinly to use as a base for a layered dessert or bake it as a cake, slice it into layers, and fill it with a cream or ganache of your choice.

Ingredients (makes 1 lb./450 g of sponge; each cake serves 4)

4 eggs
⅔ cup (4 oz./125 g) sugar
1 cup (4 oz./125 g) flour

A rimmed 12 x 16-inch (30 x 40-cm) baking sheet or two cake pans with 6-inch (15-cm) diameter

http://flamm.fr/ffd06

Preheat the oven to 350°F (180°C). Butter and flour the cake pans (**3, 4**) or line the baking sheet with parchment paper. Place the eggs and sugar in a round-bottom mixing bowl and set it over a bain-marie heated to 140°F (60°C) (**1**). Whip until the mixture reaches the ribbon stage. Sift the flour and carefully fold in half of it with a flexible spatula (**2**). When it is incorporated, fold in the remaining half, taking care not to deflate the mixture. Do not overmix. Pour onto the baking sheet to a thickness of no more than ¼ inch (6–7 mm), or into the cake pans (**5**), and even the mixture with a spatula. Bake for 15 minutes (baking sheet) to 20 minutes (for cake). The sponge should stay moist and should not color. Slide it onto a rack and let cool.

● Chef's note

To make a chocolate Genoese sponge, replace 2 ½ tablespoons (1 oz./25 g) of the flour with 3 ½ tablespoons (1 oz./25 g) unsweetened cocoa powder, sifted.

❦ Recipe ideas

Black Forest Cake >> p. 346
Strawberry and Mousseline Cream Layer Cake (*Fraisier*) >> p. 349
Mocha Cake >> p. 353
Baked Alaska >> p. 450

Succès Almond Meringue ★★

Ingredients (makes 1 lb. 5 oz./600 g of meringue)
3-4 egg whites (4 oz./120 g)
2 tablespoons (1 oz./25 g) sugar
⅓ cup (2 oz./50 g) confectioners' sugar
1 cup minus 1 tablespoon (2 ½ oz./75 g) ground almonds
2 ½ tablespoons (25 g) all-purpose flour, sifted

Preheat the oven to 350°F (180°C). Make a French meringue (see p. 176): whip the egg whites (1) until they form firm peaks. Stir in the sugar with the whisk until the mixture is firm and shiny. Combine the confectioners' sugar, ground almonds, and sifted flour (2) and, with a flexible spatula, fold them into the meringue, taking care not to deflate the mixture. Spoon into a piping bag and pipe a disk. If you wish, sprinkle with sliced almonds, chopped walnuts, and so on. You may also include broken macaron bits for added textural interest. Bake for about 10 minutes. The meringue should be dry to the touch and should not color.

Recipe ideas

Raspberry and Vanilla Bavarian Cream Layer Cake >> p. 329
Black Currant Mousse and Pear Layer Cake >> p. 350

Sponges, bases, and petits fours

Jelly Roll (Swiss Roll) ★ ★

Ingredients (makes 1 lb. 2 oz./500 g of sponge, to serve 10)
2–3 egg yolks (1 ¾ oz./50 g)
2 eggs
¾ cup (5 oz./140 g) sugar, divided
2–3 egg whites (2 ½ oz./80 g)
⅓ cup (1 ½ oz./40 g) flour
3 tablespoons (1 oz./30 g) cornstarch

Jelly roll pan (approx. 12 x 8 in./30 x 20 cm)

Preheat the oven to 400°F (200°C). Line a jelly roll pan with parchment paper. With an electric beater at high speed, whip the egg yolks, eggs, and ⅔ cup (4 ½ oz./125 g) sugar until tripled in volume, 5 to 6 minutes. Make a French meringue: whisk the egg whites energetically, lifting the whisk high to incorporate as much air as possible, until they hold firm peaks. Stir in the remaining sugar with the whisk, using a circular movement. Carefully fold the meringue mixture into the egg and sugar mixture. Sift the flour and cornstarch into the mixture and fold in carefully with a flexible spatula. Spread the batter onto the prepared jelly roll pan to a thickness of about ⅕ inch (5 mm). Bake for 6 to 7 minutes, until lightly colored and springy to the touch. It's important not to overbake this sponge, as it would be too firm to roll. Let cool on a cooling rack, covered with a cloth or sheet of parchment paper so that it does not dry out. Trim the edges if necessary. Slip the jelly roll over a sheet of parchment or waxed paper. With a pastry brush, moisten the sponge with the syrup of your choice (1). With a spatula, spread over the creamy filling of your choice (2). Begin rolling up the jelly roll tightly (3). To finish, roll the parchment paper over the jelly roll and push it with the rack to ensure that it is tightly rolled up (4).

Recipe ideas
Yule Log >> p. 333
Creamy Pistachio Log Dessert >> p. 334

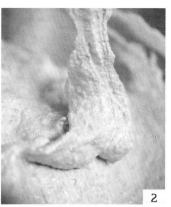

Macarons ★ ★ ★

Accurate measuring will give best results for this recipe; we recommend weighing all ingredients rather than using cup measures.

Ingredients (makes forty 1 ¼-1 ½-in./3-4-cm macarons)
1 ¾ cups (5 oz./150 g) ground almonds
Generous 1 cup (5 ¼ oz./150 g) confectioners' sugar
Scant ¼ cup (1 ¾ oz./50 g) egg whites

Italian meringue
¾ cup (5 oz./150 g) sugar
3 tablespoons (50 ml) water
¼ cup (2 oz./55 g) egg whites

Combine the ground almonds with the confectioners' sugar. Process with a blade knife so that the mixture is as fine and delicate as possible. Stir in the egg whites.
Make an Italian meringue (see p. 177): cook the sugar and water to 250°F (120°C), keeping an eye on the thermometer. When it reaches 243°F-250°F (117°C-120°C), begin whipping the remaining egg whites in a stand mixer until they hold firm peaks. Gradually pour the cooked syrup (at 250°F/120°C) over the egg whites, still whipping. Continue until the meringue has cooled completely. (It will be smooth and hold many small peaks.)
With a large scraper, gradually combine the two mixtures (1), which will deflate slightly (2), until smooth and shiny.
Spoon the mixture into a piping bag fitted with a plain tip and pipe small disks onto a silicone baking sheet (3) set on a thick baking pan, or two ordinary baking pans. Let stand for 30 minutes until a crust forms; the mixture should not stick to your fingers when touched (4). Preheat the oven to 310°F (155°C).
Bake for 12 minutes; do not let darken (5).

Recipe ideas

Glossy Chocolate Layer Cake >> p. 338
Chestnut Cream in a Macaron Shell >> p. 342
Assorted Macarons >> p. 371
Iced Yule Log >> 442

http://flamm.fr/ffd07

Florentines ★★

Ingredients (makes about 12 florentines)
½ cup (3 ½ oz./100 g) sugar
2 ½ tablespoons (2 oz./50 g) honey
½ cup (125 ml) crème fraîche or heavy cream
4 oz. (125 g) sliced almonds
3 oz. (85 g) candied fruit, chopped (angelica,
  cherries, orange peel, etc.)
2 ½ oz. (75 g) bittersweet chocolate, 60 percent cocoa

Special equipment: 2 ½-inch (6-cm) diameter silicone molds,
  sheets of food-safe acetate

Preheat the oven to 350°F (180°C).
Melt the sugar and honey in a heavy-bottom saucepan
(or a copper pot, if possible). Over low heat, gradually stir
in the cream, almonds, and candied fruit. Remove from
the heat and immediately pour into the molds. Bake until
reddened, about 12 minutes. Transfer to a cooling rack.
Meanwhile, temper the chocolate (see p. 182).
Dip one side of each florentine into the tempered chocolate
and place it, chocolate side downward, on a sheet of food-safe
acetate. (The use of this paper ensures that the chocolate
remains glossy.)
Store in an airtight container.

Almond Tuiles ★

Ingredients (makes about 12 tuiles)
¾ cup (3 ½ oz./100 g) confectioners' sugar
1 egg plus 2 egg whites
Or, if using liquid egg products: 2 ¼ oz. (60 g)
  whole eggs plus 2 oz. (50 g) egg whites
2 tablespoons (1 oz./25 g) butter, melted
1 tablespoon (10 g) flour
3 ½ oz. (100 g) sliced almonds

Preheat the oven to 350°F (180°C).
With an immersion blender, process all the ingredients,
except the sliced almonds, until smooth. Stir in the sliced
almonds.

On a silicone baking mat, spoon out small mounds of the
mixture and flatten them carefully with a fork. They should
be about 2 ½-3 inches (6-7 cm) in diameter. Space them
about 2 ½ inches (7 cm) apart, as they spread.
Bake, one batch at a time, until lightly browned at the edges,
6-8 minutes.
Immediately remove from the baking mat and drape
over bottles or a rolling pin to give them a curved shape.
Before you bake the next batch, ensure that the baking mat
(or pan) has cooled so that you can shape them properly.

Honey Lace Tuiles (egg free) ★

Ingredients (makes about 10 tuiles)
5 tablespoons (2 ½ oz./75 g) butter, room temperature
2 ½ tablespoons (2 oz./50 g) honey
¾ cup (3 ½ oz./100 g) confectioners' sugar
½ cup minus 1 tablespoon (2 oz./50 g) flour

Preheat the oven to 350°F (180°C).
In a small round-bottom mixing bowl, whip the butter with
the honey until soft. Whip in the confectioners' sugar and
flour. The mixture must be like a runny paste.
On a silicone baking sheet, spoon out small mounds and
round them out with the back of a spoon, leaving about
3 inches (7 cm) between them to spread.
Bake until lightly browned at the edges, 8-10 minutes.
Immediately remove with a spatula and shape them as
you wish, either like classic tuiles, waves, folded over on
themselves, or cut into triangles.

● **Chef's notes**
To give a stylish touch to your desserts, decorate them with these
fragile tuiles. They absorb moisture very quickly, so if you are
making them a day ahead, store in an airtight container.

Citrus-Scented Lace Tuiles ★

Ingredients (makes about 10 tuiles)
5 tablespoons (3 oz./80 g) butter, melted
½ cup (3 ½ oz./100 g) sugar
3 tablespoons (1 oz./30 g) flour
3 tablespoons (50 ml) orange juice
1 tablespoon plus 1 teaspoon (20 ml) orange liqueur

Cream the melted butter and sugar together. Beat in the flour
and then add the liquid ingredients. Mix until smooth.
Chill for 20 minutes.
Preheat the oven to 350°F (180°C).
With a teaspoon, place small balls of batter just under 1 inch
(2 cm) in diameter on a silicone baking sheet. The batter
spreads when baked so leave adequate space between them.
Bake until golden brown, about 8 minutes. Transfer to
a cooling rack or drape them over a rolling pin or in a
tuile mold.

● **Chef's note**
*Sprinkle chopped hazelnuts, almonds, or other nuts over the
tuiles before baking.*

Lace Tuiles with Red Wine ★

Ingredients (makes about 10 tuiles)
1 cup (250 ml) light red wine
3 tablespoons (2 oz./50 g) butter, melted
Scant ¾ cup (3 oz./90 g) sugar
2 ½ tablespoons (1 oz./25 g) flour

Preheat the oven to 375°F (190°C)
Pour the wine into a small saucepan and reduce to ⅓ cup
(75 ml). Beat all the ingredients together until they form
a runny paste. Place small balls of batter just under 1 inch
(2 cm) in diameter on a silicone baking sheet. The batter
spreads when baked so leave adequate space between them.
Bake until golden brown, about 8 minutes, and transfer to
a cooling rack or drape over a rolling pin or in a tuile mold.

● **Chef's note**
*These two recipes use very little flour. It is the sugar that
caramelizes to give them their lovely golden color.*

1

2

Langues de Chat (Cat's Tongue) Cookies and Cigarette Cookies ★

Ingredients (makes about 4 dozen cookies)
2 sticks (9 oz./250 g) butter, room temperature
1 cup plus scant 1 cup (9 oz./250 g) confectioners' sugar
7-8 egg whites (9 oz./250 g)
2 cups (9 oz./250 g) flour
½ teaspoon (2.5 ml) vanilla extract

Preheat the oven to 350°F (180°C). Line a baking sheet with a silicone baking mat or parchment paper. In a large mixing bowl, energetically whip the butter and confectioners' sugar until creamy. Beat in the egg whites. When the mixture is smooth, sift the flour into it and combine. Add the vanilla extract. Pipe the batter with a plain tip (1), or spoon small mounds with a tablespoon onto the prepared baking sheet and shape them into ovals with the back of the spoon. Bake, one batch at a time, until browned round the edges, about 10 minutes (2). Remove from the oven and let the cookies harden flat on a cooling rack. To make cigarette cookies, remove from oven and wrap around a rod knife sharpener to make tubes and let firm for a few seconds.

Rum and Raisin Cookies *(Palets de Dame)* ★

Ingredients (makes about 4 dozen cookies)
2 cups (9 oz./250 g) flour
2 sticks (9 oz./250 g) butter, room temperature
1 cup plus scant 1 cup (9 oz./250 g) confectioners' sugar
4-5 eggs (9 oz./250 g)
1 tablespoon (15 ml) rum
¾ cup (4 oz./125 g) raisins

Preheat the oven to 350°F (180°C).
Sift the flour into a bowl. In a large mixing bowl, energetically whip the butter and confectioners' sugar until creamy. Beat in the eggs. When the mixture is smooth, stir in all the flour until just combined. Do not overmix or the cookies will be too hard. Stir in the rum.
Spoon the batter into a piping bag and pipe small mounds, about 1 ¼ inches (3 cm) in diameter onto a silicone baking mat or lined baking sheet. Place a few raisins on each cookie (1) and bake until browned around the edges, about 10 minutes (2).
Let cool on the baking sheet and remove carefully with a spatula.

Piped Almond Shortbread ★

Ingredients (makes 8 pieces of shortbread)
1 egg white (1 oz./20 g)
7 oz. (200 g) almond paste, 50 percent almonds

Gradually beat the egg white into the almond paste to soften it. It must be soft enough for you to pipe the dough through a star tip **(1)** but should retain some firmness.
Pipe the shortbread onto a baking sheet and let stand, uncovered and preferably near an open window or in a draft for 1 hour, until a crust forms.
Preheat the oven to 400°F (200°C) and bake until the ridges turn light brown **(2)**, about 6-7 minutes.

Piped Petits Fours ★

Ingredients (makes 1 lb./450 g of shortbread,
  about 15 petits fours)
1 ¾ sticks (7 oz./200 g) butter, room temperature
Generous ½ cup (2 ½ oz./75 g) confectioners' sugar
1 egg
1 ¾ cups (8 oz./225 g) flour
¾ teaspoon (3 g) baking powder
½ teaspoon (2.5 ml) vanilla extract or 1 teaspoon finely grated
  lemon zest (optional)

Whip the butter with the confectioners' sugar until creamy. Whip in the egg. Sift the flour with the baking powder and beat it in. Stir in the flavoring if using. The texture should be soft enough for you to pipe the dough through a star tip **(1)** but should retain some firmness.
Pipe the petits fours onto a baking sheet and let stand, uncovered and preferably near an open window or in a draft for 1 hour, until a crust forms.
Preheat the oven to 350°F (180°C).
Bake until the ridges turn light brown **(2)**, about 15 minutes.

● **Chef's note**
To ensure that the patterns of these petits fours stand out clearly, it's important to let them dry out until a crust forms before baking.

1

Soft Almond Petits Fours ★

Ingredients (makes 7 oz./200 g, about 8 petits fours)
3 tablespoons (2 oz./50 g) butter, room temperature
¼ cup (2 oz./50 g) sugar
1 egg
Generous ½ cup (2 oz./50 g) ground almonds
1 ½ teaspoons (5 g) cornstarch
½ teaspoon (2.5 ml) vanilla extract
1 teaspoon (5 ml) dark rum
Hazelnuts, cherries in liqueur, candied orange
    peel etc. for decoration

1 ¼-inch (3-cm) diameter silicone molds

This recipe requires brisk whipping; use an electric
beater if you prefer.
Preheat the oven to 350°F (180°C).
Whip the butter with the sugar until creamy. Whip in
the egg. Add the almonds, cornstarch, vanilla, and rum
and whip energetically until the mixture increases
somewhat in volume and becomes pale.
Spoon the batter into a piping bag and fill small silicone
molds to two-thirds. Garnish the tops if you wish.
Bake until lightly colored, for about 12-15 minutes.

● Chef's notes
*You can also decorate these petits fours with jam
or chocolate sauce.*

Creams, mousses, and dessert fillings

Creams, mousses, and dessert fillings

Dairy products

The grass that cows chomp on and ruminate is transformed into the precious white liquid and versatile foodstuff we use every day. The composition of milk varies with the breed of animal, its feed, and health. Raw or untreated milk keeps for a very short time due to the presence of lactic fermentation agents. It undergoes homogenization and pasteurization, a process that involves heating it to destroy most of its microorganisms. In some countries, UHT or long-life milk is used: it is subjected to ultra-high temperatures and rapidly cooled, thus gaining a shelf-life of several months. Milk is available with varying percentages of butterfat. We recommend using whole milk for optimal taste in almost all of the recipes: the flavor of the final product is superior to those using skimmed milk due to the presence of the butterfat that better captures and renders the flavors of the other ingredients.

Cream is obtained by separating the fat content from milk. Today, centrifugal force is used in the process. Cream contains about ten times as much butterfat as milk and it's thanks to the butterfat that we can make whipped cream. When we whip cream, we incorporate air. The globules of fat hold the air that is essential to its expansion. With a fat content of less than 30 percent, it simply will not whip up. For best results, use cream with a minimum butterfat content of 35 percent.

If you whip your cream too much and it begins to become too firm, don't throw it out. Call your children in to see what happens next. Continue to whip and, as they watch, an agglomeration of fatty globules will begin to float within a whitish liquid, the buttermilk. Just a few moments more and some yellow-colored butter becomes separated from the liquid. Rinse it under cold water to discard the buttermilk and continue to work what has become butter.

Butter usually contains between 80–85 percent fat and 16 percent water, with traces of casein proteins and lactose. Because butter is so firm when refrigerated, it should be taken out of the refrigerator ahead of time to come to room temperature and soften before being used for baking. This is why we often specify "room temperature" in the list of ingredients.

Professional pastry makers in France use what is known as "dry" butter, which has an even lower moisture content and is easier to incorporate into puff pastries and croissants because it is so malleable.

The quality of your butter determines the taste of the final ingredient, so choose the finest possible, with the highest percentage of butterfat available. The flavor of butters varies too, as a result of the fodder given to the cows, their region and breed, and even of the season, so choose a butter with a flavor that you particularly enjoy. Browned butter is butter that has been heated until the water it contains has evaporated. The lactose caramelizes and the proteins it contains color, giving off a pleasant, nutty smell that imparts a special flavor to cakes such as *financiers*.

Keep in mind that butter captures flavors and smells, an advantage when we combine it with other ingredients. But these flavor-capturing properties can be problematic if strong odors in the refrigerator are allowed to waft around a butter cream. Store all butter-rich and creamy preparations in airtight containers or tightly covered with plastic wrap flush with the surface, and away from food with strong smells. Be aware, too, that once it has been worked with, butter turns rancid more quickly than in its original packaging.

The creamy preparations explained in this chapter are best in terms of taste and texture when served the day they are made. Because they are rich in butterfat, their quality does not keep for long. If you need to plan ahead when making a complex dessert, make sure that you leave these components to last, after you have made the sponge or other bases. Freezing is definitely not advisable (cream loses its structure and butter, because of its high butterfat content, loses its fine taste), but most of the preparations here will keep for up to three or four days, tightly covered and well refrigerated.

Almond Cream ★

This is used in the filling for the traditional *galettes des rois*, the kings' cakes eaten at Epiphany, and in *bourdaloue* tarts (with pears), *amandines*, and *pithiviers* (see p. 379). It takes on its delicious creamy texture when baked.

Ingredients (makes sufficient for one *pithiviers*
   or two *bourdaloue* tarts)
7 tablespoons (3 ½ oz./100 g) butter, room temperature
½ cup (3 ½ oz./100 g) sugar
2 eggs
1 cup plus 3 tablespoons (3 ½ oz./100 g) ground almonds
1 ½ tablespoons (15 g) cornstarch
1 teaspoon (5 ml) vanilla extract
1 tablespoon (15 ml) rum or orange liqueur
   or 1 or 2 drops of bitter almond extract

In a mixing bowl, cream the butter and whisk in the sugar until light.
Add the eggs, one by one, whisking until thoroughly combined.
Whisk in the ground almonds and then the cornstarch.
Stir in the vanilla and rum.

Bake according to the instructions: this cream is always used with a pastry base.

● Chef's notes
You can replace some or all of the ground almonds with ground hazelnuts. Adding a little pistachio paste will give the cream an attractive green color. This almond cream can be combined with an equal quantity of pastry cream to make frangipane cream, the filling for the Epiphany cake, the French galette des rois.

❙ Recipe ideas
Pithiviers Filled with Almond Cream >> p. 379
Pear and Almond Cream Tart >> p. 418

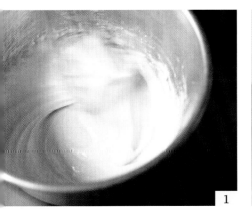
1

2

Pouring Custard (Crème Anglaise) ★★

Custard, besides being a delicious accompaniment to many cakes and desserts, is the base for a range of more complex creams, such as Bavarian, Chiboust, Diplomat, pastry, and mousseline creams, as well as egg-based ice creams.

Ingredients (makes about 1 cup/250 ml)
½ vanilla bean
1 cup (250 ml) milk
4 egg yolks
¼ cup (2 oz./50 g) sugar

Slit the vanilla bean lengthwise and scrape the seeds into the milk. In a medium heavy-bottom saucepan, heat the milk with the vanilla bean. Beat the egg yolks with the sugar until pale and thick (1). When the milk is simmering, pour half of it over the egg yolk and sugar mixture, stirring constantly (2). Return the mixture to the saucepan and cook for about 8 minutes, stirring constantly and removing the saucepan from the heat from time to time, until it reaches 185°F (85°C), or coats the back of a spoon (3). (If the egg yolks are in constant contact with high heat, they may coagulate; and do not let the custard boil, as the coagulated egg yolks would separate from the milk.)
Strain through a fine-mesh sieve into a mixing bowl and cover with plastic wrap.
Cool rapidly, preferably over an ice bath, and use according to your recipe. Custard cannot be frozen, but will keep tightly covered or in a closed jar in the refrigerator for 3 to 4 days.

● Chef's notes
If the pouring custard separates because it has been cooked over too high a temperature, you can repair the damage by immediately processing it with an immersion blender in a cold bowl.
It's important to cool pouring custard rapidly to avoid any bacteria developing. Heating it to 185°F (85°C) pasteurizes it.

Recipe idea
Floating Islands >> p. 304

3

http://flamm.fr/ffd08

Baked Creams ★

Basic Baked Cream

Ingredients (makes filling for a tart to serve 6)
½ cup (125 ml) milk
½ cup (125 ml) heavy cream
2 eggs
1 egg yolk
¼ cup (2 oz./50 g) sugar
Flavoring, such as 1 teaspoon (5 ml) vanilla or 2 teaspoons
  (10 ml) apple brandy or orange liqueur

With an electric beater or a whisk, gently beat all
the ingredients together. Be careful not to let it foam,
as bubbles would prevent a smooth surface from
forming when the tart is baked.
Strain through a fine-mesh sieve, cover with plastic wrap,
and chill if not using immediately. Use according to your
recipe: fruit tarts, for example.

Crèmes Brûlées

Ingredients (serves 4-6)
1 vanilla bean
1 cup (250 ml) milk
6 egg yolks
⅓ cup (2 ½ oz./75 g) sugar
1 cup (250 ml) heavy cream
Scant ½ cup (3 oz./80 g) light brown sugar

Slit the vanilla bean in two lengthwise and scrape the seeds
into the milk. Beat the egg yolks with the white sugar until
pale and thick. Pour the milk and cream into the egg yolk
and sugar mixture, stirring until smooth.
Cover with plastic wrap and chill for 2 hours to develop
the flavor.
Strain through a fine-mesh sieve and fill ramekins of 4-inch
(10-cm) diameter.
Preheat the oven to 200°F-210°F (90°C-100°C), no hotter,
and bake for 35 to 40 minutes, until just set.
Let cool then sprinkle with light brown sugar.
Caramelize the sugar with a kitchen torch or under
the broiler.

Cream Pots

The method for making these individual desserts is similar to that of classic crème brûlée. The proportions of the ingredients changes a little and you can flavor them according to taste.

Ingredients (serves 4-6)
3 egg yolks
¼ cup (2 oz./50 g) sugar
½ cup (125 ml) milk
½ cup (125 ml) whipping cream
Flavor of your choice, such as vanilla, coffee, or chocolate

Beat the egg yolks with the sugar until pale and thick. Pour the milk and cream into the egg yolk and sugar mixture, stirring until smooth. Stir in the flavoring.
Cover with plastic wrap and chill for 2 hours to develop the flavor.
Strain through a fine-mesh sieve and fill ramekins of 2 ¾-inch (7-cm) diameter and 1 ¼-inch (3-cm) depth.
Preheat the oven to 200°F-210°F (90°C-100°F), no hotter, and bake for 35 to 40 minutes, until just set.

Variation: Filling for savory flans (without a pastry base)
Ingredients (for a flan for 6-8)
1 cup (250 ml) milk
1 cup (250 ml) heavy cream
4 eggs
2 ½ tablespoons (1 oz./25 g) all-purpose flour
2 ½ tablespoons (1 oz./25 g) cornstarch
1 pinch salt
Freshly ground pepper
A little freshly grated nutmeg

Combine all the ingredients in the bowl of a food processor or with an electric beater until the flour and cornstarch are well incorporated.
Strain through a fine-mesh sieve and chill until needed.
Stir briskly until the flour and cornstarch, which will have sunk to the bottom, are evenly distributed again. Use with vegetables, bacon bits, and so on.

Whipped Praline Butter ★

Ingredients (makes filling for macarons [or another dessert] to serve 8)
3 ½ oz. (100 g) praline (see recipe p. 160)
7 tablespoons (3 ½ oz./100 g) butter, room temperature

In a stand mixer fitted with the paddle beater, beat the two ingredients together at low speed for 1 minute. Increase the speed until the mixture is smooth and creamy, 5-6 minutes.
Either spread it with a spatula or pipe it with a piping bag. Use this creamy spread over a *dacquoise* (p. 72), to sandwich macarons (p. 79) together, and over other sponge bases.

Panna Cotta ★

Ingredients (serves 6)
3 sheets (6 g) gelatin
½ vanilla bean
2 cups (500 ml) heavy cream
½ cup (3 oz./100 g) sugar

Soften the gelatin sheets in a small bowl of cold water. Slit the vanilla bean lengthwise and scrape the seeds into the cream. Heat the cream with the vanilla bean and the sugar until it simmers. Remove from the heat. Remove vanilla bean. Squeeze the water from the gelatin sheets and stir them into the hot mixture until dissolved.
Pour into small ramekins (2 ¾ inches/7 cm in diameter) or glasses, cool quickly, and refrigerate.

● Chef's notes
Choose the best-quality cream you can find.
Since this dessert is particularly rich, serve small portions, accompanied, if you wish, by a fruit coulis or topped with broken cookies.
To add interest, infuse the cream with citrus zest or herbs before cooking, and strain it before adding the gelatin.

● Did you know?
This dessert comes to us from northern Italy, where it has been made for many years on the farms of Piedmont and is traditionally served with hazelnuts.

Chantilly Cream ★

The all-time favorite of pastry chefs, Chantilly cream is made by whipping cream with a butterfat content of at least 35 percent until it increases in volume and holds fairly firm peaks. Sugar—15 to 20 percent—is added, as is natural vanilla. Chantilly cream is used to fill, garnish, mask, decorate, and accompany a wide range of pastries, desserts, and ice creams.

Ingredients (serves 10 as an accompaniment)
1 cup (250 ml) heavy whipping cream, well chilled
3 tablespoons (1 ½ oz./35 g) superfine sugar (Method 1)
  or ¼ cup (1 ½ oz./35 g) confectioners' sugar (Method 2)
1 teaspoon (5 ml) vanilla extract

Method 1

At least 30 minutes ahead, place a round-bottom stainless steel mixing bowl in the refrigerator.
Pour the cream into the bowl and add the sugar and vanilla. Begin whipping gently, lifting the whisk high to incorporate as much air as possible. When the cream begins to thicken, increase the speed. Continue until the cream holds firm peaks when the whisk is held up. (The peaks fold back gently on themselves.) Do not beat any further or the cream will separate. Chill immediately and use within 4 hours.

Method 2

Sift the confectioners' sugar. Pour the well-chilled cream into the bowl of a stand mixer fitted with a whisk. Beat at medium speed until the cream thickens. Add the confectioners' sugar and the vanilla and whip for a few seconds at high speed to incorporate as much air as possible. Stop when the cream holds firm peaks. (The peaks fold back gently on themselves.) Chill immediately and use within 4 hours.

● Chef's notes

It's essential to stop beating as soon as the cream reaches the right consistency.
To make Chantilly cream, ensure that the cream is well chilled. The butterfat percentage is important too: lower than 30 percent and it will not whip up. For the best taste, choose heavy whipping cream, with at least 35 percent butterfat. Try to chill the mixing bowl before you begin as this facilitates the process. If you use superfine or granulated sugar, make sure it dissolves completely in the cream. The best, of course, is confectioners' sugar, which can be incorporated in the final stages as it dissolves so quickly.

● Did you know?

In 1663, François Vatel was named "master of the kitchen" to the Prince de Condé at the Château de Chantilly, north of Paris. He was responsible for the organization, purchases, and stocks of all the food served at the impressive château. Previously, he had worked at the Château of Vaux-le-Vicomte, the inspiration behind Louis XIV's building of Versailles. It was there, in 1660, that he invented the cream that later took the name of Chantilly.

❢ Recipe ideas

Waffles >> p. 302
Black Forest Cake >> p. 346
Rum Babas >> p. 361
Fruit and Candy Cake >> p. 404

Butter Creams ★ ★ ★

Butter cream is made by emulsifying butter with a mixture of eggs, cooked sugar (like a *pâte à bombe*), and flavoring. There are several variations, including a custard-based recipe and an Italian meringue-based recipe. If you are adding flavorings, incorporate those that are powder-based (such as cocoa powder) with the syrup. Add liquid flavorings, such as vanilla extract or liqueurs, at the end.

Cooked Sugar-Based Butter Cream

Ingredients (makes sufficient for a cake to serve 8)
1 ¼ cups (9 oz./250 g) sugar
Scant ⅓ cup (70 ml) water
4 egg yolks
2 sticks (9 oz./250 g) butter, room temperature, cubed
Flavoring of your choice

http://flamm.fr/ffd09

Combine the sugar with the water to make a syrup and heat to 243°F–250°F (117°C–121°C) (1).
In the meantime, in a stand mixer fitted with a whisk, or with an electric beater, whip the egg yolks at medium speed until foamy. Increase the speed to high and gradually pour the syrup over the yolks. Continue to beat until the temperature of the mixture cools to about 86°F (30°C). It will become increasingly foamy. Retaining the medium speed, gradually add the butter and whip until the mixture reaches a creamy consistency (2) and holds peaks (3), when it is ready to use. Stir in the flavoring. Transfer to a bowl and cover with plastic wrap flush with the surface. Use according to your recipe. Butter cream keeps for 2 days, well chilled and covered, and should be stirred before use so that it regains its texture.

● **Chef's notes**
Use the finest quality butter you can find for optimal taste.
For a lighter variation, incorporate Italian or Swiss meringue (p. 176 and p. 177).

● **Did you know?**
Butter cream is classically used in the traditional French Christmas dessert, the yule log, and to assemble the mocha cake, a layered cake created by a Parisian pastry chef, Guignard, in the mid-nineteenth century. It was his predecessor, a certain M. Quillet, who had invented the butter cream used to cover the cake.

❘ **Recipe ideas**
Yule Log >> p. 333
Creamy Pistachio Log Dessert >> p. 334
Mocha Cake >> p. 353

Custard-Based Butter Cream

Ingredients (makes sufficient for a cake to serve 15)
1 cup (250 ml) milk
½ vanilla bean, seeds scraped (optional)
6 egg yolks
1 ¼ cups (9 oz./250 g) sugar
4 sticks (1 ¼ lb./500 g) butter

In a heavy-bottom saucepan, heat the milk with the vanilla bean and its seeds if using. Beat the egg yolks with the sugar until pale and thick. When the milk is simmering, pour half of it over the egg yolk and sugar mixture, stirring constantly. Return the mixture to the saucepan and cook, stirring constantly and removing the saucepan from the heat from time to time, until it reaches 185°F (85°C) or coats the back of a spoon. (If the egg yolks are in constant contact with high heat, they may coagulate.) Strain through a fine-mesh sieve and cover with plastic wrap. Quickly cool to about 85°F (30°C). Cream the butter energetically until it forms fine peaks. Gradually pour the custard over the butter (1), whisking constantly, until thoroughly combined (emulsified). If not using immediately, store at a temperature no cooler than 50°F (10°C).

Italian Meringue-Based Butter Cream

Ingredients (makes sufficient for a cake to serve 15)
2 ⅔ cups (1 ¼ lb./500 g) sugar
⅔ cup (150 ml) water
8 egg whites
1 pinch salt
4 sticks (1 ¼ lb./500 g) butter
Flavoring of your choice

In a heavy-bottom saucepan, heat the sugar and water. When it registers 230°F (110°C), begin whipping the egg whites with the salt in a stand mixer fitted with a whisk. When they hold firm peaks and the syrup registers 243°F-250°F (117°C-121°C), gradually pour the syrup into the egg whites, whisking continuously and taking care that the hot syrup does not splatter. Continue whisking until the meringue has cooled to about 85°F (30°C). It will be dense, shiny, and form many small peaks.
Cream the butter energetically with a whisk. Gradually whisk in the Italian meringue, continuing until it is completely blended (emulsified). Stir in liquid flavoring, if using.

Recipe ideas
Yule Log >> p. 333
Mocha Cake >> p. 353

Egg-Based Bavarian Cream ★★

Ingredients (makes a Bavarian cream for a sponge base
  to serve 8)
4 sheets (8 g) gelatin
1 vanilla bean (the recommended flavoring,
  but you can use others)
1 cup (250 ml) milk
4 egg yolks
⅔ cup (4 oz./125 g) sugar
1 ⅔ cups (400 ml) whipping cream

Soften the gelatin in a bowl of cold water. Slit the vanilla bean
lengthwise and scrape the seeds into the milk. In a medium
heavy-bottom saucepan, heat the milk with the vanilla bean.
Beat the egg yolks with the sugar until pale and thick. When
the milk is simmering, pour half of it over the egg yolk and
sugar mixture, stirring constantly. Return the mixture to the
saucepan and cook, stirring constantly and removing the
saucepan from the heat from time to time until it reaches
185°F (85°C) or coats the back of a spoon. (If the egg yolks
are in constant contact with high heat, they may coagulate.)
Strain the custard through a fine-mesh sieve and transfer to
a mixing bowl. Squeeze the water from the gelatin sheets and
stir into the custard until completely dissolved. Cool to about
70°F (20°C). (You can set the bowl over a larger one filled
with cold water and ice cubes.)
Whip the cream until it holds soft peaks.
With a flexible spatula or whisk, gradually fold the whipped
cream into the custard-gelatin mixture.
When the mixture is smooth, it is ready to be used and must
be poured into the mold immediately. This is because the
gelatin will start to take effect.
Chill for at least 2 hours for a large dessert and 1 ½ hours
for individual desserts.

● Chef's note

*The classic use for a Bavarian cream is in charlottes and desserts
made with ladyfingers, traditionally flavored with vanilla, coffee,
chocolate, and so on.*

❙ Recipe idea
Layered Chocolate-Coffee Creams >> p. 318

http://flamm.fr/ffd10

1

2

Fruit-Based Bavarian Cream ★★

Ingredients (makes a Bavarian cream for a sponge base
  to serve 8)
4 sheets (8 g) gelatin
1 cup (250 ml) fruit purée
4 egg yolks
½ cup (3 ½ oz./100 g) sugar
1 ⅔ cups (400 ml) whipping cream
Fruit liqueur (optional)

Soften the gelatin in a bowl of cold water. Bring the puréed
fruit to a boil. Beat the egg yolks with the sugar until pale
and thick. Remove the fruit from the heat and stir in the egg
yolk and sugar mixture. Return to the heat and cook to 185°F
(85°C). Remove from the heat, squeeze the water from the
gelatin sheets, and stir them in until completely dissolved.
Cool to about 70°F (20°C). Whip the cream until it holds firm
peaks. With a flexible spatula or whisk, carefully fold it into
the cooled fruit mixture (1, 2, 3). If you are adding a fruit
liqueur, stir it in. When the mixture is smooth, it is ready and
must be poured into the mold immediately. This is because
the gelatin will start to take effect. Chill for at least 2 hours
for a large dessert and 1½ hours for individual desserts.

● Chef's notes
*To make a charlotte that has less butterfat, you can replace some
or all of the whipped cream with Italian meringue (see p. 177).
Bavarian creams can be molded on their own or be used as
a component in more elaborate cold desserts.*

❙ Recipe idea
Strawberry-Raspberry Charlotte >> p. 337

3

Pastry Cream ★

Pastry cream is used as a base for many elaborate creamy fillings.

Ingredients (makes sufficient for 8 éclairs, for example)
½ vanilla bean
2 cups (500 ml) milk
4 egg yolks
½ cup (3 ½ oz./100 g) sugar
Scant ⅓ cup (1 ½ oz./45 g) cornstarch
  or ½ cup (2 oz./60 g) flour
2 tablespoons (1 oz./30 g) butter (optional)

Slit the vanilla bean lengthwise and scrape the seeds into the milk (1). Pour the milk into a saucepan, add the vanilla bean, and begin heating.
In a mixing bowl, briskly whisk the egg yolks, sugar, and cornstarch (2) until pale and thick. When the milk is simmering, pour half of it over the egg yolk mixture, beating continuously. Return the mixture to the saucepan with the remaining milk (3) and bring to a boil, stirring continuously. If you are using a flavor other than vanilla, add it at this stage, unless you are using a liqueur, which should only be added when the mixture has cooled. Let simmer for 2 to 3 minutes, still stirring. Transfer to a mixing bowl, whip in the butter if using, and cover with plastic wrap flush with the surface. It should look thick, smooth, and custard-colored. Let cool rapidly and use according to the recipe.
Pastry cream keeps for no more than 3 to 4 days, well covered, in the refrigerator.

● Chef's notes
Plastic wrap pressed onto the surface of pastry cream prevents a skin from forming as it cools. Pastry cream is a fragile preparation, and in pastry shops it is made as it is needed. The butter makes the texture even more unctuous. It is classically used to fill éclairs.

❘ Recipe ideas
Orange Liqueur Soufflé >> p. 274
Pastry Cream Turnovers >> p. 365

http://flamm.fr/ffd11

Mousseline Cream ★

This is one of the many creams based on pastry cream.

Ingredients
1 cup (250 ml) milk
½ cup (3 ½ oz./100 g) sugar, divided
2 egg yolks
Scant ¼ cup (1 oz./35 g) cornstarch or custard powder
1 teaspoon (5 ml) vanilla extract
1 stick plus 1 tablespoon (4½ oz./130 g) butter,
  softened, divided, and diced

In a heavy-bottom saucepan, heat the milk with half the
sugar. Beat the egg yolks with the remaining sugar until thick
and pale. Beat in the cornstarch. When the milk is simmering,
pour half of it over the egg mixture, stirring constantly.
Return the mixture to the saucepan and cook, stirring
constantly, until thickened. It should be at a temperature
of 185°F (85°C). Immediately remove from the heat and
whisk in the vanilla (1). Whisk in half the butter (2).
Transfer to a mixing bowl and cover with plastic wrap flush
with the surface. Place in the refrigerator until it has cooled
to 77°F (25°C).
Transfer the cream mixture to a stand mixer fitted with a
paddle beater. Starting at low speed and then increasing it,
add the remaining butter, continuing until the cream expands
and becomes airy. If you are using a flavoring, incorporate
it at this stage. For example, to make praline mousseline
cream, add 3 oz. (80 g) of softened praline.

❗ **Recipe ideas**
Strawberry and Mousseline Cream Layer Cake (*Fraisier*) >> p. 349
Mousseline Cream Mille-Feuille >> p. 375
Paris-Brest >> p. 376

Frangipane Cream ★

Frangipane cream comprises half pastry cream and half almond cream. It is the traditional filling for the Epiphany cake, the *galette des rois*.

Ingredients (makes filling for a *galette des rois* to serve 8)

Pastry cream
¼ vanilla bean
1 cup (250 ml) milk
2 egg yolks
¼ cup (2 oz./50 g) sugar
3 tablespoons (1 oz./25 g) cornstarch

Almond cream
7 tablespoons (3 ½ oz./100 g) butter, room temperature
½ cup (3 ½ oz./100 g) sugar
2 eggs
1 cup plus 3 tablespoons (3 ½ oz./100 g) ground almonds

A few drops bitter almond extract or a little almond liqueur

Follow the recipe for pastry cream (p. 99). Let cool rapidly. Meanwhile, make the almond cream (p. 90).
Add the almond extract or liqueur to the pastry cream. Whisk the almond cream into the pastry cream. Use with a pastry base according to your recipe.

● Chef's note
As this cream contains pastry cream, it should be used rapidly. Keep it chilled, covered with plastic wrap flush with the surface, if necessary.

● Did you know?
Frangipane cream takes its name from the Italian perfume maker, Don Cesare Frangipani, who lived in Paris in the seventeenth century.
The term crème frangipane *with the meaning it has today first appeared in a dictionary in 1732. But it was recorded in many other works as a pastry cream to which almonds were added. A* franchipane, *a pie with almond cream and chopped pistachios, is mentioned as early as 1674. There are also references to pastry cream with broken bits of macaron stirred in.*

Sabayon ★★

This cream comes to us from Italy. It accompanies desserts, poached or raw fruit, *fruits au gratin*, and ice creams.

Ingredients (serves 4 with about 1 lb./500 g prepared fruit)
5 egg yolks
Scant ½ cup (100 ml) wine
½ cup (3½ oz./100 g) sugar

Set a saucepan over a bain-marie or minimal heat. Place the egg yolks in the saucepan and add the wine and sugar. Whip continuously until the mixture reaches a creamy consistency—it should form a ribbon (ribbon stage) and register about 140°F (60°C).
Pour over fruit and bake under the broiler until browned in parts.

● Chef's note
The choice of wine or other alcoholic beverage obviously determines the taste of your sabayon. Select it so that it pairs well with the produce it accompanies.

❚ Recipe idea
Grapefruit Gratin with Hard Apple Cider >> p. 267

Creams, mousses, and dessert fillings

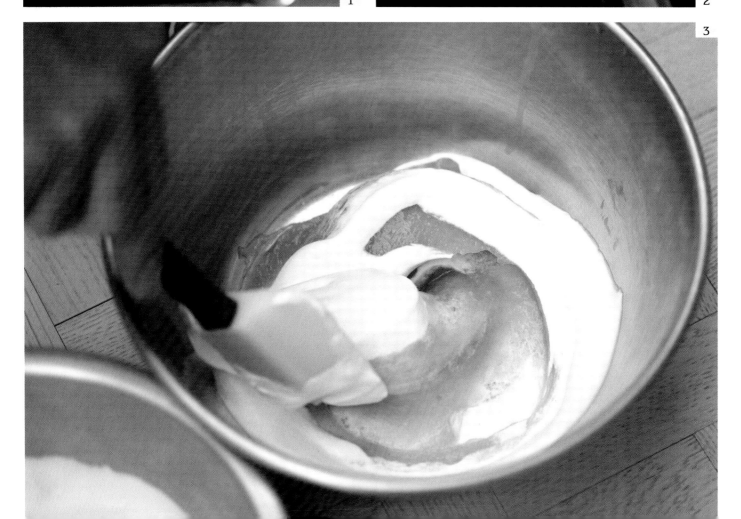

Diplomat Cream ★

This is another variation of pastry cream. It contains whipped cream as well as gelatin, so it can be molded. It is used in the eponymous Diplomat pudding, as well as fruit tarts, mille-feuilles, and in filled crêpes.

Custard-Based Diplomat Cream

Ingredients (makes 8 servings, with a pastry base)
2 ½ sheets (5 g) gelatin
¼ vanilla bean
1 cup (250 ml) milk
2 egg yolks
Scant ⅓ cup (2½ oz./65 g) sugar
2 ½ tablespoons (1 oz./25 g) cornstarch
  or 3 tablespoons (1 oz./30 g) flour
1 cup (250 ml) heavy cream

Soften the gelatin sheets in a bowl of cold water.
Slit the vanilla bean lengthwise and scrape the seeds into the milk. In a heavy bottom saucepan, heat the milk with the vanilla seeds and bean. Whip the egg yolks, sugar, and cornstarch (1) until the mixture is pale and thick. When the milk is simmering, remove from the heat and gradually pour half over the egg mixture, whisking continuously (2). Return the mixture to the saucepan and stir continuously until it simmers. Let simmer 2-3 minutes, still stirring. Remove from the heat. Remove vanilla bean. Squeeze the water from the gelatin sheets and whisk them into the custard cream.
Transfer to a mixing bowl, cover with plastic wrap flush with the surface (this will prevent a skin from forming) and chill to about 60°F (15°C). Do not leave it too long; it must not set before the whipped cream is incorporated. With an electric beater, whip the heavy cream until it forms firm peaks (the texture of a Chantilly cream).
Smooth the chilled custard cream with a flexible spatula and carefully fold in the whipped cream (3). Use according to the recipe.
Chill for about 1 ½ hours, or until set.

Recipe idea
Exotic Fruit Pouches >> p. 287

Fruit-Based Diplomat Cream

Ingredients (makes 8 servings, with a pastry base)
2 ½ tablespoons (1 oz./25 g) cornstarch
3 tablespoons (50 ml) water
1 cup (9 oz./250 g) fresh fruit purée
⅓ cup (2 oz./60 g) sugar
1 cup (250 ml) whipping cream

Dilute the cornstarch in the water. Bring the fruit purée and sugar to a simmer and stir in the cornstarch and water mixture. Simmer until thickened, 1-2 minutes. Transfer to a mixing bowl, cover with plastic wrap flush with the surface, and chill in the refrigerator. When it has cooled to 68°F-77°F (20°C-25°C), whip the cream until it holds firm peaks. With a flexible spatula, carefully fold the whipped cream into the fruit mixture. Use rapidly: do not let the gelatin begin setting before the cream is poured into its mold. Refrigerate immediately.
This cream will keep in the refrigerator, well covered (plastic wrap flush with the surface), for no longer than 24 hours.

● **Chef's notes**
Depending on the type of fruit you are using, you may need more or less sugar. The quantity given here is an indication. To change the quantities, note that you should use 1 gelatin sheet (2 g) for every 3½ oz. (100 g) of fruit purée.
It's important to let the pastry cream and fruit mixture cool to the temperatures indicated. If whipped cream is added to a mixture that is warmer, it will deflate instead of bringing a light, airy texture to it.

Chiboust Cream ★★★

Chiboust cream is the classic filling for the famous Gâteau Saint-Honoré. It also uses pastry cream as a base, incorporates gelatin, and is lightened with Italian meringue.

Ingredients (makes sufficient for a Gâteau Saint-Honoré to serve 12)

Set pastry cream	Italian meringue
5 sheets (10 g) gelatin	2 ½ cups (1 lb./480 g) sugar
½ vanilla bean	⅔ cup (160 ml) water
2 cups (500 ml) milk	8 egg whites
½ cup (3 ½ oz./100 g) sugar, divided	1 pinch salt
4 egg yolks	
Scant ⅓ cup (1 ½ oz./45 g) cornstarch or ½ cup (2 oz./60 g) flour	

Make the pastry cream.
Soften the gelatin sheets in a bowl of cold water. Slit the vanilla bean lengthwise and scrape the seeds into the milk. In a medium heavy-bottom saucepan, heat the milk with the vanilla bean and half the sugar. Beat the egg yolks with the remaining sugar until thick and pale. Beat in the cornstarch. When the milk is simmering, pour half of it over the egg mixture (1), beating constantly. Return the mixture to the saucepan with the remaining milk and bring to a boil, stirring continuously. Let simmer for 2 to 3 minutes, still stirring, until it reaches 185°F (85°C). Remove from the heat. Squeeze the water from the gelatin sheets and whisk them into the pastry cream (2). Let cool to about 122°F (50°C).

Prepare the Italian meringue.
In a heavy-bottom saucepan, begin cooking the sugar and water. When it registers 230°F (110°C), begin whipping the egg whites with a pinch of salt in a stand mixer fitted with a whisk. When they hold firm peaks and the syrup registers 243°F-250°F (117°C-121°C), gradually pour the syrup into the egg whites, whisking continuously and taking care that the hot syrup does not splatter. Continue whisking until cooled to about 122°F (50°C). It will be dense, shiny, and form many small peaks. Carefully fold the Italian meringue into the pastry cream, taking care not to deflate the mixture (3). Use rapidly: do not allow the gelatin to begin setting before the cream is poured into its mold or piped into pastries. Refrigerate immediately. This cream will keep in the refrigerator for 12 hours.

● Chef's notes
Using Italian meringue reduces the risk of contamination, enhances the texture and consistency of the cream, and gives it an attractive sheen.

If you are planning on serving your dessert the day you make it, you need not use the gelatin.

● Did you know?
Chiboust, a pastry chef, set up shop in Paris in 1840. He invented this delicious cream, naming it for the street where his establishment was located, as well as for the patron saint of bakers.

❢ Recipe idea
Gâteau Saint-Honoré >> p. 386

Custard Flan Filling ★

This custard filling is based on pastry cream and made with custard powder, which is cornstarch enriched with vanillin and yellow colorant. If you do not have this, simply use cornstarch with a little vanilla.

Ingredients (makes a filling for a tart to serve 6)
2 cups (500 ml) milk
2 egg yolks
½ cup (3½ oz./100 g) sugar
Scant ⅓ cup (1 ½ oz./45 g) custard powder
Or scant ⅓ cup (1 ½ oz./45 g) cornstarch plus 1 teaspoon (5 ml) vanilla extract

In a heavy-bottom saucepan, heat the milk. Whip the egg yolks, sugar, and custard powder or cornstarch until the mixture is pale and thick. When the milk is simmering, gradually pour half over the egg mixture, beating continuously. Return the mixture to the saucepan with the rest of the milk and stir continuously until it simmers and thickens. Let cool completely and pour into raw tart shells. Bake at 375°F (190°C) until set, lightly browned in parts, and a cake tester comes out dry.

● **Chef's note**
Add fruit like apricots, cherries, or dried fruit to the custard filling.

🍴 **Recipe idea**
Parisian Custard Tart >> p. 414

Lemon Cream ★

Method 1 (cooked and enriched with whipped cream)
Ingredients (makes sufficient for a lemon tart to serve 8)
⅔ cup (150 ml) lemon juice
3 tablespoons (50 ml) water
2 eggs plus 1 egg yolk
⅓ cup (2 ½ oz./75 g) sugar
1 ½ tablespoons (15 g) cornstarch
3 tablespoons (2 oz./50 g) butter
Scant ½ cup (115 ml) heavy cream

In a heavy-bottom saucepan, bring the lemon juice and water to a boil. Whip the eggs and egg yolk with the sugar until thick and pale. Beat in the cornstarch. When the liquid is simmering, pour it over the egg and sugar mixture, stirring constantly. Return the mixture to the saucepan and cook as you would a pastry cream, stirring constantly and removing the saucepan from the heat from time to time, until it thickens and coats the back of a spoon. (If the egg yolks are in constant contact with high heat, they may coagulate.) Take off the heat, add the butter and mix well. Transfer to a bowl to cool, cover with plastic wrap flush with the surface, and cool. Whip the cream until it holds soft peaks and carefully fold it into the lemon mixture. Pour into the cooled baked tart shell.

Method 2 (lemon cream for baking)
Ingredients (makes sufficient for a lemon tart to serve 8)
¾ cup (200 ml) lemon juice
Scant ½ cup (100 ml) water
4-5 egg yolks (3 ¼ oz./90 g)
1 cup (7 oz./200 g) sugar
¼ cup (1 ½ oz./40 g) cornstarch
3 tablespoons (2 oz./50 g) butter

In a heavy-bottom saucepan, bring the lemon juice and water to a boil. In a mixing bowl, whip the egg yolks and sugar until pale and thick. Beat in the cornstarch. When the liquid is simmering, pour it over the egg and sugar mixture, stirring constantly. Return the mixture to the saucepan and cook as you would a pastry cream, stirring constantly and removing the saucepan from the heat from time to time, until it thickens and coats the back of a spoon. (If the egg yolks are in constant contact with high heat, they may coagulate.) Take off the heat, add the butter and mix in well. Preheat the oven to 350°F (180°C).
Pour the cream into the tart shell. Bake for 20 minutes, until the lemon cream is set (the top will be dry) and lightly colored.

Chocolate Mousse ★

Old-Fashioned Chocolate Mousse

Ingredients (serves 6)
7 oz. (200 g) chocolate, 64 percent cocoa solids
2 tablespoons (1 oz./30 g) butter, softened
3 eggs, separated
¼ cup (2 oz./50 g) sugar

Melt the chocolate in a bain-marie over barely simmering water, or in brief pulses in the microwave oven, taking care not to scorch it.
Whisk the softened butter and egg yolks into the chocolate until thoroughly combined.
Whip the egg whites until they form soft peaks. Whisk in the sugar with a stirring motion until the mixture is firm and shiny.
With a flexible spatula or whisk, carefully fold the beaten egg whites into the chocolate mixture, without deflating the mixture.
Transfer to a serving bowl, cover with plastic wrap, and immediately refrigerate to set. Chill for at least 2 hours.

This chocolate mousse is best eaten on the day it is made, because of the presence of raw egg yolks. Do not keep it any longer than 24 hours.

❚ **Recipe ideas**
Gourmet Breton Traou Mad >>> p. 277
Chocolate Mousse >> p. 308

Ganache-Based Chocolate Mousse

Ingredients (makes sufficient for a layered dessert to serve 8)
Finely grated orange zest
¾ cup (200 ml) whipping cream or whole milk
7 oz. (200 g) chocolate, 64 percent cocoa solids, chopped
1 cup (250 ml) whipping cream

Add the orange zest to the cream or milk, heat, and let simmer for 2 to 3 minutes. Immediately strain over the chopped chocolate. Stir until smooth. Whip the cream until it holds soft peaks. When the ganache has cooled to 68°F-77°F (20°C-25°C), carefully fold in the whipped cream. Use according to the recipe.

Custard-Based Chocolate Mousse

Ingredients (makes sufficient for a dessert to serve 8)
3 sheets (6 g) gelatin
1 ¾ cup (450 ml) whipping cream, divided
Finely grated orange or lemon zest
2 egg yolks
¼ cup (2 oz./50 g) sugar
8 oz. (225 g) white chocolate, preferably
  couverture chocolate, chopped

Soften the gelatin in a bowl of cold water. In a heavy-bottom saucepan, heat ⅓ cup (75 ml) whipping cream with the zest. Beat the egg yolks with the sugar until thick and pale. When the cream is simmering, pour half of it over the egg mixture, stirring constantly. Return the mixture to the saucepan and cook, stirring constantly and removing the saucepan from the heat from time to time, until it reaches 185°F (85°C) or coats the back of a spoon. Immediately strain the custard over the chopped chocolate. Stir to combine. Squeeze the water from the gelatin sheets and stir into the chocolate mixture until completely dissolved. Whisk to ensure that the mixture is smooth. Whip the remaining cream until it holds firm peaks. When the chocolate mixture has cooled to about 85°F (30°C), carefully fold in the whipped cream. Use rapidly according to the recipe before it sets.

⬤ Chef's notes
To personalize your chocolate mousse, add praline or caramel. You can also add a little crunch with nougatine bits, chocolate shavings, and chopped nuts. These make a wonderful contrast with the creaminess of the mousse.

Pâte à Bombe-Based Chocolate Mousse (for layered desserts)

Ingredients (makes sufficient for a dessert to serve 10)
1 tablespoon (20 ml) water
¼ cup (2 oz./50 g) sugar
2 egg yolks
1 ¾ cups (450 ml) whipping cream
9 oz. (250 g) chocolate, 64 percent cocoa solids, chopped

Set a bowl over a bain-marie heated to 113°F-122°F (45°C-50°C). Whip the water, sugar, and egg yolks over the bain-marie until the mixture reaches the ribbon stage. It will have the consistency of a creamy mousse. Whip the cream until it holds firm peaks. Melt the chocolate over a bain-marie to 113°F-122°F (45°C-50°C). With a flexible spatula, carefully fold the whipped cream into the *pâte à bombe*. Carefully fold the melted chocolate into the mixture. Use according to the recipe.

Creams, mousses, and dessert fillings

Crémeux ★★

This cross between a ganache and a mousse can be used in a range of desserts as a thin, flavorful layer; because it is rich, pour to no more than about ⅓ inch (1 cm) thick. Use exactly the amount of water specified for the gelatin so as not to incorporate any additional liquid. The crémeux will spread best if used the same day.

Mango Crémeux

Ingredients (serves 8)
1 ½ sheets (3 g) gelatin
1 tablespoon (15 ml) water
  to soften the gelatin
3 tablespoons (1 ¼ oz./35 g)
  sugar, divided
2 tablespoons (1 ¼ oz./35 g)
  butter, divided
2 ½ oz. (70 g) fresh mango, diced
¼ vanilla bean, seeds scraped
4 oz. (110 g) mango purée
2 egg yolks

Soften the gelatin sheets in the water. Make a dry caramel with half the sugar (see p. 467). When it is a reddish color, quickly stir in 1 teaspoon (5 g) butter, the diced mango, and vanilla seeds. Whisk in the puréed mango, egg yolks, and remaining sugar. Stirring constantly, heat the mixture to 185°F (85°C). Stir in the gelatin sheets until completely dissolved and let cool to 95°F (35°C). Whisk in the remaining butter, or use an immersion blender to incorporate it. Use according to the recipe.

Caramel Crémeux

Ingredients (serves 4)
1 sheet (2 g) gelatin
2 teaspoons (10 ml) water to soften the gelatin
2 tablespoons (30 ml) milk
¼ cup (2 oz./50 g) sugar
4 tablespoons (2 oz./55 g) butter, divided
2 tablespoons (30 ml) heavy cream
1 egg yolk

Soften the gelatin in the water. Warm the milk gently. Make a dry caramel with the sugar (see p. 467). When it is a reddish color, quickly stir in 1 tablespoon (15 g) butter. Whisk in the milk, cream, and egg yolk. Stirring constantly, heat the mixture to 185°F (85°C). Stir in the softened gelatin sheet until completely dissolved and let cool to 95°F (35°C). Whisk in the remaining butter (1), or use an immersion blender to incorporate it (2). Use according to the recipe.

Nut and Caramel Tartlets >> p. 434

Strawberry Crémeux

Ingredients (serves 6)
1 ½ sheets (3 g) gelatin
1 tablespoon (15 ml) water to soften the gelatin
2 egg yolks
6 oz. (180 g) puréed strawberries
1 heaping tablespoon (½ oz./15 g) sugar
3 tablespoons (2 oz./50 g) butter

Soften the gelatin in the water. Combine the egg yolks, puréed strawberries, and sugar in a saucepan and heat to 185°F (85°C). Stir in the softened gelatin sheets until completely dissolved and let cool to 95°F (35°C). Using an immersion blender, incorporate the butter. Use according to the recipe.

Chocolate and Caramel Crémeux

Ingredients (serves 4)
3 ½ tablespoons (1 ½ oz./40 g) sugar
1 tablespoon (15 g) butter, melted
Scant ⅓ cup (70 ml) heavy cream
¾ teaspoon (5 g) glucose syrup
2 oz. (50 g) chocolate, 64 percent cocoa solids, chopped

Melt the chocolate in a bain-marie.
Make a dry caramel with the sugar. When it is a reddish color, stir in the melted butter. Heat the heavy cream with the glucose syrup to lukewarm. Gradually pour it onto the chocolate, stirring only at the center of the mixture until it is incorporated into the rest. (Work as you would to make a mayonnaise.) Use an immersion blender to ensure that the mixture is perfectly emulsified and smooth.

Chocolate Crémeux

Ingredients (serves 4)
3 tablespoons (50 ml) heavy cream
3 tablespoons (50 ml) milk
1 egg yolk
2 ½ teaspoons (10 g) sugar
1 ½ oz. (45 g) chocolate (couverture if possible),
   64 percent cocoa solids, chopped

Make a pouring custard with the first four ingredients (see p. 91). Melt the chocolate in a bain-marie over barely simmering water, or in brief pulses in the microwave oven, taking care not to scorch it. When the custard registers 185°F (85°C), gradually pour it over the chocolate, stirring only at the center of the mixture until it is incorporated into the rest. Use an immersion blender to ensure that the mixture is perfectly emulsified and smooth.

Fruit Mousse ★★

Ingredients (serves 8)
4 sheets (8 g) gelatin
1 ¼ cups (10 oz./300 g) fruit purée,
   divided
¼ cup (2 oz./50 g) sugar
1 ¼ cups (300 ml) whipping cream
Or, 10 oz. (300 g) Italian meringue
   (see recipe p. 177) made with 3 egg
   whites and 1 ¼ cups (7 oz./200 g) sugar
Or, ⅔ cup (150 ml) whipping cream and 5 oz. (150 g)
   Italian meringue

http://flamm.fr/ffd12

Soften the gelatin sheets in a bowl of cold water. Heat one-third of the fruit purée with the sugar. When it comes to a simmer, remove it from the heat. Squeeze the water from the gelatin sheets and stir into the fruit mixture until completely dissolved. Stir in the remaining fruit purée to cool the mixture to 68°F-77°F (20°C-25°C).

Using whipped cream for the mousse.
Whip the cream until it holds firm peaks. With a flexible spatula, carefully fold it little by little into the fruit mixture.

Using Italian meringue for the mousse.
In a heavy-bottom saucepan, begin cooking the sugar and water. When it registers 230°F (110°C), begin whipping the egg whites with a pinch of salt in a stand mixer fitted with a whisk. When they hold firm peaks and the syrup registers 243°F-250°F (117°C-121°C), gradually pour the syrup into the egg whites, whisking continuously and taking care that the hot syrup does not splatter. Continue whisking until the meringue has cooled to about 85°F (30°C). It will be dense, shiny, and form many small peaks.
With a flexible spatula, carefully fold it into the fruit mixture.

If using both whipped cream and Italian meringue: first fold in the Italian meringue, followed by the whipped cream.

The mousse is now ready to use and must be molded immediately.

● Chef's notes
For the best-tasting result, select seasonal fruits. If you use citrus fruits, kiwi, and pineapple, bring the entire quantity to a boil before adding the gelatin. You can save time by opting for either whipped cream or Italian meringue, but we highly recommend using both.

Icings, sauces, and cake and plate decorations

Icings, sauces, and cake and plate decorations

Fruit

All fruit grows from a flower. Fruits should be sold when they are in season. Fresh fruits are an essential part of the human diet because of the fibers, vitamins, and minerals they contain. There are two major categories of raw (untransformed) fruit:

Fleshy fruits

Dry fruits

Within the category of fleshy fruits, there are the drupes (drupaceous fruits), which have pits (a central stone) containing a kernel Examples are peaches, apricots, plums, and cherries. Other types of fleshy fruit include grapes, red currants, oranges, "pomes" such as apples, pears, and quinces, and exotic fruits such as pineapple and mangoes.

There are three types of dry fruits: achenes, which do not open and contain only one seed (like hazelnuts); beans or pods, which split open on one or two sides, often long with several seeds (vanilla and peanuts are examples); and capsules, which split open in several places (such as chestnuts).

Fruits are marketed in various forms: they can be processed, preserved, or used for fruit-based products.

Processed fruits include purées made from crushed, fleshy fruit, often with the addition of 10 percent sugar (depending on the brand). Purées are essentially used to make iced desserts, creams, mousses, Bavarian creams, and sauces.

Fruit pulps made from fleshy fruit without any additives are also available; they have the same uses as purées.

Fruit juices are made by crushing and filtering fleshy fruits; no water is added. Juices are used for drinks, iced preparations, ice creams, and sorbets.

Fruits may be dehydrated for longer preservation and are called dried fruit (bananas, dates, figs, apples, plums [prunes], grapes [raisins], etc.). They are used as they are, as decorative elements, or rehydrated with an alcoholic beverage to flavor desserts or candies. They are also found in both frozen and deep frozen form. They are considered frozen from -22°F to -31°F (-30°C to 35°C) and deep frozen from -40°F to -140°F (-40°C to -96°C).

Preserved fruit that is sterilized to be sold (in jars or cans) either comes in syrup, with 20 to 50 percent sugar), or plain, meaning simply in water. Fruit can also be preserved by soaking it in an alcoholic beverage, which may or may not have added sugar. Fruit in this form is widely used in confectionery to make candied fruit with fondant icing, and in pastry making to garnish creamy fillings, chocolate bonbons, and as decorations.

There are other fruit-based products. Jellies are preparations made with sugar and pectin-rich fruit juices. The ingredients are cooked to a sufficient degree of dehydration and consistency that enables them to be preserved. Jams are made in the same way, but use fleshy fruits.

Fruits are used for garnish and to flavor or accompany iced desserts. They can also be found in the form of compotes (stewed and puréed), marmalades, gelled fruit, and candied fruit.

Fondant Icing (for éclairs and choux puffs) ★★

Ingredients (makes icing for 8 pastries)
5 ½ oz. (160 g) fondant icing
1 tablespoon (15 ml) syrup, equal parts water and sugar
Coloring

In a bain-marie, soften the fondant icing to about 98°F (37°C). Ensure that it gets no hotter than 104°F (40°C) or it will lose its sheen; any cooler, and it will be too runny to hold. If it seems too thick, stir in a little of the syrup, until it has the consistency of runny honey and is very shiny and sticky. Stir in the coloring as needed.
Dip the pastry into the fondant (1). Wipe off any excess with a clean fingertip (2). Make sure the edge is even and let set.

❚ Recipe idea
Choux Puff *Religieuses* Filled with *Mango Diplomat Cream* >> p. 382

Coffee Glaze ★

Ingredients (makes glaze for 3-4 large cakes*)
4 sheets (8 g) gelatin
3 tablespoons (40 ml) water, to soften the gelatin
¾ cup (200 ml) milk
¾ cup (200 ml) heavy cream
2 ½ tablespoons (2 oz./50 g) glucose syrup
10 oz. (300 g) white couverture chocolate
10 oz. (300 g) ivory glazing paste (available from specialty stores)
2 g titanium dioxide (optional)
2-3 tablespoons (30-50 ml) coffee extract

* It is preferable to prepare a large quantity of glaze, such as this, as small quantities can be tricky.

Soften the gelatin sheets in the exact amount of water specified. Pour the milk, cream, and glucose syrup into a heavy-bottom saucepan and bring to a boil. Remove from the heat and stir in the couverture chocolate, ivory glazing paste, and softened gelatin sheets (they will not need to be squeezed, as they will have absorbed all the water) until completely dissolved. Take about 2 tablespoons of the mixture and dissolve the titanium dioxide in it, pressing it with a pestle if necessary, or use a wooden spoon. Add the coffee extract, but do not stir it in completely: it should be marbled.

The glazing technique.
Place the frozen dessert on a rack set over a dish deep enough to catch any drip-off (1). Pour the glaze over quickly, first covering the sides (2). With an offset spatula, carefully smooth the surface (3). Insert a flat spatula under the cake and work it round to remove the small drops of glaze at the base. Transfer the cake to the serving platter.
Keep the excess glaze, covered with plastic wrap, for another use. It will keep for 1 week. Bring it to room temperature before using.

Icings, sauces, and cake and plate decorations

Shiny Chocolate Glaze ★

Ingredients (makes sufficient for a dessert to serve 10-12)
5 sheets (10 g) gelatin
3 tablespoons plus 1 teaspoon (50 ml) water for the gelatin
Scant ½ cup (100 ml) water
⅓ cup (85 ml) heavy cream
⅓ cup (2 ½ oz./65 g) sugar
4 tablespoons (3 oz./85 g) invert sugar
½ cup (2 ½ oz./65 g) unsweetened cocoa powder

Soften the gelatin sheets in the water. The gelatin should
absorb all the water. In a saucepan, bring the water, heavy
cream, sugar, and invert sugar to a boil. Stir in the cocoa
powder until completely smooth. Simmer for 2 minutes,
stirring frequently. Remove from the heat. Stir in the softened
gelatin sheets until completely dissolved. Process briefly
with an immersion blender.

The glazing technique.
The optimal temperature for this glaze is 86°F (30°C),
to be poured onto a cold dessert or cake.
Place the dessert on a rack set over a dish deep enough to
catch any drip-off. With a ladle, pour the glaze smoothly over
the cake **(1)**. Be careful not to let the ladle touch the icing, not
even to smooth it over. Continue until completely covered,
tipping the rack as much as necessary for the glaze to drizzle
down the sides **(2)**. Lightly rap the rack so that any excess
glaze drops off. This action also removes bubbles and ensures
that the layer of glaze is as fine as possible. If necessary,
smooth with a spatula.
Keep the excess glaze, covered with plastic wrap, for another
use. It will keep for 1 week.

Recipe ideas
Glossy Chocolate Layer Cake >> p. 338
White Chocolate Mousse with Litchi-Apple Compote >> p. 344

1

2

Glaze for Opéra Cake ★

Ingredients (makes glaze for one Opéra to serve 8)
4 oz. (125 g) brown glazing paste
2 oz. (50 g) bittersweet couverture chocolate
1 tablespoon (12 ml) grapeseed oil

Combine the ingredients over a bain-marie
and heat to 104°F (40°C).
Let cool to 86°F (30°C) and use immediately.

The glazing technique.
For an Opéra, leave the cake in its ring so that no glaze
drizzles down the sides. For other cakes, pour the glaze
smoothly over the top with a ladle, ensuring the ladle
does not touch the cake. Continue until completely covered
(it is very runny and will drip down the sides easily).
With a spatula or an offset spatula, smooth over the top
very thinly (less than ⅛-inch/2-3 mm).

❙ Recipe idea
Opéra Coffee and Chocolate Layer Cake >> p. 354

http://flamm.fr/ffd13

Ivory Glaze ★

Ingredients (makes sufficient for a dessert to serve 10-12)
2 sheets (4 g) gelatin
1 tablespoon plus 1 teaspoon (20 ml) water
½ cup (125 ml) milk
⅓ cup (75 ml) heavy cream
1 ½ tablespoons (1 oz./25 g) glucose syrup
5 ¼ oz. (150 g) white couverture chocolate
5 ¼ oz. (150 g) ivory glazing paste
1.5 g titanium dioxide (optional)
1 ½ teaspoons (7 ml) rum (optional)

Soften the gelatin sheets in the water. Pour the milk, cream,
and glucose syrup into a heavy-bottom saucepan and bring
to a boil. Remove from the heat and stir in the white
couverture chocolate, ivory glazing paste, and softened
gelatin sheets (they will not need to be squeezed, as they
will have absorbed all the water) until completely dissolved.
If using titanium dioxide, take about 2 tablespoons of the
mixture and dissolve the titanium dioxide in it, pressing
it with a pestle if necessary, or use a spatula. Incorporate
it thoroughly into the glaze and add the rum, if using.

The glazing technique.
Place the frozen or very cold dessert on a rack set over a dish
deep enough to catch any drip-off. Pour the glaze over quickly,
working first to cover the sides. With an offset spatula,
carefully smooth the surface. Insert a flat spatula under
the cake and work it round to remove the small drops
of glaze at the base. Transfer the cake to the serving platter.
Keep the excess glaze, covered with plastic wrap, for another
use. It will keep for 1 week.

● Did you know?
Titanium dioxide is a white colorant that is found in toothpaste.
Used in glaze or icing, it gives a shiny white color and enhances
other colorants that may be added.

Icings, sauces, and cake and plate decorations

Chocolate Velvet
(for spraying) ★

Ingredients (makes sufficient for at least two cakes for 8)
3 ½ oz. (100 g) cocoa butter
3 ½ oz. (100 g) couverture chocolate (you can use bittersweet, milk, or white)

In a bain-marie, or at low power in the microwave oven, heat the cocoa butter and couverture chocolate to 122°F (50°C). Make sure that the surface you will be working on, as well as the walls behind it, are protected from the spray.
Pour the hot mixture into an electric spray gun and spray evenly over a frozen dessert.
When the hot mixture comes into contact with a cold surface, it forms tiny droplets, creating a velvety-looking appearance. Chocolate velvet spray keeps for 4 weeks in the refrigerator and simply needs to be reheated to 122°F (50°C) to use.

● **Chef's note**
You can also buy ready-made velvet spray in cans. All you need to do is heat them to 122°F (50°C) in a bain-marie and follow the manufacturer's instructions.

Caramel Sauce
with Salted Butter ★

Ingredients (serves 10 as an accompaniment)
⅔ cup (4 ½ oz./125 g) sugar
½ cup (125 ml) heavy cream
2 teaspoons (10 g) salted butter
¾ teaspoon (3g) fleur de sel or other flaky salt

Make a dry caramel with the sugar (see p. 467). While it is cooking, heat the cream. The caramel should be only lightly colored, so remove it from the heat before it reddens. Stir in the butter and gradually pour in the cream, stirring constantly. The caramel will harden a little as you add the cream, so continue to stir until it comes to a boil again. Remove from the heat and stir in the fleur de sel. Serve immediately.

Pear Butter ★

Ingredients (serves 8 as an accompaniment)
12 oz. (400 g) pears
Juice of 1 lemon
2 sticks (8 oz./225 g) butter, divided
½ cup (3 ½ oz./100 g) sugar
3 cups (750 ml) hard pear cider
1 pinch ground cinnamon
Scant ½ cup (100 ml) heavy cream

Peel and dice the pears. Toss them lightly in the lemon juice to prevent them from browning.
Heat 4 tablespoons (2 oz./50 g) butter and the sugar in a pan over high heat and quickly sauté the pear pieces. Do not let them color.
Stir in the hard pear cider and add the cinnamon. Turn the heat down to low and simmer gently until reduced by one-half or even by two-thirds. Stir in the cream and bring to a boil. Reduce until the mixture has thickened. Transfer to a mixing bowl and add the remaining butter, mixing with an immersion blender. Strain through a fine-mesh sieve to make a smooth sauce.
Serve warm.

● **Chef's note**
Instead of pears, you can use apples. Substitute hard apple cider for the pear cider. Another alternative is to use plums with Armagnac. In which case, use only ⅔ cup (150 ml) Armagnac.

Techniques

Icings, sauces, and cake and plate decorations

Chocolate Sauces ★

Chocolate Cream Sauce

Ingredients (serves 6 as an accompaniment)
3 ½ oz. (100 g) bittersweet chocolate, 64 percent cocoa
½ cup (125 ml) crème fraîche or heavy cream

Chop the chocolate. Bring the cream to a boil and pour it over the chocolate. Let stand for a few minutes for the heat to melt the chocolate. Stir until smooth. Serve warm.

Chocolate-Orange Sauce

Ingredients (serves 6-8 as an accompaniment)
3 ½ oz. (100 g) bittersweet chocolate, 64 percent cocoa
½ cup (125 ml) milk
1 tablespoon (20 g) glucose syrup
Zest of ¼ orange
2 teaspoons (10 g) butter

Chop the chocolate. Bring the milk and glucose syrup to a boil with the orange zest. Pour through a fine-mesh sieve over the chocolate. Let stand for a few minutes to melt the chocolate. Stir until smooth and mix in the butter. Serve warm.

 Recipe idea
 Brownies ›› p. 396

White Chocolate Sauce

Ingredients (serves 6-8 as an accompaniment)
3 ½ oz. (100 g) white chocolate
¼ vanilla bean
½ cup (125 ml) milk
1 tablespoon (20 g) glucose syrup
2 teaspoons (10 g) butter

Chop the chocolate. Slit the vanilla bean lengthwise and scrape the seeds into the milk. Bring the milk and glucose syrup to a boil with the ¼ vanilla bean. Remove the vanilla bean and pour the hot liquid over the chocolate. Let stand for a few minutes to melt the chocolate. Stir until smooth and mix in the butter. Serve warm.

Chocolate, Passion Fruit, and Caramel Sauce

Ingredients (serves 10 as an accompaniment)
2 oz. (50 g) milk chocolate
⅔ cup (4 ½ oz./125 g) sugar
2 teaspoons (10 g) butter
⅔ cup (180 ml) passion fruit juice

Chop the chocolate. Make a dry caramel with the sugar (see p. 467), cooking it until it is lightly colored. Stir in the butter, and gradually pour in the passion fruit juice, stirring constantly. When it comes to a boil, remove from the heat and stir in the milk chocolate until smooth.

Chocolate-Caramel Sauce

Ingredients (serves 8-10 as an accompaniment)
2 oz. (50 g) milk chocolate
⅔ cup (4 ½ oz./125 g) sugar
⅔ cup (180 ml) heavy cream
2 teaspoons (10 g) butter

Chop the chocolate. Make a dry caramel with the sugar (see p. 467), cooking it until it is lightly colored. In the meantime, bring the cream to a boil. Stir the butter into the caramel, and gradually pour in the cream, stirring constantly. When the liquid returns to a boil, remove from the heat and stir in the chocolate until smooth.

Strong Bittersweet Chocolate Sauce

Ingredients (serves 12 as an accompaniment)
3 ½ oz. (100 g) bittersweet chocolate, 64 percent cocoa
Scant ½ cup (100 ml) water or milk
Scant ½ cup (100 ml) heavy cream
⅓ cup (2 ½ oz./70 g) sugar
6 tablespoons (1 ½ oz./40 g) unsweetened cocoa powder
1 tablespoon (20 g) butter

Chop the chocolate. Bring the water, cream, and sugar to a boil. Stir in the chocolate. Sift in the cocoa powder. Bring back to a boil, stirring constantly, and let simmer for 2 to 3 minutes, continuing to stir. Remove from the heat and beat in the butter. Serve warm.

Eggnog ★

This is a variation on pouring custard, *crème anglaise* (see p. 91). It is thicker, and other types of strong alcohol can be added.

Ingredients (serves 12 as an accompaniment)
1 cup (250 ml) milk
1 cup (250 ml) heavy whipping cream
¼ cup (2 oz./50 g) sugar
3 egg yolks
2 tablespoons (30 ml) eau-de-vie

In a heavy-bottom saucepan, bring the milk, cream, and sugar to a boil. Turn the heat to low and simmer until reduced by half. Whisk in the egg yolks and add the eau-de-vie. Bring to a boil again, stirring constantly, until the mixture coats the back of a spoon or reaches 185°F (85°C). Cool rapidly, cover with plastic wrap, and chill until needed. Eggnog sauce is generally served cold, but it can also be served warm.

Suzette-Style Fruit Butter ★

Ingredients (makes sauce for 8 crêpes)
⅓ cup (2 oz./60 g) sugar
5 tablespoons (2 ½ oz./70 g) butter, divided
Scant ½ cup (100 ml) orange juice
Finely grated zest of ½ orange
3 tablespoons (40 ml) Grand Marnier or other orange liqueur

In a small, heavy-bottom saucepan, make a dry caramel with the sugar (see p. 467). When it is reddish (330°F/165°C), stir in 1 tablespoon (20 g) butter, and gradually pour in the orange juice, stirring constantly to stop the caramelization process. Add the orange zest. Bring to a gentle boil and simmer until thickened. Stir in the liqueur and reduce again slightly. Remove from the heat and whip in the remaining butter. Keep warm until needed.

● **Did you know?**
There are various stories about the origin of the dessert known as Crêpes Suzette. One is that the Prince of Wales and future King Edward VII so liked the creation by Henri Charpentier, who was chef at a Monte Carlo hotel, that it was named after his companion. Other chefs, however, also claim to have invented it.

❙ **Recipe idea**
❙ Crêpes Suzette-Style >> p. 264

Icings, sauces, and cake and plate decorations

Sauce for Fruits au Gratin ★★

This sauce is ideal to pour over seasonal fruit baked in the oven, and is particularly good with cooked strawberries.

Ingredients (serves 4 as an accompaniment)
½ cup (125 ml) wine, preferably white
Scant ½ cup (3 oz./80 g) sugar
5 egg yolks
¾ cup (200 ml) whipping cream

In a bain-marie, gently heat the wine, sugar, and egg yolks, whipping energetically. The temperature must not exceed 150°F (65°C). Continue whipping until the mixture doubles in volume. It should be very foamy. Do not allow the mixture to come into contact with direct heat as the yolks might coagulate and form small yellow specks.
Remove from the heat. With an electric beater, whip the mixture until it cools to room temperature.
Whip the cream until it holds soft peaks and fold it carefully into the wine-egg mixture.

Wine Sauce ★

Ingredients (serves 8 as an accompaniment)
3 cups (750 ml) wine, preferably white
⅔ cup (4½ oz./125 g) sugar
1 cinnamon stick
1 star anise
1 vanilla bean, slit lengthwise, seeds scraped out
1 tablespoon (10 g) cornstarch, diluted in a little water

Put the wine, sugar, cinnamon stick, star anise, vanilla seeds, and bean into a heavy-bottom saucepan. Bring to a boil and simmer until reduced by half. Whisk in the diluted cornstarch. Process with an immersion blender and strain through a fine-mesh sieve. It should have a custard-like texture, and be of pouring consistency.
Cool rapidly and use cold to accompany fruit.

● **Chef's note**
For extra flavor, poach the fruit in the wine as you reduce the sauce.

Citrus Sauce with Butter ★

Ingredients (serves 4 as an accompaniment)
½ vanilla bean
Scant ½ cup (100 ml) citrus juice, or a combination of orange, grapefruit, lemon, mandarin, etc.
½ cup (3½ oz./100 g) sugar
3 tablespoons (50 ml) water
Scant 1 tablespoon (8 g) cornstarch
2 teaspoons (10 g) butter

Slit the vanilla bean lengthwise and scrape the seeds into the citrus juice. Add the sugar and bring to a boil in a heavy-bottom saucepan. Whip in the cornstarch diluted in a little water. Bring to a boil again, stirring constantly, until thick, with the consistency of custard. Remove from the heat and stir in the butter.

● **Chef's notes**
This sauce, similar to pouring custard, is excellent with fruit cooked en papillote or with pancake pouches.

Set Puréed Fruit ★

Ingredients (serves 6)
5 sheets (10 g) gelatin
2 cups (1¼ lb./500 g) puréed fruit, such as mango, litchis, or strawberries, divided
½ cup (3½ oz./100 g) sugar

Soften the gelatin sheets in a little cold water.
Heat 3 tablespoons (2 oz./50 g) of the puréed fruit with all of the sugar, either in a small saucepan or briefly in the microwave oven. Squeeze the water from the gelatin sheets and dissolve them completely in the heated fruit purée.
Pour the mixture into the remaining purée and let cool.
It should have the texture of a jelly.
Pour into a rimmed tray and let set. Cut with a cookie cutter to make decorative shapes. You can also use this set fruit to marble plates (see p. 125). It will be less watery than a plain coulis.

Sabayon Sauce ★★

Ingredients (serves 4-6 with about 14 oz./400 g fruit)
Approx. ½ cup (100-125 ml) wine, such as dry white wine,
  sparkling wine, champagne, or sweet wine
½ cup (3 ½ oz./100 g) sugar
4 egg yolks
A little finely grated citrus zest (optional)

In a bain-marie, heat the wine, sugar, and egg yolks (1),
whisking constantly until the thermometer registers about
150°F (65°C) and the mixture is doubled in volume, about
5-7 minutes. It should be very foamy. Do not let the mixture
come into contact with direct heat as the yolks might
coagulate and form small yellow specks. Add zest if using.
Use as soon as it is ready—pour over uncooked fruit
and serve.

● Chef's note
*Depending on how sweet the wine is, you can reduce the quantity
of sugar.*

Icings, sauces, and cake and plate decorations

Icings, sauces, and cake and plate decorations

1

Marbling a plate ★★

This is a fun technique that provides a decorative background for plated desserts and adds a decidedly professional touch. Use two or three colors for contrast.

   The recipes for dark and white glazes given on pages 116 and 117 provide a base to work on. And combining white glaze with colorants will give you endless combinations to try out. Fruit coulis are both attractive and delicious, as are pouring custard and the other sauces for which recipes are given.

One approach is to start with pouring custard. To make a "background" to cover the plate, pour just enough of the recipe to make a thin layer.
Color a little of the custard in orange and use a paper decorating cone to make dots of orange around the rim. Repeat with chocolate-flavored custard, alternating the two colors. With a small wooden skewer or toothpick, draw a circle through the dots (1). This will make heart-like shapes for an attractive border around the dessert, which you can then place in the center of the plate.

Alternatively, cover the plate with the sauce used for the background and draw differently colored lines following the shape of the rim. With a toothpick, draw lines in whichever direction you like (2).

To make a spider web pattern, cover the plate with the sauce, a pouring custard, for example. With a paper decorating cone filled with chocolate sauce, start from the center and draw a spiral, leaving less than ½ inch (1 cm) between the lines. With a toothpick, starting from the center, draw a line toward the rim of the plate (3), move the toothpick slightly to one side, and draw a line toward the center. Continue until the entire plate is covered with the pattern.

Use your imagination to personalize your plate decorations and vary the patterns and colors as you wish.

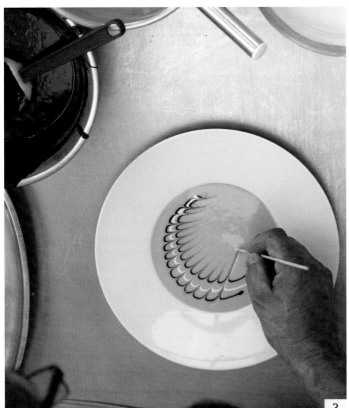

2

3

Masking a dessert ★★

To mask a dessert or cake is to cover it evenly with a cream, couverture chocolate glaze, almond paste, jam, and so on, to make it more attractive. Masking also covers any blemishes.

Place the dessert on a cardboard plate of the same diameter so that you can hold it more easily if necessary.
Hold the dessert at eye level with one hand and, using a plain spatula (1), apply a thin layer of cream. Smooth the sides to even the surface—this initial stage is very important, particularly if you intend to make the striped pattern.
Place the dessert on the work surface and cover the top with a thin layer of cream. Smooth until the surface is even.

To make stripes, use a large serrated knife (2). Work from right to left, downward, making sure the lines are parallel. Make one continuous movement without lifting the knife. Hold the cake at eye level and smooth the sides of the cake. If you wish, lightly press in chopped or sliced roasted almonds, chocolate sprinkles, or streusel crumbs, to decorate the sides or the base of your dessert. Chill until set.

To mask a cake with almond paste, lightly flour the work surface with cornstarch or potato starch and roll the paste out very thinly. Carefully drape it over the rolling pin and set it over the cake, still in its ring, making sure there are no air bubbles or folds. Use the rolling pin to cut the paste to the right size by pressing over the rim of the ring.

❦ **Recipe ideas**
White Chocolate Mousse with Litchi-Apple Compote ›› p. 345
Strawberry and Mousseline Cream Layer Cake (*Fraisier*) ›› p. 349
Black Currant Mousse and Pear Layer Cake ›› p. 350
Opéra Coffee and Chocolate Layer Cake ›› p. 354

1

2

Gelled Layers ★

These are included in layered desserts, small cakes, and desserts in small glasses. They may be crémeux (see p. 108), fruity preparations, or delicate mousses, and they enrich the composition of a dessert by adding color and textural interest.

Ingredients (makes sufficient for a dessert to serve 0)
2 ½ sheets (5 g) gelatin
1 tablespoon plus 2 teaspoons (25 ml) water
10 oz. (300 g) puréed raspberries
3 eggs (6 oz./180 g)
⅓ cup (2 ½ oz./75 g) sugar
7 tablespoons (3 ½ oz./100 g) butter

Soften the gelatin sheets in the water (they will absorb all the water if you use the precise quantity indicated). In a heavy-bottom saucepan, heat the puréed raspberries, eggs, and sugar, whisking constantly, until the thermometer registers 185°F (85°C). Stir the gelatin into the mixture until completely dissolved. Chill to 95°F (35°C). Add the butter and process with an immersion blender. Pour into the desired molds. Freeze for 1 ½ hours, until set. Unmold and use in a layered dessert.

● Chef's note
When making a crémeux, it is important to incorporate the butter when the mixture has cooled to between 86°F and 95°F (30°–35°C) so as not to break up its structure. The crémeux is an emulsion of liquid in fat. The mixture must be held together so that the crémeux maintains its smooth, rounded texture.
This gelled layer goes well with a vanilla Bavarian cream, for example.

Icings, sauces, and cake and plate decorations

Fruit Coulis ★

Ingredients (serves 4)
2 ½ tablespoons (1 oz./30 g) sugar
3 tablespoons (50 ml) water
3 ½ oz. (100 g) fresh fruit (strawberries, mangoes,
    black currants, etc.)
Juice of ½ lemon
Flavoring, such as rum (1 tablespoon/15 ml)

Heat the sugar and water to make a syrup. Process the fruit
with the lemon juice (1) until smooth. Gradually add the syrup
to the puréed fruit (2) until it reaches the desired consistency
(you may not need it all). It should be slightly thick. Let cool
rapidly. If you wish, strain through a fine-mesh sieve.

Confectioners' Sugar-Based Coulis ★

Ingredients (serves 3-4)
3 ½ oz. (100 g) fresh fruit (strawberries, red currants, raspberries,
    cherries, peaches, apricots, pineapple, etc.)
Juice of ½ lemon (optional)
¾ cup to 1 generous cup (3 ½-5 ¼ oz./100-150 g) starch-free
    confectioners' sugar

Blend the fruit and add the lemon juice to prevent oxidation,
if necessary. Add the confectioners' sugar as needed,
depending on how sour the fruit is.
If you are using particularly liquid fruit, such as citrus fruit,
grapes, papaya, add 1 sheet (2 g) softened gelatin to a little
heated purée and then incorporate the mixture into the fruit
purée.

● **Chef's notes**
*You will need to add lemon juice if you are using fruits such as
banana, apples, or pears. If you are using fruits with small seeds,
such as kiwi, raspberries, red currants, mulberries, grapes,
or blueberries, it's best to use a juicer rather than an immersion
blender. This will ensure that the taste of the seeds does not
leak into the sauce. For wild strawberries, use a vegetable mill.
You can make starch-free confectioners' sugar by blending
or processing fine sugar until it forms a powder.*

1

2

Gelled Fruit Coulis ★

Ingredients (serves 6-8)
5 sheets (10 g) gelatin
3 tablespoons plus 1 teaspoon (50 ml) water
1 lb. (450 g) puréed apricots
½ cup (3½ oz./100 g) sugar

Soften the gelatin sheets in the water (they will absorb all the water if you use the precise quantity indicated). Heat one-quarter of the apricot purée with the sugar to about 185°F (85°C). Stir the softened gelatin sheets into it until completely dissolved. Pour into the remaining purée and mix well. The coulis is ready to be molded, so pour it immediately and chill.

● **Chef's note**
The less the fruit is heated, the more flavor it retains. This is why we advise only heating one-quarter of the quantity.

Gelled Fruit Coulis with Pectin ★

Ingredients (serves 6)
1 heaping tablespoon (½ oz./15 g) sugar
$\frac{1}{10}$ oz. (3 g) pectin NH
7 oz. (200 g) puréed raspberries
1 heaping tablespoon (1 oz./25 g) glucose syrup
½ oz. (15 g) invert sugar

Combine the sugar and pectin NH. Heat the puréed raspberries with the glucose syrup and invert sugar to 113°F (45°C). Stir in the sugar and pectin mixture. Simmer for 2 minutes and immediately pour into the mold. Chill until set.

● **Chef's note**
Pectin NH is a reversible gelling agent, which means you can soften the mixture by reheating it.

Crémeux have a lower sugar content than jams and are used in desserts and verrines, individual desserts served in shot glasses. With their colors and flavors, they brighten up all manner of desserts.

Pistachio Crémeux ★

Ingredients (makes sufficient for a dessert to serve 6-8)
2 ½ sheets (5 g) gelatin
1 tablespoon plus 2 teaspoons (25 ml) water
1 ½ cups (350 ml) heavy cream
4-5 egg yolks (3 oz./90 g)
¼ cup (2 oz./50 g) sugar
2 oz. (60 g) pure pistachio paste (see chef's note)

Soften the gelatin sheets in the water. In a heavy-bottom saucepan, bring the cream to a boil.
Whip the egg yolks with the sugar until pale and thick. Gradually pour the hot cream over the egg yolk mixture, stirring constantly. Stir in the gelatin until completely dissolved. Stir in the pistachio paste, return to the heat, and cook until the thermometer registers 185°F (85°C). Pour into the mold, cool rapidly, and freeze until set, about 1 ½ hours. Turn out of the mold and use according to the recipe.

● **Chef's note**
Pistachio paste is certainly one of the adulterated aromatic pastes on the market, so ensure you buy it only from a reputable store.

Orange Crémeux ★

Ingredients (makes sufficient for a dessert to serve 6-8)
2 sheets (4 g) gelatin
1 tablespoon plus 1 teaspoon (20 ml) water
⅔ cup (165 ml) milk
⅔ cup (165 ml) heavy cream
4 egg yolks
Scant ½ cup (3 oz./80 g) sugar
1 tablespoon (15 ml) orange liqueur
Finely grated zest of 1 orange

Soften the gelatin sheets in the water.
In a heavy-bottom saucepan, bring the milk and cream to a boil.
Whip the egg yolks with the sugar until the mixture is thick and pale. Gradually pour the hot milk and cream over the egg yolk mixture, stirring constantly. Stir in the gelatin until completely dissolved. Stir in the orange liqueur and add the orange zest. Return to the heat and cook until the thermometer registers 185°F (85°C). Pour into the mold, cool rapidly, and freeze until set, about 1 ½ hours.

Cutting citrus segments ★

Citrus segments make an attractive decoration and can also be used as part of a fruit salad.

Ingredients
Citrus fruits (orange, grapefruit, lemon, lime, etc.)

Cut off the top and bottom of the fruit, and stand it on one of the cut ends. With a sharp knife, cut off the skin, including the white pith, which is bitter and looks unattractive. With the same knife, remove the segments of flesh between the white membranes. Remove any seeds. Press the trimmings for their juice, which can be used for another recipe.
Segments can be used either raw or candied. (They can be candied by leaving them to soak in syrup for extended periods.) Store in an airtight container, chilled, for up to 2 days.
Note that they are very fragile, so handle them carefully.

Recipe ideas
Grapefruit Gratin with Hard Apple Cider >> p. 267
Summer Fruit Soup >> p. 306

Fruit Chips ★

Chips of fruit or vegetables are easy to make. All you need is a sharp knife and a little practice in fine slicing. You can also use a Japanese mandolin or meat slicer. The idea is to make the finest possible slices, about $\frac{3}{10}$ inch (1 mm), and then dry them out slowly.

Spread the fruit slices completely flat on a silicone baking sheet or baking sheet lined with parchment paper. Bake at between 125°F and 140°F (50°C-60°C) for about 3 hours, making sure that they do not color. Store in an airtight container.

● **Chef's note**
You can also let the slices dry out overnight on a radiator, an economical and effective way of preparing them.

1

2

3

Almond Paste Decorations ★★

Almond Paste Rose

The rose is a universally loved flower, whether natural or made of almond paste. There are many varieties, but the petals are always delicate.

Ingredients
Almond paste (see p. 167)

You can color your roses by adding liquid or powdered edible colorants. For a marbled effect, put together layers of differently colored almond paste (1). Roll into a log shape. Cut thin slices and place them between two sheets of food-safe acetate. Press down with your thumbs to make them as thin as possible. Roll the first petal in on itself, forming a conical tip. Roll the second petal close to this core, ensuring that it is the same height. After that, add successive petals, overlapping them by about one-third (2). It's best to use an odd number of petals on the outer round, for example five or seven. To individualize the roses, turn back some petals gently, pinch others slightly, and make small folds (3).

● **Chef's note**
If you don't have food-safe acetate, you can use parchment paper dusted with starch, but the petals won't be quite as fine.

Almond Paste Carnation

Carnations tend to look a little ruffled, and so the petals should be somewhat ragged.

Prepare the almond paste, combining two colors, if you wish, as described for the rose (p. 132).
Make a log about 20 inches (50 cm) long with a ½-inch (8-10-mm) diameter.
Working on a lightly dusted surface (use potato starch or cornstarch), crush the log with the palm of your hand. Use the back of a soup spoon to thin the paste, working lengthwise until it is very fine. Holding a small kitchen knife flat, slip it towards the edges to tear them. Cut slices about 2 inches (4-5 cm) long. Fold each one like an accordion, placing them on the work surface as you make them. Gather them all together lightly and fold them out horizontally. When they are all gathered together, pinch them as you turn the flower so that they open out and form a half-pompom shape.

Moistening sponge layers ★

Ingredients
Syrup or fruit juice, as specified in the recipe

With a pastry brush, dab or lightly brush the sponge as evenly as possible, dipping the brush into the syrup as often as possible.
Some recipes may call for both sides of the sponge to be moistened, while others may require moistening twice on one side.

● Chef's note
The sweetness and flavor of the syrup varies according to the other components of the recipe.

⦙ Recipe ideas
Strawberry-Raspberry Charlotte >> p. 337
Black Forest Cake >> p. 346
Mocha Cake >> p. 353

Icings, sauces, and cake and plate decorations

1

2

Sugar Decorations ★ ★ ★

Ingredients (makes 8-10 decorations)
1 cup (7 oz./200 g) sugar
¼ cup (60 ml) water
1 tablespoon (20 g) glucose syrup

Equipment: variously shaped round-bottom bowls or molds,
   or ladles, lightly oiled with neutral oil

Spoon-dropped caramel decoration

Combine the ingredients in a heavy-bottom saucepan and
cook to 310°F-330°F (155°C-165°C), a straw color. To stop the
cooking process, immediately dip the bottom of the saucepan
in a bowl of cold water, otherwise residual heat causes the
caramel to continue cooking. Let the caramel cool a little.
Turn the molds upside down. With a soup spoon, drizzle the
caramel back and forth over them (1), working regularly
to create a decorative pattern, either zigzags or a random
crisscrossing that will hold together to form either a basket
(see facing page, bottom) or a decoration.

Spun sugar (angel's hair)

Dip a fork or cut whisk (2) into the caramel. If it forms
a thin thread, it is ready to use. Pull caramel threads from
the saucepan and shake the fork or whisk to and fro over

a metal surface until you have as much as you need. Gather
it up when it is cool enough (but not yet firm). This is the
traditional decoration for croquembouche (see pp. 368-69).

Caramelized Nuts ★

Ingredients
About 30 almonds or hazelnuts
1 cup (7 oz./200 g) sugar
¼ cup (60 ml) water
1 tablespoon (20 g) glucose syrup

Preheat the oven to 350°F (180°C). Toast the nuts for about
10 minutes. Let cool and insert a toothpick into each. Prepare
a base to work from. Set a piece of polystyrene securely set
on a high shelf, so that the caramel can form a thread. You can
also place the polystyrene on top of a stable vase. Combine
the ingredients in a heavy-bottom saucepan and cook to
310°F-330°F (155°C-165°C), a straw color. To stop the cooking
process, immediately dip the bottom of the saucepan in a
bowl of cold water. Let the caramel cool a little. Dip the nuts
into the caramel. Keep them downward and insert the other
end of the toothpick into the piece of polystyrene (3). The
caramel flows down and forms a thread. Let firm before using.

3

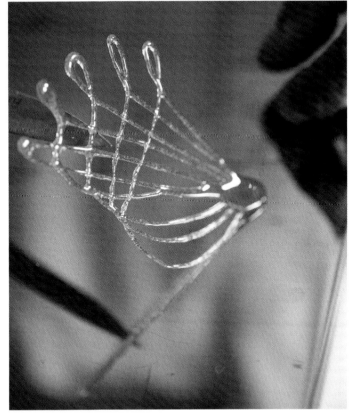

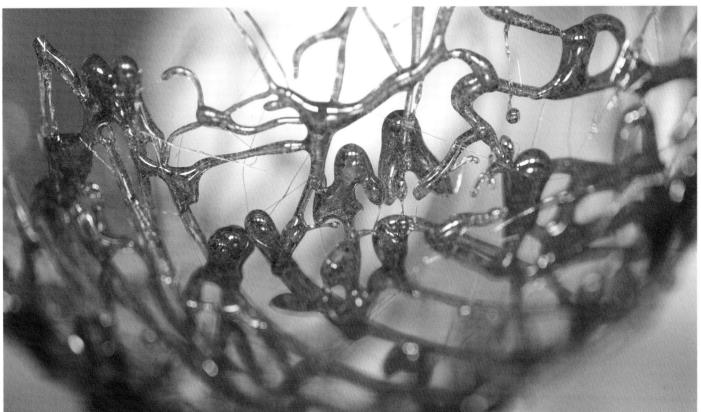

Icings, sauces, and cake and plate decorations

Bubble Glucose ★

Ingredients (makes sufficient to decorate a dessert to serve 8)
About ½ cup (5 oz./150 g) glucose syrup
Food coloring (optional)

Preheat the oven to 320°F (160°C).
With a metal spatula, spread thin ovals of glucose on a silicone baking sheet. If using food coloring, add a few drops to the glucose on the sheet. Bake for about 30 minutes, leaving the oven door ajar if possible, until the glucose begins to swell and form bubbles.
When you remove them, they should be transparent and retain their bubbles. If not, return the tray to the oven to dry the glucose out further.
Let cool on the baking sheet. If you wish, drape the ovals while still soft over a rolling pin for an attractive curved shape. They are very fragile, so handle them carefully.

Pastillage ★★

Ingredients (makes 2 ¼ lb./1 kg of pastillage)
4 sheets (8 g) gelatin
3 tablespoons (40 ml) water
2 teaspoons (10 ml) lemon juice or white vinegar
1 cup plus 1 scant cup (9 oz./250 g) confectioners' sugar
A few drops of coloring (optional)

Soften the gelatin sheets in the water (they will absorb all of
it). Heat the mixture briefly to dissolve and combine it with
the lemon juice. Sift the confectioners' sugar onto a work
surface and make a well in the center. Pour in the softened
gelatin and lemon juice (1). Working with one hand and a
rubber scraper, knead the paste to incorporate the liquid into
the sugar (2), adding coloring if desired. Then knead with
your hands (3, 4) until smooth. It will harden very quickly
and should have the texture of shortcrust pastry. To roll
out the pastillage, lightly dust the work surface (marble,
if possible) with corn starch. Roll to the desired shapes and let
dry, uncovered, turning regularly so they dry evenly, for about
2-3 hours. Stick your pieces together for decorations or
to make a base, using royal icing (see p. 140). Store unused
pastillage, completely covered with plastic wrap, for up
to 2 days.

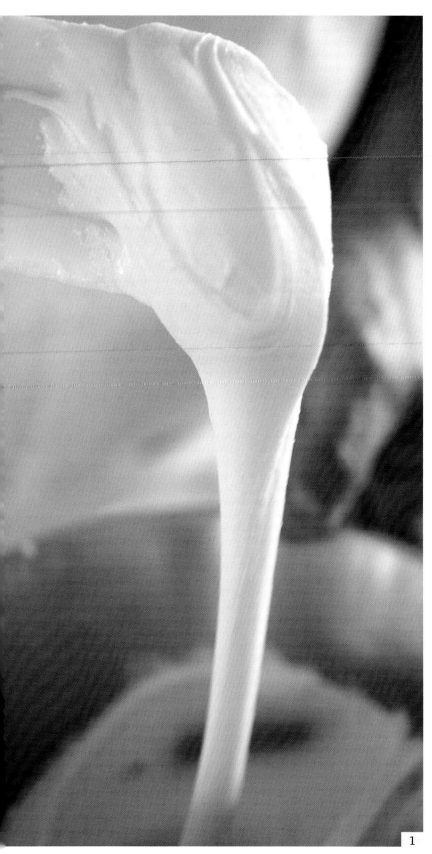

Royal Icing ★

Ingredients (makes 2 ¼ lb./1 kg of royal icing)
3 cups plus scant 1 cup (1 ¼ lb./500 g) confectioners' sugar
7 egg whites
1 tablespoon plus 1 teaspoon (20 ml) lemon juice
  or white vinegar
A few drops of coloring (optional)

Sift the confectioners' sugar. In a clean, dry bowl, beat one-quarter of the confectioners' sugar with the egg whites using a wooden spatula (1). Continue beating energetically, gradually adding the remaining confectioners' sugar, until the royal icing is thickened (2). Stir in the lemon juice and coloring, if using. Check the consistency: it should form small peaks with tips that hold at the end of the spatula, but be fluid enough to be used with a paper decorating cone. Add more confectioners' sugar if necessary. As soon as it is piped, it will set.

● Chef's note
Royal icing can be kept for no longer than 24 hours, covered completely with plastic wrap.

❚ Recipe idea
Croquembouche >> p. 368

Rock Sugar (for sculpting) ★★

1

2

Ingredients
5 ¼ cups (2 ¼ lb./1 kg) sugar
1 ½ cups (350 ml) water
3 oz. (80 g) royal icing (see facing page)
Colorant (optional)

Preheat the oven to 400°F (200°C). Line a large ovenproof
bowl or mold with parchment or waxed paper.
In a large, heavy-bottom saucepan (1), cook the sugar with
the colorant, if using, until the thermometer registers 295°F
(145°C). Remove the cooked sugar from the heat and whisk
in the royal icing until thoroughly combined. The mixture will
foam and double in volume, but then immediately deflate.
As soon as this happens, quickly pour it into the prepared bowl
(2, 3). Place the bowl in the oven for 2 minutes, no longer.
Remove and immediately turn out of the mold (4, 5).
The sugar is now like porous stone (6), and can be cut,
sculpted, or simply broken into shards.

● Chef's note
*It's important to use a sufficiently large saucepan because the
mixture doubles in volume, if only temporarily, and is very hot.*

3

4

5

6

Icings, sauces, and cake and plate decorations

Stencils and printed sponges ★

Using stencils

To make unusually shaped bases for tarts or tartlets, for example, or other pieces using a firm dough, place the stencil on a silicone baking sheet (1). With an offset spatula, spread the dough evenly within the outlines. With a small, sharp knife, carefully trim the edges, remove the stencil, and bake according to instructions.

Printed Sponge

Ingredients

2 tablespoons (1 oz./25 g) butter, softened
3 tablespoons (1 oz./25 g) confectioners' sugar
1 egg white minus 1 teaspoon (1 oz./25 g), lightly beaten
2 ½ tablespoons (1 oz./25 g) flour
Food coloring

Whisk the butter with the confectioners' sugar until light and fluffy. Incorporate the egg white. Pour in all of the flour and mix until smooth. Stir in the coloring of your choice. Spread the cigarette paste (piping batter) thinly on a silicone baking sheet (2). With your fingers (3) or an icing comb (4), draw patterns (5). Chill the baking sheet until set, about 20-30 minutes and pour the raw sponge batter over it. Bake according to instructions and carefully peel away the baking sheet (6).

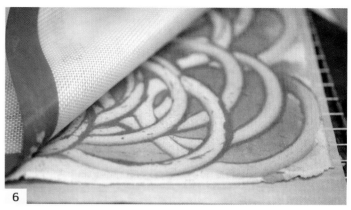

Marbling a mille-feuille ★★

Ingredients

Clear glaze
White fondant icing
Couverture chocolate

Special equipment: a paper decorating cone (see p. 147)

Gently heat the clear glaze. With a brush, lightly cover the layer of baked puff pastry. Over a bain-marie, heat the white fondant to 104°F (40°C). Over another bain-marie, or in brief pulses at medium power in the microwave oven, melt the chocolate. It should be no hotter than 113°F-122°F (45°C-50°C). Pour it into a paper decorating cone and set aside so that the chocolate does not run. Pour the white fondant over the puff pastry and smooth it with a stainless steel spatula (1). You may need to smooth it from one side to another a second time; it should be as even as possible. With the paper decorating cone, make stripes of chocolate from one side to the other, keeping about ½ inch (1 cm) between them (2). When you reach one side, round off the turn (instead of making a sharp angle) to create the effect of parallel lines. With a paring knife and working at a slight angle, scrape lightly through the lines from top to bottom (3). Let cool until set and then remove any drips of fondant.

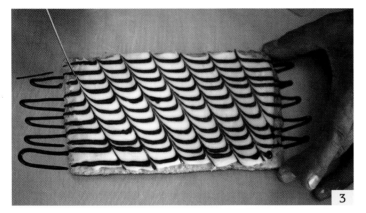

Marbling a glazed topping ★

Ingredients (makes sufficient for three desserts to serve 6)
4 sheets (8 g) gelatin
1 tablespoon plus 1 teaspoon (40 ml) water for the gelatin
⅔ cup (150 ml) water
1 cup (7 oz./200 g) sugar
Red food coloring

Special equipment: a long, plain stainless steel spatula

Soften the gelatin in the water. Bring the ⅔ cup (150 ml) water and sugar to a boil. Remove from the heat and stir in the gelatin until completely dissolved. Pour half of it into a small mixing bowl and color it red. Cool both glazes to 77°F-83°F (25°C-30°C), when they are ready to use. Place the dessert, still in its dessert ring, on a paper plate or serving platter. The dessert ring is used to ensure that the marbling is smooth. Cover the dessert with the transparent glaze and dot some of the red glaze here and there over the surface (**1**). Slide the stainless steel spatula over the top, making small movements so as not to cover the entire surface, to create a veined marbled effect (**2**). Position the spatula flat on one side of the dessert ring and, pressing down on the rim, move it across to the other side to ensure that the surface is perfectly smooth (**3**). Remove the dessert ring (**4**) and refrigerate until serving.

🥄 **Recipe idea**
Strawberry and Mousseline Cream Layer Cake (*Fraisier*) ›› p. 349

Assembling a charlotte ★

Charlottes are generally made in special charlotte molds, but they may also be made in high dessert rings, lined with ladyfingers, either individual or baked in a strip. All sorts of creamy mixtures are used to fill them.

Place the dessert ring on a piece of golden cardboard or serving platter.
Cut the ladyfingers to a length just under ½ inch (1 cm) higher than the dessert ring. Stand the ladyfingers touching one another, rounded side upward, around the inside (1), or place the strip of ladyfinger sponge around the rim, making sure that the ends fit snugly together.
Cut out a disk of sponge (either Genoese sponge or ladyfinger) to fit into the bottom, again making sure that there is no gap with the lining on the sides. Lightly moisten it just before setting it at the bottom (1).
Pour in the mousse or creamy filling (2, 3), adding pieces of fruit, or a thin gelled layer of fruit (crémeux), if using.
Pour in the remaining mousse, filling the charlotte to the top (4) and chill according to directions, until set.

● **Chef's note**
Because ladyfingers and other sponges do not stick to the dessert ring, there is no need to use food-safe acetate to line the ring.

▌ **Recipe idea**
Strawberry-Raspberry Charlotte >> p. 337

Icings, sauces, and cake and plate decorations

Decorating a *pithiviers* ★

For a clear, shiny pattern on the top of this cake (see p. 378 and illustration pp. 380-381), you will need to baste your puff pastry twice, using 1 egg, lightly beaten.

When the cake is assembled and the edges scored with the sharp edge of a knife (below right), brush the top of the cake, taking care not to let any egg run over the edges. This would prevent the puff pastry from rising evenly. Chill for about 10 minutes.

When this first layer is absorbed by the pastry, brush it a second time. The albumin contained in the egg coagulates and acts as a protective cover. It also provides color.

Begin by making a small hole in the center of the top layer of puff pastry. This allows the steam from the frangipane to escape during baking. Then, with the back edge of a small knife, draw out arcs starting from the center. Take care not to cut too deeply into the pastry. Another traditional pattern is crisscrossing lines. Chill again for 20 minutes before baking.

❦ **Recipe idea**
Pithiviers Filled with Almond Cream >> p. 379

Making and writing with a paper decorating cone ★ ★

Paper decorating cones are very useful for writing inscriptions on cakes or for other delicate patterns with royal icing or chocolate.

Material
Wax or parchment paper

Cut a right (right-angled) triangle 6 inches (15 cm) high and 10 inches (25 cm) long.
Roll the small side around your hand onto the large side and continue rolling until you can fold the tip inside the cone to keep it in place. (You may even use a paper clip.) Note that it should be closed opposite the fold.

Half-fill the cone (with melted chocolate, royal icing, or whatever you're using), and fold it closed. With a pair of scissors, snip off a small hole at the tip. The size depends on the pattern you will be drawing.
With the icing in the paper cone, you can produce fine motifs or write a message on your dessert or cake. It takes considerable practice, so persevere! You will find examples of decorating motifs on page 233.

http://flamm.fr/ffd14

Glazing a log-shaped cake and dessert ★★

This is a delicate procedure and it may take practice before you master the technique of glazing a cake smoothly. It requires precision and a sure hand.

The cake must be very cold, so make sure it has been in the refrigerator (or if necessary, the freezer) for several hours. Heat the glaze to 77°F-83°F (25°C-30°C). Add the coloring (1). Place the dessert on a pastry rack set over a dish large enough to catch any excess that drips off.

Fill a large ladle with the glaze and pour it in one go over the dessert. You must work quickly and evenly so that the glaze does not accumulate more thickly in any one spot than another (2).

Again working quickly, use a stainless steel spatula to push any excess glaze to the edges. Just before you reach the edges, lift the spatula so that you do not damage them. Lightly rap the rack and wait for the drops to stop falling. Immediately transfer the dessert to a serving platter, chill to set, and decorate (3).

● **Chef's note**

Always prepare a little extra glaze to avoid patching up gaps.

❙ **Recipe ideas**

Creamy Peach and Orange Log Dessert >> p. 330

Yule Log >> p. 333

Creamy Pistachio Log Dessert >> p. 334

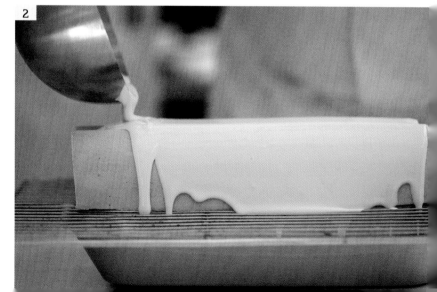

Icings, sauces, and cake and plate decorations

3

Confectionery, jams, and candy decorations

Confectionery, jams, and candy decorations

Sugar

Whether sugar is derived from sugar cane or beets, it is the result of a long industrial process that transforms the raw product into small, white crystals through a series of treatments. Sugar cane is grown essentially in tropical regions, and sugar beet is cultivated in temperate regions. The refining process starts when the beets and cane are harvested. The beet is thoroughly washed to rid it of the earth and stones that cluster around the roots. It is finely sliced and washed under very hot water, which dissolves and captures the sugar. This part of the process is called diffusion. Cut sugar cane is shredded and crushed and then washed with very hot water.

Clarified cane and beet juices, now richer in sugar, also have many natural impurities. The syrup must be clarified by liming it and treating it with carbon dioxide. This triggers a chemical reaction that traps all the impurities in a lime carbonate that we call sucrate. All that then remains to be done is to evaporate the water and collect the sugar. It is heated in a vacuum so that no caramelizing can take place. Gradually the substance crystallizes. It is still soaking in some juice, but centrifugation rapidly extracts it.

When cooked on its own, sugar melts at 320°F (160°C) and is transformed into caramel. To cook it, add one-third of its weight in hot water.

Candy sugar is made by slowly crystallizing hypersaturated syrup. In the industrial process, wires are stretched within the containers that contain a hypersaturated syrup and placed in a steam bath at about 95°F (35°C). There is no vibration or movement. The crystals form slowly on the sides on the wires. They gradually form clusters of crystallized sugar.

Artisanal candying is a far quicker process and results in smaller crystals settling on a range of confections from almond paste and chocolates to filled dried fruit.

Make a syrup with a very refined sugar (this is important to avoid impurities). Use 4 ¾ lb. (2.2 kg) for every 4 cups (1 liter) water. Bring to a boil, skimming frequently and washing down the sides of the saucepan with a brush dipped in clean water. When it reaches boiling point, remove from the heat and cover with plastic wrap. Let cool completely without stirring the syrup at all or touching the saucepan—it must not be subjected to any vibration or movement.

When dissolved crystals are so highly concentrated, they will tend to cluster together again. If you stir the mixture at all, they will come together in an uncontrolled way and clog the entire syrup. Organized crystallization is the aim—as one would expect from a master candy maker.

During the cooling phase, you will have ample time to prepare the confections you are going to candy. Place them on a candying stand, not too close to one another. Gradually pour the syrup until the confections are completely covered—the syrup should cover them by about ½ inch (1 cm). Prepare a piece of parchment paper the size of the candying rack and make small holes, about ½ inch (1 cm) square. Place it over the syrup. Leave in a place where the candying process will not be disturbed and let the magic work as long as you like: 24 hours, 36 hours, 3 days, or even 6 months if you have the patience. The longer you let the confections rest, the more spectacular the result will be.

Unlike when gelled fruit confections are rolled—in crystallized sugar, for example—in this technique the crystals of candy sugar join together and form a coating that protects whatever is inside from the air, keeping it nice and soft.

The little windows in the paper allow you to peep in to see how the thickness is progressing. If you just break the coating of a single confection, you will have an idea of what has happened below the paper. If you're happy with the result, carefully lift it up, raise the candying stand and let drain for 30 minutes. Place it in a well-ventilated spot and let dry.

When you are working with sugar, the ingredients and material will reach hot temperatures, so be very careful. For pulled sugar, it is advisable to don disposable gloves.

Sugar burns quickly and the contents of your saucepan demand your undivided attention—if you exceed the temperature specified in the recipe, there is a good chance that you won't be able to use it: burned sugar cannot be rescued so you will have to start over.

Always have a large pan of cold water ready to dip the bottom of the saucepan in to halt the caramelizing process (see p. 467).

For decorative pieces and candies, use the purest sugar you can find to avoid impurities, which cause crystallization. In all the candy recipes that follow, cream of tartar is used to prevent sugar crystallization.

Soft Caramels
with Salted Butter ★ ★

Ingredients (makes about 30 candies)
1 ¼ cups (9 oz./250 g) sugar
⅓ cup (75 ml) heavy cream
⅓ cup (75 ml) water
Heaping ¼ teaspoon (1 g) cream of tartar
3 tablespoons (1½ oz./45 g) salted butter, diced
¼–½ teaspoon (1 ml) vanilla extract

8 x 4-inch (20 x 10-cm) rimmed baking pan

In a heavy pan, place the sugar, cream, water, and cream of tartar. Heat to 240°F (116°C) (1) and stir in the butter. Continue heating to 280°F (138°C). Immediately remove from the heat, stir in the vanilla, and pour into a rimmed baking pan or between two square rulers set on parchment paper (2)–it should be no thicker than just under ½ inch (1 cm). Let cool slightly. While it is still warm, turn it onto a cutting board and cut into squares (or other shapes).
Let cool completely and wrap in cellophane paper.

● Chef's notes
If you wish, you can also use unsalted butter or butter made with salt crystals.
If you prefer softer caramels, cook the mixture only to 262°F (128°C). For harder caramels, continue to a maximum of 300°F (150°C).

Caramel Shards ★

Small pieces of caramel shards add textural interest to chocolate mousses and other creamy fillings.

Ingredients (makes 10 oz./300 g or serves 10)
½ cup (3 ½ oz./100 g) superfine (caster) sugar
Scant ⅓ cup (3 ½ oz./100 g) glucose syrup
¾ teaspoon (3 g) fleur de sel
Scant ½ cup (100 ml) heavy cream

In a heavy pan, cook the sugar, glucose syrup, fleur de sel, and heavy cream to 300°F (150°C) (1, 2).
Immediately pour over a silicone baking sheet (3) and cover with a second silicone sheet or parchment paper. Roll out (4).
Let cool.
Break into small decorative shards.
Alternatively, pour the caramel in a thin layer into lollipop molds and insert a stick. Let harden and wrap in cellophane. These lollipops will be very hard.

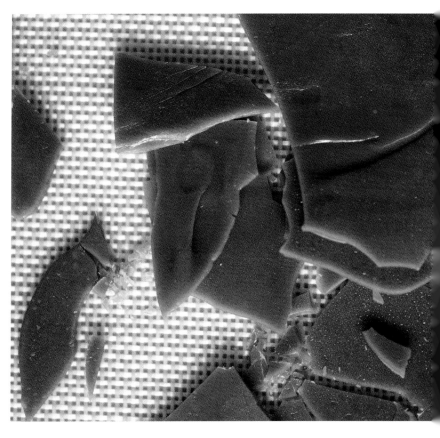

Gelled Fruit ★ ★

Ingredients (makes thirty to forty 1-in./2.5-cm candies)

9 oz. (250 g) prepared fruit pulp, 10 percent sugar

⅕ oz. (6 g) yellow pectin

1 oz. (27 g) superfine (caster) sugar

⅙ oz. (5 g) 50/50 solution citric acid (see chef's note)

½ cup (3 ½ oz./100 g) granulated sugar, plus a little extra for coating

2 ½ tablespoons (2 oz./50 g) glucose syrup

Special equipment: confectionery frame

In a heavy saucepan, begin heating the fruit pulp. Do not let it boil. Combine the yellow pectin with the superfine sugar. Whisk the mixture into the hot fruit pulp (1) and heat to 225°F (107°C), stirring the liquid frequently. Stir in the citric acid solution and immediately pour the mixture into a confectionery frame to a thickness of 1 inch (2.5 cm) (2). Let cool and harden.

Sprinkle a cutting board with the granulated sugar and turn the gelled fruit onto the board. Cut into the desired shapes (3), rinsing the knife frequently and wiping it down with cotton wool soaked in alcohol so that it does not stick. Coat the cubes of gelled fruit in sugar.

● Chef's notes

To make the solution of citric acid, combine an identical quantity of water with pure citric acid and measure out the quantity you require.

Yellow pectin and citric acid trigger a gelling process that cannot be reversed. This means that the gelled fruit cannot be heated and re-liquefied.

Gelled fruit can also be inserted into various layered desserts. If you are making the recipe for this purpose, cut out appropriate shapes and do not coat them in sugar. Lightly brush them with alcohol so they do not stick together.

http://flamm.fr/ffd15

Almond Paste-Filled Dried Fruits ★

Ingredients (makes 24)
24 pieces of dried fruit, such as apricots, prunes, dates, and figs
1 lb. (480 g) white and/or colored almond paste (see p. 167)
Scant ⅛ cup (100 ml) water
1 ¼ cups (10 oz./300 g) sugar
2 ½ tablespoons (2 oz./50 g) glucose

Special equipment: small skewers, one for each piece of fruit

With a pair of scissors, slit the fruit horizontally along its length (1) just deep enough to extract the pit if present. Make a small log of almond paste (½ inch/1 cm diameter) (2) and cut pieces to fit the opening. Enclose the fruit over the almond paste (3). Cook the water, sugar, and glucose to 300°F (150°C) and insert a skewer carefully into the filled fruit, dipping them one by one (4). Place the skewers, well separated so that the individual fruits do not come into contact, on a raised surface so that the excess syrup can drip off. When cool and dry, remove the little tip of solidified syrup with a pair of scissors (5) and slide the fruit into a paper case without touching it. Carefully remove the skewers.

● Chef's note
For added textural interest, enclose a walnut, almond, or hazelnut, or even a piece of candied fruit, such as pineapple or citrus, in the almond paste and proceed as above.

Confectionery, jams, and candy decorations

Red Nougat ★★

Ingredients (makes 1 lb. 5 oz./600 g of nougat)
5 oz. (150 g) blanched almonds
Scant ½ cup (100 ml) water
1 ¼ cups (10 oz./300 g) granulated sugar
5 tablespoons (3 ½ oz./100 g) glucose syrup
A few drops of red food colorant

Toast the almonds in a 350°F (180°C) oven for 8 minutes.
Carefully cut an almond in two. It should be white inside.
If not, leave the other almonds for 2 more minutes. Remove
as soon as they are lightly toasted outside but still white
inside. Let cool slightly, but note that they should be warm
when you incorporate them into the syrup.
In a heavy-bottom pan, cook the water, sugar, glucose,
and colorant to 310°F (155°C). Stir in the warm almonds **(1)**.
Pour the mixture thinly into a rimmed silicone baking pan,
smooth with an offset spatula, and let cool **(2)**.
Roughly cut into pieces using poultry shears and store
in an airtight box as any moisture will spoil them.

● **Did you know?**
Red nougat is a candy typically sold at country fairs in France.

White Nougat ★★

Ingredients (makes 30-40 individual nougats)
9 oz. (250 g) blanched almonds
¾ cup (9 oz./250 g) acacia honey, or other light-colored honey
¾ cup (9 oz./250 g) glucose syrup
1 ½ egg whites (1 ½ oz./45 g)
2 oz. (50 g) shelled pistachios

Special equipment: two sheets of edible rice paper (alternatively,
use parchment paper but remove before eating)

Toast the almonds in a 350°F (180°C) oven for 8 minutes.
Carefully cut an almond in two. It should be white inside.
If not, leave the other almonds for 2 more minutes. Remove
as soon as they are lightly toasted outside but still white
inside. Let cool slightly, but note that they should be warm
when you incorporate them into the syrup.
In a heavy pan, heat the honey and glucose. Meanwhile, whip
the egg whites until they hold firm peaks. When the honey
and glucose mixture reaches 250°F (120°C), pour one-quarter
of it over the beaten egg whites, whisking as you pour.
(This is the same technique as for Italian meringue, p. 177.)
Let the remaining honey and glucose mixture cook to 310°F
(155°C) as you continue whisking the egg white mixture.
Gradually pour the remaining syrup over the egg white
mixture, whisking until it cools completely. Replace the whisk
of the stand mixer with the paddle beater and incorporate the
still warm almonds and the pistachios (1). Continue beating
with the paddle beater at medium speed until the mixture
has dried out. If you wish, you may finish cooking it
with a kitchen torch. This will take about 30 minutes.
To test for doneness: dip a knife into the mixture and
immediately transfer it into a bowl of ice water; rap the
knife hard on the edge of the work surface; the nougat
should detach itself easily from the knife and break.
Pour the nougat over the rice paper between two steel square
rulers to a thickness of just under 1 inch (2 cm). Make sure
that the thickness is even all over and cover with the second
sheet of rice paper. Set a baking sheet over it and weigh
it down with packets of sugar, rice, etc. Leave for at least
12 hours before cutting.

● Chef's note
*Like caramels, the longer you cook the mixture, the firmer
the nougat will be.*

❙ Recipe idea
Nougat Blancmange with Pear Coulis >> p. 292

Praline Paste ★

Ingredients (makes 11 oz./300 g of praline paste)
Scant 1 cup (5 oz./150 g) hazelnuts
3 tablespoons (40 ml) water
¾ cup (5 oz./150 g) granulated sugar
2 teaspoons (10 g) butter

Toast the hazelnuts in a 350°F (180°C) oven for 8 to 10 minutes. Note that they should still be warm when you incorporate them into the recipe. In a heavy-bottom saucepan, cook the water and sugar until it forms a reddish caramel. Remove from the heat and immediately stir in the butter and warm hazelnuts. Pour onto a silicone baking sheet (1) and let cool. Chop roughly with a knife and process in a food processer fitted with a blade knife in several additions, to avoid overheating the motor (the paste goes through several stages (2, 3), until it forms a creamy paste. Transfer to a container and cover with plastic wrap. Praline paste keeps for up to 3 months in an airtight container at room temperature.

❡ Recipe ideas

Creamy Pistachio Log Dessert >> 334
Crisp and Creamy Layered Chocolate Dessert >> 341
Paris-Brest >> p. 376
Iced Praline Lollipops >> 462

Marshmallow ★★

Ingredients (makes 1 lb./450 g of marshmallow)
7 ½ sheets (15 g) gelatin
5 tablespoons (75 ml) water for the gelatin
1 ¼ cups (9 oz./250 g) sugar
Scant ½ cup (100 ml) water
1 tablespoon plus 1 teaspoon (25 g) glucose syrup
1 egg white
Flavoring of your choice
Colorant of your choice (optional)
Equal parts confectioners' sugar and cornstarch for dusting

Lightly dust a rimmed silicone baking sheet with the mixture of confectioners' sugar and cornstarch. Soften the gelatin sheets in the water specified. Cook the sugar, water, and glucose syrup to 260°F (127°C). Heat the gelatin very briefly in the microwave oven to dissolve it, and lightly whip the egg white. When the syrup registers 260°F (127°C), remove from the heat and gradually pour it over the melted gelatin (1). It will immediately become foamy. Gradually pour this mixture over the egg white, whipping for about 15 minutes, until it reaches the consistency of a meringue. Stir in the flavoring and colorant and immediately pour onto the baking sheet (2), making sure it is even. Let set and cut into ribbons for skewers (3), or other shapes.

Plum Jam ★

Ingredients (makes three to four 1-lb./450-g jars)
2 ¼ lb. (1 kg) pitted plums
4 cups (1 ¾ lb./800 g) granulated sugar

Special equipment: a large pan (the jam becomes very foamy),
  preferably copper

Begin the recipe a day (or 12 hours) ahead. Coat the pitted
plums in the sugar (**1**) and let them macerate in a large bowl,
covered with a clean cloth. Stir once or twice so that the sugar
melts more easily.
The following day, make the jam. In a large pan, preferably
copper, bring the plums and sugar to a boil over high heat,
skimming when necessary (**2**). Continue to skim as necessary
for 25 to 30 minutes. To test for doneness, drop a little jam
on a cold plate (**3**). As soon as the last drop holds firm
without running at all, the jam is ready.
Immediately fill sterilized jam jars to the top (**4**), close,
and turn upside down until cooled. This sterilizes any
air remaining in the jars.

● Chef's notes
*If you have an instant-read or candy thermometer, you can cook
the jam to between 220°F (105°C), when it will be very tasty, or to
225°F (107°C), when it will be firmer and keep better.
If you have pectin-enriched sugar available, you can make the
jam far more quickly, but the traditional cooking method given
here is much tastier.*

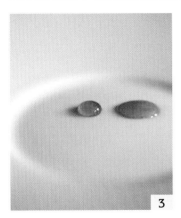

1

2

3

Spiced Rhubarb and Strawberry Compote ★

Ingredients (serves 4-6)
10 oz. (300 g) rhubarb
7 oz. (200 g) strawberries
½ cup (3 ½ oz./100 g) sugar
3 tablespoons (50 ml) water

1 vanilla bean
1 star anise
1 cinnamon stick

Trim the bases of the rhubarb stalks and peel off the tough outer skin (1). Wash the strawberries, carefully pat them dry, and hull them. Cut the fruit into pieces (not too small) (2). Place the fruit and sugar in a large pot, copper if possible. Slit the vanilla bean in two lengthwise, scrape the seeds into the fruit mixture, and add the bean, star anise, and cinnamon stick. Over high heat, bring the ingredients to a boil. Immediately reduce the heat to low and gently stew the fruit. The pieces of fruit should remain more or less intact and the flavors should not meld too much. This should take about 30 minutes. Taste to check when the compote is ready. Remove flavorings. Cool quickly, cover in plastic wrap or store in an airtight container, and chill for 2 to 3 days before serving (3).

Raspberry Jelly ★

Ingredients (makes six 1-lb/450-g jars)
2 ¼ lb. (1 kg) raspberries
5 cups (2 ¼ lb./1 kg) sugar
A few drops of lemon juice (optional)

Blend the raspberries to make a purée. Alternatively, bring them to a boil and strain to remove the seeds.
Place the purée in a medium saucepan with the sugar over high heat and bring to a boil. Skim the foam from the top, maintaining the boil over high heat for 20 to 25 minutes. Stir frequently and check the texture (1). To test for doneness, drop a little jelly on a cold plate (2). As soon as a drop holds firm without running at all, the jelly is ready (3). If using lemon juice, stir it in to help the jelly set.
Raspberry jelly is relatively quick and easy to make because it is a fruit that is naturally high in pectin, a gelling agent.

● **Chef's note**
A copper pot always gives better results for jams and jellies. Copper diffuses heat more evenly than other materials; the presence of copper oxide enhances the solidification of pectin.

Quince Jelly ★

Ingredients (makes four to five 7-oz./200-g jars)
1 ⅔ lb. (750 g) quinces
½ vanilla bean
2 ⅔ cups (1 lb. 2 oz./500 g) sugar (approximately, see below)
Finely grated zest of 1 orange

One stage of this recipe involves squeezing juice out of hot fruit. You may want to use clean disposable gloves to protect your hands. You will also need to weigh the juice, so have a scale handy. Because of the fruit's hardness, the jelly may take several hours to prepare.

With a brush, remove the fine hair on the skin of the quinces.
Cut into quarters without removing the skin or the seeds.
Quinces are very hard fruit, so cut carefully.
Place in a large pot and pour in enough water to just cover them. With the lid on, cook them gently over low heat until you can easily slide a knife into the pieces.
While the fruit is cooking, slit the vanilla bean lengthwise and scrape out the seeds into a small bowl. Finely dice the bean and add to the seeds.
Set a colander over a large mixing bowl and drain the quince pieces, keeping the cooking liquid. With a clean cloth, press down on the fruit to extract any remaining juice. The fruit will be very hot so work carefully. Reserve the pieces of fruit for another use.
The juices are particularly flavorful and rich in pectin.
Weigh the juice and prepare the equivalent amount of sugar.
Place all the juice, sugar, vanilla seeds and diced bean, and the orange zest, in a pot, preferably copper, over high heat for maximum evaporation.
To test for doneness, drop a little jelly on a cold plate. As soon as a drop holds firm without running at all, the jelly is ready.
The color, when done, is amber red. It is transparent and you will be able to see the vanilla seeds and orange zest.
Immediately pour into the small jam jars, close, and turn them upside down until cooled. This ensures that any remaining air in the jars is sterilized and means that the jelly will keep well.

● **Chef's note**
Quinces taste good with other fruit, such as apples and raspberries. If you add them to your jelly, the test for doneness is identical.

Crisp Nut Cookies ★

Ingredients (makes twelve to fifteen 2-2 ½-in./3-4-cm cookies)
Scant ¼ cup (50 ml) milk
1 stick (4 oz./125 g) butter
¾ cup (5 oz./150 g) sugar
¹⁄₁₀ oz. (3 g) pectin NH
2 ½ tablespoons (2 oz./50 g) glucose syrup
5 oz. (150 g) chopped almonds
3 ½ oz. (100 g) chopped pistachios
3 ½ oz. (100 g) chopped hazelnuts

Preheat the oven to 375°F (190°C).
In a heavy-bottom saucepan, bring the milk, butter, sugar, pectin NH, and glucose syrup to a boil. Stir in the nuts.
Immediately pour into small silicone molds.
Bake for 15 to 20 minutes, until nicely caramelized.
Turn out onto a cooling rack.

● **Chef's note**
You can make any shape that takes your fancy, by using differently shaped silicone molds.

Confectionery, jams, and candy decorations

Nougatine ★ ★

Ingredients (makes 12 oz./350 g of nougatine)
3 ½ oz (100 g) chopped almonds
¾ cup (5 oz./150 g) sugar
Scant ⅓ cup (3 ½ oz./100 g) glucose syrup
2 teaspoons (10 g) butter

Use nougatine as a component of a dessert, as a decoration, or break it up and include it in cookies, ice creams, and so on.

Preheat the oven to 350°F (180°C). Lightly roast the chopped almonds for 6 minutes. They should still be warm when you stir them into the caramel. In a heavy-bottom saucepan, copper if possible, heat the sugar and glucose syrup (1). When the temperature reaches 340°F (170°C) and the caramel is a reddish color, remove from the heat and stir in the butter and chopped nuts (2). Pour onto a silicone baking sheet (3), spread out a little, and let cool. As soon as the nougatine is cool enough to handle (it must still be malleable), roll it out as thinly as possible (4) and cut it out to the desired shapes (5). To make curved shapes, drape triangles around a tube (6) or in a tuile pan. Let cool completely and store in an airtight container. Humidity will spoil the texture.

● Chef's notes

For variations on this classic nougatine, substitute some of the almonds with sesame seeds or other nuts.
It's important to cook the caramel to 340°F (170°C), when it reaches an attractive reddish color. If it is undercooked, it will lack taste, and if it's overcooked, it will be bitter.

❗ Recipe ideas
Semolina Cake >> p. 315
Croquembouche >> p. 368
Cookies >> p. 400
Iced Nougat >> p. 463

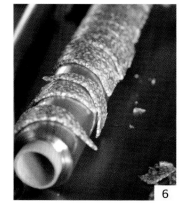

http://flamm.fr/ffd16

Poppy Seed Nougatine ★★

Ingredients (makes 11 oz./300 g of nougatine)
9 oz. (250 g) fondant icing
2 teaspoons (10 g) butter
Heaping ½ cup (3 oz./80 g) poppy seeds

In a heavy-bottom saucepan, copper if possible, caramelize the fondant icing. When it reaches 330°F-347°F (165°C-170°C), remove from the heat. Immediately stir in the butter and poppy seeds. Pour onto a silicone baking sheet, spread out a little, and let cool. As soon as the nougatine is cool enough to handle (it must still be malleable) roll it out as thinly as possible and cut it out to the desired shapes. To make curved shapes, drape triangles around a tube or in a tuile pan. Let cool completely until it is hard and will break like glass. Store in an airtight container. Humidity will spoil the texture.

Almond Paste ★

Ingredients (makes 1 lb. 2 oz./500 g of almond paste)
3 ½ oz. (100 g) whole almonds
1 ¼ cups (10 oz./300 g) sugar
Scant ½ cup (100 ml) water
1 ½ tablespoons (1 oz./30 g) glucose

Drop the almonds into a pot of boiling water for 1 minute. Drain them and place on sheets of paper towel. With your fingers, pop the almonds out of their skins. In a heavy-bottom pot, cook the sugar, water, and glucose to 250°F (120°C). Add the almonds (1). Stir continuously for a few minutes with a wooden spoon (2). After a few minutes, the mixture becomes slightly crumbly: the water is absorbed and the mixture is dry and lumpy. Transfer it to a sheet of parchment paper. Process the almonds in the bowl of a food processor

fitted with a blade knife in several additions so as not to overheat the motor. The almond paste goes through several stages (3). It first resembles a coarse powder and then reaches a fatty consistency. This is due to the extraction of the oil contained in the almonds (54 percent). When it reaches this texture, immediately cover it in plastic wrap so that it does not form a crust. Use according to the recipe.

● Did you know?
Marzipan is a traditional confectionery that is particularly popular in many European countries, from Portugal to Norway, Belgium to Greece. Lübeck in Germany has a long tradition of manufacturing high-quality marzipan, and mazapán de Toledo (Spain) has protected status within the European Union. Almond paste is available with varying proportions of almonds and sugar. The finest quality contains around 66 percent almonds and 33 percent sugar. The next grade contains 50 percent of each. For confectionery, almond paste with 33 percent almonds and 66 percent sugar tends to be used. The lowest grade has 25 percent almonds. Follow the instructions on the recipe when selecting which type to use.

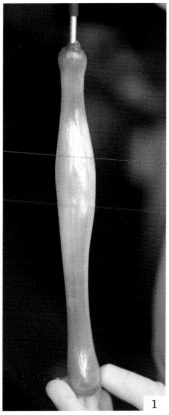

http://jflamm.fr/jffd17

1

2

Blown Sugar Swan ★ ★ ★

Working with blown sugar is an art that requires a great deal of practice before you acquire the skills. Persevere and you will stun your guests with your creations.

Ingredients
2 ⅔ cups (1 lb. 2 oz./500 g) sugar
⅔ cup (180 ml) water
Scant ⅓ cup (3 ½ oz./100 g) glucose syrup
⅓ teaspoon (1 g) cream of tartar
A little alcohol-based food coloring

Special equipment: an insulated ladle, disposable gloves, a blowing pump, a blowing tube, a heating lamp, and a fan

Caution: This technique involves handling sugar at a very high temperature, so take extreme care. Use the most refined sugar possible to ensure that there are no impurities.

Combine all the ingredients except the food coloring in a heavy-bottom saucepan and cook to 320°F (160°C), skimming constantly as soon as the mixture begins to boil. Dip a brush in water and brush the sides down frequently to remove any traces of foam and sugar crystals. Pour the mixture onto a silicone baking sheet, making a cylindrical shape, and incorporate the food coloring. Now the sugar must cool evenly so that no blemishes or harder zones form; it must remain malleable. As soon as the sugar is cool enough to handle, put on the disposable gloves and begin pulling it until it becomes shiny and satiny **(1)**. Hold it near the heating lamp (or the open door of a heated oven). Fold it over itself several times and then inward as if you were making a ball, ensuring that the top is smooth and the underside has the folds. Maintaining the sugar near the source of heat, flatten the ball and shape it into a mushroom cap. One side must be hollow (to insert the blowing pump) and the thickness must be regular. Heat the metal part of the pump and insert it into the hollow of the cap. Pressing firmly, enclose the metal part with the sugar. Start pumping air very slowly in small puffs **(2)**. Continue pumping to shape the head, taking care not to press too hard on the sides, which could close together. Pull the head away from the body–this will form the neck–still making little puffs with the pump. With two fingers, pinch the end to make the beak. Place the sculpture in front of the fan to cool down completely. Heat a sharp knife over a kitchen torch and, with a sawing motion, cut the tail off from the rest of the sugar. (The heat melts the sugar to enable you to do this.) To make the wings, use the pulled sugar technique.

1

2

Candied Rose Petals ★

Ingredients
1 egg white, very fresh
1 pinch salt
¾ cup (5 oz./150 g) sugar
Petals from 3 or 4 unsprayed roses

Lightly beat the egg white with the salt, just to liquefy it.
With a brush, carefully spread the egg white on both sides
of the petals, making sure to coat them evenly (1).
Dust the petals on both sides with sugar and place them
on a piece of parchment paper (2).
Set carefully on a radiator or in an oven at 85°F (30°C)
and leave for 12 hours, until dry.

⬤ Chef's notes
*Use this method to candy the petals of other flowers,
like fragrant violets, nasturtiums, and pansies.
Store for 2 to 3 months in an airtight container.*

Boiled Candies (*Berlingots*) ★★

Berlingots are tetrahedron-shaped hard French candies that have been popular since the nineteenth century.

Ingredients (makes 1 lb. 9 oz./700 g or about 50 *berlingots*)

2 ⅔ cups (1 lb. 2 oz./500 g) sugar
⅔ cup (180 ml) water
Scant ⅓ cup (3 ½ oz./100 g) glucose syrup
⅓ teaspoon (1 g) cream of tartar
3-4 drops essential oil, such as mint, lemon, or orange
A little alcohol-based food coloring
1 pinch powdered citric acid (optional)

Combine all the ingredients except the essential oil and coloring in a heavy-bottom saucepan and cook to 320°F (160°C), skimming constantly as soon as the mixture begins to boil. Dip a brush in water and brush the sides down frequently to remove any traces of foam and sugar crystals. Pour the mixture onto a silicone baking sheet (1) in two equal parts. Stir the essential oil into one half and the coloring into the other half (2). Add the citric acid if using. As soon as the sugar is cool enough to handle, put on disposable gloves, if using, and pull it until it becomes shiny and satiny (3).
Press the two pieces together and twist them evenly (4). Shape into a thin log, just under ½ inch (1 cm) in diameter. With a heated pair of scissors, cut off pieces of the same length as the diameter (5), twisting as you do so to form a tetrahedron, the typical shape of *berlingots*.

● Did you know?

The berlingot *made in Carpentras (in the south of France) has white stripes and is larger than the* berlingot *produced in Nantes (in Brittany), which is more opaque.*

Colored Ribbons ★ ★ ★

Ingredients (makes 2 lb. 14 oz./1.3 kg or about 60 ribbons)
5 cups (2 ¼ lb./1 kg) sugar
1 ½ cups (350 ml) water
⅓ teaspoon (1 g) cream of tartar
Assorted powdered food colorings, diluted in alcohol

Special equipment: an insulated ladle, disposable gloves,
    a heating lamp, and a fan

Combine all the ingredients except the food colorings in a
heavy-bottom saucepan and cook to 330°F (165°C), skimming
constantly as soon as the mixture begins to boil. Immediately
pour three or four equal parts on a silicone baking sheet and
color quickly so that the sugar does not cool down too fast. As
soon as the sugar is cool enough to handle, put on disposable
gloves, if using, and pull it near a source of heat (an oven with
the door ajar, if you don't have a heating lamp) until it becomes
shiny and satiny without allowing it to harden. Shape each
piece into a log (they may be different sizes) **(1)** and place them
side by side as you think best to combine the dark and light
colors **(2)**. Press them together lightly so that they stick to one
another. Pull them until the pieces are about 20 inches (50 cm)
long and cut them in half through the center **(3, 4)**. Working
under the lamp, juxtapose the colors and repeat the operation
until you have the number of stripes you want **(5)**. Stretch the
ribbon for the last time as long as you can without cracking
it. It is easier if you can work with another person. Place the
ribbon on the work surface and cut it out according to your
decoration **(6)**. Shape the pieces into rings **(7)** and make knots
if you wish, or any other shape.

● **Chef's note**
*To make very wide ribbons, begin by pressing two or three logs
of the same color (red, for example) together, and then add a
separating log (black, for example), followed by four or five logs
of another color (green, for example). Pull and cut as above.*

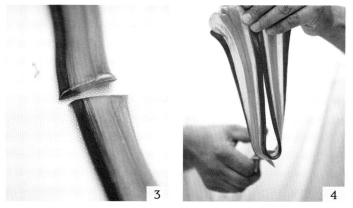

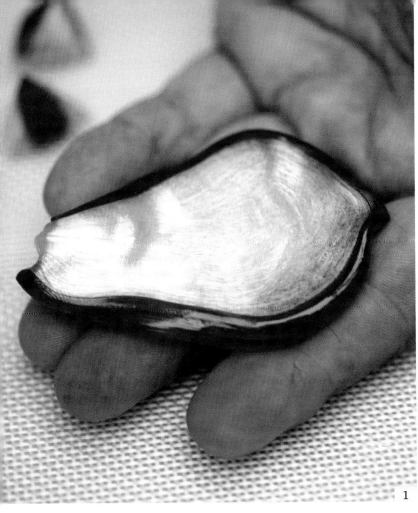

1

Lollipops ★

Ingredients (makes 1 lb. 9 oz./700 g or about 20 lollipops)
2 ⅔ cups (1 lb. 2 oz./500 g) sugar
⅔ cup (175 ml) water
Scant ⅓ cup (3 ½ oz./100 g) glucose syrup
⅓ teaspoon (1 g) cream of tartar
3-4 drops essential oil, such as mint, lemon, or orange
A little alcohol-based food coloring
1 pinch citric acid (optional)

Combine all the ingredients except the essential oil and
coloring in a heavy-bottom saucepan and cook to 320°F
(160°C), skimming constantly as soon as the mixture begins
to boil. Dip a brush in water and brush the sides down
frequently to remove any traces of foam and sugar crystals.
Pour the mixture onto a silicone baking sheet and add
the essential oil and coloring. Add the citric acid, if using.
Divide the sugar up and shape the lollipops–round, oval,
or with imprints—and make them in one or more colors **(1)**.
Insert a lollipop stick **(2)**.

● Chef's notes

A pinch of citric acid adds zing to fruity flavors.
Using lollipop molds will facilitate your task: pour the sugar into
them as soon as you remove it from the heat and add the colors
and flavors of your choice before inserting the stick.

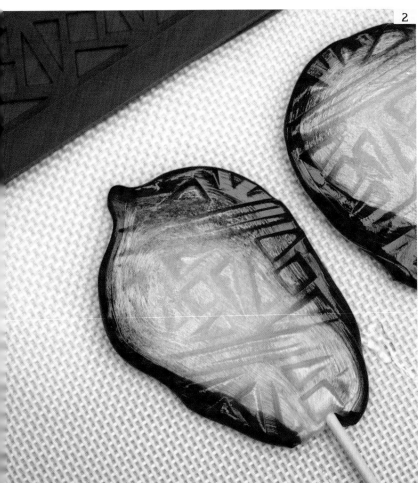

2

Confectionery, jams, and candy decorations

Bubble Sugar ★★

Ingredients (makes 1 lb. 9 oz./700 g of bubble sugar)
2 ⅔ cups (1 lb. 2 oz./500 g) sugar
⅔ cup (175 ml) water
Scant ⅓ cup (3 ½ oz./100 g) glucose syrup
⅓ teaspoon (1 g) cream of tartar
3-4 drops essential oil, such as mint, lemon, or orange
Liquid food coloring

Gently crumple sheets of wax or parchment paper.
Combine all the ingredients except the essential oil and
coloring in a heavy-bottom saucepan and cook to 320°F
(160°C), skimming constantly as soon as the mixture begins
to boil. Dip a brush in water and brush the sides down
frequently to remove any traces of foam and sugar crystals.
Pour the syrup little by little on the creased paper. Add a few
drops of essential oil and coloring. Carefully hold it up, tilting
it from side to side to spread the coloring through the sugar.
It will form small bubbles and resemble stained glass.
Place on the work surface and let cool completely.
Break into pieces according to the decorations you
require. Store in an airtight container.

1

2

Barley Sugar ★ ★

Ingredients (makes 1 lb. 9 oz./700 g of barley sugar)
2 ⅔ cups (1 lb. 2 oz./500 g) sugar
⅔ cup (175 ml) water
Scant ⅓ cup (3 ½ oz./100 g) glucose syrup
⅓ teaspoon (1 g) cream of tartar
3-4 drops essential oil (mint, lemon, orange, etc.)
Liquid food coloring

Combine all the ingredients except the essential oil and coloring in a heavy-bottom saucepan and cook to 320°F (160°C), skimming constantly as soon as the mixture begins to boil. Dip a brush in water and brush the sides down frequently to remove any traces of foam and sugar crystals. Pour onto a silicone baking sheet in two equal parts. Add an essential oil to one half and color the other half. As soon as it is cool enough to handle, pull the two pieces separately until they are shiny and satiny. Press them together and twist neatly. Make a log with a diameter of just under ½ inch (1 cm) (1). Heat a pair of scissors and cut 4-inch (10-cm) sticks (2). If you wish, you can bend one end to make walking sticks.

Confectionery, jams, and candy decorations

Meringues

When making meringues, make sure the bowl is perfectly clean and dry. Any traces of fat or moisture will prevent the meringue from turning out perfectly. If you're working by hand with a whisk or hand-held beater, it's best to use a round-bottom bowl for maximum air incorporation.

French Meringue ★

Ingredients
3 egg whites (3 ½ oz./100 g)
1 scant cup (7 oz./200 g) sugar

In a round-bottom mixing bowl, lightly beat the egg whites to liquefy them. Then whip energetically, lifting the egg whites high, to incorporate as much air as possible. When the egg whites hold soft peaks (they will bend over slightly when lifted with the whisk or spatula), stir in the sugar with brisk, circular movements of the whisk. The meringue must be compact and smooth, and form thin tips when the whisk is lifted up. Bake according to directions, if making meringues, or incorporate into the recipe.

Recipe ideas
Layered Blinis with Mulberries >> p. 295
Creamy Pistachio Log Dessert >> p. 334
Strawberry-Raspberry Charlotte >> p. 337
Marble Cake >> p. 399

Swiss Meringue ★

Ingredients
3 egg whites (3 ½ oz./100 g)
1 scant cup (7 oz./200 g) sugar

Prepare a bain-marie with the water heated to between 125°F-130°F (52°C-55°C). In a round-bottom mixing bowl, lightly beat the egg whites to liquefy them. Pour in the sugar and whip energetically, lifting the egg whites high, to incorporate as much air as possible. When the mixture begins to foam, set the bowl over the bain-marie and whisk until the mixture thickens, triples in volume, and becomes shiny. At this stage, it should register 113°F (45°C) on a thermometer. Remove from the heat and continue to whisk until the meringue cools to room temperature. Incorporate into the recipe.

Recipe idea
A Contemporary Vacherin with Four Fruit Sorbets >> p. 439

1

2

Italian Meringue ★★

This hot preparation, made with cooked sugar, is firm enough to use for decoration. It is also an essential component of almond macarons and some iced desserts.

Ingredients
1 cup (7 oz./200 g) sugar
3 ½ tablespoons (55 ml) water
3 egg whites (3½ oz./100 g)
1 pinch salt

In a heavy-bottom saucepan, begin cooking the sugar and water. When it registers 230°F (110°C), begin whipping the egg whites with a pinch of salt in a stand mixer fitted with a whisk. When they hold firm peaks and the syrup registers 243°F–250°F (117°C–121°C), gradually pour the syrup into the egg whites, whisking continuously and taking care that the hot syrup does not splatter. Continue whisking until the meringue has cooled to about 85°F (30°C). It will be dense, shiny, and form many small peaks.

Recipe ideas
Assorted Macarons >> p. 371
Lemon Meringue Tart >> p. 425
Baked Alaska >> p. 450

http://flamm.fr/ffd18

Confectionery, jams, and candy decorations

Working with chocolate

Chocolate

The story of chocolate can be traced to the hinterlands of Central America, to the Equatorial forest where abundant rains and heat create a climate that produces luxuriant vegetation. In the midst of this grows a perpetually flowering tree with leaves that look surprisingly like those of the chestnut tree so familiar to us. The flowers, leaves, and fruit of the tree were of course known to the indigenous peoples, who roasted its seeds and used it to make a spicy drink that they called *xocoatl*. The cellars of Emperor Moctezuma were filled with the oval fruit, which he used as currency.

Worldwide, there are three varieties of cocoa tree: Forastero, Trinitario, and Criollo. Their fruit, the pod, contains seeds, and when the seeds are roasted they take on the name of cocoa beans. The seeds are beautifully arranged in a white, slightly sour pulp within the pod. The seeds are fermented and dried so that they can be transported. Pure cocoa paste (also known as chocolate liqueur) is obtained by crushing roasted cocoa beans.

Cocoa powder is made by subjecting pure cocoa paste to high pressure, 6,000 lb./sq. in. (500 kg/sq. cm). This partially extracts the cocoa butter; the remaining substance is crushed to make cocoa powder.

Cocoa butter is the firming agent of chocolate. Without it, Easter eggs would not shine, melted chocolate would not have that unctuous fluidity, and chocolate bars would not snap and then crunch when eaten. In Europe, chocolate manufacturers are legally allowed to replace up to 5 percent cocoa butter with another vegetable fat, but generally they do not do this in the case of high-quality couverture chocolate. Chocolate is termed "couverture" because of its high cocoa butter content (31 percent for dark chocolate), which gives it the fluidity to leave a fine layer, a light *couverture* (covering) over chocolate candies, for example.

Couverture chocolate is chocolate obtained after a complicated process that involves crushing, grinding, and refining until it is reduced to particles smaller than 50 microns. Sugar is added, and sometimes vanilla. This means that in bittersweet chocolate, everything that is not chocolate is sugar. Powdered milk is added to milk chocolate.

The difficulty in working with chocolate is getting the temperatures right. It should never be heated beyond 122°F (50°C), so this means never setting it over a bain-marie at full boil. You can melt it in the microwave oven, but work in brief pulses and never at maximum power (no more than 350 W) so as not to scorch it. Make sure all your implements and surfaces are perfectly clean, and that the chocolate does not come into contact with any water.

Tempering is indispensable because of the presence of cocoa butter, a complex substance that contains several groups of molecules with different points of fusion and crystallization. The aim of tempering is solely to enable crystallization to take place in an orderly fashion.

● Did you know?

White chocolate contains no chocolate paste. It does, however, contain cocoa butter, to which sugar and milk powder are added.

http://flamm.fr/ffd19

 is placed; side text: Techniques

181

Working with chocolate

Decorating with chocolate ★★

Tempering chocolate

To start with, chocolate has to be tempered. Pastry chefs use what is called couverture chocolate. With a high cocoa butter content, it easily becomes fluid and leaves a fine layer or cover (*couverture*) when used to coat candies and make molds. It must be melted and then put through a cycle of temperature changes in order to crystallize uniformly. Tempering is the procedure that enables chocolate to retain its sheen, snap satisfyingly, and melt in the mouth. There are several tempering methods.

Tempering using a tempering stone

1. Melt the chocolate, preferably over a bain-marie with barely simmering water, or carefully in a microwave oven so that it does not scorch. It should heat to no more than 122°F (50°C).
2. Take two-thirds of the melted chocolate and spread it over a granite work surface (or other cold surface). With a spatula or offset spatula, spread and turn it constantly (it must not form grains) until it cools to 79°F-81°F (26°C-27°C).
3. Return this chocolate to the bowl containing the remaining third and check the temperature, which should reach 86°F-88°F (30°C-31°C). While you are using the chocolate, ensure that it remains at this temperature. You can do this by checking the temperature of the bain-marie regularly.

Tempering by seeding

This method involves adding couverture chocolate in the form of pistoles, chunks, or chopped pieces to already melted chocolate. Melt two-thirds of the couverture chocolate, heating it to 122°F (50°C). Stir in the remaining one-third of the unmelted chocolate. This triggers the reaction we want, arranging the chocolate molecules so that they are shiny and easily snapped when set.

Tempering by natural cooling

When the chocolate has melted (it should be no warmer than 122°F/50°C), take the bowl from the heat and let the chocolate cool naturally, stirring from time to time, until it reaches the desired temperature, 86°F-88°F (30°C-31°C). It will take some time so use this method if you are not in a hurry.

Ingredients

2 oz. (50 g) syrup at 1.2624 on the density scale
14 oz. (400 g) glucose syrup
2 ¼ lb. (1 kg) couverture chocolate, melted
 (no hotter than 122°F/50°C)

Pour the syrup and glucose syrup into the melted chocolate without stirring. Wait for the ingredients to cool to the right temperature. After 15 minutes, stir very gently and briefly. As soon as the mixture becomes pasty, cover it with plastic wrap and refrigerate.
Just before you begin to work with it, soften it for 2 to 3 seconds in the microwave oven, or knead it with your hands, like modeling clay.

● Chef's notes

If you have white chocolate, process it in the bowl of a food processor so that you can manipulate it like modeling clay. Keep in mind that chocolate spoils when it comes into contact with water. Keep all work surfaces clean and dry, and always use perfectly dry equipment.

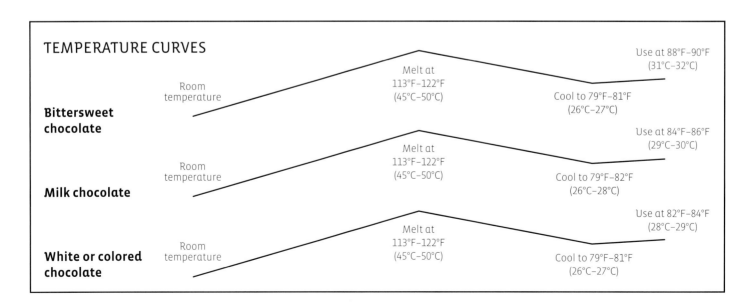

TEMPERATURE CURVES

Bittersweet chocolate
Room temperature — Melt at 113°F–122°F (45°C–50°C) — Cool to 79°F–81°F (26°C–27°C) — Use at 88°F–90°F (31°C–32°C)

Milk chocolate
Room temperature — Melt at 113°F–122°F (45°C–50°C) — Cool to 79°F–82°F (26°C–28°C) — Use at 84°F–86°F (29°C–30°C)

White or colored chocolate
Room temperature — Melt at 113°F–122°F (45°C–50°C) — Cool to 79°F–81°F (26°C–27°C) — Use at 82°F–84°F (28°C–29°C)

Chocolate cigarettes (1)

Make these delicate rolls of chocolate by using a large knife to scrape tempered chocolate, when it is finely spread on a marble surface, just as it begins to set. If you scrape it too soon, the chocolate sticks to the knife, and if you wait too long, it cracks and doesn't roll up.

To make rolled chocolate with stripes, spread tempered white chocolate on the surface and scrape it with a large-toothed comb. Wait until it sets and spread tempered bittersweet chocolate over it before scraping rolls with the knife.

Flames on transfer paper (2)

Spread a thin layer of melted colored cocoa butter on a plastic transfer sheet or a sheet of food-safe acetate. Spread tempered bittersweet chocolate over it and let it begin to set. With a kitchen knife, make arcs in the chocolate and immediately roll it up diagonally without tightening the sheet. Unroll only when you are ready to use it. It will make thin, twisted flame shapes to use as decorations.

● Chef's note

Depending on the color of your cocoa butter transfers, you can also spread a thin layer of white chocolate before spreading the bittersweet chocolate. White chocolate brings out the patterns very well.

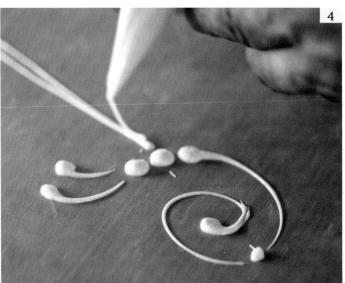

Ruffled chocolate (3)

Ruffled or fanned chocolate is quite magical. On a very hot, but not burning, metal sheet, spread melted couverture chocolate and place it in the refrigerator. When the chocolate has cooled, bring it to room temperature. Wait for just the right moment to scrape it with a triangular metal pastry scraper. The trick is to first make a small roll of chocolate with the thumb and index finger of the left hand, while the right hand pushes the scraper forward. It's hard to explain but easy to make; it just takes a little practice. You'll soon be able to judge the "right moment" when the chocolate rolls without sticking to the scraper.

Paper decorating cone (4)

Mastering decorations with a paper decorating cone is like practicing musical scales to play an instrument. You have to repeat the curves and curlicues until you get the hang of it. The friezes you make either by sliding the cone or dropping the icing from it will become more and more even with practice. It's a technique that can bring as great a pleasure as good handwriting (see p. 147 and p. 233).

Two-colored openwork roll

The technique involved here is delicate but the effect
is stunning.

Half-fill a paper decorating cone with tempered white
chocolate and another with tempered bittersweet chocolate.
On a sheet of food-safe acetate, draw out a close-knit
crisscross pattern (it should be able to hold together later).
Wait a few minutes until the chocolate begins to set, and roll
it over itself, ensuring that the sides meet, then roll up the
entire sheet. Keep the edges together with an elastic band
or a piece of Scotch tape. Refrigerate immediately.
Remove the food-safe acetate only when you are ready to use
the decoration.

● **Chef's note**

*If you use a microwave oven to melt couverture chocolate,
do not exceed 350 W so that it does not scorch. Pulse in several
brief stages, stirring each time, until the chocolate has melted.*

1

Chocolate bubble wrap (1)

Sprinkle a sheet of bubble wrap with edible sparkling powder (gold or bronze, for example). Temper the couverture chocolate and spread it thinly over the bubble wrap. Either leave the bubble wrap flat, fold it, or drape it over a bowl or mold.
Let set and gently pull off the plastic.

Molds for small chocolate figures

Create small chocolate figures or objects by making gelatin molds.

Ingredients
2 cups (500 ml) water
2 ½ cups (1 lb. 2 oz./500 g) sugar
6 oz. (175 g) powdered gelatin

Place the selected object (small figure, Christmas balls, etc.) in the refrigerator. It should be at 35°F-37°F (2°C-3°C) maximum.

Heat the water. Combine the sugar and powdered gelatin. Pour the water over the dry ingredients and, in a heavy-bottom saucepan, heat without boiling until a clear syrup forms. Skim off any impurities. Check the temperature: it should be no hotter than 113°F (45°C).
Pour it over the object to mold.
Let harden in the refrigerator. Cut the block in half, taking care not to spoil the object, and put the mold together again with Scotch tape or elastic bands.

For instructions on how to mold chocolate, see p. 188.

For instructions on how to mold chocolate, see p. 188.

 Chef's note
For simple, inexpensive molds, use solid transparent plastic objects that you can easily find at hobby shops.

Chocolate Cornflake Cookies ★

Ingredients (makes 7 oz./200 g, to serve 4)

3 ½ oz. (100 g) milk couverture chocolate

2 oz. (50 g) cocoa butter or 3 tablespoons (2 oz./50 g)
  clarified butter

2 oz. (50 g) cornflakes

Special equipment: a pair of disposable gloves

Melt the chocolate and cocoa butter to 122°F (50°C).
Place the cornflakes in a round-bottom bowl and pour
the hot mixture over them.
Wearing disposable gloves, coat the cornflakes in the
chocolate by hand. Shape small mounds on a lined
or silicone baking sheet.
Place in the refrigerator to set.
Store in an airtight container. These cookies will keep
for several weeks.

● Did you know?

In French, these cookies are called roses des sables, *literally
"roses of the sands," because they resemble the rock formation
colloquially known as the desert rose.*

Chocolate Ganache ★

Ingredients (makes 12 oz./350 g)

4 oz. (125 g) milk couverture chocolate

4 oz. (125 g) bittersweet couverture
  chocolate

⅓ cup (75 ml) heavy cream

Finely grated zest of ¼ orange (optional)

3 tablespoons (50 ml) orange liqueur
  (optional)

http://flamm.fr/ffd20

Over a bain-marie, melt both the chocolates. The temperature
must not exceed 113°F-122°F (45°C-50°C).
Meanwhile, bring the cream to a boil (add the orange zest
at this point, if using, to infuse the cream).
Pour the chocolate into the heavy cream in several additions,
whisking each time until fully emulsified. Add the orange
liqueur, if using.
Pour onto a rimmed silicone baking sheet and let set. Cut to
the desired shapes and dip in tempered couverture chocolate
to make ganache-filled chocolates. Alternatively use a piping
bag to pipe out bite-sized rosettes of the ganache, or use
in a baked tart crust.

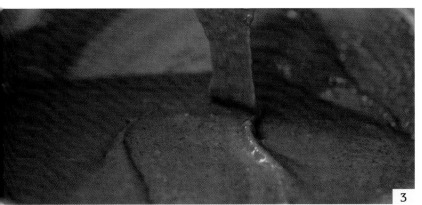

Praline Filling
for Coated Chocolates ★

Ingredients (makes filling for about 10 chocolates)
2 oz. (50 g) milk couverture chocolate, 36 percent cocoa
3 ½ oz. (100 g) praline (see recipe p. 160), softened

Special equipment: confectionery frame

In a bain-marie, melt the milk chocolate. The chocolate should be no hotter than 122°F (50°C) (1). Remove from the heat and stir in the praline with a flexible spatula (2). Continue until smooth (3). Let cool at room temperature until it reaches a creamy consistency. Place a confectionery frame over a silicone baking sheet or food-safe acetate. Pour the mixture into it and let set at about 60°F (16°C) for 12 hours or in the refrigerator for 5 to 6 hours. Coat the top of the praline lightly with tempered chocolate to form an undercoat (see p. 188), then cut into shapes (4). Place the undercoated side on the tines of a fork and dip into the tempered chocolate (5). Dip it in three or four times. Scrape the dipping fork against the edge of the bowl so that the layer on the base is not too thick. Transfer to a baking sheet lined with a plastic sheet or parchment paper.

Undercoating (*chablonnage*)

Spreading a very fine layer of tempered chocolate over a set ganache filling makes it easier to cut and coat it. You will need some tempered chocolate (more than you will actually use) and a spatula (or offset spatula). Spread the tempered chocolate evenly and thinly over the surface of the tray of ganache filling before it is cut. This fine layer will be the base of your coated chocolate bonbons. Immediately cut it into the desired shapes.

Hand-dipped chocolate

You will probably only use about 20 percent of the total weight of the ganache to be coated, but it is advisable to temper considerably more so that you can dip the bonbons and give them a proper outer layer. It can always be re-tempered for another use. Set the bonbon with the undercoated side downward on the tines of a dipping fork. Place it in the tempered chocolate, ensuring that it is completely submerged. Retrieve the bonbon and dip it in about three more times. The coating should not, however, be too thick. Wipe the dipping fork and chopstick regularly as you work to remove the chocolate that sticks to them. Carefully transfer to a piece of food-safe acetate (preferably) or parchment paper to set. You may need to use a chopstick to slide the chocolates off the fork so as not to damage them.

Praline Filling

Ingredients (makes about 15 chocolates)
2 oz. (65 g) milk couverture chocolate
1 oz. (25 g) cocoa butter
9 oz. (250 g) praline (see recipe p. 160)

In a bain-marie, melt the chocolate and cocoa butter. Alternatively, use the microwave oven at no more than 350 W, pulsing in brief stages. The mixture should be no hotter than 122°F (50°C). Remove from the heat. With a spatula, mix in the praline until smooth. Let cool at room temperature until it reaches a creamy consistency. Spoon into a piping bag fitted with a plain tip and pipe bite-sized rosettes. Place in the refrigerator until thoroughly chilled. Finely coat the top with tempered chocolate to make the base of the chocolate candies (see "Undercoating," above), cut to the desired shapes, and dip in tempered chocolate (see "Hand-dipped chocolate," above).

Almond Paste Filling

Ingredients (makes about 25 chocolates)
1 ¼ cups (10 oz./300 g) sugar
Scant ½ cup (100 ml) water
1 ½ tablespoons (1 oz./30 g) glucose syrup
3 ½ oz. (100 g) whole almonds

Follow the instructions in the recipe for almond paste (p. 167). Keep in a cool place, about 60°F (15°C), for 24 hours. Finely coat the top with tempered chocolate to make the base of the chocolate candies (see "Undercoating," left), cut to the desired shapes, and dip in tempered chocolate (see "Hand-dipped chocolate," left).

● **Chef's note**
If the almond paste is at the right temperature, it will be easier to work with and will not become oily.

Molding chocolate

To ensure your chocolate molds are spotlessly clean and grease-free, clean them with cotton wool and 90° alcohol. Holding the mold over the bowl of tempered chocolate, fill the cavities with a ladle, letting it flow swiftly across. Tilt the mold from side to side until the tempered chocolate coats the entire surface of each and every cavity. Turn the mold upside down so that any excess chocolate can drip back into the bowl, and tap it lightly. Set the mold upside down on a baking sheet lined with parchment paper and wait a few minutes, until it begins to set. Before it has hardened, scrape the top clean so that the edges of the molding are perfectly trim, and let set completely. Pipe the ganache filling into the lined cavities. When it has set, form the base: ladle more tempered chocolate over, wait until it begins to set, and scrape off any excess. Chill for about 30 minutes, until the chocolates begin to release from the sides. Bring back to room temperature and unmold. For more advice, see the troubleshooting table (p. 242).

Hazelnut Filling for Molded Chocolates

Ingredients (makes about 20 chocolates)
Scant 1 cup (5 oz./150 g) hazelnuts
3 tablespoons (40 ml) water
¾ cup (5 oz./150 g) granulated sugar
2 teaspoons (10 g) butter
1 ¼ oz. (35 g) cocoa butter

Special equipment: molds; 90° alcohol; 2 confectionery rulers; 1 baking sheet lined with parchment paper; 1 ladle

Prepare the chocolate molds (see "Molding chocolate," p. 188). Make the hazelnut paste. Toast the hazelnuts in a 350°F (180°C) oven for 10 minutes. In a heavy-bottom saucepan, cook the water and sugar until it forms a reddish caramel. Remove from the heat and immediately stir in the butter and warm hazelnuts. Pour onto a silicone baking sheet and let cool. Chop roughly with a knife and process in the bowl of a food processer until it forms a creamy paste. Heat the cocoa butter to 122°F (50°C), taking the same precautions as for couverture chocolate. Remove from the heat and incorporate the hazelnut paste. Let cool to 80°F (27°C). Spoon into a piping bag and pipe into the molded chocolate. Set aside for 12 hours and close the molds with tempered chocolate.

Milk Praline Filling for Molded Chocolates

Ingredients (makes about 20 chocolates)
3 ½ oz. (100 g) milk couverture chocolate, 36 percent cocoa
12 oz. (350 g) praline (see recipe p. 160)

Prepare the chocolate molds (see "Molding chocolate," p. 188).
In a bain-marie, melt the chocolate. Alternatively, melt it in the microwave oven, in brief pulses and using no more than 350 W. Ensure that the temperature of the chocolate is no higher than 120°F (49°C). Remove the chocolate from the heat and add the praline with a firm spatula or wooden spoon. When the mixture has cooled to 81-83°F (27-28°C), spoon it into a piping bag. Pipe into the chocolate molds and let set for 12 hours. Cover with tempered chocolate.

Cognac Truffles ★

Ingredients (makes about 18 truffles)
2 ½ oz. (75 g) milk couverture chocolate
2 ½ oz. (75 g) bittersweet couverture chocolate (64 percent cocoa)
⅓ cup (80 ml) heavy cream
Scant 1 cup (3 ½ oz./100 g) unsweetened cocoa powder
Chocolate for coating
1 tablespoon plus 2 teaspoons (25 ml) cognac

In a bain-marie, melt the two types of chocolate to 113°F-122°F (45°C-50°C). Meanwhile, bring the cream to a boil. Gradually whisk the melted chocolate into the hot cream until thoroughly blended (this is called an emulsion). Gradually whisk in the cognac. Let cool until almost set, but soft enough to pipe. Spoon into a piping bag and pipe small balls, about the size of a large hazelnut. Place in a cool place, about 50°F (10°C) and let set. Melt the chocolate for coating. Wearing disposable gloves if you wish, roll the centers in chocolate (1) then cocoa powder (2).

These praline layers add an interesting texture to multilayered desserts. The essential ingredient is crushed Gavotte crêpe dentelle cookies, a buttery crêpe batter that is baked to a delicate crisp and crumbles on contact. In fact, professionals buy them already crushed. If these aren't available, you can substitute any delicate crisp sweet wafer, as long as you crush it finely.

Crunchy Praline Layer ★

Ingredients (makes 1 lb. 1 oz./500 g, sufficient
  for a dessert to serve 12)
7 oz. (200 g) bittersweet couverture chocolate,
  64 percent cocoa
3 ½ oz. (100 g) hazelnut paste
8 oz. (230 g) Gavotte crêpe dentelle cookies, crushed

Over a bain-marie, melt the couverture chocolate to no more than 122°F (50°C).
Remove from the heat and gently stir in the hazelnut paste, followed by the crushed dentelle cookies. While it is still malleable, roll it between two sheets of parchment paper or spread it very thinly over a sponge base.

❦ Recipe idea
Crisp and Creamy Layered Chocolate Dessert >> p. 341

Crisp Praline Layer ★

Ingredients (makes 9 oz./260 g, sufficient for a dessert
  to serve 6)
1 oz. (25 g) milk couverture chocolate
1 oz. (25 g) cocoa butter
3 oz. (80 g) hazelnut paste
2 oz. (50 g) praline paste (see recipe p. 160)
3 oz. (80 g) Gavotte crêpe dentelle cookies, crushed

Melt the couverture chocolate with the cocoa butter in a bain-marie. The temperature must not exceed 118°F (48°C). Remove from the heat and stir in the hazelnut paste and praline. Gently stir in the crushed dentelle cookies. Pour the mixture onto a silicone baking sheet to make a thin layer of about ⅕ inch (5 mm) and freeze.

❦ Recipe idea
Crisp and Creamy Layered Chocolate Dessert >> p. 341

Candied Orange Peel Dipped in Chocolate (*Orangettes*) ★ ★

Ingredients
2 oranges
2 cups (500 ml) water
Scant ½ cup (100 ml) orange juice
1 ¼ cups (10 oz./300 g) sugar
2 ½ oz. (75 g) bittersweet couverture chocolate,
  64 percent cocoa

Make at least one day ahead.

Peel the oranges, leaving no white pith on the flesh.
Cut the peel into narrow strips, about ⅕ inch (5 mm) wide. Place them in cold water and bring to a boil to blanch them. Repeat the procedure; this should remove some of the bitterness.
In a heavy-bottom saucepan, place the water, orange juice, and sugar to make a syrup. Bring to a boil, remove from the heat, and place the orange peel in it. Cover with plastic wrap and let cool. Leave the peel in the syrup for at least 12 hours. Remove the peel with a slotted spoon and drain, returning any excess syrup to the saucepan. Bring the syrup to a boil again, let simmer for 2 minutes, and carefully drop the orange peel back into it. Switch off the heat, cover with plastic wrap, and let the peel continue to cook gently as it cools.

You may repeat the procedure as many times as is necessary for the peel to soften sufficiently.
Drain well, patting it to remove any excess moisture.
Melt the chocolate and dip the candied peel in it with a dipping fork (see "Hand-dipped chocolate," p. 188).
Place on food-safe acetate paper to set.

● Chef's note
The number of times a fruit needs to be boiled and soaked in syrup depends on its hardness. Candying may take several days in some cases.

Chocolate Mendiants ★

Ingredients (makes 10 mendiants)
4 oz. (125 g) bittersweet couverture chocolate,
  64 percent cocoa
10 roasted blanched almonds
10 roasted blanched hazelnuts
10 walnuts
10 unsalted shelled pistachios
10 strips of candied orange peel

Over a bain-marie, melt the couverture chocolate to 122°F (50°C). Cool it to 79°F-81°F (26°C-27°C) and return it to the bain-marie for a few seconds to reheat it to 88°F-90°F (31°C-32°C), when it is ready to use.
Spoon the chocolate into a piping bag and pipe small mounds onto a sheet of food-safe acetate set on a baking sheet **(1)**.
Place a cloth over the work surface and lightly rap the baking pan on it to settle the chocolate and ensure that the disks are evenly shaped.
On each disk of chocolate, place an almond, a hazelnut, a pistachio, a walnut, and a strip of orange peel **(2)**. Let the chocolate crystallize: it will firm up and shrink slightly.
Carefully remove the disks from the paper and store in an airtight container at room temperature.

● Chef's note
You can also make mendiants with milk or white chocolate, respecting the tempering curve, different for each type of chocolate. To make them even more attractive, marble them or draw stripes with a paper decorating cone.

Iced desserts

Vanilla

Liquid extract is the most widely used form of this spice. But, in nearly all cases, whether it is light or dark, it is artificial—identical in nature, because the molecule is exactly the same, but synthesized by chemists. It's not that vanilla is so rare that it had to be reinvented, but its price makes us think twice before using it.

Vanilla is the fruit of a creeping orchid. Its vine flourishes in the shade of trees and it requires a great deal of rain. So it is essentially found in the tropics, with the main producers being Madagascar and Réunion in the Indian Ocean, and Polynesia, which produces the renowned Tahitian vanilla. This is a different variety and it is processed differently. *Vanilla tahitensis* is not boiled, while *Vanilla planifolia*, commonly known as Bourbon vanilla, is scalded in boiling water for a few minutes after it has been harvested. Harvesting methods, on the other hand, are similar, and carried out by hand. The flowers appear in bunches and bloom one by one. Every morning, vanilla pollinators comb the orchid looking for the flowers to pollinate so that the fruit can grow. The technique was discovered by Edmond Albius, a twelve-year-old slave on what was then Bourbon Island (Réunion) and is still used today, over one hundred and fifty years later. The labor-intensive technique required to produce the fruit goes some way to explaining the high price of the subtly perfumed black bean.

A vanilla bean should be neither too plump, nor too dry. It is shiny and has a wonderful smell. It must be slit in two lengthwise to scrape out the small black seeds contained inside—the seeds of the orchid.

To use vanilla beans, proceed as described above and place both bean and seeds in milk. Bring the milk with the seeds and bean to a boil. Then remove from the heat, cover, and leave for at least 10 minutes to infuse before continuing your recipe.

● Chef's notes

In the past, flavored sugars were very popular. You can flavor your sugar with vanilla (follow instructions below) but also lemon or orange zest, rose petals, and many more ingredients, to add a little extra zing to your recipes.

To make vanilla sugar, place a slit vanilla bean in a jar, cover with sugar, and close tightly. After a week or so, you will have a deliciously flavored sugar to use in baking.

So do not discard used vanilla beans. Wash them well and dry them out on a radiator or in the sun. You can also reuse them to decorate cakes and individual desserts.

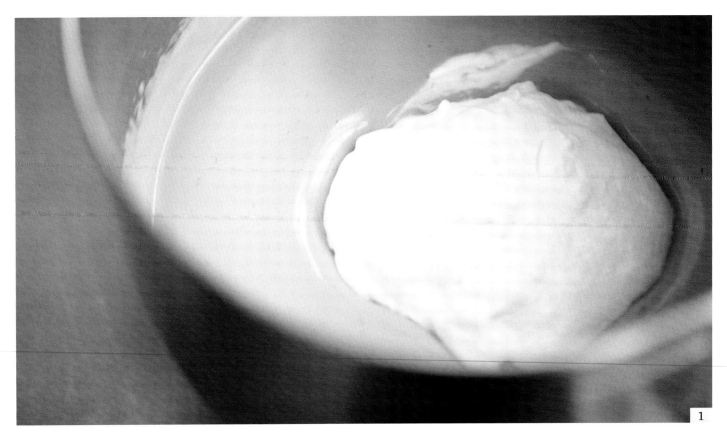

Iced Parfaits ★★

Parfaits are iced desserts that incorporate whipped heavy cream. To ensure that they are well frozen, it's best to make them a day ahead.

Fruit Parfait (basic recipe)

Fruit parfaits are light desserts made by poaching fruit pulp, egg yolks, and sugar in a bain-marie, and adding whipped cream.

Ingredients
9 oz. (250 g) fruit pulp
10 egg yolks (or, if using an egg product: 7 oz./200 g egg yolks)
¾ cup (5 oz./150 g) sugar
3 cups (750 ml) heavy cream
Liqueur (optional)

Poach the fruit pulp, egg yolks, and sugar in water, heating to 185°F (85°C). Alternatively, cook directly on the heat, simmering gently at 195°F (90°C).
Take off the heat and stir until cooled. Whip the heavy cream and fold in (1, 2, 3).
If using a liqueur, weigh it out to 3-6 percent of the weight of the cream and incorporate it into the whipped cream. Freeze.

Milk-Based Iced Parfait

This dessert uses a pouring custard to which whipped cream is added.

Ingredients
8 egg yolks (or, if using an egg product: 5 ½ oz./160 g egg yolks)
1 ¼ cups (9 oz./250 g) sugar
1 cup plus 2 teaspoons (250 ml) whole milk
1 ¾ cups (450 g) heavy cream
Flavoring

Prepare a pouring custard with the egg yolks, sugar, and milk, using a bain-marie. Whip the cream, add the flavoring, and fold into the pouring custard. Freeze.

Iced Honey Parfait

Ingredients
Scant ½ cup (3 ½ oz./100 g) acacia honey
4 egg yolks (or, if using an egg product: 3 oz./80 g egg yolks)
1 cup (250 ml) heavy cream

Heat the honey to 244°F (118°C). Beat the egg yolks. Pour the honey over the egg yolks, whisking constantly, as you would for a *pâte à bombe* (see right), until cooled. Whip the cream and carefully fold it into the mixture. Pour into ramekins or small glasses and freeze for at least 2 to 3 hours.

Pâte à Bombe ★ ★

The *pâte à bombe* is a light mixture used in other preparations, the base for parfaits and iced bombes. It is made by whisking egg yolks and sugar together. There are several methods for making it; the method that involves poaching in a bain-marie is superior to the one that uses cooked sugar.

Cooked sugar method

Ingredients
¾ cup (5 oz./150 g) sugar
3 tablespoons (50 ml) water
10 egg yolks (or, if using an egg product: 7 oz./200 g egg yolks)

Combine the sugar and water and cook to 250°F (120°C). Meanwhile, beat the egg yolks. Pour the hot syrup over the egg yolks, whisking until the mixture cools completely.

Poaching method

Ingredients
15 egg yolks (or, if using an egg product: 10 ½ oz./300 g egg yolks)
1 ½ cups (10 ½ oz./300 g) sugar

In a bain-marie, heat the egg yolks and sugar until the yolks begin to coagulate around the edges (131°F/55°C). Whisk energetically until the mixture is foamy and reaches the ribbon stage (see recipe for Genoese sponge, p. 76).

Pouring custard method

Ingredients
2 cups (500 ml) milk
Scant ⅔ cup (4 oz./120 g) sugar
16 egg yolks (or, if using an egg product: 11 ½ oz./320 g egg yolks)

Make a pouring custard, heating the mixture to 185°F (85°C). Whip until completely cooled.

● **Did you know?**
The pâte à bombe *mixture is not the same thing as an iced bombe dessert.* Pâte à bombe *uses egg yolks heated with sugar and beaten. A bombe glacée is a domed iced dessert.*

Soufflés ★

A soufflé is, essentially, a parfait to which an Italian meringue has been added. Desserts comprising a mixture of fruit pulp or juice, Italian meringue, and whipped cream make up a sub-category of soufflés. Add fruit soaked in liqueur or partially candied or dried fruit soaked in liqueur.

Iced Liqueur Soufflé (basic recipe)

Ingredients
10 egg yolks (or, if using an egg product: 7 oz./200 g egg yolks)
¾ cup (5 oz./150 g) sugar
3 tablespoons (50 ml) water
7 oz. (200 g) Italian meringue, made with 2 oz. (55 g)
  egg whites, generous ½ cup (3 ¾ oz./110 g) sugar,
  and 2 ½ tablespoons (35 ml) water
3 cups (750 ml) heavy cream
¼-⅓ cup (60-75 ml) liqueur or brandy

There are three steps: 1. Make the *pâte à bombe* (see p. 197); 2. Make the Italian meringue (see p. 177) and incorporate it into the *pâte à bombe*; 3. Whip the cream, stirring in the liqueur at the last minute, and fold it into the mixture.

The method for Iced Liqueur Soufflé can be used for other variations:

Iced Fruit Soufflé

Ingredients
10 egg yolks (or, if using an egg product: 7 oz./200 g egg yolks)
¾ cup (5 oz./150 g) sugar
3 tablespoons (50 ml) water
9 oz. (250 g) fruit pulp
7 ¾ oz. (220 g) Italian meringue, made with 2 egg whites
  (2 oz./60 g), scant ⅔ cup (4 oz./120 g) sugar, and 3 tablespoons
  (40 ml) water
2 ¾ cups (700 ml) heavy cream, whipped
3 ½ tablespoons (50 ml) fruit brandy

Follow the method above (basic recipe), incorporating the fruit pulp into the *pâte à bombe* (step 1) before adding the Italian meringue.

Iced Banana Soufflé

Ingredients
11 ½ oz. (325 g) puréed banana
Juice of 1 lemon, if using fresh banana
9 oz. (250 g) *pâte à bombe*
10 ½ oz. (300 g) Italian meringue, made with 3 oz. (82 g)
  egg whites, generous ¾ cup (5 ¾ oz./163 g) sugar,
  and 3 tablespoons plus 2 teaspoons (55 ml) water
1 ½ cups (350 ml) heavy cream, whipped
2 tablespoons plus 1 teaspoon (35 ml) rum

Iced Tangerine Soufflé

Ingredients
1 cup (250 ml) tangerine juice
1 lb. 2 oz. (500 g) *pâte à bombe*
7 oz. (200 g) Italian meringue, made with 2 oz. (55 g) egg
  whites, generous ½ cup (3 ¾ oz./110 g) sugar, and
  2 ½ tablespoons (35 ml) water
3 ½ cups (850 ml) heavy cream, whipped
2 tablespoons plus 2 teaspoons (40 ml) tangerine liqueur

Iced Nougatine Soufflé

Ingredients

Nougatine (see recipe p. 166)	Italian meringue
3 tablespoons (40 ml) water	Scant ⅔ cup (4 oz./120 g) sugar
½ cup (3 ½ oz./100 g) sugar	3 tablespoons (40 ml) water
1 tablespoon (20 g) glucose syrup	2 egg whites (2 oz./60 g)
2 ½ oz. (70 g) egg yolks	1 pinch salt
1 cup (250 ml) heavy cream	

Following the recipe on p. 166, make a thin layer of nougatine and chop it finely.
Make a *pâte à bombe*. In a heavy-bottom saucepan, heat the water, sugar, and glucose syrup to 250°F (121°C). Meanwhile, beat the egg yolks. Pour the hot syrup over the yolks, whisking until cooled.
Make the Italian meringue (see p. 177), using the quantities indicated above. Take 4 oz. (125 g) Italian meringue to use in the soufflé. Incorporate into the *pâte à bombe*. Whip the cream and fold it into the mixture. Carefully stir in the finely chopped nougatine. Pour into a mold and freeze for at least 2 to 3 hours.

⬤ **Chef's note**
We advise that you use these quantities to make your Italian meringue, using the remainder in another dish. Smaller amounts are trickier to work with.

Iced Mousses ★

Iced fruit mousses are light desserts that comprise Italian meringue, fruit (in the form of either pulp or juice), and whipped cream. A thickener may be added. Iced fruit mousses are not churned.

Iced Raspberry Mousse

Ingredients
1 cup (250 ml) heavy cream
1 lb. 2 oz. (500 g) raspberry purée
1 ¼ lb. (550 g) Italian meringue (see p. 177), made with
  5 ¼ oz. (150 g) egg whites, 1 ¼ cups (10 oz./300 g) sugar,
  and 7 tablespoons (100 ml) water

Whip the heavy cream to a Chantilly texture.
Fold the raspberry purée into the Italian meringue (1, 2).
With a flexible spatula, fold the whipped cream into the
mixture. Pour into small glasses or ramekins and freeze
for 2 to 3 hours.

*The method for Iced Raspberry Mousse can be used
for other variations:*

Iced Strawberry Mousse

Ingredients
1 ⅔ cups (400 ml) heavy cream
1 lb. 2 oz. (500 g) strawberry purée
9 oz. (250 g) Italian meringue (see p. 177), made with 2 ½ oz.
  (70 g) egg whites, ¾ cup (5 oz./140 g) sugar, and 3 tablespoons
  (40 ml) water

Iced Mango and Passion Fruit Mousse

Ingredients
2 cups (500 ml) heavy cream
1 ¼ cups (9 oz./250 g) sugar
10 oz. (300 g) puréed mango
¾ cup (200 ml) passion fruit juice
9 oz. (250 g) Italian meringue (see p. 177), made with 2 ½ oz.
  (70 g) egg whites, ¾ cup (5 oz./140 g) sugar, and 3 tablespoons
  (40 ml) water

Milk-Based Iced Mousses ★★

Milk-based iced mousses are light desserts comprising pouring custard, whipped cream, and sometimes Italian meringue. They are not churned.

Iced Rum and Raisin Mousse

Ingredients
3 oz. (75 g) raisins
Water and sugar for a syrup
1 cup (250 ml) heavy cream, well chilled
3 tablespoons (50 ml) white rum

Custard base
1 vanilla bean
1 cup (250 ml) milk
7 egg yolks (8 oz./140 g)
1 cup (7 oz./200 g) sugar
1 ¼ oz. (50 g) invert sugar, melted

Place the raisins in a small pot of hot water and bring to a boil. Drain and repeat the procedure.
Make a syrup with equal parts sugar and water and pour the drained raisins into it. Pour into a glass jar, adding some rum if you wish, and close with a rubber seal. Sterilize in a bain-marie. Let macerate for at least 8 hours or overnight. This method allows you to preserve the raisins and ensures you have a supply of plump, macerated raisins.

Prepare the custard base: slit the vanilla bean lengthwise and scrape the seeds out into the milk. In a medium heavy-bottom saucepan, heat the milk with the vanilla bean. Beat the egg yolks with the sugar and melted invert sugar until pale and thick. When the milk is simmering, pour half of it over the egg yolk and sugar mixture, stirring constantly. Return the mixture to the saucepan, then cook, stirring constantly and removing the saucepan from the heat from time to time, until it reaches 185°F (85°C) or coats the back of a spoon. (If the egg yolks are in constant contact with high heat, they may coagulate.) Strain the custard through a fine-mesh sieve, transfer to a mixing bowl, and cover with plastic wrap. Chill rapidly to about 68°F (20°C).
Whip the cream and fold it carefully into the cooled custard base.
Drain the raisins and stir them in with the rum.
Pour into molds and freeze for 2 to 3 hours.

The method for Iced Rum and Raisin Mousse can be used for other variations:

Iced Orange-Chocolate Mousse

Ingredients
1 cup (250 ml) milk
Finely grated zest of 1 orange (unsprayed)
7 egg yolks (5 oz./150 g)
⅔ cup (4 oz./125 g) sugar
Scant ½ cup (3 ½ oz./100 g) glucose syrup
Scant ⅓ cup (3 ½ oz./100 g) invert sugar
13 oz. (375 g) bittersweet chocolate, 50 percent cocoa solids, chopped
1 ½ cups (350 g) heavy cream
3 tablespoons plus 1 teaspoon (50 ml) orange liqueur

In a heavy-bottom saucepan, heat the milk with the orange zest. Beat the egg yolks with the sugar until pale and thick. When the milk is simmering, pour half of it over the egg yolk and sugar mixture, stirring constantly. Return the mixture to the saucepan and incorporate the glucose syrup and invert sugar. Stir constantly and remove the saucepan from the heat from time to time, until it reaches 185°F (85°C) or coats the back of a spoon. Strain the custard through a fine-mesh sieve, over the chopped chocolate. Let stand for a few moments to melt and stir until smooth. Cover with plastic wrap flush with the surface and chill rapidly to about 68°F (20°C). Whip the cream and fold it carefully into the chilled chocolate custard base. Stir in the orange liqueur and pour into molds. Freeze for 2 to 3 hours.

Iced Praline Mousse

Ingredients
1 cup (250 ml) milk
6 egg yolks (4 oz./140 g)
⅔ cup (4 oz./125 g) sugar
2 ¼ cups (550 ml) heavy cream
8 oz. (225 g) praline paste (see recipe p. 160)

Iced Arabica Coffee Mousse

Ingredients
1 cup (250 ml) milk
7 egg yolks (5 oz./150 g)
1 cup (7 oz./200 g) sugar
2 ¼ cups (550 ml) heavy cream
⅔ cup (1 ¼ oz./35 g) instant Arabica coffee
⅓ oz. (8 g) coffee extract

Sorbets ★★

Sorbets are iced preparations made with puréed fruit, water, and sugar. No fats are added and the minimum fruit content is normally 25 percent; however, sorbets made with certain fruits may have a lower percentage. By "fruit" we mean all edible parts of the fruit or its juice, extracts, concentrates, lyophilized powders, etc., and it is used either fresh or in the form of correctly preserved products, using appropriate techniques.

Strawberry Sorbet

Ingredients
Scant ½ cup (100 ml) water
1 ¼ cups (9 oz./250 g) sugar
1 ½ lb. (650 g) puréed strawberries

Ideally, prepare the day before needed.

Heat the water to 77°F (25°C) and add the sugar (1), whisking until it is fully dissolved. It can be pasteurized by heating to 185°F (85°C) for 3 minutes. Blend (2) and then remove from the heat and let cool for a few minutes, covered with plastic wrap. Leave to mature for at least 4 hours in the refrigerator. Stir in the puréed fruit. You may blend the mixture at this stage for a finer texture. Process in an ice-cream maker according to the manufacturer's instructions, transfer to an airtight container, and freeze at 0.4°F (-18°C).

● Did you know?
Churned iced preparations are recipes that require cooling with constant stirring, exactly what an ice-cream maker does. There are three categories of churned preparations:
- *sorbets*
- *egg-enriched ice creams*
- *custard-based ice creams*

Categories vary depending on the type and quantities of ingredients. For example, a full fruit sorbet has a minimum of 45 percent fruit, while an ice cream contains cream and an egg-enriched ice cream contains egg yolks. Ice-cream professionals work like veritable chemists to balance their recipes. They use ingredients like stabilizers, atomized glucose, and invert sugar. Here we will merely suggest a few recipes without delving into the complexities of the trade. All preparations that do not contain stabilizers are intended for home consumption and must be eaten within 24 hours of being made.
Sugar is indispensable in making ice cream and plays an important role in the final texture. Its anti-freezing properties prevent the preparation from becoming unpleasantly hard. Alcohol, too, significantly softens ice creams and sorbets.

For the sorbet and ice cream recipes that follow, it is advisable to measure your ingredients using the metric system and to weigh the liquid ingredients for best results. The precise quantities make it difficult to convert into imperial or volume measures.

Sorbets with Stabilizers ★★

General method
Combine the stabilizer with 10 percent of the sugar. Heat the water. When it reaches 77°F (25°C), add the remaining sugar, atomized glucose, and invert sugar and skim milk powder if used. At 113°F (45°C), add the stabilizer combined with the sugar. Cook to 185°F (85°C), process, and chill rapidly to 39°F (4°C). Cover with plastic wrap and chill for at least 4 hours at 39°F (4°C) for the flavor to develop. Add the fruit pulp (and lemon juice if used) and blend. Process in an ice-cream maker, transfer to an airtight container, and freeze at 0.4°F (-18°C).
These sorbets can be kept for about one to two months in the freezer.

Strawberry Sorbet

Ingredients
4 g SL 64 stabilizer
133 g sugar
194 g water
85 g atomized glucose
1000 g puréed strawberries

Apricot Sorbet

Ingredients
4 g SL 64 stabilizer
140 g sugar
220 g water
25 g lemon juice
105 g atomized glucose
30 g invert sugar
1000 g puréed apricots

Litchi Sorbet

Ingredients
6 g SL 64 stabilizer
260 g sugar
514 g water
120 g atomized glucose
1100 g puréed litchis

Pêche de Vigne Sorbet

Ingredients
4 g SL 64 stabilizer
170 g sugar
221 g water
20 g lemon juice
105 g atomized glucose
1000 g puréed heirloom peaches

Raspberry Sorbet

Ingredients
4 g SL 64 stabilizer
186 g sugar
332 g water
97 g atomized glucose
1000 g puréed raspberries

Black Currant Sorbet

Ingredients
5 g SL 64 stabilizer
225 g sugar
409 g water
126 g atomized glucose
40 g invert sugar
1000 g puréed black currants

Cherry Sorbet

Ingredients
4 g SL 64 stabilizer
125 g sugar
221 g water
120 g atomized glucose
30 g invert sugar
1000 g puréed cherries

Pineapple-Ginger Sorbet

Ingredients
6 g SL 64 stabilizer
348 g sugar
306 g water
120 g atomized glucose
1200 g puréed pineapple
20 g fresh ginger rhizome

Lemon-Basil Sorbet

Ingredients
10 g SL 64 stabilizer
775 g sugar
1348 g water
1000 g lemon juice
133 g atomized glucose
67 g skim milk powder
20 g fresh basil

Mango-Orange Sorbet

Ingredients
4 g SL 64 stabilizer
328 g sugar
260 g water
105 g atomized glucose
10 g invert sugar
500 g orange juice
500 g puréed mango

Egg-Enriched Ice Creams with Stabilizers ★★

Egg-enriched ice creams are made by freezing a pasteurized mixture made of milk, cream, sugar, and eggs, flavored with fruit, fruit juice, or authorized natural flavorings.

Egg-Enriched Coffee Ice Cream

Ingredients
1036 g milk
369 g heavy cream
60 g egg yolks
77 g skim milk powder
274 g sugar
60 g atomized glucose
6 g SE 30 emulsified stabilizer (Cremodan SE 30)
50 g instant coffee

General method
Ideally, prepare the day before needed.

In a saucepan, combine all the liquid ingredients (milk, cream, and egg yolks) and heat to 104°F (40°C) (1). For the chocolate ice cream (p. 204), add the melted couverture

chocolate with the liquid ingredients. Vigorously whisk in the dry ingredients (powdered milk, sugar, atomized glucose or invert sugar, cocoa powder if used, stabilizer) (2), then increase the temperature to 185°F (85°C), whisking continuously. Add the instant coffee, or other flavoring. Blend (3) and allow to cool for a few minutes, covered with plastic wrap. Leave to mature and chill for at least 4 hours in the refrigerator at 39°F (4°C), to let the flavor develop. Process in an ice-cream maker, transfer to an airtight container, and freeze at 0.4°F (-18°C).

Egg-Enriched Pistachio Ice Cream

Ingredients
1036 g milk
180 g heavy cream
130 g egg yolks
55 g skim milk powder
220 g sugar
70 g invert sugar
7 g SE 30 emulsified stabilizer
80 g pure, unsweetened pistachio paste
    (add at 122°F/50°C)

Egg-Enriched Vanilla Ice Cream

Ingredients
1036 g whole milk
1 vanilla bean (to flavor the milk)
250 g heavy cream
144 g egg yolks
75 g skim milk powder
260 g sugar
80 g atomized glucose
7 g SE 30 emulsified stabilizer

Egg-Enriched Orange Liqueur Ice Cream

Ingredients
1036 g whole milk
130 g egg yolks
55 g skim milk powder
150 g sugar
80 g atomized glucose
7 g SE 30 emulsified stabilizer
100 g orange liqueur

Egg-Enriched Chocolate Ice Cream

Ingredients
1036 g whole milk
140 g heavy cream
144 g egg yolks
160 g couverture chocolate, 64 percent cocoa, melted
70 g skim milk powder
180 g sugar
120 g invert sugar
40 g unsweetened cocoa powder
8 g SE emulsified stabilizer

Custard-Based Ice Cream ★

Vanilla Ice Cream

Ingredients
Scant ½ cup (100 ml) milk
Scant ½ cup (100 ml) heavy cream
6 egg yolks
1 vanilla bean
½ cup (3½ oz./100 g) sugar

Ideally, prepare the day before needed.

In a saucepan, combine all the liquid ingredients (the milk, cream, and egg yolks). Slit the vanilla bean lengthwise and scrape the seeds into the mixture. Heat to 104°F (40°C). Whisking vigorously, add the sugar. Pasteurize by increasing the heat to 185°F (85°C) for 3 minutes. Blend and let cool, covered with plastic wrap. Leave to mature and chill for at least 4 hours at 39°F (4°C), to allow the flavors to develop. Pour into an ice-cream maker and proceed according to the manufacturer's instructions. Transfer to a mold or airtight container and freeze at 0.4°F (-18°C).

Custard-Based Ice Creams with Stabilizers ★★

General method
Combine the stabilizer with 10 percent of the sugar.
Pour the milk or water and powdered milk into a saucepan.
At 77°F (25°C), add the remaining sugar, atomized glucose, and/or invert sugar.
At 95°F (35°C), pour in the cream or butter.
At 104°F (40°C), add the egg yolks, if used.
At 113°F (45°C), add the stabilizer combined with sugar.
Add the flavorings and cook to 185°F (85°C).
Blend and chill rapidly to 39°F (4°C).
Cover with plastic wrap and mature for at least 12 hours at 39°F (4°C).
Blend. Process in the ice-cream maker and immediately pour into a mold or airtight container.
Freeze at 0.4°F (-18°C).

Chocolate Ice Cream

Ingredients
5 g SE 30 emulsified stabilizer
200 g sugar
1036 g whole milk
70 g skim milk powder
85 g invert sugar
200 g heavy cream
55 g egg yolks
30 g unsweetened cocoa powder
150 g bittersweet couverture chocolate,
   64 percent cocoa

Coffee Ice Cream

Ingredients
6 g SE 30 emulsified stabilizer
305 g sugar
1036 g whole milk
75 g skim milk powder
50 g atomized glucose
350 g heavy cream
55 g egg yolks
29 g instant coffee granules

● **Chef's note**
For a more authentic taste, infuse roughly chopped roasted coffee beans in the milk. However, it is instant coffee that will give the coffee ice cream its color.

Banana Ice Cream

Ingredients
8 g SE 30 emulsified stabilizer
270 g sugar
1036 g whole milk
160 g skim milk powder
110 g atomized glucose
700 g heavy cream
60 g egg yolks
800 g puréed bananas

Coconut Ice Cream

Ingredients
8 g SE 30 emulsified stabilizer
220 g sugar
1036 g whole milk

100 g skim milk powder
100 g invert sugar
200 g butter
60 g egg yolks
300 g puréed coconut

Praline Ice Cream

Ingredients
6 g SE 30 emulsified stabilizer
80 g sugar
1036 g whole milk
70 g skim milk powder
80 g invert sugar
100 g heavy cream
60 g egg yolks
250 g almond-hazelnut praline paste
   (add at 122°F/50°C)

Vanilla Ice Cream

Ingredients
6 g SE 30 emulsified stabilizer
295 g sugar
1036 g whole milk
65 g skim milk powder
1 vanilla bean
50 g atomized glucose
390 g heavy cream
55 g egg yolks

● **Did you know?**
In all formulae used to make ice cream, stabilizers and emulsifiers prove useful by ensuring that the texture is smooth, creamy, and light (they help it expand). In addition, they act as preservatives.

Granitas ★

A granita is a variation of a sorbet, made with fruit, wine, or other alcohol, and has no stabilizer. Its density means it is slightly crystallized and granular. The density of a fruit granita is approximately 1074 D. We use the Brix degree system to make granitas, adjusting them to between 17°Bx and 23°Bx. Use a refractometer only for fruit granitas, as the alcohol in wine, liqueur, and eau-de-vie granitas falsifies the reading. Granitas are easily made by simple freezing. When the liquid is frozen, it is scraped with a fork. It may, however, be churned before it is scraped.

Tangerine-Champagne Granita

Ingredients
1 ¼ cups (300 ml) tangerine juice
¾ cup (200 ml) water
1 cup (7 oz./200 g) sugar
2 ¾ cups (700 ml) champagne

General method
Ideally, prepare the day before needed.

Bring the tangerine juice and water to a boil with the sugar. Simmer for 3 minutes, remove from the heat, and cool rapidly. Pour in the champagne. Pour into a large, deep dish so that you have a thin layer of liquid. Place in the freezer for 15 minutes. With a fork, scrape the mixture to break up the ice crystals on the surface. Return to the freezer and repeat the procedure every 25 minutes for 2 hours. Scrape well just before serving.

Grapefruit and Rosé Wine Granita

Ingredients
¾ cup (200 ml) grapefruit juice
Scant ½ cup (100 ml) water
1 ¼ cups (9 oz./250 g) sugar
2 ¾ cups (700 ml) rosé wine

Pêche de Vigne Granita

Ingredients
13 oz. (375 g) puréed pêche de vigne (heirloom peaches)
1 ¾ cups (445 ml) water
1 scant cup (6 oz./180 g) sugar

Vodka-Orange Granita

Ingredients
Scant ½ cup (100 ml) orange juice
1 ¼ cups (300 ml) water
Scant ½ cup (3 oz./90 g) sugar
3 tablespoons plus 1 teaspoon (50 ml) vodka

Mojito Granita

Ingredients
Scant ¼ cup (50 ml) lime juice
1 ¼ cups (300 ml) water
A little finely grated lime zest
A few mint leaves, chopped
½ cup (3 ½ oz./100 g) sugar
3 tablespoons plus 1 teaspoon (50 ml) white rum

Cassatas ★

Cassatas are light iced desserts made with a mixture of Italian meringue and whipped cream, and garnished with candied fruit soaked in liqueur or wine. It is also possible to add nuts, dried fruit, or nougat. Cassatas are not churned. Traditionally, cassatas are served in molds lined with ice creams or sorbets.

Cognac and Nougatine Cassata

Ingredients
Scant ½ cup (100 ml) heavy cream
2 oz. (50 g) Italian meringue (see p. 177), made with 1 oz. (30 g) egg whites, scant ⅓ cup (2 oz./60 g) sugar, and 4 teaspoons (20 ml) water*, cooled
1 tablespoon plus 2 teaspoons (25 ml) Cognac, 40 percent alcohol
2 oz. (50 g) nougatine pieces (see recipe p. 166)

* It is preferable to make more Italian meringue than is required and then to weigh out the 2 oz. (50 g) necessary for this recipe. The remainder can be used to make decorative meringues.

General method
Ideally, prepare the day before needed.

Whip the heavy cream with an electric beater. Carefully fold the whipped cream into the cooled Italian meringue. Stir in the Cognac and nougatine pieces. Freeze.

Orange-Hazelnut Cassata

Ingredients
Scant ½ cup (100 ml) heavy cream
¼ cup (2 oz./50 g) sugar (to be mixed into the whipped cream)
3 ½ oz. (100 g) Italian meringue (see p. 177), made with
    1 oz. (30 g) egg whites, scant ⅓ cup (2 oz./60 g) sugar,
    and 4 teaspoons (20 ml) water
2 tablespoons plus 1 teaspoon (35 ml) orange liqueur
2 oz. (50 g) chopped hazelnuts

Spoom ★

Spoom is a classic sorbet, made without the addition of a stabilizer, to which a double quantity of Italian meringue is added. We highly recommend using pasteurized egg whites for this type of recipe. The mixture is light and foamy. The Italian meringue may be added before or after churning. Spoom is best made with sour fruits or liqueurs.

Pineapple-Champagne Spoom

Ingredients
3 tablespoons (40 ml) water
⅓ cup (2 oz./60 g) sugar
14 oz. (400 g) puréed pineapple
½ cup (125 ml) champagne
7 oz. (200 g) Italian meringue (see p. 177), made with
    2 oz. (55 g) egg whites, generous ½ cup (3 ¾ oz./110 g) sugar,
    and 2 ½ tablespoons (35 ml) water

Heat the water to 77°F (25°C) and whisk in the sugar until it is fully dissolved. Pasteurize by heating to 185°F (85°C) for 3 minutes. Blend, remove from the heat and let cool for a few minutes, covered with plastic wrap. Leave to chill and mature for at least 4 hours in the refrigerator. Stir in the puréed pineapple and champagne and blend well. Process in the ice-cream maker according to the manufacturer's instructions. As soon as it comes out of the ice-cream maker, carefully incorporate the Italian meringue into the mixture and immediately freeze at 0.4°F (-18°C).

Iced Nougat ★ ★

Iced nougat is a light dessert comprising Italian meringue made with honey or sugar, whipped cream, and roasted nuts, candied fruits, and nougatine bits. Iced nougat desserts are not churned.

Ingredients
¼ cup (2 oz./55 g) sugar
Scant ⅓ cup (3 ½ oz./100 g) honey
½ vanilla bean, seeds scraped
4 egg whites (4 oz./120 g)
2 cups (500 ml) heavy cream, well chilled
3 ½ oz. (100 g) chopped almonds, lightly roasted
3 ½ oz. (100 g) chopped hazelnuts, lightly roasted
3 ½ oz. (100 g) unsalted pistachios
2 oz. (60 g) diced candied orange peel
2 oz. (60 g) diced candied cherries
3 ½ oz. (100 g) nougatine, broken into small bits
    (see recipe p. 166)

Prepare an Italian meringue, making a syrup with the sugar, honey, and vanilla seeds. In a stand mixer fitted with a whisk, begin whipping the egg whites. When the syrup registers 250°F (120°C), pour it carefully over the egg whites, whisking continuously. Continue whisking until the meringue has cooled to 85°F (30°C). Whip the cream until it holds firm peaks and carefully fold it into the meringue. Carefully stir in the nuts, candied fruit, and nougatine bits. Pour into silicone molds or one loaf pan and immediately place in the freezer for at least 4 hours.
Serve with fruit coulis (see p. 128) or custard (see p. 91).

Iced Nougat with Orange Liqueur

Ingredients
¾ cup (9 oz./250 g) honey
5 egg whites (5 oz./150 g)
3 ½ oz. (100 g) diced candied orange peel, soaked in orange
    liqueur
2 oz. (50 g) diced candied orange peel
3 ½ oz. (100 g) chopped almonds, lightly roasted
3 ½ oz. (100 g) chopped hazelnuts, lightly roasted
4 oz. (110 g) chopped pistachios
3 ½ cups (850 ml) heavy cream
3 tablespoons plus 1 teaspoon (50 ml) orange liqueur

Make an Italian meringue with the honey (heated to 250°F/120°C) and egg whites (see method above). Stir in both types of candied orange peel and nuts. Whip the cream and carefully fold it in. Stir in the orange liqueur and freeze for at least 4 hours.

Cooking techniques

Stewing fruit ★

Fruit turnovers, some tarts, and desserts cooked en papillote (in parcels), require fruit that is already cooked. Stewing is the method generally advised. It involves slow, gentle cooking to soften fruit, either partially or completely.

Wash and peel the fruit **(1)** and rub it with (or dip it in) lemon juice if necessary (deciduous and many other types of fruit brown as they oxidize, and the acid in lemon juice slows or prevents the process).

Cut it into cubes, as far as possible of the same size so they cook evenly. If you are working with apples and pears, for example, the cubes will have to be squeezed with lemon juice again to prevent the newly exposed surfaces from browning.

Place the fruit in a pot and add just a little water or another liquid, depending on the recipe (for example wine or hard cider). The liquid vaporizes and facilitates the cooking process **(2)**. You may need to add more liquid as the fruit cooks.

Add the flavoring (spices, herbs, extracts, or grated zest) if using. Cover with a lid and cook over low heat, stirring from time to time so that the sugar contained in the fruit does not caramelize.

Stir in the sugar and remove any hard ingredients, such as cinnamon sticks or star anise.

If your recipe calls for a soft texture, process the fruit until smooth.

● Chef's notes

Firm fruits that contain starch (such as bananas and chestnuts), and fruits that have a particularly high sugar content, such as prunes, require more liquid at the start of the cooking process. They must be carefully watched, as they tend to caramelize fairly quickly.

❙ Recipe idea
Apple Turnovers >> p. 366

1

Candying (crystallizing) ★

Candying requires slow, gentle cooking in a sugar syrup to concentrate the sugar content in the food. Traditionally, the technique is used to candy fruit and vegetables.

Ingredients
2 ⅔ cups (1 lb. 2 oz./500 g) sugar
2 cups (500 ml) water
Confectioners' sugar for dusting

Prepare the fruit or vegetables. If you are using citrus peel or chestnuts, they must be blanched (cooked briefly in boiling water). Citrus peel needs to be blanched at least three times to remove some of its bitterness (1).
Combine approximately 1 ½ cups sugar and water in a heavy-bottom saucepan and heat to 225°F (107°C). Immerse the fruit or peel in the hot syrup (you may use a metal basket). Remove the saucepan from the heat and let cool (2). This is the first sugar bath.
Strain the syrup into another bowl. Add 25 percent more sugar than you used for the first sugar bath. Return the fruit to the syrup, bring to a boil, let cool, and strain again. Repeat the procedure altogether from three to seven times, depending on the bitterness of the ingredient.
Drain (3) and dust with confectioners' sugar.

● Chef's notes
Flavor the syrup with spices such as cinnamon, vanilla, or star anise.
If you wish to store the candied fruit, it is essential to sterilize the jars.
Citrus peel includes a little of the white pith, whereas "zest" refers to the colored part only.

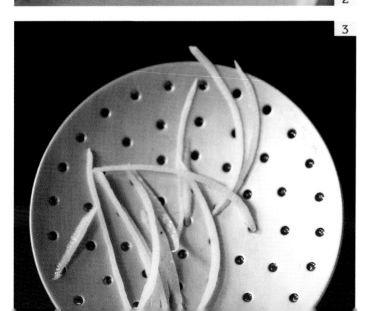

2

3

1

Baking blind (prebaking) ★★

This technique involves baking a tart shell before filling it.

Any pastry shell that will contain a filling with a lot of moisture (fruit or custard) should be partially baked; a tart shell that will hold ingredients that will not be cooked more (for example, a ganache or cooked lemon cream) should be fully baked. If you are using a tart ring, place it on a baking sheet lined with parchment paper or a silicone baking sheet. Line the tart pan with the dough. Place a square of food-safe heat-resistant plastic wrap over the dough, leaving an overhang of about 6 inches (15 cm). Alternatively, use parchment paper, but be careful to smooth over any creases. Press the wrap (or parchment paper) down to cover the dough (1). To hold it in place, fill it either with flour or sugar (2). Fold the four corners of the wrap to the center (3) and begin baking according to the recipe. If you are using a pastry ring, remove the ring and the plastic wrap with the flour or sugar 5 to 10 minutes before the recommended baking time so that the dough colors evenly and dries out properly.

Recipe idea
Lemon Meringue Tart>> p. 425

2

3

Cooking semolina ★

Ingredients
½ vanilla bean
4 cups (1 liter) milk
1 cup (5 oz./150 g) medium grain semolina
Scant ⅔ cup (4 oz./120 g) sugar

Slit the vanilla bean lengthwise and scrape the seeds into the milk. Heat the milk with the vanilla seeds and bean. When it simmers, pour in the semolina (1), stirring with a whisk. Simmer gently, stirring constantly, for about 15 minutes (2), until the semolina is soft. Constant stirring is essential to prevent burning at the bottom, which would give the semolina a bad taste. Remove from the heat, take out the vanilla bean, and stir in the sugar.
Transfer to a mixing bowl and cover with plastic wrap flush with the surface to prevent a skin from forming.

● Chef's note
You may need to change the quantity of semolina, depending on the creaminess you require for your recipe.

❢ Recipe idea
Semolina Cake >> p. 315

1

2

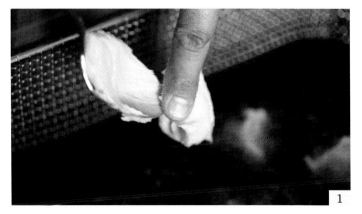

1

2

3

Deep-fat frying ★

Deep-fat frying is a technique that involves immersing an ingredient in a heated bath of fat. The temperature depends on the type of fat, which should be selected according to the ingredients, as well as the size of the food you're frying.

Prepare the food to be fried (fritters, donuts, etc.) and heat the oil bath to the temperature indicated in the recipe. Larger items should be fried at about 340°F (170°C) as they need to cook more slowly, whereas for smaller items you can heat the oil to up to 375°F (190°C), the average temperature being about 350°F (180°C).
If you are cooking delicate food, dust it with flour to form a fine protective crust that prevents the flesh from breaking up. If you are frying food that is not coated in a batter, make sure it is patted dry before immersing it in the oil bath (1).
Turn the food so that all sides are uniformly colored.
For some recipes the fritters will turn over by themselves. Remove the food with a slotted spoon (2), let the fat drip off, and then place on paper towel to drain.
If you are making fritters, dust them with confectioners' sugar (3) over the paper towel or plate.

● **Chef's notes**
Never hold food over a hot oil bath when you sprinkle it with salt or sugar.
Change the oil regularly. You may use it up to ten times, providing you use it for the same type of food.
Do not fry different types of food (meat, fish, vegetables, fruit, and so on) in the same oil, otherwise the taste will be spoiled.
After use, place it, tightly closed, in a dark place, to prevent the fat from oxidizing.

Macerating ★

Macerating means placing an ingredient in a liquid—fruit juice, spiced syrup, wine, or other alcoholic beverage, depending on the recipe—in order to soften it and impart extra flavors. Dried fruit is macerated to plump it up and add moisture and flavor.

Prepare the fruit (wash, peel, cut or slice as required, etc.). Splash, sprinkle, or cover the fruit with the chosen liquid and leave to sit in it for a few hours or overnight. The time necessary depends on the ingredient used and its initial dryness.

Peeling fruit ★

This technique involves removing the skin or outer envelope of fruit. In many cases, peeling fruit makes for a more refined taste.

To prepare soft fruit, such as peaches and nectarines: remove the stem and use a small kitchen knife to make a cross-shaped incision (1) at the other end.
Immerse the fruit in a pot of boiling water for about 10 seconds, until the skin begins to peel away from the incision.
Remove from the water (2) and immediately dip into a bowl of ice water. The drop in temperature means that the fruit will not cook.
With the kitchen knife, pull the skin away carefully (3) and place the fruit on paper towel.

To peel shelled almonds and walnuts: immerse them in a pot of boiling water for about 10 seconds. To remove the skins, press the nuts between your fingers and squeeze the skin off. For walnuts, you may also use a kitchen knife.

To peel shelled hazelnuts: roast them at 350°F (180°C) for 6 to 7 minutes. Transfer them to a kitchen towel to cool and rub them between your hands.

● **Chef's note**
Some skins are worth keeping to use as decoration—they can be fried.

1

2

3

Cooking en papillote
(in parcels) ★★

This method of cooking entails wrapping food in greased parchment paper to blend the flavors of the garnish and the main ingredient, ensuring that all the components retain their moisture.

Prepare and cut the main ingredients to equal size to ensure even cooking.
Cut the parchment paper to notebook or foolscap size. Lightly grease or oil it. If you wish, to ensure that the papillote is sealed, brush the edges with lightly beaten egg white and a pinch of salt.
Place the ingredients on one half of the paper (1), making sure that the main ingredient and the garnish are attractively arranged (2).
You may drizzle the food with a little wine, syrup, or whatever complements your recipe, sprinkle it with sugar, and flavor it with spices.
Fold the other half of the parchment paper over (3). Fold the edges over on themselves several times. Press down hard on the folds (4) and, to ensure the papillote remains closed, secure with paper clips.

Cook in the oven at a medium temperature: if the oven is too hot, the paper will darken and the food inside will not necessarily cook.
When the papillote has puffed up, let it cook for an additional 5 to 6 minutes.

● Chef's notes
It's best to serve the papillotes closed; that way, the guests can enjoy the aromas as they open them.
Aluminum foil is not generally used these days. If an acidifier, like lemon juice or wine, is part of the recipe, it causes the food to oxidize. Parchment paper is more resistant to tears.

1

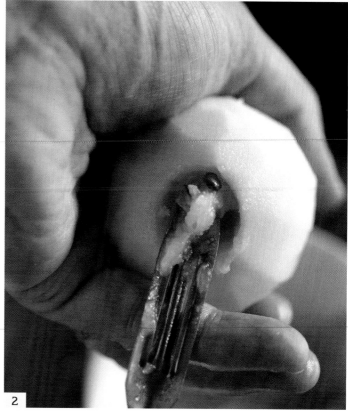

2

3

Poaching ★

Poaching involves cooking a food—generally whole—in a liquid, such as syrup, fruit juice, milk, etc.

Pour the liquid into a saucepan, flavoring it, if you wish, with spices, aromas, or herbs (1).
Bring to a boil, and let the flavorings infuse. The infusion time is variable.
Prepare the ingredient (2) and place it in the liquid (3).
Simmer gently until cooked. The cooking time depends, of course, on the size of the ingredient. Do not allow to boil—this might damage the fruit.
Let cool either in the cooking liquid or on paper towel, depending on the recipe.

Sautéing ★

Sautéing is a quick cooking process carried out in a sauté pan or skillet, with or without fat. The food—often fruit—is sometimes caramelized as an extension of the process; the fruit is sautéed until it begins to brown, sprinkled with sugar, and sautéed further until caramelized and tender.

Prepare and cut the ingredients. Preheat the sauté pan or skillet, with or without a little fat (1).
Sear the ingredients until colored. Flavor as you wish, with vanilla, citrus zest, or spices (2). Turn over until colored on all sides. Sprinkle with sugar if necessary (3). When the ingredients are cooked and removed from the pan, you may deglaze the pan with fruit juice, wine, or other alcoholic beverage to make an accompanying sauce that can be thickened with a little butter.

Practical Guide

Molds and pans

1. Round cake pans (left) and dessert rings (right)
2. Square dessert ring
3. Rectangular cake and loaf pans
4. Hexagonal dessert ring and round tart rings
5. Log-shaped mold
6. Tuile mold
7. Silicone baking sheet
8. Charlotte mold
9. Savarin or baba mold

Material for working with chocolate

1. Food-safe acetate transfer sheet (for working
   with chocolate, cocoa butter, and edible gold dust)
2. Plastic chocolate comb
3. Electric spray gun (for velvet icing)
4. Egg-shaped polycarbonate mold
5. Roll of cellulose acetate plastic

6. Stainless steel triangle spatula
7. Rubber spatula with integrated thermometer
8. Dipping forks (for candies)
9. Wood grain design comb
10. Edible gold dust (for decoration)
11. Assorted blades (for sculpting)

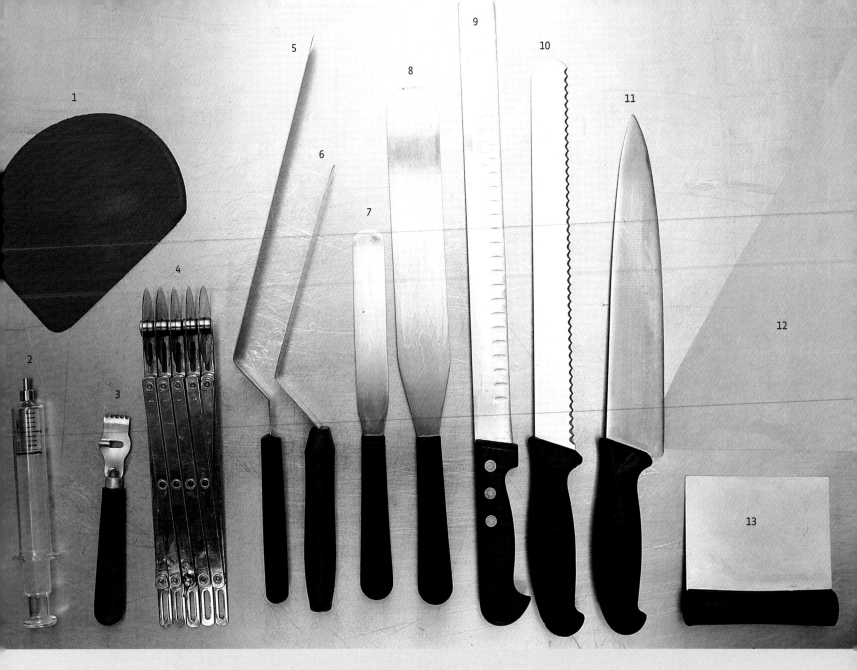

Knives and small tools

1. Plastic scraper
2. Glass syringe (for sugar, coulis, and sauces)
3. Citrus zester
4. Five-wheel adjustable dough divider
5. Large stainless steel offset spatula
6. Small stainless steel offset spatula
7. Small spatula or palette knife
8. Large spatula or palette knife
9. Slicing knife (for high-precision slices of fruits like pineapple and mango)
10. Serrated knife (for sponges and puff pastry)
11. Double-edged slicing knife
12. Triangle of paper for decorating cone
13. Stainless steel pastry blender

Basic material

1. **Stand beater and accessories** (whisk, dough hook, and paddle beater)
2. **Electronic kitchen scale and high-precision small scale**
3. **Electronic timer**
4. **Stainless steel shaker**
5. **Immersion blender**
6. **Plastic bowl**
7. **Stainless steel mixing bowl**
8. **Round-bottom stainless steel bowl** (for whipping egg whites and cream)
9. **Chinois** (fine-mesh conical strainer) **with food mill**
10. **Siphon or gourmet whip** (works with gas cartridges)

Papayas

Coconut

Star fruit or carambola

Pineapple

Mangoes

Passion fruit

Kaffir lime

Pomegranate

Prickly pear

Exotic fruit

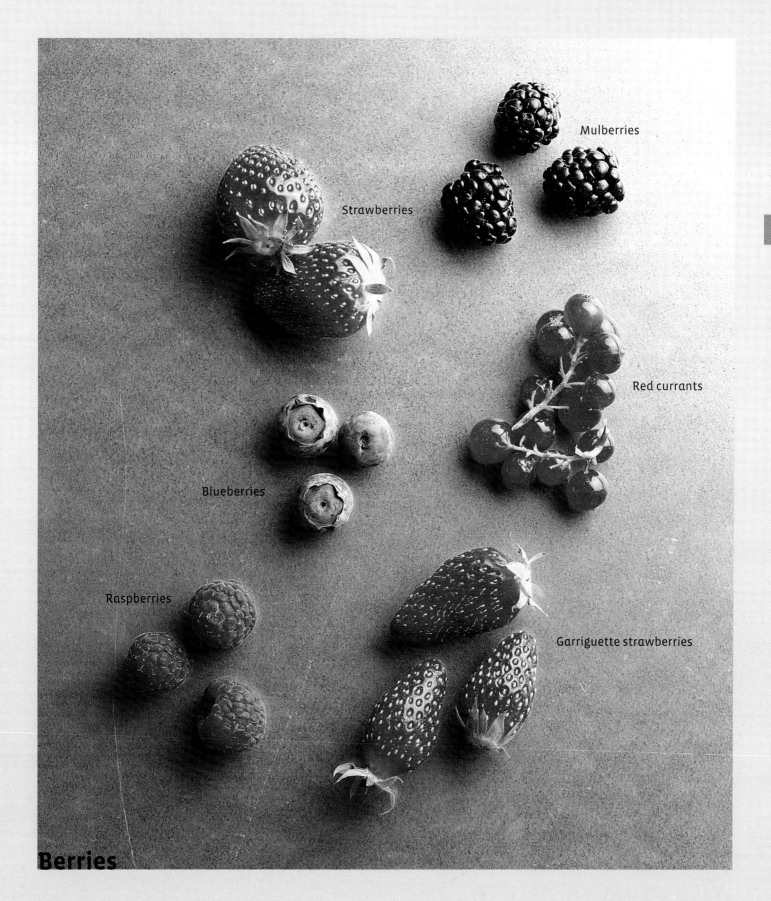

Mulberries

Strawberries

Red currants

Blueberries

Raspberries

Garriguette strawberries

Berries

Apricots

Plum

Nectarines

Peaches

Cherries

Orchard fruits

Candied cherries

Candied cedrat or citron

Dried figs

Dried apricots

Prunes or dried plums

Candied watermelon

Dried dates

Candied angelica stems

Candied orange peel

Dried and candied fruit

Pecans

Peanuts (with shell and shelled)

Pine nuts

Hazelnuts

Blue poppy seeds

Blanched almonds

White sesame seeds

Pistachios

Walnuts (with shell and shelled)

Nuts and seeds

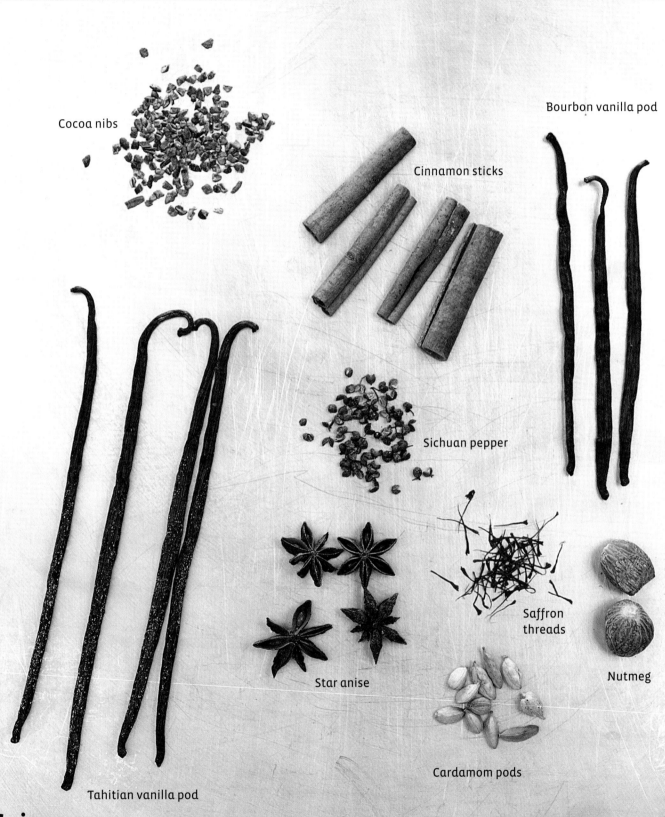

Cocoa nibs

Cinnamon sticks

Bourbon vanilla pod

Sichuan pepper

Saffron threads

Nutmeg

Star anise

Cardamom pods

Tahitian vanilla pod

Spices

Burnet

Marsh mallow

Borage flowers

Marigold

Pineapple sage

Wormwood or absinthe

Nasturtiums

Pansies

Mint

Verbena

Aromatic herbs and flowers

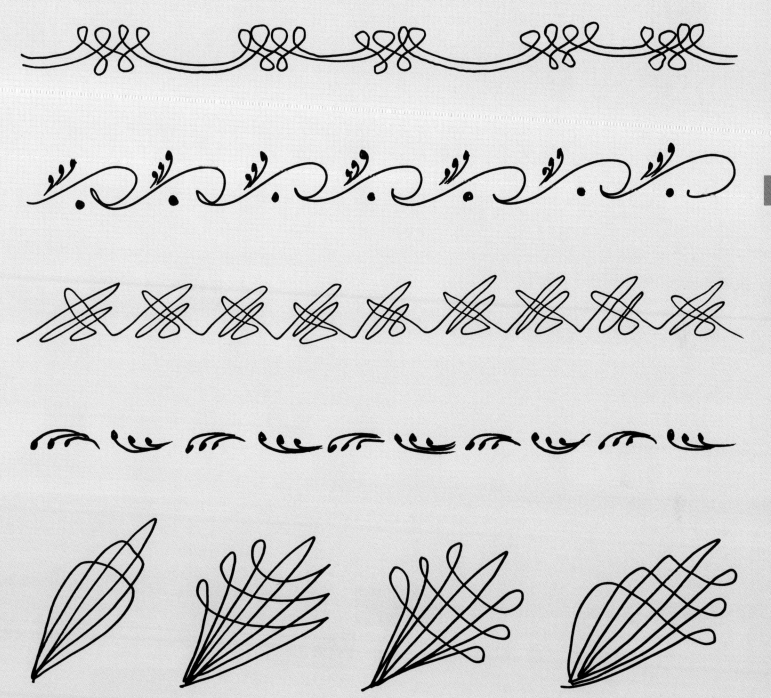

Designs to make with paper decorating cones

Fruit and nut seasons

Type of fruit	Northern Hemisphere season	Southern Hemisphere season
Almond	June–September	March–April
Apple	July–March	December–September
Apricot	May–September	December–February
Avocado pear	February–June	August–December
Banana	January–December	October–August
Blackberry	May–August	December–February
Black currant	June–August	December–February
Blood orange	December–March	August–September
Blueberry (Bilberry)	May–September	December–February
Cherry	June–August	November–January
Chestnut	November–January	March–June
Citron	October–February	Not usually grown
Clementine	November–January	April–February
Coconut	Not usually grown	October–December
Cranberry	October–February	Not usually grown
Date	August–December (available dried all year round)	February–April (available dried all year round)
Elderberry	September–November	March–May
Fig	June–September	December–April
Grape	September–October	December–May
Grapefruit	September–November	June–February
Guava	November–March	February–July
Hazelnut	August–October	March–June
Huckleberry	July–September	Not usually grown
Kiwi	January–August	February–August
Cumquat	November–March	April–October
Lemon	January–March	All year round
Lime	September–December	January–August
Litchi	April–June	November–February
Mango	March–September	October–March

Type of fruit	Northern Hemisphere season	Southern Hemisphere season
Mangosteen	May–October	February–March
Medlar	October–December	April–June
Melon	July–October	October–February
Mirabelle plum	August–September	Not usually grown
Mulberry	August–September	January
Orange	January–March	All year round
Papaya	Not usually grown	March–November
Passion fruit	July–March	October–June
Peach	June–September	December–April
Peanut	September–October	April–May
Pear	September–January	January–June
Persimmon (Sharon fruit)	September–December	March–June
Physalis (Cape gooseberry)	June–July	December–January
Pine nut	July–November	July–October
Pineapple	March–July	October–February
Pistachio	September–November	March–April
Plum	May–October	December–April
Pomegranate	October–January	March–May
Prickly Pear	August–January	January–July
Quince	October–December	February–June
Raspberry	June–September	December–March
Red currant	July–August	January–February
Rhubarb	January–May	February–August
Star fruit (carambola)	July–September	January–February
Strawberry	June–August	October–February
Tangerine (Mandarin)	October–April	April–February
Tomato	June–September	November–May
Walnut	October–January	March–June
Watermelon	August–October	December–May
Wild strawberry	August	January–February

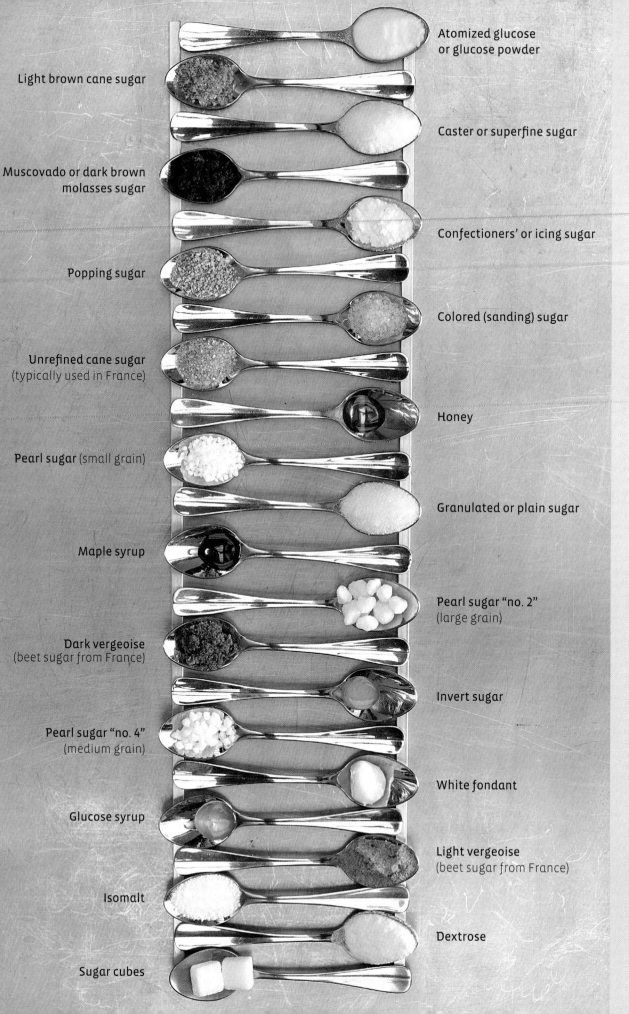

Atomized glucose
or glucose powder

Light brown cane sugar

Caster or superfine sugar

Muscovado or dark brown
molasses sugar

Confectioners' or icing sugar

Popping sugar

Colored (sanding) sugar

Unrefined cane sugar
(typically used in France)

Honey

Pearl sugar (small grain)

Granulated or plain sugar

Maple syrup

Pearl sugar "no. 2"
(large grain)

Dark vergeoise
(beet sugar from France)

Invert sugar

Pearl sugar "no. 4"
(medium grain)

White fondant

Glucose syrup

Light vergeoise
(beet sugar from France)

Isomalt

Dextrose

Sugar cubes

Sugar

The main syrups

Syrups	Proportions	Use for
For dipping or poaching	• 4 cups (1 liter) water • 1 ¼–2 ½ cups (10 oz.–1 ¼ lb./300 g–500 g) sugar • Flavoring	• Savarin • Baba • Poached fruit
For moistening	• 4 cups (1 liter) water • 5 ¼–7 cups (2 ¼–3 lb./1–1.35 kg) sugar • Flavoring	• Desserts • Sponges • Cookies
Candy syrup	• 4 cups (1 liter) water • 4 ¾ lb. (2.2 kg) sugar • Let cool to 77°F (25°C) in an airtight container • Pour over candies or fruit placed on candy rack. Let stand for 24 to 36 hours, until coated.	• Dried fruit stuffed with marzipan • Cake decorations • Molded almond paste

Temperatures for commonly used syrups

Sugar for	Temperatures
Syrup	200°F (100°C)
Gelled fruit paste	221°F–223°F (105°C–106°C)
Italian meringue	243°F–250°F (117°C–121°C)
Pâte à bombe	243°F–250°F (117°C–121°C)
Decorative sugar (poured, spun, blown, pulled)	300°F–311°F (150°C–155°C)
Caramel (sauce and decoration)	356°F (180°C)

Cooked sugar and caramel

We strongly advise you to use a candy or instant-read thermometer when cooking sugar.

Stage	Temperatures	Uses
Coated	217°F (103°C)	• Jams and jellies
Small thread or small gloss	223°F (106°C)	• *Pâte de fruits* (fruit jellies)
Large thread or large gloss	230°F (110°C)	• Florentine cookies
Soft-ball	237°F (114°C)	• Soft caramels
Hard-ball	244°F (118°C)	• Soft fondant, almond paste
Light or soft crack	250°F (121°C)	• Italian meringue, butter cream, hard fondant
Hard crack	275°F–293°F (135°C–145°C)	• White nougat, marshmallow
Grand cassé	293°F–311°F (145°C–155°C)	• Thread stage, poured or spun sugar, soufflé, blown sugar
Light caramel	329°F (165°C)	• Croquembouche, etc., poured or spun sugar, soufflé, blown sugar
Caramel	356°F (180°C)	• Caramel sauce with salted butter
Blackjack or dark caramel	375°F–400°F (190°C–200°C)	• Blackjack for inedible decoration

Ice-cream making equipment

1. Ice-cream spatula
2. Curved ice-cream scoop
3. Oval ice-cream scoop (for quenelles)
4. Large ice-cream scoop
5. Small ice-cream scoop

6. Refractometer
7. Stainless steel high dessert ring
8. Silicone mold to form thin layers (resistant to -83°F/-64°C)
9. Stainless steel bombe molds
10. Equipment for making ice-cream cones
11. Silicone lollipop (or popsicle) molds with sticks

Ice-cream making

Well-known sundaes

Name	What's in it?	The story behind it
Peach Melba	• 2 scoops of vanilla ice cream • Whole peaches, gently poached in vanilla syrup • Red currant jelly • Chantilly cream • Sliced toasted almonds	The illustrious chef Auguste Escoffier was working at the Savoy Hotel in London and created this dessert while Nelly Melba, the Australian opera singer, was performing there.
Colonel	• Lemon sorbet • Vodka	
Poire Belle-Hélène	• 2 scoops of vanilla ice cream • Pear halves poached in syrup • Warm chocolate sauce • Chantilly cream • Sliced toasted almonds	This dessert was created around 1864 in homage to Offenbach's famous opera, *La Belle Hélène*.
Banana split	• A banana, split in half lenghtwise • 3 scoops of vanilla and/or chocolate ice cream • Chocolate sauce or fruit coulis • Chantilly cream	
Café liégeois	• 2 scoops of soft coffee ice cream made from a coffee infusion • Chantilly cream	An iced version of the famous Belgian coffee drink.
Chocolat liégeois	• Churned chocolate served in a tall glass • Chantilly cream	
Dame blanche	• 2 scoops of vanilla or almond milk ice cream • Chocolate sauce	The name of this dessert means "white lady." It probably takes its name from the successful opera by Boieldieu, produced in 1825.

List of primary ingredients in ice-cream making

Fats

Product	% water	% total solids	% fat	% milk solids	% sweetening capacity
Whole milk	88	12	3.60	8.40	Milk solids / 2 × 16
Low fat milk			1.80		
Skim milk	90	9.30	0.06	9.28	Milk solids / 2 × 16
Evaporated milk	75	25	7.50	17.50	Milk solids / 2 × 16
Sweetened condensed milk	30	70	9	20	Milk solids / 2 × 16
Powdered milk (26% fat)	3	97	26	71	Milk solids / 2 × 16
Powdered milk (0% fat)	3	97	0	97	Milk solids / 2 × 16
Cream (30% fat)	63.56	36.44	30	6	Milk solids / 2 × 16
Cream (35% fat)	59.02	40.98	35	5	Milk solids / 2 × 16
Cream (40% fat)	54.48	45.52	40	5	Milk solids / 2 × 16
Dairy butter (82% fat)	12	84	82	2	Milk solids / 2 × 16
Dairy butter (80% fat)	18	82	80	2	Milk solids / 2 × 16
Clarified (or concentrated) butter (99.98% fat)	0.02	99.98	99.98	0	Milk solids / 2 × 16
Egg yolks	50	50	33	0	Milk solids / 2 × 16

Sweeteners

Product	Origin	% sweetening capacity	% total solids
Sucrose (regular table sugar)	Derived from beet or cane sugar. Composed of two molecules: glucose and fructose	100	100
Glucose syrup or crystals	Hydrolyzed from starches (extracted from apples, potatoes, rice, corn, sweet potato)	40 in general (from 38 to 68 according to DE*)	78
Glucose powder	Dehydrated glucose syrup	47	95
Invert sugar crystals or invert sugar syrup	Hydrolyzed from sucrose (fructose and glucose)	Approx. 127	78
Dextrose	Pure glucose (hydrolyzed from cornstarch)		95
Liquid sorbitol E420	Made from hydrogenated sugar from the fruit of the rowan tree (adding hydrogen)	75	70
Sorbitol powder E420	Evaporation of liquid sorbitol	30	100
Isomalt E953	Hydrolyzed from sucrose followed by hydrogenation	30	95
Fructose	Natural fruit and vegetable components (hydrolyzed sucrose)	50	
Honey	Flower nectar extracts (by honeybees)	173	78
Maple syrup	Maple sugar (North America)	130	80
Lactose	Milk (4.2%) and other dairy products	16	
Maltose	Hydrolyzed from starches from different grains, such as corn or barley. Composed of two glucose molecules	33	
Brown or demerara sugar	First extract from the crystallization of sugar cane juice, unrefined	100	100
Muscovado or dark brown molasses sugar	Raw sugar from the crystallization of thick, dark sugar cane syrup. Origin Philippines. Dried and ground	100	100
Stevia (leaf)	From the stevia plant family. Origin South America	35 times that of sucrose	17

* Dextrose Equivalent

Fruits and nuts

Name	% solids	% commonly used in sorbet
Almond	94	—
Apricot	14	50 to 70
Avocado	32	30 to 50
Banana	25	50 to 60
Blackberry	16	45 to 60
Blood orange	11	55 to 70
Blueberry	15	40 to 50
Cantaloupe	8	60 to 80
Cherry (morello)	19	40 to 50
Chestnut	49	30 to 40
Coconut	56.2	55 to 70
Comice pear	17	60 to 70
Currant	15	40 to 50
Fig	23	45 to 60
Gooseberry	16	40 to 50
Grape	21	50 to 60
Grapefruit	10	35 to 45
Green (Anjou) pear	14	50 to 60
Guava	15	40 to 50
Hazelnut	93	—
Huckleberry	16	40 to 50
Kiwi	16	50 to 60
Lemon	9	20 to 30
Lime	9	15 to 25
Litchi	15	45 to 55
Mandarin orange	12	45 to 55
Mango	15	50 to 60
Mint	16.5	—
Orange	10	55 to 70
Papaya	15	60 to 70
Passion fruit	15	30 to 45
Pineapple	14	45 to 60
Plum	19	45 to 55
Plum (mirabelle)	18	50 to 60
Pomegranate	20	60 to 70
Prune	67	30 to 40
Raspberry	14	45 to 55
Red peach	13	60 to 70
Strawberry	11	50 to 70
Strawberry (wild Mara)	11	50 to 70
Strawberry (wild)	12	50 to 70
Walnut	93	—
Watermelon	7	60 to 70
White peach	14	60 to 70
Williams pear	13	60 to 70
Yellow peach	13	60 to 70

Chocolate

Tempering chocolate: Troubleshooting guide
We recommend you use couverture chocolate when making recipes that involve tempering.

Problem	Causes	The remedy
The couverture chocolate thickens while you are working with it	• Significant cooling (crystallization) of the chocolate	• Add a little hot melted chocolate or place under a source of heat, such as a heat gun
The chocolates do not shine	• Couverture chocolate not properly tempered • Storage and/or refrigerator too cold • Molds or acetate sheets not clean	• The temperature in the kitchen should range between 65°F and 75°F (19°C and 23 °C) and the refrigerator should be between 46°F and 54°F (8°C and 12°C) • Molds and acetate sheets should be perfectly clean: wipe with cotton wool
The chocolates do not unmold neatly or break	• Cold couverture chocolate in a warm (room temperature) mold	• Respect the tempering curves • Ensure the molds are clean: wipe with cotton wool • Molds must be at room temperature: 72°F (22°C)
The chocolates whiten when unmolded (dull color, shrinkage)	• Cold couverture chocolate in a cold mold	• Respect the tempering curves • Check the temperature • Molds must be at room temperature: 72°F (22°C)
The chocolates stick in the molds; streaks appear in the chocolate	• Cold couverture chocolate in a hot mold	• Respect the tempering curves • Check the temperature • Molds must be at room temperature: 72° F (22° C)
The chocolates split or the surface cracks	• Temperature has been lowered too rapidly	• Wait for the chocolate to set before placing in the refrigerator at between 46°F and 54°F (8°C and 12°C)
The chocolates whiten (bloom)	• Chocolate still too hot and placed in a refrigerator that's too cold • Placed near a source of humidity (condensation)	• Respect the tempering curves • Check the temperature • The refrigerator should be between 46°F and 54°F (8°C and 12°C)
There are traces on the chocolate	• Molds not clean and badly wiped, leading to a lack of gloss	• Remove any grease from the molds with cotton wool and 90° alcohol • Then rub the molds well with dry cotton wool

Specialty French desserts

Regional specialties

France has a wide and varied range of desserts. Here is a selection of regional specialties that you can find if you travel through the country,[1] some of which bear the same names but are made differently. Translations are given where possible.

Alsace

- *Beignet de carnaval* (carnival donut): leavened dough usually made in a round shape and sometimes garnished with fruit.
- *Berewecke*: a mildly spiced loaf of dried and candied fruit, usually made before Christmas.
- *Galette au streusel*: rustic leavened dough topped with cinnamon and almond streusel.
- *Galette des rois* (Epiphany cake): the Alsatian version is made of brioche dough and shaped into a crown.
- *Gâteau de santé* (health cake): vanilla-flavored cake, sometimes marbled with cocoa.
- *Kugelhopf*: a kirsch-scented, yeast-based cake in the shape of a turban, with whole almonds and raisins.
- *Mannala*: a leavened cake shaped like a gingerbread man with raisins for eyes, sold in December.
- *Mendiant*: a type of bread pudding garnished with black cherries and other fruit.
- *Nid d'abeille* (bees' nest): honey-based, crown-shaped cake with pastry cream in the center.
- *Pet de Nonne* (literally, "nun's fart"): small, light, sweet donut puff.
- Plum and rhubarb tarts.
- Strudel, apple: apple quarters and raisins, flavored with cinnamon, rolled in strudel dough.
- *Tarte de linz:* Linzer tart with jam.

Aquitaine

- *Canelé*: a fluted little cake, caramelized on the outside with a sweet, soft crumb, a specialty of Bordeaux.
- *Casse museau* (literally, "jaw breaker"): this cake is double baked and extremely hard to break. An irregularly shaped cookie that keeps well, filled with pastry cream and sprinkled with confectioners' sugar.
- *Crespet*: large, fried, hollow choux pastry flavored with orange flower water, orange zest, and rum.
- *Croquet de Bordeaux*: small, very dry, stick-shaped cookie with chopped almonds.

- *Gâteau basque* (Basque cake): flat, round cake comprising two layers of short pastry filled with rum-scented pastry cream or black cherry jam.
- *Gâteau des rois bordelais* (Bordelais Epiphany cake): leavened dough shaped into a crown and decorated with slices of candied citron and sanding sugar.
- *Macaron de Saint-Émilion*: small almond macaron baked on special paper.
- *Pastis landais*: soft yeast dough in a cylindrical shape, flavored with Pastis (the aniseed drink) and orange flower water, sprinkled with pieces of crushed sugar cubes.
- *Rousquille*: dry, figure-eight-shaped cookie flavored with aniseed and orange flower water.
- *Tourtière*: a pie of fine layers of dough filled with Armagnac-flavored apple slices.

Auvergne

- *Brioche de Riom*: rustic brioche made with milk and eggs.
- *Cornets de Murat*: cornet-shaped dough garnished with Chantilly cream or flavored almond paste.
- *Fouace*: brioche with candied fruit.
- *Pompe aux pommes*: apple turnover made with puff or short pastry.
- *Puy de Dôme*: conical-shaped Genoese sponge garnished with ice cream and masked with meringue. The dessert may take its name from an extinct volcano in central France.
- *Tarte de Vic-sur-Cère* or *Tarte bourbonnaise*: shortcrust tart filled with a *fromage blanc* mixture.

Brittany

- *Craquelin*: crunchy cake or cookie made of unsweetened dough, often shaped like a nest.
- *Crêpe*: fine disk of batter cooked quickly on both sides, either in a crêpe pan or on a cast-iron crêpe maker.
- *Crêpe dentelle* (lace crêpe): small buttery cookie made of cooked crêpe batter that is rolled up and cooled until very crisp. It flakes easily and can be used to add a crunchy texture to desserts.
- *Far Breton*: an egg-rich flan baked with dried plums.
- *Galette bretonne*: pure butter shortbread made with salted butter.
- *Gâteau breton*: a thick, risen dough with one-quarter salted butter.
- *Kouign Amman*: very buttery, sweet puff pastry that caramelizes when baked.

---

1. These specialties are taken from *L'inventaire du patrimoine culinaire*, Albin Michel/CNAC.

- *Palet Breton*: thick, risen, round cookie made with salted butter.
- *Pommé rennais*: lightly puffed pastry filled with apple jam.

Burgundy

- *Biscuit de chablis*: a light, crunchy rectangular cookie baked until golden brown.
- *Brioche aux pruneaux*: a light yeast dough with prunes.
- *Cacou*: unpitted black cherry clafoutis.
- *Cassissine*: a jellied candy made from black currants, with a black currant liqueur center. The Dijon area is known for its black currants.
- *Cion*: *fromage blanc* (farmer's cheese) tart.
- *Croquet aux amandes*: crisp almond cookie, often rectangular.
- *Gaufrette mâconnaise*: fine, cigarette-shaped rolled wafer.
- *Gimblette*: small, ring-shaped spice cookie.
- *Gougère*: savory choux puff with Comté cheese.
- *Massepain* (marzipan): small, soft, round cookie made with sugar, almonds, and egg white.
- *Pain d'épices de Dijon* (Dijon spice bread): honey-based yeast dough with spices.

Center

- *Beignets de fleur d'acacia*: acacia flower fritters.
- *Pet de Nonne* (literally, "nun's fart"): small, shaped choux pastry that is deep-fried and rolled in sugar.
- *Pithiviers*: puff pastry pie filled with almond cream.
- *Poirat*: poached pear pie.
- **Tarte Tatin** (apple upside-down cake): caramelized apple halves covered with pastry, baked, and turned upside down. (See p. 249 for the history of this dessert.)

Champagne-Ardenne

- *Biscuit rose de Reims*: pink ladyfinger cookie from Reims. The surface is white with a thick sprinkling of confectioners' sugar.
- *Caisse de Joinville*: almond meringue baked in small rectangles until golden.
- *Croquignole*: very dry, crisp cookie made of sugar, flour, and egg white. Alternate cookies are colored pink.
- *Massepain de Reims*: round almond cake (closely related to the basic almond macaron) with a hollow in the center made with a small piece of wood dipped in sugar.
- *Nonette de Reims*: small, round spice bread garnished with raspberry jam or orange marmalade. A traditional gift on Saint Nicholas' feast day.
- *Pain d'épice de Reims*: variously shaped spice loaves made with rye flour and honey.
- *Tarte au quemeu*: a cheese tart made with fresh cheese from Langres.
- *Tarte aux prunes rouges*: shortcrust tart shell covered with rings of red plum (*quetsches*) halves, sprinkled with confectioners' or granulated sugar.

Corsica

- *Bugliticcia*: a fritter.
- *Canestra*: brioche pastry.
- *Canistrellu*: small, cylindrical, delicate pastries made with oil, white wine, and aniseed.
- *Castagnacciu*: soft cake made with chestnut flour.
- *Falculella*: Half-inch thick sweet pastry with mild soft cheese (brocciu), baked on chestnut leaves.
- *Fenuchjettu d'Ajaccio*: a firm, figure-eight-shaped cake flavored with aniseed that is briefly boiled before baking.
- *Fiadone*: another cake made with brocciu and flavored with lemon zest.
- *Frappa*: aniseed and citrus-flavored fritter sprinkled with confectioners' sugar.
- *Fritella au brocciu*: a small fritter filled with brocciu.
- *Fugazza* or *inuliata*: a round cake flavored with aniseed, white wine, and oil, baked for Holy Week.
- *Imbrucciata*: a tart filled with lemon zest-scented brocciu.
- *Panzarottu*: a fritter made with rice or potatoes, eau-de-vie, and grated lemon zest.
- *Pastella au brocciu*: shortcrust turnover filled with brocciu.

Franche-Comté

- *Biscuit de Montbozon*: soft, oval cookie flavored with orange flower water. The recipe was brought to the village of Montbozon by Louis XVI's pastry chef after the execution of the king.
- *Charlotte aux pommes* (apple charlotte): baked dessert with a brioche base and sides, filled with apples.
- *Galette de Goumeau*: brioche dough topped with an orange flower-scented cream.
- *Gâteau de ménage* (household cake): buttery brioche topped with an egg cream.
- *Gaufre comtoise*: a waffle.
- *Pain d'épices de Vercel*: a spice bread made with honey and wheat flour.
- *Téméraire*: cake filled with apples and raisins, flambéed with *marc de Jura*, a locally produced eau-de-vie.

Île-de-France

- *Amandine*: almond cream tartlet scattered with sliced almonds.
- *Brioche de Nanterre*: brioche dough baked in two rows of buns.
- *Chouquette*: small, light choux puff sprinkled with sanding sugar.
- *Confit de pétale de rose*: jelly with rose petals.
- *Flan parisien*: vanilla-scented flan filling baked in a shortcrust pastry shell.
- *Galette feuilletée sèche ou fourrée*: round puff pastry layers (*sèche*), or a pie (*fourrée*) filled with almond cream.
- *Macaron lisse* (widely known as a macaron): a soft cookie made with almonds, sugar, and egg whites, flavored in many ways. The Parisian macaron comprises two macarons sandwiched

together with a filling. The cookies themselves are generally colored to suggest the flavor of the filling.

- *Manqué*: a variation of a Savoy sponge, with the addition of butter.
- *Moka/Mocha*: a layered sponge cake garnished with coffee-flavored butter cream. The sides are sprinkled with sliced almonds. (See p. 248 for the history of this dessert.)
- *Niflette*: a specialty of the Seine et Marne department, the town of Provins in particular. A cake traditionally made for All Saints' Day, it is a disk of puff pastry garnished with orange flower-scented pastry cream.
- *Opéra*: rectangular cake made of layers of a light almond sponge sandwiched together with coffee-scented butter cream and chocolate ganache. (See p. 248 for the history of this dessert.)
- *Paris-Brest*: a crown-shaped cake made of praline cream-filled choux pastry and sprinkled with sliced almonds. (See p. 248 for the history of this dessert.)
- *Puits d'amour* (literally, "well of love"): a small, puff pastry cake, one round set over the other, with the second hollowed out to form a well that is filled with pastry cream or red currant jelly.
- *Saint-Honoré*: a disk of shortcrust or puff pastry covered with a ring of choux pastry, topped with caramelized choux puffs that are filled with Chiboust cream. (See p. 249 for the history of this dessert.)
- *Savarin*: a large or small, crown-shaped cake of yeast dough, soaked with sugar syrup and liqueur (usually rum or kirsch), and garnished with either Chantilly or pastry cream, or fruit. Not to be confused with rum babas. (See p. 249 for the history of this dessert.)
- *Sucre d'orge des religieuses de Moret* (barley sugar of the nuns of Moret): a small, pyramid-shaped, yellow-amber candy.
- *Tarte bourdaloue*: a sweet shortcrust pastry shell filled with poached pear halves nestling in an almond-based cream. (See p. 248 for the history of this dessert.)

Languedoc-Roussillon

- *Alléluia de Castelnaudary*: a dry citron-flavored cake with sugar icing.
- *Biscotin de Bédarieux*: small, rounded, soft cake flavored with lemon and orange.
- *Biterroise*: a soft brioche with raisins and applesauce, flavored with orange flower water.
- *Bras de gitan* (literally, "gypsy's arm"): jelly roll with rum-flavored pastry cream.
- *Brioche anisée*: round, aniseed-scented flavored brioche.
- *Coque catalane*: oval brioche with fresh or dried fruit.
- *Coque Saint-Aphrodise*: very soft brioche flavored with lemon and orange flower water.
- *Crème catalane*: baked cream sprinkled with sugar that is caramelized just before serving.
- *Croquant de Mende*: rectangular, dry, and golden, this is a vanilla-scented cookie with almonds or hazelnuts.

- *Croquignoles d'Uzès*: small hard cookie made with a caramelized pastry and filled with a whole almond or hazelnut. It's one of the thirteen traditional desserts served to end Christmas dinner in this region.
- *Fougasse d'Aigues-Mortes*: square, egg-rich brioche flavored with orange flower water.
- *Limoux*: crown-shaped brioche covered with pieces of candied fruit and sprinkled with sanding sugar.
- *Millas*: lightly sweetened corn flour cake that is sometimes served salted.
- *Minerve*: sliced brioche covered with sugar icing.
- *Oreillettes* (literally, "small ears"): dry, friable, round fritter.
- *Pain paillasse de Lodève*: rustic sourdough bread with a firm crust and a dark crumb.
- *Pastisson de Beaucaire*: sweet-savory paté made with candied citron and Mediterranean lime in puff pastry.
- *Tourteau à l'anis*: a crown-shaped brioche flavored with aniseed and lemon.

Limousin

- *Aréna*: a cake that bears the name of its creator, Paulin Aréna, and won an award in a 1908 national pastry contest. Its secret recipe includes almond paste.
- *Boulaigous limousine*: a thick, rustic pancake that is eaten with locally produced honey or jam.
- *Clafoutis*: unpitted cherries baked in a flan-like batter, widely made during the brief cherry season.
- *Cornue*: a Y-shaped brioche that can be traced back to the twelfth century, traditionally distributed at Easter time.
- *Creusois*: a hazelnut-based cake whose original recipe, written in the Middle Ages, was recently rediscovered and is followed to the letter by a few authorized pastry makers.
- *Flognarde*: a flan-like batter that ressembles clafoutis (but is lighter), incorporating apples or pears.
- *Madeleine de Saint-Yrieix*: less well known than the *madeleines de Commercy* mentioned by Proust, these are flavored with bitter almonds. Tradition has it that the shape recalls the scallop, a sign of St. James's Way, the pilgrims' route to Santiago de Compostela.
- *Mique*: a dumpling made from yeast dough that is either used as an accompaniment to meat dishes or spread with jam for breakfast.

Lorraine

- *Baba*: a butter-rich yeast dough with currants or raisins, generally soaked in rum. It is said to have been created in the early eighteenth century when King Stanislas Leszczynski of Poland, exiled to Lorraine, complained that the local *kugelhopf* was too dry. Rum was poured over it and the dish was named after a hero in his favorite book, *The Thousand and One Nights*.
- *Croquet de Saint-Mihiel*: crisp, long cookie made from one third unblanched almonds from Provence.

- *Macaron de Boulay*: another version of the ground almond-egg white recipe, colored yellow. It is shaped using spoons and has the form of a pyramid.
- *Macaron de Nancy*: a macaron created by the nuns of the convent of Les Dames du Saint Sacrement. It is soft inside and baked until brown and cracked on the outside.
- *Madeleine de Commercy*: individual cakes with a rounded shell, described by Marcel Proust as a "seashell cake so strictly pleated outside and so sensual inside."
- *Nonette de Remiremont*: small, mounded, spice bread cake made with pine honey from the Vosges forests.
- *Pain-d'anis de Gérardmer*: a dry cookie with 3 percent aniseed.
- *Saint-Epvre*: two disks of almond meringue with vanilla-scented butter cream incorporating crushed nougatine.
- *Tarte aux mirabelles* (Mirabelle plum tart): a fresh plum tart made with the locally grown, small, yellow Mirabelle plums that are harvested in August. It is emblematic of Lorraine cuisine.
- *Visitandine de Nancy*: very soft, round or oval cakes made with almonds, sugar, butter, and egg whites. The recipe is said to have been invented in monasteries to use up leftover egg whites.

Midi-Pyrénées

- *Croquant de Cordes*: a delicate crunchy almond cookie from the town of Cordes-sur-Ciel.
- *Croustade aux pommes*: a light puff pastry filled with sliced apples that have been soaked in Armagnac.
- *Flône*: a short pastry crust filled with a mixture whose main ingredient is fresh ewe's milk cheese.
- *Fougasse* (or *fouasse*) *aveyronnaise*: a crown-shaped brioche usually sprinkled with sanding sugar.
- *Gâteau à la broche*: traditionally cooked on a roasting spit in the fireplace, this cake resembles a pine tree. The dough solidifies as the spit turns and successive layers are added. It is celebrated at its own annual festival.
- *Gâteau aux pignons*: tart with a sweet shortbread crust filled with a pine nut frangipane.
- *Gimblette d'Albi*: ring-shaped cookie with candied citron that is boiled before being baked.
- *Massepain de Montbazens*: a round cake with fluted sides that is made without any butter or oil.
- *Navette albigeoise*: diamond-shaped shortcrust cookie (the shape of a weaver's shuttle), decorated with whole almonds, made from a recipe that has been traced back to the eighteenth century.
- *Pain à l'anis*: small, light brioche dough sprinkled with aniseed and sugar.
- *Pompe à l'huile* (literally, "oil pump"): bread made with walnut oil and citrus zest.
- *Rissole*: crescent-shaped fritter filled with prunes.
- *Tarte encalat*: a tart made with cows' milk curd cheese.

Nord-Pas-de-Calais–Picardy

- *Carré de Lille*: dark, anise-flavored spice loaf.
- *Craquelin de Boulogne*: sweet puff pastry caramelized in the oven and shaped in a figure of eight.
- *Dartois*: rounds of donut-like dough topped with red currant jelly or almond cream.
- *Galette flamande*: brioche with dried fruit, sometimes garnished with cream and flavored with rum.
- *Gaufre fourrée*: thin waffle rolled into a cone or stick and filled with *vergeoise* (soft brown beet sugar) softened in butter.
- *Macaron d'Amiens*: cookie-like macaron made with almond paste, fruit, and honey.
- *Nieulle*: small cookie traditionally made in the town of Armentières in September. In the sixteenth century they were thrown to the crowds from the town hall.
- *Tarte au sucre* (sugar tart): shortbread pastry crust filled with a light brown sugar mixture.

Normandy

- *Bourdalot*: whole apple or pear wrapped in dough and baked.
- *Bourdin*: puff pastry with quartered Calville apples.
- *Brasillé*: puff brioche pastry made with salted butter and decorated with a scored ear of corn on top.
- *Galette à l'anis*: small, round, aniseed-flavored cookie, prepared like a Genoese sponge and then dried in the oven.
- *Mirliton de Pont-Audemar*: a roll of puff pastry filled with praline mousse closed in at each end with bittersweet chocolate.
- *Mirliton de Rouen*: puff pastry tartlet garnished with almond cream.
- *Sablé normand*: small, buttery, crumbly shortbread cookie.
- *Tarte normande*: shortcrust pastry tart with a layer of applesauce topped with thin slices of apples.
- *Teurgoule*: rice pudding flavored with cinnamon and slow-cooked in a special ceramic dish.

Pays-de-la-Loire

- *Brioche vendéenne*: a particularly soft-textured, braided brioche flavored with eau-de-vie and orange flower water.
- *Croquant de l'Anjou*: thin, aniseed-flavored, round cookie.
- *Fion* (means "flan" in local dialect): flan batter with a strong flavor of cinnamon, as well as vanilla and orange flower water, baked in a crust.
- *Fouace nantaise*: rustic, leavened, dense dough from Nantes, shaped like a star.
- *Foutimasson* or *bottereau*: small leavened fritter that swells when fried and is sprinkled with sugar. It is made for Mardi Gras.
- *Gâche vendéenne*: an oval brioche that is richer than the *brioche vendéenne* because of the addition of cream.
- *Galette Saint-Michel*: small, round, dry buttery cookie.
- *Gâteau nantais*: a round, rum-scented sponge cake with almonds topped with apricot jelly and covered with white icing.

- *Pâté de prunes d'Angers*: whole plums wrapped in dough and baked.
- *Sablé de Retz*: small, round cookie with coconut.

Poitou-Charentes
- *Angélique de Niort*: stalk of candied angelica, an aromatic plant introduced into France by the Vikings and cultivated there by monks.
- *Broyé de Poitou*: a dry, dense cookie and a close relative of the *galette charentaise* from the same region.
- *Corinette*: a small cake made using a madeleine batter but with a thin, elongated shape.
- *Cornuelle*: triangular cookie made of shortbread or puff pastry, depending on where it is made, and often sprinkled with aniseed.
- *Fouace*: a brioche that was originally baked in the ashes. The name comes from the Latin *panis focacius* (bread of the hearth).
- *Grimolle*: crêpe batter that includes apple or pear slices and is baked underneath a cabbage leaf. It is similar to the clafoutis.
- *Macaron de Lusignan*: small, flour-free cake with a high percentage of ground almonds.
- *Marguerite d'Angoulême*: a confection made with bittersweet chocolate flavored with candied orange peel and shaped like a daisy.
- *Merveille*: a fritter that can be made in any shape, but is often rectangular, made with baking powder. It is generally eaten during Mardi Gras.
- *Millas*: a flan made with corn flour.
- *Pine*: triangular, risen cake that is first boiled and then oven-dried.
- *Tourteau fromager*: dessert comprising a shortcrust pastry with a lightly sweetened goat's-milk cheese filling, whose blackened top looks burned.

Provence-Alpes-Côte d'Azur
- *Biscotin d'Aix*: small sphere of orange flower-scented, very firm shortbread pastry, with a roasted hazelnut in the center.
- *Calisson d'Aix*: a diamond-shaped candy made of almond paste and candied melon topped with royal icing.
- *Chichi-frégi*: leavened doughnut batter flavored with orange flower water, shaped into a horseshoe, fried, and sprinkled with sugar. It is often sold at fairs and street markets.
- *Croquant*: rectangular dry cookie with honey and almonds.
- *Fougasse*: flat bread made with olive oil and slit before baking to form holes.
- *Gâteau des rois*: This version of the Epiphany cake, with a favor baked inside, is a brioche with candied fruit, orange peel, and sanding sugar.
- *Navette*: a dry, stick-shaped cookie scored along the top and flavored with orange flower water. There are numerous variations.

- *Oreillette*, *bugne*, *merveille*, etc. All leavened or risen batters that are given various shapes and fried, traditionally eaten at Mardi Gras.
- *Pompe à huile* (literally, "oil pump"): flattened bread made with olive oil and slit before baking to form holes.
- *Soufflé à la réglisse* (licorice soufflé): stiffly beaten egg whites folded into licorice-scented pastry cream and baked in butter and sugar-lined molds.

Rhône-Alpes
- *Bescoin*: saffron and aniseed-flavored brioche loaf, twisted at each end.
- *Brioche de Saint-Génix*: a brioche made with pink candied almonds.
- *Copeau*: fine, twisted, dry cookie flavored with orange flower water that takes its name from the wood shavings it resembles.
- *Croquette aux amandes*: small, dry almond cookie, cut up after it has been baked.
- *Galette bressane*: brioche dough covered with cream and sprinkled with sugar.
- *Gâteau aux noix*: a walnut tart.
- *Gâteau de Savoie*: light, Savoy sponge.
- *Pain de courge*: pumpkin loaf, a type of brioche with very small pieces of squash.
- *Pain de Modane*: brioche with candied fruit, sometimes filled with pastry cream or frangipane cream.
- *Pogne*: crown-shaped brioche flavored with orange flower water.
- *Suisse de valence*: a shortbread dough with candied orange peel, shaped like a gingerbread man.
- *Tarte au quemeu*: cream cheese tart.

Famous desserts and the story behind them

Baked Alaska (omelette norvégienne)

This dessert is indirectly linked to the American physicist Benjamin Thompson Rumford, who in 1804 discovered that the tiny bubbles in beaten egg whites have insulating properties. Because a meringue cover does not conduct heat, it bakes while preventing the ice cream below from melting. Rumford apparently said that the recipe was a byproduct of his experiments. The idea was taken up in France by a chef named Balzac when he worked at the Grand Hôtel in Paris. He set ice cream over a sponge layer, covered it with meringue, and then flambéed it all.

Bourdaloue

This cake was created in Paris, by a pastry chef named Fasquelle. A shortcrust pastry base holds pear halves poached in a vanilla syrup, nestling on a bed of frangipane cream.

Charlotte

There are many types of charlottes. They were apparently created at the court of England as a tribute to Queen Charlotte, wife of King George III (1738–1820). The charlotte was a pudding made of brioche slices soaked in flavored milk and filled with a gelled fruit purée. Early in the nineteenth century, Antonin Carême invented the charlotte à la parisienne as we know it today: finger biscuits line a high, round mold (named a charlotte mold), into which a Bavarian cream or fruit mousse is poured.

Crêpe Suzette

Although this is certainly a French dessert, the date of its creation is not known. Henri Charpentier, a maître d'hôtel in Monte Carlo, claimed to have invented it as early as 1896, but this seems unlikely. The story goes that while he was preparing crêpes for the then Prince of Wales, the liqueur he was pouring over them caught fire. The future king liked the result so much that he suggested the dessert take the name of his companion, Suzette.

Mille-feuille

It takes a great deal of skill to make this cake. It uses puff pastry, numerous layers of fine dough (1,479, to be precise), which swells when the water vaporizes during baking. Three layers of puff pastry are used, separated by two layers of pastry cream. The top is dredged with confectioners' sugar or covered with fondant icing marbled with chocolate. Puff pastry was known in ancient times by the Greeks and Arabs, but it was Antonin Carême who perfected it, and he is credited with the invention of this classic pastry.

Moka/Mocha

This layered sponge cake filled with coffee-flavored butter cream and whose sides are covered with sliced almonds takes its name from a variety of coffee grown in Ethiopia. It was created in two steps over two generations of pastry makers. A M. Quillot invented the coffee-scented butter cream, and his successor, Guignard, made the cake as we know it today.

Opéra

Two major Parisian pastry chefs claim the creation of the Opéra, a layered cake of Joconde sponge, coffee-scented butter cream, and ganache. According to Paul Bugat, who bought the Pâtisserie Clichy at place de la Bastille in 1955, it was the founder of the pastry shop, a certain Monsieur Riss, who created the cake in the 1920s. He gave it the name of his establishment, Le Clichy, and Bugat continued to sell it under this name at 5, boulevard Beaumarchais, near the Bastille. Late in the 1950s, a relative of the family, Monsieur Gavillon, who owned the Dalloyau pastry shop, apparently tasted Le Clichy and found it so delicious that he started selling it at his own establishment under the name of l'Opéra. The Dalloyau company disagrees with this version of the story and asserts that Monsieur Gavillon himself invented the cake in 1954. They even fêted its thirtieth anniversary in 1984. We will not take sides in the dispute, but it can be said for certain that the two cakes are as alike as two peas in a pod. Even if, years ago, two different pastry shops sold the cake under different names, today the Opéra is one of the best known of Paris's glorious cakes.

Paris-Brest

According to the 1984 edition of the Larousse gastronomique cookery encyclopedia, this cake was an invention of a pastry chef in the outskirts of Paris. He created it during a bicycle race between the cities of Paris and Brest in Brittany. The chef's shop was located on the route of the race and he decided to make a wheel-shaped cake. But who exactly was the creator and where exactly was his pastry shop?

The Durand family, who owned a pastry shop on avenue Longueil in Maisons-Lafitte, maintain that it was Louis Durand who created the cake in 1909, not in 1891 (as the Larousse suggests). Is it any coincidence that, in 1910, a book by Darenne and Duval entitled Traité de la pâtisserie moderne (Treatise on Modern Pastry) gives the recipe for this cake, calling it the Paris-Nice? Whatever the case, no one can dispute the success of the recipe. It is one of the most popular specialties of Île-de-France.

Peach Melba

Auguste Escoffier created this famous dessert late in the nineteenth century in honor of Nellie Melba, the Australian opera singer, when she was singing in London and Escoffier was working at the Savoy Hotel there. Escoffier later worked with César Ritz at the Ritz Hotel in Paris. The dessert is made of lightly poached peaches on a bed of vanilla ice cream, drizzled with raspberry coulis.

Religieuse (literally, "nun")

Frascatti, a pastry chef and ice-cream maker in Paris, invented this amusing individual dessert in the mid-nineteenth century. It is made of two differently sized choux puffs filled with chocolate or coffee pastry cream and topped with fondant icing, with the smaller puff set over the larger one, almost like a head. A ruffle of butter cream between the two puffs resembles a collar, and the name is said to have come from the color of the original icing, similar to that of nuns' homespun robes.

Saint-Honoré

This spectacular cake was certainly created in Paris, but its exact origins are unknown. Some say it was dedicated to St Honoré, the patron saint of bakers, which would explain its name. Others claim that the inventor was the pastry chef Auguste Julien, who, in the 1840s, worked with Chiboust, the chef who created the cream used to garnish the cake and whose establishment was located on the rue Saint-Honoré in Paris.

Savarin

Yeast doughs have been made since ancient times; the term includes breads, brioches, and *viennoiseries* (pastries such as croissants and fruit buns, often eaten for breakfast in France). The savarin is derived from a yeast dough made with wheat flour, water, and salt, to which eggs and butter are added. The savarin is differentiated from the *Kugelhopf* by the fact that it does not have any raisins. It is baked in a ring-shaped mold, soaked in flavored syrup, and garnished in the center with Chantilly cream. The savarin was first made in 1845 by Auguste Julien in tribute to Brillat-Savarin, the author of *La Physiologie du goût* (The Physiology of Taste), published in 1825.

Sorbet

Sorbets are the first known iced desserts and apparently originated in China, from where they travelled to Persia and Arabia. The name is derived from the Arab or Assyrian word *shorbet*, and when it was introduced to the Italians, they called it *sorbetto*, later Gallicized to *sorbet*. The principle has remained unchanged through the ages. Fruit juice was filtered through silk cloth and sweetened with honey. Extracts of plants were added at the end of the process to prevent crystallization. Since the late eighteenth century, ice-cream makers have created countless varieties of sorbets. Sorbets differ from ice creams in that they contain neither fat (milk or cream) nor eggs.

Tarte Tatin (apple upside-down cake)

In the late nineteenth century, the two Tatin sisters ran a modest inn with a restaurant in Lamotte-Beuvron, in the Sologne region of game-filled forests. They prepared home-style food for the hunters and other travelers who stopped by there. It just so happened that Curnonsky, a famous gastronomic critic, writer, and witty intellectual, was eating a meal there one day in 1926. He was so taken with their apple tart that he described it to a Parisian restaurateur. The dessert was so simple and delicious that, a few years later, it featured on the menus of practically every restaurant in Paris, and then in the rest of France. But the story goes that it was originally made by accident, or because the sisters were in a hurry, the pastry being placed over the caramelized apples.

Recipes

Hot
desserts

Jérôme Chaucesse

Pastry chef at the Hôtel de Crillon, Paris

"I grew up with the classics of fine French pastry. I love them dearly, and I also like to revisit them, giving them a contemporary feel and style. One of my new creations is a variation on one of my particular favorites, the Poire Belle-Hélène. I've turned a simple sundae into a sophisticated, luxury dessert. The pear is cooked two ways: infused and Tatin-style; there is a suspended Bourbon vanilla ice cream, Polignac sliced almonds, and it's all drizzled with a sauce that has two chocolates, both milk and bittersweet, spiced up with ginger and black pepper. It's to die for! My conception of pastry combines elegance and stylish design to make for a flavor sensation."

Pear Belle-Hélène,
Bourbon Vanilla Ice Cream,
and Spiced Chocolate Sauce

Serves 10
Preparation time: 50 minutes
Chilling and freezing time: 4 hours
Cooking time: 30 minutes

Prepare the cooked upside-down pears.
Peel and seed the pears. At two-thirds of the length from the stem, cut them horizontally in two.

For the syrup, pour the water into a saucepan and add the sugar, orange juice, and ginger. Slit the vanilla bean in two and scrape the seeds into the mixture. Place the vanilla bean in the mixture. Bring to a boil. Poach the upper part of the pears. Stir in the eau-de-vie. Transfer to a bowl and chill.

Make the caramel for the Tatin-style pears.
Caramelize the sugar using the dry method (see "Caramelization," p. 467). Stir in the butter. Quickly coat the remaining part of the pears on both sides. Stir in the eau-de-vie and finish cooking the pears in the oven (approx. 15 minutes at 350°F/180°C).

Make the almond tuiles.
Combine all the ingredients and roll out on a silicone baking sheet or sheet of parchment paper lined with plastic wrap. Bake at 320°F (160°C) for a few minutes. Cut out disks the same diameter as the serving glasses and pierce small holes at regular intervals around the edge with a plain icing tip. Return to the oven to finish baking for 1 or 2 minutes. When cooled, store in an airtight container.

Prepare the vanilla ice cream.
Bring the milk and cream to a boil. Slit the vanilla bean in two lengthwise, scrape the seeds out into the milk and cream mixture, add the vanilla bean, and infuse. Remove the bean. Combine half the sugar with the stabilizer and stir it into the milk.

Whip the egg yolks with the remaining sugar and atomized glucose until pale and thick.

Stir into the milk-cream mixture and cook to 185°F (85°C).

Chill for 4 hours to mature the flavors. Process in an ice-cream maker.

Mold the ice cream into plastic cones. Turn out and insert a pear stem made of chocolate into the tip. Stick the ice cream onto the bottom of an almond tuile and freeze until needed.

Ingredients
10 Bartlett pears

Syrup
4 cups (1 liter) water
2 cups (15 oz./400 g) sugar
3 tablespoons (50 ml) orange juice
2 oz. (60 g) fresh ginger, finely grated
1 vanilla bean
3 tablespoons (50 ml) pear eau-de-vie
(such as Poire Williams)

Caramel
1 cup (7 oz./200 g) sugar
3 tablespoons (2 oz./50 g) butter
2 tablespoons (25 ml) pear eau-de-vie
(such as Poire Williams)

Almond tuiles
⅓ cup (2 oz./60 g) sugar
3 tablespoons (1 oz./30 g) flour
2 oz. (50 g) egg whites (approx. 1 ½ egg whites)
1 tablespoon (16 g) melted butter
1 ⅓ cups (4 oz./100g) sliced almonds

Vanilla ice cream
1 ⅔ cups (400 ml) milk
Scant ½ cup (100 ml) heavy cream
1 vanilla bean
½ cup (3 ½ oz./100 g) sugar, divided
5–6 egg yolks (3 ½ oz./100 g)
¹⁄₁₀ oz. (2 g) stabilizer
⅔ oz. (20 g) atomized glucose
10 chocolate (pear) stems (see p. 182, Decorating with chocolate)

Make the Chantilly-mascarpone cream.

Slit the vanilla bean in two lengthwise and scrape the seeds out. Combine the vanilla seeds and all the other ingredients in the bowl of a stand mixer fitted with a whisk. Whisk until the mixture holds firm peaks. Chill.

Prepare the Polignac almonds.

Discard any broken or discolored almonds. Heat the water and dissolve the sugar in it to make a syrup; carefully stir the almonds into the syrup. Toast on a baking sheet at 320°F (160°C) until golden. When cooled, store in an airtight container until needed.

Prepare the spiced chocolate sauce.

Bring the milk and cream to a boil. Add the glucose, ginger, pepper, and cinnamon. Infuse for 5 minutes and strain over the two chocolates. Blend.

Assemble and finish the dish.

Slice the cooked caramel-coated pears and place them at the bottom of the glasses. Set a tuile with the pear-shaped ice cream upside down into a glass. Pipe small beads of Chantilly cream around the rims of the glasses. Dot with seven Polignac almonds. Place a poached pear in the center and stick a little gold leaf on the stem. Drizzle the pear with warm spiced chocolate sauce.

Chantilly-mascarpone cream
1 vanilla bean
1 cup (250 ml) heavy cream
Scant ¼ cup (50 ml) mascarpone
Scant ¼ cup (1 oz./30 g) confectioners' sugar

Polignac almonds
⅓ cup (1 oz./25 g) sliced almonds
1 teaspoon (4 ml) water
1 teaspoon (4 g) sugar

Spiced chocolate sauce
Scant ⅓ cup (75 ml) milk
¼ cup (62 ml) heavy cream
1 oz. (25 g) glucose syrup
1 teaspoon (4 g) fresh ginger, finely grated
1 grind of the pepper mill
Scant ½ teaspoon (1 g) ground cinnamon
2 oz. (65 g) Caraïbes couverture chocolate
(bittersweet, 66 percent cocoa)
⅔ oz. (20 g) Jivara couverture chocolate
(milk, 40 percent cocoa)

A little edible gold leaf for garnish

Apple Fritters ★

Serves 6
Preparation time: 45 minutes
Marinating time: 1 hour
Chilling time: 30 minutes
Cooking time: 25 minutes

Peel and core the apples with an apple-corer. Cut them into ½-inch (1-cm) thick slices. Arrange them flat in a dish, drizzle with the apple brandy, and sprinkle with sugar. Let marinate for at least 1 hour.

Make the fritter batter.
Place the flour, salt, and 1 ½ tablespoons (⅔ oz./20 g) of the sugar in a mixing bowl and whisk to combine. Make a well in the center. Pour in the egg yolks, oil, and a little beer. Whisk briskly for a few minutes then gradually pour in the remaining beer, whisking continuously until the batter is smooth. Chill the batter for at least 30 minutes.
Whip the egg whites. When they form soft peaks, stir in the remaining sugar with a whisk. Carefully fold the egg whites into the batter.

Fry the fritters.
Heat an oil bath to 350°F (180°C).
Using a fork or skewer, dip the apple slices into the batter. Carefully place each slice in the hot oil, taking care not to burn yourself. Cook them in small batches so as not to lower the temperature of the oil too much.
When the batter turns a nice golden color, turn the fritters over. Continue to cook for a few more minutes and then transfer to sheets of paper towel to drain. Place them quickly on a serving dish and drizzle with apricot coulis.

⬤ **Chef's note**
You can make fritters using other types of fruit and even vegetables.
If you use bananas, replace the apple brandy with white rum.

Technique
Deep-fat frying >> p. 214

Ingredients
4 firm apples
3 tablespoons (50 ml) Calvados
or other apple brandy
3 ½ tablespoons (1 ½ oz./40 g) sugar

Fritter batter
1 ⅔ cups (7 oz./200 g) flour
½ teaspoon (2 g) salt
⅓ cup (2 oz./60 g) sugar, divided
2 egg yolks
2 tablespoons (30 ml) oil
Scant 1 cup (220 ml) beer
3-4 egg whites (4 oz./120 g)

Oil for frying

½ cup (120 ml) apricot coulis
or lightly sweetened
apricot purée to serve

Ingredients

1 vanilla bean
5 tablespoons (3 oz./80 g) butter
1 pineapple
½ cup (3 ½ oz./100 g) light brown sugar
3 tablespoons (50 ml) brown rum
1 cup (9 oz./250 g) rum raisin ice cream to serve

Special equipment: a fine-pointed
   metal skewer or a trussing needle

Caramelized Pineapple Skewers ★

Serves 4
Preparation time: 20 minutes
Drying time: 1 hour
Cooking time: 1 hour 15 minutes

Preheat the oven to 100°F-120°F (30°C-40°C). Slit the vanilla bean in four lengthwise and place in the oven to dry out for 1 hour.

Place the butter in a bain-marie and heat gently to clarify. You can also clarify it in the microwave oven.

Peel the pineapple, ensuring that all the eyes are removed, and cut into 1-inch (3-cm) slices. Cut the slices into regular 1-inch (3-cm) cubes. Insert the skewer or needle through each cube to pierce a hole. Thread a piece of vanilla bean through three pineapple cubes and repeat with the other three pieces to make four skewers.

Heat a heavy-bottom pan and pour in the clarified butter. Sauté the skewers until lightly colored, turning them so that they are evenly colored, and sprinkling them regularly with the sugar. Pour in the rum, flambé, and remove from the heat.

Place each skewer in a dessert dish with a generous scoop of rum-raisin ice cream.

● Chef's notes

Victoria pineapple is one of the most popular despite its small size—it is particularly sweet. Other very sweet varieties include Hawaiian Gold and Super Sweet. The Smooth Cayenne variety is the most frequently found; these pineapples have a high acid content but their flavor is mellowed by their high sugar content.

If you use a large pineapple, you can make larger quantities of this dessert using more vanilla beans.

Pineapples are tropical fruit and will not ripen after being harvested. Since fully ripe pineapples are too fragile for long-distance transport, by far the best pineapples you will find are shipped by air. Look out for the label specifying how it was transported.

● Did you know?

Christopher Columbus gave Queen Isabella of Spain a gift of pineapples from Guadeloupe in the late fifteenth century. They are actually berries that grow around a central stalk.

Churros (*Chichis*) ★

Serves 4
Preparation time: 20 minutes
Cooking time: 20 minutes

Bring the water to a boil with the salt, 1 tablespoon (15 g) sugar, and the orange flower water. Pour in all the flour, remove from the heat, and beat energetically with a wooden spoon or spatula until smooth.
Heat an oil bath to 350°F (180°C). Spoon the batter into the cookie press and pipe tubes of different lengths directly into the hot oil.
Cook until they are golden. With a slotted spoon, remove the churros and transfer them to a tray lined with paper towel to drain. Immediately sprinkle with the remaining sugar and serve hot.

● **Chef's note**
Churros are excellent served with chocolate sauce (see p. 120).

 Technique
Deep-fat frying >> p. 214

Ingredients
¾ cup (200 ml) water
Scant ½ teaspoon (2 g) salt
¼ cup (2 oz./55 g) sugar, divided
Scant ½ teaspoon (2 ml) orange flower water
1 ⅔ cups (7 oz./200 g) flour
Oil for frying

Special equipment: a cookie press
or piping bag fitted with a large star tip

Ingredients

1 vanilla bean
1 cup (250 ml) milk
6 egg yolks
⅓ cup (2 ½ oz./75 g) sugar
1 cup (250 ml) heavy cream
Scant ½ cup (3 oz./80 g)
   light brown sugar

Crème Brûlée

Serves 5

Preparation time: 15 minutes
Chilling time: 2 hours
Cooking time: 40 minutes

Slit the vanilla bean in two lengthwise and scrape the seeds into the milk.
Beat the egg yolks with the sugar until thick and pale. Pour the milk and
cream into the egg yolk and sugar mixture, stirring until smooth.
Cover with plastic wrap and chill for 2 hours to develop the flavor
Strain through a fine-mesh sieve and fill five ramekins.
Preheat the oven to 200°F–210°F (90°C–100°C), and bake for 35 to 40 minutes,
until just set. Let cool and sprinkle with light brown sugar. Caramelize the
sugar with a kitchen torch or under the broiler for 2 to 3 minutes, watching
carefully.

Technique
Baked creams >> p. 92

Hot desserts

Crêpes Suzette-Style ★

Serves 8
Preparation time: 20 minutes
Chilling time: 30 minutes
Cooking time: 30 minutes

Prepare the crêpe batter.
Sift the flour and salt into a mixing bowl. Break the eggs, one by one, into the dry ingredients, mixing them in thoroughly each time. Beat in a little of the milk. Then pour in the remaining milk and beat in briskly until the batter is smooth and liquid. Stir in the vanilla extract. Strain through a fine-mesh sieve. Stir in the melted butter.
Chill for 30 minutes.

Make the crêpes.
Heat a crêpe pan over high heat with a drop of neutral oil and cook 16 crêpes, turning them over when the edges begin to brown.

Prepare the Suzette-style butter.
In a small, heavy-bottom saucepan, make a dry caramel with the sugar (see p. 467). When it is reddish (330°F/165°C), stir in 1 tablespoon (20 g) butter, and gradually pour in the orange juice, stirring constantly, to stop the caramelization process. Stir in the orange zest. Bring to a gentle boil and reduce over low to medium heat until thickened. Stir in the Grand Marnier and reduce slightly again. Remove from the heat and whip in the remaining butter. Keep warm.

Finish the dish.
Fold the crêpes into four and place them, four at a time if possible, in a gently heated skillet. Pour in the Suzette-style butter to soak them. Turn the crêpes over and repeat the operation. Serve immediately.

Techniques
Crêpe batter >> p. 40
Suzette-style fruit butter >> p. 121

Ingredients

Crêpe batter
2 cups (9 oz./250 g) flour
½ teaspoon (2 g) salt
3 small eggs (5 oz./150 g)
2 cups (500 ml) milk,
room temperature
½ teaspoon (2 ml) vanilla extract
3 tablespoons (1 ½ oz./40 g) butter,
melted until browned
(*beurre noisette*)
A little neutral oil for frying

Suzette-style butter
⅓ cup (2 oz./60 g) sugar
5 tablespoons (2 ½ oz./70 g)
butter, divided
Scant ½ cup (100 ml) freshly
squeezed orange juice
Finely grated zest of ½ orange
3 tablespoons (40 ml) Grand Marnier
or other orange liqueur

Berry Crumble ★

Serves 5
Preparation time: 10 minutes
Cooking time: 20 minutes

Preheat the oven to 350°F (180°C).
Sift the flour and combine with the sugar and ground almonds.
Working with your hands, rub the butter into the dry ingredients until the texture is sandy.
Butter an ovenproof dish and spread the mixed berries evenly at the bottom.
Sprinkle the crumble mixture over, ensuring that it is around ¾ inch (1.5 cm) thick all over.
Bake for about 20 minutes, until the top is lightly browned.

● Chef's note
Crumble is very good served warm with a scoop of vanilla ice cream or a red berry sorbet. Choose seasonal fruits whenever possible for best results, but avoid any that are too juicy, particularly citrus fruits.

Ingredients
1 cup (4 oz./120 g) flour
Scant ⅔ cup (4 oz./120 g) sugar
Scant ½ cup (1 ½ oz./40 g) ground almonds
1 stick (4 oz./120 g) butter, room temperature
3 oz. (80 g) black currants, destalked
3 oz. (80 g) mulberries
3 oz. (80 g) red currants, destalked
3 oz. (80 g) raspberries
3 oz. (80 g) blueberries

Ingredients
4 pink grapefruit

Sabayon
5-6 egg yolks (3 ½ oz./100 g)
Scant ½ cup (100 ml) hard apple cider,
 rosé if possible
½ cup (3 ½ oz./100 g) sugar

Techniques
Sabayon sauce >> p. 123
 Cutting citrus segments >> p. 130

Grapefruit Gratin
with Hard Apple Cider ★

Serves 4
Preparation time: 20 minutes
Cooking time: 10 minutes

Carefully peel the grapefruit, removing all the white pith. Remove the segments from between the membranes (see p. 130).

Prepare the sabayon.
Place the egg yolks in a bain-marie and pour in the hard apple cider and the sugar. (Depending on the sweetness of the cider, you can reduce the quantity of sugar.) Whip the mixture until doubled in volume and a thermometer registers about 150°F (65°C), about 5-7 minutes. Do not let it come into contact with direct heat as the yolks might coagulate and form small yellow specks.

Assemble and finish.
Set the oven to broil.
Arrange the grapefruit segments in an ovenproof dish. Pour the sabayon over and bake until the top begins to brown in places.

● **Chef's note**
You can replace the hard cider with a sweet wine. The sweeter the wine, the less sugar you will need.

Apple Tarts ★★

Serves 6
Preparation time: 3 hours 30 minutes
Chilling time: 3 hours
Cooking time: 20 minutes

Prepare the puff pastry.
Make puff pastry following the method on page 366.
Roll out to a thickness of just under ⅛ inch (2 mm), cut out six 5-inch (12-cm) circles, and carefully return the dough to the refrigerator for 1 hour.

Assemble and bake.
Preheat the oven to 375°F (190°C).
Peel, core, and quarter the apples and finely slice. Arrange on the pastry circles, overlapping closely, in a spiral. Sprinkle with sugar so that they color nicely when baked. If you wish, you can baste them lightly with a beaten egg for an even more attractive result.
Bake for 20 minutes, until lightly browned.

Prepare the caramel sauce with salted butter.
Make a dry caramel with the sugar (see p. 467). While it is cooking, heat the cream. The caramel should be only lightly colored. Stir the butter in and gradually pour in the cream, stirring constantly. The caramel will harden a little as you add the cream, so continue to stir until it comes to a boil again. Remove from the heat and stir in the fleur de sel.

Prepare the vanilla-cinnamon ice cream.
Make a pouring custard (see technique p. 91), substituting the cream for the milk. Add the cinnamon stick to the mixture as it cooks. When the temperature reaches 185°F (85°C), or the mixture coats the back of a spoon, immediately remove from the heat. Strain through a fine-mesh sieve and process in an ice-cream maker. Freeze.

Finish the dish.
Place a tart on each plate with a scoop of ice cream. Drizzle with the salted butter caramel sauce.

Ingredients

Puff pastry
1 ⅔ cups (7 oz./200 g) all-purpose flour
Scant teaspoon (4 g) salt
Scant ½ cup (100 ml) water
1 ¼ sticks (5 oz./150 g) butter
or margarine, room temperature

Filling
10 oz. (300 g) apples
¼ cup (2 oz./50 g) sugar
1 egg, beaten (optional)

Caramel sauce with salted butter
⅔ cup (4 ½ oz./125 g) sugar
½ cup (125 ml) heavy cream
2 teaspoons (10 g) salted butter
1 small pinch fleur de sel
or other flaky salt

Vanilla-cinnamon ice cream
1 vanilla bean
Scant ½ cup (100 ml) heavy cream
6-7 egg yolks (4 oz./120 g)
½ cup (3 ½ oz./100 g) sugar
1 stick cinnamon

Techniques
Puff pastry >> p. 24
Pouring custard (crème anglaise) >> p. 91
Caramel sauce with salted butter >> p. 119

Molten Chocolate Cakes ★

Serves 6
Preparation time: 20 minutes
Chilling time: 2 hours
Cooking time: 15 minutes

Melt the chocolate with the butter in a bain-marie over simmering water.
Combine the eggs and both sugars in a mixing bowl. Place in a bain-marie
at 140°F (60°C) and whisk energetically until the mixture reaches the ribbon
stage, thick and creamy. Take off the heat, then sift the flour and baking
powder together and fold gently into the mixture until just combined.
Incorporate the melted chocolate and butter and mix carefully.
Chill for 2 hours.
Preheat the oven to 340°F (170°C).
Butter and lightly flour the cake molds.
Melt the white chocolate and cocoa butter over gently simmering water in a
bain-marie. Divide evenly between six small molds and let set.
Fill the cake molds to one-third with the chocolate batter. Place a white
chocolate heart in each one and pour in the remaining batter to two-thirds
of the depth.
Bake for about 15 minutes. The tops must be cooked, but the center should
be melting; a cake tester should come out showing melted chocolate. Serve
immediately.

● Chef's notes
*Molten cakes are delicious served with custard, which you can flavor as you like
or leave plain.*
Chilling the batter ensures that the core will be molten when the cakes are baked.

Technique
Genoese sponge >> p. 76

Ingredients
10 oz. (300 g) chocolate, 70 percent cocoa
2 ¼ sticks (9 oz./250 g) butter
5 eggs
3 ½ tablespoons (1 ½ oz./40 g) sugar
Scant ½ cup (3 oz./80 g) light brown sugar
¾ cup plus 3 tablespoons (3 ½ oz./110 g) flour
Scant 1 teaspoon (3 g) baking powder
3 oz. (100 g) white chocolate
1 oz. (25 g) cocoa butter
(or unsalted butter)
2 teaspoons (10 g) butter and
1 tablespoon (10 g) flour for the molds

Special equipment: six small molds
for the white chocolate centers, heart-shaped
if possible, and six cake molds

Ingredients

Raspberry coulis

4 oz. (125 g) raspberries
Juice of ½ lemon
⅔ cup (3 oz./80 g) confectioners' sugar

Fruit filling

16 vine or flat peaches
Juice of 1 lemon
2 vanilla beans
½ cup (3 ½ oz./100 g) sugar
5 tablespoons (3 oz./80 g) butter
1 combava (kaffir lime)
Egg white to seal the parcels (optional)

Peaches Papillote ★

Serves 8
Preparation time: 30 minutes
Cooking time: 10 minutes

Prepare the raspberry coulis.
Process the raspberries with the lemon juice. Stir in the sugar and strain through a fine-mesh sieve. Cover the bowl with plastic wrap.

Prepare the filling.
Preheat the oven to 320°F-340°F (160°C-170°C).
Peel the peaches: Dip them briefly in boiling water and immediately cool under cold water. Remove the skins. Cut into quarters and remove the pits. Coat the quarters with lemon juice so they do not brown.
Cut eight rectangles of parchment paper measuring 10 by 12 inches (25 by 30 cm) to make the papillotes (parcels). Arrange eight peach quarters in the center of each sheet. Slit the vanilla beans in two lengthwise and scrape the seeds out. Sprinkle the peaches with the vanilla seeds and cut the vanilla bean halves in two, placing a piece of vanilla bean in each papillote.
Sprinkle the peaches with the sugar and dot with the butter.
Finely grate a little combava zest over the fruit.
Fold the parchment paper over and twist closed. Press the folds down firmly and ensure that each papillote is closed with paper clips at the corners. (To seal, lightly beat an egg white and brush the outside edges of the parcels).
Bake for about 10 minutes. When the parcels begin to swell, let them cook for 4 to 5 minutes more. If the paper begins to brown, turn the oven down slightly. The fruit should remain firm and not stew.
As soon as the parcels are ready, serve them, accompanied by the coulis.

⬤ **Chef's note**
This hot dessert contrasts delightfully with a scoop of sorbet.

 Techniques
Fruit coulis ›› p. 128
Peeling fruit ›› p. 216
Cooking en papillote (in parcels) ›› p. 217

Orange Liqueur Soufflé ★

Serves 6
Preparation time: 1 hour 15 minutes
Cooking time: 20 minutes

Prepare the pastry cream.
Slit the vanilla bean lengthwise and scrape the seeds into the milk. Pour the milk into a saucepan, add the vanilla bean, and begin heating. In a mixing bowl, briskly whisk the egg yolks, sugar, and cornstarch until pale and thick. When the milk is simmering, pour half of it over the egg yolk mixture, beating continuously. Return the mixture to the saucepan with the remaining milk and bring to a boil, stirring continuously. Let simmer for 2 to 3 minutes, still stirring. Stir in the Cointreau. Remove the vanilla bean. Transfer to a mixing bowl, cover with plastic wrap flush with the surface, and immediately place in the refrigerator to chill.

Prepare the ladyfingers.
Preheat the oven to 400°F (200°C). Whisk the egg whites with the sugar until firm and shiny. Lightly beat the egg yolks and, with a flexible spatula, fold them carefully into the meringue, taking care not to deflate it. Sift the flour and cornstarch together and fold in carefully. Spoon the batter into a piping bag fitted with a plain tip and pipe out ladyfingers approx. 2 ½ inches (7-8 cm) long. Sprinkle lightly with confectioners' sugar, wait 5 minutes, and sprinkle again. Bake for about 10 to 15 minutes, but do not let them color. Let cool on a cooling rack.

Make the soaking syrup.
Heat the water and sugar until the sugar is dissolved. Let cool and add the Cointreau.

Prepare the soufflé mixture.
Preheat the oven to 350°F (180°C) and set a baking sheet in the middle of the oven to heat. Brush the soufflé molds with melted butter and sprinkle with sugar. Lightly beat the egg yolks and stir them into the pastry cream. Whip the egg whites until they hold soft peaks and stir in the sugar. Fold into the pastry cream taking care not to deflate the mixture.

Assemble the soufflé.
Moisten the ladyfingers with the syrup. Half-fill the molds with the soufflé mixture. Place a layer of ladyfingers over this and then fill to the top with the mixture. Smooth with a spatula. With your thumb, wipe away a fraction of an inch (0.5 cm) of the mixture from around the rim. This helps the soufflé rise vertically. Place the molds on the heated baking sheet and bake for about 15 minutes, until nicely risen and slightly browned on the top.
Immediately dust with confectioners' sugar and bring to the table.

● Chef's note
To bake a soufflé, it's best to use conventional rather than fan heat, which might cause the soufflé to rise at an angle.

Ingredients

Pastry cream
¼ vanilla bean
1 cup (250 ml) milk
2-3 egg yolks (1 ½ oz./40 g)
¼ cup (2 oz./50 g) sugar
2 ½ tablespoons (1 oz./25 g) cornstarch
2 teaspoons (10 ml) Cointreau
or other orange liqueur

Ladyfingers
3 eggs, separated
Scant ½ cup (3 oz./80 g) sugar
½ cup (2 oz./65 g) flour
1 ½ tablespoons (½ oz./15 g) cornstarch
Confectioners' sugar for sprinkling

Soaking syrup
¼ cup (60 ml) water
2 ½ tablespoons (1 oz./30 g) sugar
2 tablespoons (30 ml) Cointreau
or other orange liqueur

Soufflé mixture
2 egg yolks
3-4 egg whites (4 oz./120 g)
½ cup (3 ½ oz./100 g) sugar
2 tablespoons (1 oz./25 g) butter, melted,
and 1 ½ tablespoons sugar for the molds

Six 3-inch (7-cm) molds

Techniques
Ladyfingers >> p. 73
Pastry cream >> p. 99
Moistening sponge layers >> p. 133
French meringue >> p. 176
Soufflés >> p. 198

Ingredients

Traou mad
1 ½ sticks (6 oz./170 g) salted butter, room temperature
¾ cup (5 oz./150 g) sugar
5-6 egg yolks (3 oz./100 g)
2 cups (9 oz./250 g) flour
2 teaspoons (8 g) baking powder

Topping
1 ¾ lb. (800 g) apples
Juice of 1 lemon
3 tablespoons (2 oz./50 g) salted butter
¼ cup (2 oz./50 g) sugar
Scant ½ cup (100 ml) hard apple cider, rosé if possible

Salted butter caramel mousse
⅔ cup (4 ½ oz./125 g) sugar
⅓ cup (80 ml) heavy cream
1 tablespoon (20 g) butter, room temperature
1 teaspoon (3 g) fleur de sel
1 cup (250 ml) whipping cream

Spun sugar decoration
1 cup (7 oz./200 g) sugar
¼ cup (60 ml) water
1 tablespoon (20 g) glucose syrup

Eight 3-inch (8-cm) dessert rings

Gourmet Breton Traou Mad ★★

Serves 8
Preparation time: 45 minutes
Cooking time: 30 minutes

Prepare the traou mad.
Preheat the oven to 350°F (180°C). Line a baking sheet with parchment paper. In a stand mixer fitted with the paddle beater, or with an electric beater or whisk, cream the butter with the sugar until very soft. Stir in the egg yolks, scraping down the sides, until fully incorporated. Sift the flour and baking powder together and work in with your fingertips. The dough will now have a grainy texture.
Roll the dough to a thickness of ⅕ inch (5 mm). With a 3-inch (8-cm) cookie cutter, cut out eight disks. Place the disks of dough in pastry rings of the same diameter and bake for 17 minutes, until golden. Transfer to a rack and let cool.

Prepare the topping.
Peel the apples and rub them with lemon juice. Cut them into quarters. In a heavy-bottom pan, heat the butter and sauté the quarters, sprinkling them with the sugar, until lightly browned. They should be cooked through but not too soft. Remove the apple quarters and deglaze the pan with the hard cider. Let the juices reduce until thickened.

Make the salted butter caramel mousse.
In a small heavy-bottom saucepan, heat the sugar until it is a light caramel color. Immediately remove from the heat, stir in the heavy cream, and whip in the butter. Stir in the fleur de sel and let cool. Whip the whipping cream until it forms soft peaks. Carefully fold it into the caramel and chill.

Prepare the spun sugar.
Make a syrup with the sugar, water, and glucose syrup and cook to 310°F-330°F (155°C-165°C), when it should be a light yellow color. Remove from the heat and let cool a little. With a fork, make the spun sugar, shaking it over a metal bar. Squeeze the threads into a ball and place on parchment paper.

Assemble and decorate.
Using the dessert rings, place the traou mad bases on the plates. Arrange the apple quarters over them. Spoon the mousse into a piping bag, and just before serving, pipe dots over the apples. Remove the dessert rings and drizzle a little reduced juice over the top. Decorate with the spun sugar.

● Chef's note
Traou mad, traditionally a buttery cookie, is a Breton specialty from Pont-Aven. The name means "good thing." Here we revisit it, adding two other Breton specialties—apples and salted caramel.

 Techniques
Traou mad ›› p. 58
Chocolate mousse ›› p. 106
Sugar decorations ›› p. 134

Kouign Amman,
a specialty of Brittany ★ ★

Serves 8
Preparation time: 40 minutes
Chilling time: 1 hour 50 minutes
Cooking time: 20 minutes

Prepare the dough.
Place the flour, water, and yeast in a food processor fitted with a dough hook. Knead for 2 minutes at low speed, and let rest for 30 minutes at room temperature, covered with a clean cloth.
Knead at medium speed until the dough is smooth and elastic, 15-20 minutes altogether. You may need to add a little more warm water. The dough must be firm; it should not stick to your fingers and should pull away from the sides of the bowl. After 10 minutes, add the salt and knead for an additional 5 minutes. Transfer the dough to a bowl and cover with a clean cloth. Let rise for 35 to 40 minutes at room temperature, until doubled in volume. Punch down, transfer to a baking sheet, cover with plastic wrap, and chill for at least 30 minutes.

Finish and bake.
Soften the two types of butter together. Roll the dough out, as you would for puff pastry (see technique p. 26) and place the butter in the center of the cross-shaped dough. Sprinkle the work surface with the sugar, make one simple turn, chill for 20 minutes, and repeat the procedure twice.
Roll the dough into a rectangle just under ½ inch (1 cm) thick and 8 inches (20 cm) wide. Cut out 3-inch (8-cm) disks and place them in the silicone molds. Let the dough rise for 30 to 40 minutes in a warm, draft-free place.
Preheat the oven to 400°F (200°C) and bake for about 20 minutes, until the dough turns a caramel color. Remove from the oven and turn the cakes over in the molds so that they can absorb the caramel on both sides.
Kouign amman is best served warm.

● **Chef's notes**
Kouign amman (pronounced kween-a-mun) originated in the southern part of the region of Brittany. In Breton, the name means "butter cake."

Techniques
Puff pastry >> p. 24
Sandwich loaf dough >> p. 49

Ingredients
Basic dough
2 cups (9 oz./250 g) flour
Minimum ⅔ cup (150 ml) water
at 77°F-83°F (25°C-30°C)
¼ cake (0.15 oz./5 g) fresh yeast
1 teaspoon (5 g) salt

Sugar-butter finish
7 tablespoons (3 ½ oz./100 g) butter,
room temperature
7 tablespoons (3 ½ oz./100 g)
salted butter, room temperature
1 cup (7 oz./200 g) sugar

Eight 3-inch (8-cm) silicone molds,
measuring about 1 inch (2-3 cm) deep

Cold desserts

Alexis Bouillet

Junior World Pastry Champion,
Professional Olympiads 2011

As an apprentice, I began working in luxury hotels. In the kitchens, we were given two key phrases: "beautiful" and "good, very good." The finest basic ingredients are a prerequisite in this universe, together with know-how, but it's even more important to love the work and be passionate about it. I have always liked simple things. Here, however, without being simplistic, I've revisited a tartlet and made it sexier, with familiar but powerful flavors: vanilla, for its mildness and unique taste, and creamy caramel, which brings back memories of my childhood. When I was a child, I would pick berries in my grandmother's garden, and so the idea of using raspberries in this "Red Power" dessert came naturally to me—they have a tangy, strong character, and work perfectly with vanilla. I love artistic presentations, and so I've showcased the two petits fours in an artistic piece made of sugar. The themes are wild nature and its flowers. The creation here results, in part, from the work I undertook at the international competition at which I won the title of Junior World Pastry Champion.

Vanilla and Caramel Tartlets and "Red Power" Petits Fours

Prepare the vanilla-scented pastry shell.
Slit the vanilla bean and scrape the seeds out. Make an emulsion with the butter, confectioners' sugar, and vanilla seeds. Add the salt and flour. Incorporate the egg white. Pipe 1 ¼-inch (3 ½-cm) circles and bake at 350°F (180°C) for 14 minutes.

Prepare the vanilla-mascarpone cream.
Soften the gelatin in a little cold water. Combine the milk, cream, egg yolk, sugar, and vanilla seeds to make a pouring custard. Cook to 185°F (85°C). Squeeze the water from the gelatin and incorporate it into the custard. Pour the custard over the mascarpone, combine, and chill for at least 2 hours. Whip the mixture until firm and pipe into hemispherical silicone 1-inch (2.5-cm) molds. Place in the freezer.

Prepare the semi-liquid caramel.
Heat the cream, vanilla seeds, and salt. Make a light caramel with the sugar. Stir the butter into the sugar to stop the caramelization process and incorporate the cream mixture thoroughly. Process with an immersion blender and let cool.

Make the caramel glaze.
Soften the gelatin in a little cold water. Using the dry method, make a light caramel with the sugar. Stir in the butter to stop the caramelization process. Stir in the cream and bring to a boil. Dissolve the potato starch in the water and stir it into the caramel mixture. Squeeze the water from the gelatin, stir it in, and blend the mixture.

Assemble the tartlets.
Pipe the semi-liquid caramel onto the pastry shells. Turn the half-spheres of vanilla-mascarpone cream out of the molds and glaze them with the caramel glaze heated to 77°F (25°C). Decorate with a small piece of edible gold leaf and chopped almonds.

To prepare the "Red Power" petits fours, first make a madeleine sponge.
Whisk the eggs, sugar, and vanilla together until thick and pale. Sift the flour with the baking powder and incorporate. Stir in the hot butter and milk. Pipe the mixture into 1 ¾-inch (4-cm) silicone molds. Bake at 350°F (175°C) in two stages, 4 minutes each time. Turn out of the molds and trim with a 1 ¼-inch (3-cm) diameter cutter.

Prepare the stewed raspberries.
Heat the raspberry purée and invert sugar to 113°F (45°C). Combine the sugar and pectin and pour the mixture into the purée. Bring to a boil for 15 seconds. Half-fill 1-inch (2.5-cm) diameter flexible spherical molds. Place in the refrigerator.

Makes 40 petits fours
Preparation time: 2 hours
Cooking time: 30 minutes
Chilling time: 2 hours

Ingredients

Vanilla-scented pastry shell
1 vanilla bean
1 ½ sticks (6 ½ oz./184 g) butter
Generous ½ cup (2 ½ oz./70 g) confectioners' sugar
1 pinch salt
1 cup plus 2 tablespoons (4 ½ oz./146 g) flour
1 ½ oz. (38 g) egg white

Vanilla-mascarpone cream
1 sheet (2 g) gelatin
4 tablespoons plus 1 teaspoon (64 ml) milk
4 tablespoons plus 1 teaspoon (64 ml) heavy cream
1 oz. (25 g) egg yolk
2 teaspoons (10 g) sugar
1/10 oz. (3 g) vanilla seeds
½ cup (4 oz./120 g) mascarpone

Semi-liquid caramel
Scant ⅓ cup (70 ml) heavy cream
1/8 oz. (4 g) vanilla seeds
1 pinch salt
3 tablespoons (1 ¼ oz./35 g) sugar
1 tablespoon (20 g) butter

Caramel glaze
7 ½ sheets (15 g) gelatin
3 cups (1 ¼ lb./574 g) sugar
2 tablespoon (24 g) butter
1 cup plus scant 1 cup (482 ml) heavy cream
¼ cup (1 ½ oz./42 g) potato starch
Scant ⅓ cup (70 ml) water

For decoration
Edible gold leaf
Chopped almonds

Madeleine sponge
2 eggs (3 ½ oz./100 g)
Scant ½ cup (3 oz./92 g) sugar
⅓ oz. (8 g) vanilla seeds
⅔ cup (3 oz./82 g) flour
¾ teaspoon (3 g) baking powder
6 tablespoons (3 oz./90 g) butter, melted and still hot
2 tablespoons plus 1 teaspoon (34 ml) milk

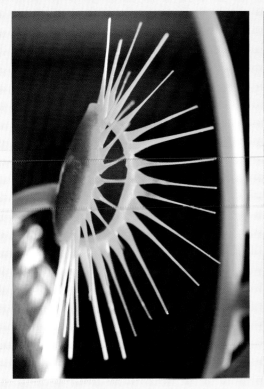

Make the raspberry Bavarian cream.

Soften the gelatin in a little cold water. Combine the milk, 3 tablespoons heavy cream, egg yolk, and sugar to make a pouring custard. Cook to 185°F (85°C). Squeeze the water from the gelatin sheets and incorporate into the custard. Stir in the raspberry purée and chill to 77°F (25°C). Whip the remaining 5 tablespoons heavy cream until it holds soft peaks and fold it into the raspberry mixture. Pour the Bavarian cream over the stewed raspberries, filling the molds, and freeze.

Prepare the gelled vanilla Chantilly cream.

Soften the gelatin in a little cold water. Combine ¾ cup (200 ml) of the cream with the mascarpone, vanilla, and sugar. Squeeze the water from the gelatin. Heat the remaining cream with the gelatin and incorporate into the cream-mascarpone mixture. Process with an immersion blender and chill for at least 2 hours.

Assemble the "Red Power" petits fours.

Turn the frozen spheres out of the molds. Whip the vanilla Chantilly cream and pipe it with a Saint-Honoré tip, for example, to make flame-shapes over the spheres, so that they look like flowers. Spray with "red velvet" and place on the madeleine sponge. Decorate with a few drops of red glaze.

Stewed raspberries
9 oz. (262 g) raspberry purée
1 ¼ oz. (36 g) invert sugar
3 tablespoons (1 ¼ oz./36 g) sugar
⅛ oz. (4 g) pectin NH

Raspberry Bavarian cream
1 ½ sheets (3 g) gelatin
3 tablespoons (45 ml) milk
3 tablespoons (45 ml) plus 5 tablespoons (72 ml) heavy cream
1 egg yolk (⅔ oz./18 g)
½ tablespoon (7 g) sugar
3 ½ oz. (96 g) raspberry purée

Gelled vanilla Chantilly cream
½ sheet (1 g) gelatin
1 cup (250 ml) heavy cream, divided
Scant ¼ cup (2 oz./50 g) mascarpone
⅒ oz. (4 g) vanilla bean
Scant ⅓ cup (2 ¼ oz./65 g) sugar

For decoration
Cocoa butter "Red Velvet" spray
Red glaze

Ingredients

Crêpe batter
1 cup (4 oz./125 g) flour
½ teaspoon (2 g) salt
1 ¾ tablespoon (20 g) sugar
1 egg plus 1 egg yolk (3 oz./75 g)
1 cup (250 ml) milk, warmed
½ teaspoon (2 ml) vanilla extract
1 tablespoon (20 g) butter, melted until brown
A little oil for frying

Diplomat cream
2 ½ sheets (5 g) gelatin
¼ vanilla bean
1 cup (250 ml) milk
2 egg yolks (1 ½ oz./40 g)
Scant ⅓ cup (2 ½ oz./65 g) sugar
3 tablespoons (1 oz./30 g) cornstarch
1 cup (250 ml) heavy cream

Filling
2 mangoes
3 tablespoons (1 ½ oz./40 g) butter
3 ½ tablespoons (1 ½ oz./40 g) light brown sugar
1 tablespoon (20 ml) white rum
1 passion fruit

Exotic Fruit Pouches ★

Serves 8
Preparation time: 1 hour 15 minutes
Chilling time: 30 minutes
Cooking time: 30 minutes

Prepare the crêpe batter.
Sift the flour into a mixing bowl and stir in the salt and sugar. Make a well in the center. Pour in the eggs and with a whisk, energetically mix them into the dry ingredients, adding a little warm milk. Pour in the remaining milk and whisk until the batter is smooth and liquid. Stir in the vanilla extract and browned butter and chill for 30 minutes.
In a 7-inch (18-cm) crêpe pan, heat a drop of oil over high heat and cook the crêpes, turning them over when the edges begin to brown. Repeat to make eight crêpes.

Make the Diplomat cream.
Soften the gelatin sheets in a bowl of cold water.
Slit the vanilla bean in two lengthwise and scrape the seeds into the milk. In a heavy-bottom saucepan, heat the milk with the vanilla seeds and bean. Whip the egg yolks, sugar, and cornstarch until the mixture is pale and thick. When the milk is simmering, gradually pour half over the egg and sugar mixture, whipping continuously. Return the mixture to the saucepan and stir continuously until it simmers. Let simmer 2-3 minutes, still stirring. Remove the vanilla bean.
Remove from the heat. Squeeze the water from the gelatin sheets and whisk them into the custard cream. Transfer to a mixing bowl, cover with plastic wrap flush with the surface (this will prevent a skin from forming) and chill to about 60°F (15°C). Do not leave it too long; it must not set before the whipped cream is incorporated. With an electric beater, whip the heavy cream until it forms firm peaks.
Smooth the chilled custard cream with a flexible spatula and carefully fold in the whipped cream. Return to the refrigerator.

Prepare the filling.
Peel the mangoes and cut them into small cubes (dice). Heat the butter in a skillet and quickly color the diced mangoes, sprinkling them with sugar so that they caramelize. Flambé with the rum and let cool.

Assemble the dish.
Place a crêpe on a large plate. Spoon the Diplomat cream into a piping bag and pipe a generous serving into the center of the crêpe. Arrange diced mangoes over the cream and top with a little passion fruit pulp. Lift the edges of the crêpe toward the center and fasten with a toothpick to form a pouch. Serve with any remaining fruit.

Techniques
Crêpe batter >> p. 40
Diplomat cream >> p. 103

Strawberry Bubble ★ ★ ★

Serves 8
Preparation time: 1 hour 30 minutes
Cooking time: 30 minutes

Prepare the blown sugar bubbles.
Caution: this technique involves handling sugar at a very high temperature. Take every precaution possible and be extremely careful.
In a heavy-bottom saucepan, heat all the ingredients to 320°F (160°C). Pour onto a silicone mat and wait for the mixture to cool slightly. Being careful not to burn yourself, begin pooling it toward the center so that it cools evenly. When the temperature has cooled to 165°F-175°F (75°C-80°C), place it under an infrared lamp. Take a piece of the cooked sugar and fit it snugly at the end of a tube; there should not be any gaps. Working in front of a fan, gradually blow into the tube, molding the bubble as you blow, until it reaches the desired size. With a heated knife, cut the bubble from the tube. The heat melts the sugar and this makes the opening. This technique takes considerable practice but will never fail to impress once mastered.

Make the strawberry mousse.
Soften the gelatin sheets in a bowl of cold water.
Heat one-third of the strawberry purée with the sugar. Remove from the heat. Squeeze the water out of the gelatin sheets and stir them into the heated mixture until completely dissolved. Incorporate the remaining strawberry purée to cool the mixture. The temperature should be between 70°F and 80°F (20°C-25°C). Whip the cream until it forms soft peaks. With a whisk, carefully fold it into the purée until completely combined. Chill, but do not let set until it has been piped into the containers.

Prepare the red currant jelly.
Soften the gelatin sheets in a bowl of cold water. Heat the puréed red currants with the sugar. Squeeze the water out of the gelatin sheets and stir them into the heated mixture until completely dissolved.

Assemble the dish.
Spoon the strawberry mousse into a piping bag and fill the sugar globes, or glasses (see chef's note), to three-quarters. Top with a small piece of cookie or sponge and set a half-strawberry on it. This prevents the fruit from sinking into the mousse. Make small mounds of light brown sugar on each plate to hold the sugar globes in place. Garnish with the bunches of red currants and drizzle with the red currant jelly.

● Chef's note
You can simplify this recipe considerably by using clear glass containers instead of the sugar globes.

Techniques
Fruit mousse >> p. 109
Blown sugar swan >> p. 168
Bubble sugar >> p. 174

Ingredients

Blown sugar
2 ½ cups (1 lb./500 g) sugar
⅔ cup (150 ml) water
7 oz. (200 g) glucose syrup
A few drops of pink food coloring

Strawberry mousse
4 sheets (8 g) gelatin
10 oz. (300 g) puréed strawberries
¼ cup (2 oz./50 g) sugar
Scant ½ cup (100 g) heavy cream, well chilled

Red currant jelly
2 sheets (4 g) gelatin
9 oz. (250 g) puréed red currants
¼ cup (2 oz./50 g) sugar, depending on the sourness of the berries

For garnish and serving
8 cookies of your choice, or 8 disks of sponge, cut to the size of the containers
1 cup (7 oz./200 g) light brown sugar
4 fresh strawberries, sliced in half
8 small bunches of red currants

Ingredients

Raspberry coulis
4 oz. (125 g) puréed raspberries
1 heaping tablespoon (15 g) sugar

Apricot coulis
5 ½ oz. (160 g) pitted apricots
1 heaping tablespoon (15 g) sugar
3 tablespoons (40 ml) water

Bubble glucose
¼ cup (3 oz./80 g) glucose syrup

Vanilla Bavarian cream
4 sheets (8 g) gelatin
1 vanilla bean
1 cup (250 ml) milk
4 egg yolks
⅔ cup (4 ½ oz./125 g) sugar
1 ⅔ cups (400 ml) heavy cream

Garnish
8 ladyfingers, cubed
Assorted fresh fruits

Techniques
Ladyfingers ›› p. 73
Egg-based Bavarian cream ›› p. 97
Bubble glucose ›› p. 138

Vanilla Bavarian Cream with Two Fruit Coulis ★

Serves 8
Preparation time: 45 minutes
Cooking time: 1 hour 30 minutes
Chilling time: 30 minutes

Make the raspberry coulis.
In a small saucepan, combine the ingredients and bring to a simmer over medium heat. Let simmer for 1 minute. Process with an immersion blender or with the blade knife in the food processor and strain through a fine-mesh sieve.

Make the apricot coulis.
In a small saucepan, combine the ingredients and bring to a simmer over medium heat. Let simmer for 10 minutes. Process with an immersion blender or with the blade knife in the food processor and strain through a fine-mesh sieve.

Prepare the bubble glucose.
Preheat the oven to 300°F (150°C).
With a metal spatula, spread thin ovals of glucose syrup over a silicone baking sheet. Bake for about 1 hour, depending on the size, until the glucose rises and forms bubbles. When removed from the oven, the ovals must be transparent and retain their bubbles. If the bubbles disappear, return the baking sheet to the oven and let dry some more. If you add a few drops of alcohol-based food coloring to the crystal glucose, the effect will be even more attractive.

Prepare the vanilla Bavarian cream.
Soften the gelatin in a bowl of cold water. Slit the vanilla bean in two lengthwise and scrape the seeds into the milk. In a medium heavy-bottom saucepan, heat the milk with the vanilla bean. Beat the egg yolks with the sugar until thick and pale. When the milk is simmering, pour half of it over the egg yolk and sugar mixture, stirring constantly. Return the mixture to the saucepan and cook, stirring constantly and removing the saucepan from the heat from time to time, until it reaches 185°F (85°C) or coats the back of a spoon. (If the egg yolks are in constant contact with high heat, they may coagulate.) Strain the custard through a fine-mesh sieve and transfer to a mixing bowl. Squeeze the water from the gelatin sheets and stir into the custard until completely dissolved. Cool to about 70°F (20°C). (You can set the bowl over a larger one filled with cold water and ice cubes.) Whip the cream until it holds soft peaks. With a flexible spatula or whisk, gradually fold the whipped cream into the custard-gelatin mixture until it is smooth.

Assemble the dish.
Spoon the Bavarian cream into a piping bag and pipe into small shot glasses, alternating the layers with the two fruit coulis and adding cubes of ladyfingers. Garnish with fresh fruit of your choice and decorate with pieces of bubble glucose.

Nougat Blancmange with Pear Coulis ★

Serves 8
Preparation time: 15 minutes/Chilling time: 3 hours
Cooking time: 30 minutes

Make the blancmange base.
Soften the gelatin sheets in a bowl of cold water. Slit the vanilla bean in two lengthwise, scrape the seeds into the milk, and add the vanilla bean. In a heavy-bottom saucepan, heat the milk, sugar, and nougat paste until the paste dissolves. Simmer for 1 minute. Remove from the heat. Squeeze the water from the gelatin sheets and stir into the milk and nougat mixture until completely dissolved. Immediately pour into the molds and chill.

Prepare the pear coulis.
Peel the pears and rub them with lemon juice. Cut into small dice. In a saucepan over low heat, cook the fruit dice gently with the sugar until completely softened (about 30 minutes). Process until smooth.

Assemble the dish.
Turn out of the molds, garnish with pear chips, and drizzle with the coulis.

⬤ **Did you know?**
Blancmange was first made in the Middle Ages, when chicken breasts were used to make a white meat jelly, and almonds and honey to make a milk jelly.

Ingredients
Blancmange base
9 sheets (18 g) gelatin
1 vanilla bean
4 cups (1 liter) milk
Scant 1 cup (6 oz./180 g) sugar
3 oz. (80 g) white nougat paste
(see recipe p. 159, or store-bought)

Pear coulis
10 oz. (300 g) pears
1 tablespoon (15 ml) lemon juice
2 tablespoons (1 oz./25 g) sugar

Garnish
Pear chips (see p. 131)

Eight small molds

Techniques
Fruit coulis >> p. 128
Fruit chips >> p. 131

Ingredients

2 egg whites (2 oz./60 g)

⅓ cup (2 ½ oz./70 g) sugar

10 oz. (300 g) *fromage frais*
  or other cheese (see chef's note)

3 ½ oz. (100 g) blueberries, fresh,
  or lightly sautéed and cooled

Fromage Frais with Blueberries ★

Serves 4

Preparation time: 20 minutes

Chilling time: 1 hour

In a round-bottom mixing bowl, whisk the egg whites until they form soft peaks. Stir in the sugar and whisk until firm and shiny. Carefully fold the mixture into the cheese and stir in the blueberries. Spoon into glasses or small bowls and chill before serving

● Chef's notes

Substitute farmer's cheese or smoothed cottage cheese (blend cottage cheese until smooth) for fromage frais, a fresh cheese with a high moisture content often served as a dessert in France. Ricotta or low-fat cream cheese can also be substituted. Serve this dessert with baked petits fours or small cookies. Vary the fruit with the seasons.

Technique

French meringue >> p. 176

Ingredients

Blinis
1 cup (4 oz./125 g) flour
1 small pinch salt
1 egg yolk
1 cup (250 ml) milk, room temperature
2 egg whites (2 oz./60 g)
1 ¾ tablespoons (20 g) sugar
1 tablespoon (20 g) butter, melted
  until lightly browned
A little oil for frying

Diplomat cream
2 sheets (4 g) gelatin
¼ vanilla bean
½ cup (125 ml) milk
1 egg yolk
3 tablespoons (1 ¼ oz./35 g) sugar
1 ½ tablespoons (15 g) cornstarch
½ cup (125 ml) heavy cream

Garnish
5 oz. (150 g) mulberries
1 bunch verbena

Layered Blinis with Mulberries ★

Serves 8
Preparation time: 1 hour 15 minutes
Cooking time: 40 minutes

Make the blinis.
Sift the flour into a mixing bowl and stir in the salt. Add the egg yolk and whisk vigorously with a little of the milk. Pour in the remaining milk, whisking energetically until the batter is smooth and fluid. Strain through a fine-mesh sieve.
Whisk the egg whites and sugar to make a French meringue (see p. 176). Fold it carefully into the batter, taking care not to deflate the mixture. Stir in the browned butter. Add a drop of oil to a blini pan over high heat and cook 16 blinis. Alternatively, use a pastry ring placed in a pan. When they are lightly colored on both sides, transfer to a rack to cool.
If necessary, trim them with a cookie cutter so that they are nicely shaped.

Prepare the Diplomat cream.
Soften the gelatin sheets in a bowl of cold water.
Slit the vanilla bean lengthwise and scrape the seeds into the milk. In a heavy-bottom saucepan, heat the milk with the vanilla seeds and bean. Whip the egg yolk, sugar, and cornstarch until the mixture is pale and thick. When the milk is simmering, gradually pour half of it over the egg mixture, whisking continuously. If you wish to incorporate any flavorings, this is the moment, with the exception of alcohol which must be added to the cream once it has cooled. Return the mixture to the saucepan over the heat and stir continuously until it simmers. Let simmer for 2 to 3 minutes, still stirring.
Remove from the heat. Remove the vanilla bean. Squeeze the water from the gelatin sheets and whisk them into the custard cream.
Transfer to a mixing bowl, cover with plastic wrap flush with the surface (to prevent a skin from forming) and chill to about 60°F (15°C). Do not leave it too long; it must not set before the whipped cream is incorporated. With an electric beater, whip the heavy cream until it forms firm peaks. Smooth the chilled custard cream with a flexible spatula and carefully fold in the whipped cream.

Assemble the dish.
Drop a small spoonful of Diplomat cream into the center of the dessert plates. Place a blini over the cream.
Arrange the mulberries around the rim of the blini and in the center, leaving enough space for a small dollop of Diplomat cream between them. Pipe the cream between the mulberries. Cover with a second blini and garnish with mulberries and verbena leaves.

Techniques
Blini batter >> p. 41
Chantilly cream >> p. 94
Diplomat cream >> p. 103
French meringue >> p. 176

Tropical Fruit Carpaccio ★

Serves 5
Preparation time: 40 minutes
Chilling time: 1 hour plus overnight
Cooking time: 10 minutes

Peel the mango and pineapple. Cut each into very fine slices, under ⅛ inch (2 mm) thick, if possible using a meat slicer or mandolin, or else a knife with a fine blade.

Prepare the syrup.
Bring the water and sugar to a boil. Remove from the heat and add the hyssop and Szechuan pepper. Infuse for 1 hour.
Strain and bring to a boil again. Divide between two saucepans and carefully place the fruit slices in the syrup, the mango in one saucepan and the pineapple in the other. Let simmer for 2 to 3 minutes and remove from the heat.
Let cool and macerate overnight in the refrigerator.

Make the decorative syrup.
In a small, heavy-bottom saucepan, cook the balsamic vinegar with the sugar until thickened.

Finish the dish.
Cut the fruit slices into 1 ¾-inch (4-cm) squares and arrange them in a checkerboard pattern on flat plates. Garnish with hyssop leaves and a little Szechuan pepper. Drizzle with the balsamic vinegar syrup to make an attractive pattern.

● **Did you know?**
The first dish to bear the name "carpaccio" seems to date to the mid-twentieth century. Finely sliced raw beef was presented under this name in a Venetian restaurant, in honor of an exhibition devoted to the painter Vittore Carpaccio (1460–1526).

Technique
Macerating >> p. 215

Ingredients
1 mango, ripe but firm
1 pineapple

Syrup
3 cups (750 ml) water
1 ½ cups (10 oz./300 g) sugar
1 sprig hyssop
15 grains of Szechuan pepper

Decorative syrup
Scant ½ cup (100 ml) balsamic vinegar
¼ cup (2 oz./50 g) sugar

Garnish
A few hyssop leaves
A few grains of Szechuan pepper

Ingredients

Chestnut sponge

8 oz. (225 g) chestnut cream (*crème de marron*)
½ cup plus 1 tablespoon (4 oz./110 g) sugar
1 stick plus 1 tablespoon (4 ½ oz./135 g)
 butter, softened
2 eggs
2 tablespoons (25 ml) brown rum
¾ cup plus 2 tablespoons (3 ½ oz./100 g) flour
½ teaspoon (2 g) baking powder

Decorated chocolate disks

7 oz. (200 g) bittersweet chocolate

Chestnut cream panna cotta

1 ½ sheets (3 g) gelatin
½ vanilla bean
2 oz. (50 g) chestnut cream (*crème de marron*)
¼ cup (2 oz./50 g) sugar
1 cup (250 ml) heavy cream

Cocoa nibs for garnish

Eight 4-inch (10-cm) pastry rings and eight
 1 ¾-inch (4-cm) diameter silicone molds,
 measuring 2 inches (5 cm) deep
Special equipment: transfer sheet for chocolate

Chestnut Sponge with Chestnut Cream Panna Cotta ★

Serves 8
Preparation time: 40 minutes
Cooking time: 25 minutes
Freezing time: 2 hours

Prepare the chestnut sponge.
In the bowl of a stand mixer fitted with the paddle attachment, beat the chestnut cream and sugar at low speed until smooth. With the paddle still turning, add the butter and eggs until fully incorporated. Stir in the rum. Sift the flour with the baking powder and incorporate into the batter. Stop the mixer as soon as the flour is fully incorporated.
Preheat the oven to 350°F (180°C).
Butter the pastry rings and dust them lightly with flour. Spoon the batter into a piping bag and pipe spirals about ½ inch (1 cm) thick. Alternatively, spoon the batter into the rings and smooth very well with an offset spatula. Bake for 10 minutes, just until the top is set. Do not overbake or the cakes will dry out. They must remain moist inside.

Make the decorated chocolate disks.
Temper the chocolate (see p. 182). Pour it thinly onto the transfer sheet.
Let cool in a dry place. Working quickly, use a cookie cutter to stamp out 1 ¼-inch (3-cm) disks, but leave them on the transfer sheet. Let cool completely in the refrigerator. Peel them off carefully only when you assemble the dessert.

Prepare the chestnut cream panna cotta.
Soak the gelatin in a bowl of cold water. Slit the vanilla bean in two lengthwise and scrape the seeds into the chestnut cream. Add the vanilla bean, chestnut cream, and sugar to the cream and bring to a boil. Simmer for 1 minute and remove from the heat. Remove the vanilla bean.
Squeeze the water from the gelatin sheets and stir them into the cream-chestnut mixture until completely dissolved. Pour the panna cotta into the silicone molds. Freeze for at least 2 hours.

Assemble the dish.
Turn each panna cotta onto a chestnut sponge. Sprinkle with cocoa nibs. Defrost for 15 to 30 minutes in the refrigerator and decorate with the chocolate disks.

● **Chef's note**
Crème de marron, also known as chestnut spread, is made of chestnuts, sugar, and vanilla, and sometimes glucose and candied chestnuts.

Techniques
Panna cotta >> p. 93
Decorating with chocolate >> p. 182

Crème Caramel ★

Serves 6

Preparation time: 15 minutes
Cooking time: 45 minutes

Ingredients
Scant 1 cup (6 oz./180 g) sugar, divided
3 tablespoons (50 ml) water, divided
2 cups plus scant ½ cup (600 ml) milk
4 eggs
1 teaspoon vanilla extract

Preheat the oven to 195°F-200°F (90°C-100°C).

In a small heavy-bottom saucepan, make a caramel with ½ cup (3 ½ oz./100 g) sugar and half the water (see p. 467). When it turns a reddish-brown (330°F/165°C), immediately remove from the heat and stir in the remaining water. Quickly pour it into the bottom of six ramekins and swirl it around so that it coats them evenly.

In a large heavy-bottom saucepan, heat the milk. In a round-bottom mixing bowl, lightly whisk together the eggs, remaining sugar, and vanilla extract. Do not let it become foamy. Whisk in the hot milk without creating any bubbles.

Pour the mixture into the six ramekins.

Bake for 35 to 40 minutes, until the mixture is firm. It must not wobble when the ramekins are gently moved. If you wish, turn the crème caramels out onto plates and serve with the caramel dripping appetizingly over the sides and into the plates.

Ingredients

10 oz. (300 g) strawberries
5 oz. (150 g) drained canned cherries
1 teaspoon (5 ml) lemon juice
1 sprig verbena
Scant ½ cup (100 ml) whole milk
A little freshly ground pepper

Strawberry-Cherry Gazpacho ★

Serves 5
Preparation time: 30 minutes
Chilling time: 1 hour

Wash and hull the strawberries. Dry them carefully and cut them into quarters. Add the cherries, lemon juice, and half the verbena leaves. Process in a blender (or with an immersion blender) and strain through a fine-mesh sieve into a mixing bowl. Cover with plastic wrap and chill.

Whip the milk until it is foamy. (It is important to use whole milk because the fat content is necessary to trap the air bubbles).

Pour the gazpacho into glasses. Clear glasses will showcase the color of the gazpacho best. Spoon in a little foamy milk and sprinkle with freshly ground pepper. Garnish the glasses with a few verbena leaves.

● **Chef's note**
This refreshing, simple dessert can be made with other seasonal fruits of your choice, and it could also be served as a pre-dessert.

Cold desserts

Cold desserts

Waffles ★

Makes 10 waffles
Preparation time: 30 minutes
Cooking time: 30 minutes

You can make the waffle batter using either the egg white-based method or the baking powder method. Both options are given below.

Method 1.
Make an egg white-based waffle batter.
In a mixing bowl, whisk the egg yolks with 1 tablespoon sugar until the mixture is pale and creamy. Sift the flour into a large mixing bowl and make a well in the center. Whisk in the egg yolk and sugar mixture. Gradually pour in the milk, stirring constantly, and whisk in the salt, vanilla, and butter. Whisk the egg whites until they hold firm peaks. Add the remaining sugar and stir with the whisk until the meringue is firm and shiny.
With a flexible spatula, carefully fold the meringue into the batter base. Grease the waffle maker and heat it. Cook the waffles for 2 to 3 minutes, until an even golden color. Transfer immediately to a rack to cool slightly so that they don't reabsorb any moisture.

Method 2.
Make a waffle batter with baking powder.
Melt the butter and beat it with the sugar and vanilla sugar until creamy. Separate one egg. Set the white aside. Beat the two remaining eggs with the egg yolk into the butter and sugar mixture.
Sift the flour and baking powder into the batter and fold in. Gradually pour in the milk, mixing it in carefully so that no lumps form.
Whisk the egg white until it forms firm peaks. Stir the salt in with the whisk. Fold the egg white into the batter, working carefully so as not to deflate the mixture.
Grease the waffle maker and heat it. Cook the waffles for 2 to 3 minutes, until an even golden color. Transfer immediately to a rack to cool slightly so that they don't reabsorb any moisture.

Prepare the Chantilly cream.
Whip the cream until it holds firm peaks. Stir in the sugar and vanilla. With a piping bag fitted with a star tip, pipe the Chantilly cream over each waffle, arrange a few pieces of fruit over it, and cover with another waffle.

● Chef's notes
If you replace half the milk with beer, the batter will be even lighter and have a slightly different taste. You can use all sorts of flavors for the batter, so be creative—lemon zest and orange flower water are some suggestions. Traditionally, waffles are served with chocolate sauce.

Ingredients
Waffle batter, egg white-based
2 egg yolks
3 tablespoons (1 ½ oz./40 g) sugar, divided
2 cups (9 oz./250 g) flour
1 cup (250 ml) milk
2 teaspoons (10 g) salt
1 teaspoon (5 ml) vanilla extract
3 tablespoons (2 oz./50 g) butter, softened (or melted and cooled)
3–4 egg whites (4 oz./120 g)

Waffle batter with baking powder
5 tablespoons (3 oz./80 g) butter
2 ½ tablespoons (1 oz./30 g) sugar
1 sachet vanilla sugar,
or 1 tablespoon homemade vanilla sugar,
or 1 tablespoon sugar with ½ teaspoon vanilla extract
3 eggs
1 ⅔ cups (7 oz./200 g) flour
1 ½ teaspoons (6 g) baking powder
1 cup (250 ml) milk
Heaping ½ teaspoon (3 g) salt

Chantilly cream
⅔ cup (150 ml) heavy cream
2 ½ tablespoons (20 g) confectioners' sugar
½ teaspoon vanilla extract

Assorted fruit of your choice to serve

Techniques
Chantilly cream >> p. 94
French meringue >> p. 176

Floating Islands ★

Serves 8
Preparation time: 45 minutes
Cooking time: 30 minutes
Chilling time: 1 hour

Prepare the French meringue.
Whisk the egg whites until they hold firm peaks. Add the sugar and whisk vigorously until the meringue is firm and shiny.

Make the pouring custard.
Slit the vanilla bean lengthwise and scrape the seeds into the milk. In a medium heavy-bottom saucepan, heat the milk with the vanilla bean. Beat the egg yolks with the sugar until pale and thick. When the milk is simmering, pour half of it over the egg yolk and sugar mixture, stirring constantly. Return the mixture to the saucepan and cook, stirring constantly and removing the saucepan from the heat from time to time, until it reaches 185°F (85°C) or coats the back of a spoon. (If the egg yolks are in constant contact with high heat, they may coagulate.) Strain the custard through a fine-mesh sieve, transfer to a mixing bowl, cover with plastic wrap, and let chill in the refrigerator.

Cook the floating islands.
Heat the milk in a large heavy-bottom saucepan. When it is simmering, shape the French meringue into "floating islands" with a soup ladle and poach them in the milk for 3 to 4 minutes, turning them over frequently. To test for doneness, cut one of them in half with a knife. The inside should be firm. Lift them carefully onto paper towel to drain and immediately place in the refrigerator.

Make the caramel decoration.
Follow the instructions on p. 134, using the quantities given here.

Assemble the dish.
Pour the custard into large bowls or soup plates and place a floating island in the center. Top with the caramel decoration and scatter with sliced, roasted almonds.

Techniques
Pouring custard (crème anglaise) >> p. 91
Sugar decorations >> p. 134
French meringue >> p. 176

Ingredients

French meringue
8 egg whites
Scant ½ cup (3 oz./80 g) sugar

Pouring custard
1 vanilla bean
2 cups (500 ml) milk
4 egg yolks
⅓ cup (2 ½ oz./75 g) sugar
4 cups (1 liter) milk

4 cups (1 liter) milk to cook the meringue

Caramel decoration
¾ cup (5 oz./150 g) sugar
3 tablespoons (50 ml) water
2 oz. (50 g) crystal glucose

2 oz. (50 g) sliced, roasted almonds
for decoration

Summer Fruit Soup ★

Serves 4

Preparation time: 30 minutes
Marinating time: overnight or 12 hours
Cooking time: 5 minutes

Slit the vanilla bean in two lengthwise and scrape the seeds into the water.
Bring the water and sugar to a boil to make a syrup and add the lime zest
and vanilla bean.
Make small scoops of melon. Cut the apricots in half and remove the pits.
Place the fruit in the boiling syrup. Remove from the heat and marinate the
fruits. Let cool, and chill for at least 12 hours.
Arrange the fruit and syrup in deep bowls and garnish each with a bunch
of red currants.

● **Chef's note**

With the changing seasons, you can make infinite variations on this basic recipe.

Ingredients
1 vanilla bean
⅔ cup (150 ml) water
⅓ cup (3 oz./80 g) sugar
Finely grated zest of ½ lime,
unwaxed or organic
1 melon
8 apricots
8 bunches red currants,
for garnish

Ingredients

A few sprigs fresh mint

¾ cup (4 oz./120 g) medium grain
  semolina

⅔ cup (150 ml) fresh orange juice

2 ½ tablespoons (1 oz./30 g) sugar

8 oz. (250 g) assorted fresh fruit,
  such as strawberries, peaches, red currants,
  black currants, and raspberries

Fruit Tabbouleh ★

Serves 4

Preparation time: 10 minutes/Chilling time: overnight

A day ahead.
Pick the larger leaves of mint and shred them. Combine the semolina, orange juice, sugar, and shredded mint leaves in a mixing bowl. Cover with film and chill overnight.

Assemble the dish.
Dice half the fruit, excluding the strawberries. Slice enough strawberries to fit round four servings. Place a dessert ring on a plate and stand strawberry slices around the inside of the rim. Carefully stir the diced fruit into the semolina and fill the ring with it, pushing down gently. Remove the ring and arrange the remaining fruit on the plate. Repeat to make the other three servings.

● Chef's note
Citrus butter is a good accompaniment.

Chocolate Mousse ★

Serves 5
Preparation time: 15 minutes
Cooking time: 2 minutes
Chilling time: 2 hours

Ingredients
7 oz. (200 g) bittersweet chocolate,
64 percent cocoa
2 tablespoons (1 oz./30 g) butter, softened
3 eggs, separated
¼ cup (2 oz./50 g) sugar

Melt the chocolate in a bain-marie over barely simmering water, or in brief pulses in the microwave oven, taking care not to scorch it.

Whisk the softened butter and the egg yolks into the chocolate until thoroughly combined.

Whip the egg whites until they form soft peaks. Whisk in the sugar with a stirring motion until the mixture is firm and shiny.

With a flexible spatula, carefully fold the beaten egg whites into the chocolate mixture, without deflating the mixture.

Immediately pour into small glasses.

Cover with plastic wrap to prevent the mousses from absorbing other odors in the refrigerator. Chill for at least 2 hours.

Serve the same day, as raw egg yolks do not keep.

● **Chef's note**

You can add good-quality chocolate chips or chopped chocolate to the mousse, and serve it with almond tuiles (see p. 80).

Technique
Chocolate mousse >> p. 106

Ingredients

Panna cotta
12 sheets (24 g) gelatin
1 vanilla bean
4 cups (1 liter) milk
1 cup (7 oz./200 g) sugar

Coulis
3 ½ oz. (100 g) mango
2 teaspoons (10 ml) lemon juice
2 ½ tablespoons (1 oz./30 g) sugar

Panna Cotta with Mango Coulis ★

Serves 4
Preparation time: 30 minutes
Cooking time: 30 minutes

Make the panna cotta.
Soften the gelatin sheets in a large bowl of cold water.
Slit the vanilla bean in two lengthwise and scrape the seeds into the milk. In a medium heavy-bottom saucepan, heat the milk with the sugar and the vanilla bean. As soon as it starts simmering, remove from the heat and take out the vanilla bean. Squeeze the water from the gelatin sheets and incorporate them into the milk, stirring until dissolved.
Pour into four ramekins and chill rapidly.

Prepare the coulis.
Dice the mango and cook it over low heat with the lemon juice until softened.
Stir in the sugar and blend until perfectly smooth.
When the panna cotta has set, pour a little mango coulis on top so that it looks like an egg yolk.

● Chef's notes
The lemon juice in the coulis adds a little zing to the mixture, thanks to the citric acid it contains. Citric acid is as indispensable to the pastry chef as salt is to the cook.
Serve the panna cotta with small cookies or baked petits fours.

 Techniques
Panna cotta >> p. 93
Fruit coulis >> p. 128

Mango Sushi ★

Serves 4
Preparation time: 1 hour 15 minutes
Maturing time: 4 hours
Cooking time: 30 minutes
Chilling time: 30 minutes

Prepare the rice pudding.
Slit the vanilla bean in two lengthwise and scrape the seeds into the milk. In a medium heavy-bottom saucepan, heat the milk with the vanilla bean and seeds.
Place the rice in an equal volume of cold water and bring to a boil. As soon as the water boils, strain the rice and pour it into the hot milk. Simmer over low heat for about 30 minutes, stirring every 5 minutes, until cooked through. Note that different types of rice require different cooking times, so you will need to check for doneness.
Remove the vanilla bean and stir in sugar to taste. Cover the surface with plastic wrap to prevent a skin from forming and chill.

Make the pomegranate sorbet.
Heat the water to 77°F (25°C) and whisk in the sugar until it is fully dissolved. Still whisking, add the atomized glucose and stabilizer, then heat to 185°F (85°C) while continuing to stir the mixture and cook at this temperature for 3 minutes to pasteurize. Remove from the heat and let cool to room temperature. Blend and leave to cool for a while, covered with plastic wrap. Allow it to chill and mature for at least 4 hours in the refrigerator. Stir in the pomegranate purée and blend for a good minute in order to obtain a perfect mixture. Process in an ice-cream maker according to the manufacturer's instructions, transfer to an airtight container, and freeze at 0.4°F (-18°C).

Assemble the dish.
Peel the pineapple and cut it into sticks 2 inches (10 cm) long and ⅕ inch (5 mm) thick.
Slice the mangoes very finely with the skin, if possible using a slicing machine. Use only the whole slices. Remove the skin and place the slices on plastic wrap. Spread the rice pudding over the mango slices and place a pineapple stick in the center. Using the plastic wrap, roll the mango with rice to make a cylinder, making it as tight as possible. Make two to three cylinders per person.
Arrange the sushi on pairs of chopsticks set on rectangular plates. Place a pomegranate seed on top of each sushi. With a spoon, make quenelles of pomegranate sorbet and place one on each plate next to the sushi.

Technique
Sorbets >> p. 201

Ingredients

Rice pudding
½ vanilla bean
3 cups (750 ml) milk
¾ cup (5 oz./150 g) short grain rice
Sugar to taste

Pomegranate sorbet
(it is advisable to measure the ingredients for the sorbet using the metric system and to weigh the liquid ingredients)
64 g water
43 g sugar
28 g atomized glucose
1.3 g stabilizer SL 64
330 g pomegranate purée

½ pineapple
2 mangoes
1 pomegranate

Rice Pudding ★

Serves 4
Preparation time: 15 minutes
Cooking time: 40 minutes

Pour the water into a saucepan and add the rice. Bring to a boil. Bring the milk to a boil with the flavoring. As soon as the water begins to boil, drain the rice and place it in the milk. Simmer gently, or bake in the oven, covered, at 285°F (140°C) until soft, about 30 minutes. Different types of rice require different cooking times, so you will need to check for doneness.

Using a flexible spatula or wooden spoon, combine the egg yolks, sugar, and cornstarch. Stir into the cooked rice, return to low heat, and bring to a simmer. It should thicken like a pastry cream.

Transfer to four ramekins and cover with plastic wrap flush with the surface (to prevent a skin from forming) until cool enough to serve.

● Chef's note

Add an interesting note to this traditional rice pudding with diced dried fruit, candied fruit, or even poached fruit.

Ingredients
Scant ½ cup (100 ml) water
⅔ cup (4 ½ oz./130 g) short grain rice
4 cups (1 liter) milk
Flavoring, such as 1 teaspoon grated orange zest or 1 teaspoon vanilla extract
4 egg yolks
Scant ⅔ cup (4 oz./120 g) sugar
1 ½ tablespoons (15 g) cornstarch

Ingredients

¼ cup (1 oz./35 g) raisins

3 tablespoons (40 ml) white rum

Butter to grease the molds

2 cups (500 ml) milk

½ cup (3 oz./90 g) fine semolina

1 egg yolk

¼ cup (2 oz./50 g) sugar

1 oz. (35 g) nougatine pieces

Scant ½ cup (100 ml) mango coulis
  (see recipe p. 311)

Semolina Cake ★

Serves 4

Preparation time: 35 minutes

Cooking time: 20 minutes

Chilling time: 1 hour

Soak the raisins in the rum until needed.

Butter four molds or dessert rings. Heat the milk until it almost reaches boiling point. Pour in all the semolina, stirring energetically with a whisk. Cook over low heat for 15 to 20 minutes, stirring continuously, until the semolina is softened. Remove from the heat and stir in the egg yolk to thicken the mixture. Drain the raisins and stir them into the semolina with the sugar. Add some of the nougatine pieces.

Spoon into the molds and cover with plastic wrap flush with the surface. Chill. Turn out onto plates and serve with the mango coulis and remaining nougatine pieces.

Techniques

Nougatine >> p. 166

Cooking semolina >> p. 213

Ingredients

Ladyfinger sponge

3 large eggs, separated
Scant ½ cup (3 oz./80 g) sugar
½ cup (2 oz./65 g) flour
1 ½ tablespoons (15 g) cornstarch
Confectioners' sugar for sprinkling

Coffee syrup

Scant ½ cup (100 ml) espresso or strong coffee
2 ½ tablespoons (1 oz./30 g) sugar
2 tablespoons (25 ml) coffee liqueur

Tiramisu cream

1 cup (8 oz./250 g) mascarpone
¾ cup (200 ml) heavy cream

French meringue

3 egg whites
1 ¾ tablespoons (20 g) sugar

A little cocoa powder for dusting

Tiramisu ★★

Serves 8
Preparation time: 1 hour
Cooking time: 20 minutes
Chilling time: 2 hours

Prepare the ladyfinger sponge.
Preheat the oven to 400°F (200°C).
Whisk the egg whites with the sugar until firm and shiny. Lightly beat the egg yolks and fold them carefully into the meringue mixture with a flexible spatula, taking care not to deflate it. Sift the flour and cornstarch together and fold in carefully. Spoon the batter into a piping bag fitted with a plain tip and pipe lengths in a strip to form a layer on a lined baking sheet. Sprinkle lightly with confectioners' sugar, wait 5 minutes, and sprinkle again. Bake for 10 to 12 minutes, but do not let it color. Let cool on a cooling rack.

Make the coffee syrup.
Heat the coffee with the sugar until dissolved. Stir in the liqueur and let cool.

Prepare the tiramisu cream.
With an electric beater, whip the mascarpone and heavy cream until the mixtures holds firm peaks.

Make the French meringue.
Whip the egg whites until they hold soft peaks. Stir in the sugar until the mixture is firm and shiny.

Assemble the dish.
With a flexible spatula, fold the meringue into the tiramisu cream, taking care not to deflate the mixture.
For each serving, cut out three disks of ladyfinger, ensuring they will be suitable sizes for each layer within the glass. With a pastry brush, moisten them well with the syrup.
Spoon a thin layer (under ½ inch or 1 cm) of tiramisu cream into the base of each glass. Place a disk of ladyfinger sponge over it. Repeat the procedure twice, finishing with a layer of tiramisu cream. Smooth the top with a spatula. Chill immediately. Just before serving, dust the top with cocoa powder, sprinkling it through a small strainer. If you wish, you can add height to your glasses by adding a small square of ladyfinger sponge. Serve within 24 hours.

Techniques

Ladyfingers >> p. 73
Moistening sponge layers >> p. 133
French meringue >> p. 176

Layered Chocolate-Coffee Creams ★

Serves 8

Preparation time: 1 hour
Cooking time: 15 minutes
Chilling time: 2 hours

Make the speculoos biscuit.

Preheat the oven to 350°F (180°C).
Combine all the ingredients in the bowl of a food processor fitted with a blade knife and process until combined. Gather into a ball and roll out the dough thinly, to less than ⅛ inch (3 mm) thick.
Transfer to a silicone baking sheet and bake for 7 to 8 minutes, until lightly browned. Transfer to a cooling rack.

Prepare the mascarpone layer.

Slit the vanilla bean lengthwise and scrape out the seeds. Place the mascarpone, heavy cream, sugar, and vanilla seeds in the bowl of a food processor fitted with a whip. Beat until the mixture holds firm peaks. Cover with plastic wrap and chill.

Make the Bavarian coffee cream.

Soften the gelatin sheets in a bowl of cold water.
Heat the milk in a medium heavy-bottom saucepan. Beat the egg yolks with the sugar until thick and pale. When the milk is simmering, pour half of it over the egg yolk and sugar mixture, stirring constantly. Return the mixture to the saucepan and cook, stirring constantly and removing the saucepan from the heat from time to time, until it reaches 185°F (85°C) or coats the back of a spoon. (If the egg yolks are in constant contact with high heat, they may coagulate.) Strain through a fine-mesh sieve into a mixing bowl. Squeeze the water from the gelatin sheets and stir in until completely dissolved. Cool the custard to about 70°F (20°C).
Whip the cream until it holds soft peaks. Briefly whisk the cooled custard mixture to smooth it. With a whisk, and working carefully so as not to deflate the mixture, gradually fold the whipped cream into the Bavarian cream. Add coffee extract to taste.

Assemble the dish.

Half-fill a paper decorating cone with chocolate glaze and make a marble pattern in the glasses. Half-fill the glasses with the Bavarian cream. Drizzle in just enough coffee liqueur to cover the layer. Spoon in the mascarpone cream, either to the top, flattened, or shape it like a dome. Crush the speculoos and sprinkle on the top. Decorate with the chocolate glaze.

⚑ Techniques

Egg-based Bavarian cream >> p. 97
Shiny chocolate glaze >> p. 116
Making a paper decorating cone >> p. 147

Ingredients

Speculoos biscuit
3 tablespoons (2 oz./50 g) salted butter
¼ cup (2 oz./50 g) light brown sugar
1 heaping tablespoon (15 g) sugar
1 scant teaspoon (2 g) ground cinnamon
½ teaspoon (2 g) baking powder
⅛ teaspoon (1 g) salt
1 teaspoon (5 ml) milk
½ egg
¾ cup plus 2 tablespoons (3 ½ oz./100 g) all-purpose flour
¼ teaspoon (1 g) vanilla extract

Mascarpone layer
1 vanilla bean
⅔ cup (5 oz./150 g) mascarpone
⅔ cup (150 ml) heavy cream
⅓ cup (2 oz./60 g) sugar

Bavarian coffee cream
2 sheets (4 g) gelatin
½ cup (125 ml) milk
2 egg yolks (1 ½ oz./40 g)
¼ cup (2 oz./55 g) sugar
¾ cup (200 ml) heavy cream
Coffee extract to taste

Shiny chocolate glaze (see recipe p. 116)
A little Kahlua or other coffee liqueur

Ingredients

Flour-free chocolate sponge
8 egg yolks (5 oz./150 g)
5-6 egg whites (6 ½ oz./190 g)
1 ¼ cups (8 ½ oz./240 g) sugar
⅔ cup (2 ½ oz./75 g) unsweetened
  cocoa powder

Gelled sweet wine
2 ½ sheets (5 g) gelatin
¾ cup (200 ml) Pineau de Charentes
  or other fortified wine
6 raspberries

Black currant mousse
4 sheets (8 g) gelatin
10 oz. (300 g) puréed black currants
¼ cup (2 oz./50 g) sugar
1 ¼ cups (300 ml) heavy cream

Garnish
6 small bunches of black currants
A little cocoa powder for dusting

Techniques
Flour-free chocolate sponge >> p. 71
Fruit mousse >> p. 109

Black Currant Mousse with Gelled Sweet Wine ★

Serves 6
Preparation time: 1 hour 15 minutes
Cooking time: 30 minutes
Chilling time: at least 5 hours

Prepare the flour-free chocolate sponge.
Preheat the oven to 340°F (170°C). Beat the egg yolks well. Whip the egg whites until they form soft peaks. Stir in the sugar until the mixture is firm and shiny. Carefully fold the egg whites into the egg yolks. Sift in the cocoa powder and, with a flexible spatula, stir it in until just combined.
Spread the mixture out on a baking sheet to about ¼ inch (5 mm) and bake for 15 to 20 minutes, until it springs back to the touch; the inside should remain moist. Carefully transfer it to a cooling rack (it is very fragile).

Make the gelled sweet wine.
Soak the gelatin sheets in a bowl of cold water. Heat the wine and let boil for 1 minute, until the alcohol has evaporated. Remove from the heat. Squeeze the water from the gelatin and stir it in until completely dissolved.
Pour it into six small glasses and place a raspberry in the middle. Chill until set, at least 5 hours.

Prepare the black currant mousse.
Soak the gelatin sheets in a bowl of cold water. Heat one-third of the purée with the sugar. When it simmers, remove from the heat. Squeeze the water from the gelatin sheets and stir into the purée until completely dissolved. Stir in the remaining purée to cool the mixture. Whip the cream until it holds firm peaks. When the purée mixture cools to between 70°F and 80°F (20°C-25°C), carefully fold the cream in with a whisk.

Assemble the dish.
Cut six disks of chocolate sponge to the same diameter as the serving glasses and six slightly larger ones. Place the six smaller disks over the gelled wine in each glass. Spoon the black currant mousse into a piping bag and pipe it over the sponge, filling the glasses to three-quarters. Decorate with the small bunches of black currants and the larger disks of sponge.

⬤ Chef's notes
Use this recipe to make mousses with other fruits or berries.
Instead of the cream, you can use an equivalent weight of Italian meringue.

⬤ Did you know?
Pineau comes from the Charentes region in southwestern France. It is made with a lightly fermented grape must to which cognac is added to stop the fermentation, and is then aged in oak barrels.

Pistachio, Vanilla, and Raspberry Layered Cake ★★★

Serves 8
Preparation time: 1 hour 45 minutes
Cooking time: 50 minutes
Chilling time: 1 hour

Make the French meringue.
Whip the egg whites until they form firm peaks. Stir in the sugar with a whisk until the mixture is firm and shiny.

Make the pistachio sponge.
Preheat the oven to 350°F (180°C).
Place the pistachio paste, sugar, egg yolks, and egg whites in the bowl of a stand mixer fitted with a paddle and beat at medium speed until the mixture is foamy.
With a flexible spatula, fold in the flour until just combined. Then carefully fold in the French meringue mixture.
Pour into the rectangular pan and smooth with a spatula. Bake for 12 to 15 minutes, until the top is done and it springs back to the touch; it should remain soft inside. Transfer to a rack to cool.

Prepare the raspberry fruit jelly.
Combine the yellow pectin with 2 tablespoons (1 oz./25 g) sugar. Heat the raspberry purée but do not boil. Pour it over the pectin-sugar mixture, add the remaining sugar and glucose syrup and heat to 225°F (107°C). Stir in the citric acid and pour onto a baking sheet or a frame a little smaller than the baking pan. Leave to set.

Make the Bavarian vanilla cream.
Soften the gelatin sheets in a bowl of cold water. Slit the vanilla bean lengthwise and scrape the seeds into the milk. In a medium heavy-bottom saucepan, heat the milk with the vanilla bean. Beat the egg yolks with the sugar until pale and thick. When the milk is simmering, pour half of it over the egg mixture, beating constantly. Return the mixture to the saucepan, remove the vanilla bean, and cook, stirring constantly and removing the saucepan from the heat from time to time, until it reaches 185°F (85°C) or coats the back of a spoon. (If the egg yolks are in constant contact with high heat, they may coagulate.)

Squeeze the water from the gelatin sheets and stir into the custard until completely dissolved. Strain through a fine-mesh sieve, transfer to a mixing bowl, and cover with plastic wrap flush with the surface. Let cool to about 70°F (20°C). Whip the cream until it holds firm peaks. With a whisk, stir the custard mixture to smooth it. Still working with a whisk, gradually fold in the whipped cream, taking care not to deflate it. The Bavarian cream is ready for use immediately.

Assemble the dish.
Place the sponge in a pastry frame. If necessary, cut the raspberry fruit jelly so that it is slightly narrower than the sponge. Center it over the sponge. Pour the Bavarian vanilla cream on top and smooth it with an offset spatula. Chill for 1 hour.

Prepare the glaze and finish.
Soak the gelatin in 3 tablespoons cold water. Bring the remaining water and sugar to a boil. Remove from the heat. Squeeze the water from the gelatin and stir it into the syrup until completely dissolved. Divide into two and color one half green and the other half yellow. Let cool to between 75°F and 85°F (25°C-30°C). Rapidly apply the green glaze, making a wavy pattern, and then apply the yellow glaze. Remove the pastry frame and, with a heated knife, cut out narrow rectangular shapes.
Individual serving plates can be decorated with marbled custard or fruit coulis (see p. 125).

Techniques
Egg-based Bavarian cream >> p. 97
Gelled fruit >> p. 156
French meringue >> p. 176

Ingredients

French meringue
3-4 egg whites (4 ¼ oz./125 g)
¼ cup (2 oz./50 g) sugar

Pistachio sponge
2 oz. (60 g) pistachio paste
¼ cup (2 oz./50 g) sugar
1-2 egg yolks (1 oz./30 g)
2 egg whites (2 ¼ oz./65 g)
½ cup plus 1 teaspoon (2 ½ oz./65 g) flour

Raspberry fruit jelly
⅕ oz. (6 g) yellow pectin
1 cup plus 2 tablespoons (8 oz./225 g)
   sugar, divided
9 oz. (250 g) raspberry purée,
   10 percent sugar
2 oz. (50 g) glucose syrup
⅙ oz. (5 g) citric acid solution 50/50

Bavarian vanilla cream
4 sheets (8 g) gelatin
1 vanilla bean
1 cup (250 ml) milk
4 egg yolks (3 oz./80 g)
⅔ cup (4 ½ oz./125 g) sugar
1 ⅔ cups (400 ml) heavy cream

Glaze
4 sheets (8 g) gelatin
¾ cup (200 ml) water, divided
1 cup (7 oz./200 g) sugar
Green and yellow food coloring

A rectangular cake pan, measuring about
   5 x 12 inches (12 x 30 cm),
   at least ¾ inch (1.5 cm) deep
Special equipment: pastry frame

Layered desserts

Laurent Le Daniel

Meilleur Ouvrier de France, pâtisserie

The idea for this dessert came from what we call in pastry a "surprise." I've dressed up small cakes so that the outside does not give away what's inside—this is unusual, as generally the decoration of a cake provides some idea of its contents. A chocolate cake is decorated with chocolate; we find hazelnuts on a cake flavored with hazelnuts, and so on. But here, we ask our clients to trust us. The red outer coating may suggest red berries, but in reality that isn't the case. Every week, we change the ingredients but use the same type of presentation. Of course, the other cakes displayed in our boutiques meet more conventional criteria.

Surprise

Prepare the pistachio *dacquoise*.
Whip the egg whites with the sugar until they hold firm peaks. Mix together the ground almonds, confectioners' sugar, and flour and fold carefully into the meringue mixture. Stir in the pistachio paste. Spread on a 16 x 24-inch (40 x 60-cm) baking sheet, dust with confectioners' sugar, and bake at 350°F (180°C) for 25 minutes.

Make the mango-apricot compote.
Combine the pectin and sugar. Dice the fruits and place in a saucepan. Add the puréed fruit and incorporate the pectin-sugar mixture. Bring to a boil, stirring. Divide the compote among small, flexible molds, about 1 oz. (25 g) per mold. Freeze until set.

Make the almond supreme.
Soak the gelatin sheets in a bowl of cold water. Slit the vanilla bean in two and scrape the seeds into 1 ½ cups (350 ml) cream. Heat with the milk, almond paste, and vanilla bean. Beat the egg yolks with the sugar until pale and thick. Incorporate the mixture into the cream-almond mixture and proceed as for a pouring custard. Squeeze the water from the gelatin and incorporate into the almond-custard mixture. Let cool, blend, and stir in the Amaretto. Lightly whip the remaining cream and fold it in carefully.

Assemble the dish.
Half-fill a cubed flexible mold with the almond supreme. Place the frozen compote in the center, pour in a little more almond supreme, and close with a square of pistachio *dacquoise*. Freeze until firm and turn out of the molds. Cover with red glaze and decorate with a pink macaron on one of the sides.

Makes 50 individual pastries
Preparation time: 45 minutes
Cooking time: 30 minutes
Freezing time: 3 hours

Ingredients

Pistachio *dacquoise*
9–10 egg whites (10 oz./300 g)
1 ¼ cups (8 ½ oz./240 g) sugar
2 ¾ cups (8 ½ oz./240 g) ground almonds
Scant cup (4 oz./120 g) confectioners' sugar, plus a little extra for dusting
½ cup (2 oz./55 g) flour
2 oz. (65 g) pistachio paste, softened

Mango-apricot compote
⅔ oz. (18 g) pectin
2 ¾ tablespoons (1 oz./33 g) sugar
14 oz. (400 g) mangoes
14 oz. (400 g) apricots
11 oz. (330 g) puréed mango
11 oz. (330 g) puréed apricot

Almond supreme
11 ½ sheets (23 g) gelatin
1 vanilla bean
5 ½ cups (1.3 liters) heavy cream, divided
1 ½ cups (350 ml) milk
4 oz. (125 g) almond paste, 65 percent almonds
8 egg yolks (5 oz./145 g)
Scant 1 cup (7 oz./190 g) sugar
2 ½ tablespoons (38 ml) Amaretto

Red glaze as needed
50 pink macaron cookies

Ingredients

Printed sponge
2 tablespoons (1 oz./25 g) butter, softened
3 tablespoons (1 oz./25 g) confectioners' sugar
1 egg white minus 1 teaspoon (1 oz./25 g), lightly beaten
2 ½ tablespoons (1 oz./25 g) flour
Pink food coloring

Genoese sponge
2 eggs
Scant ⅓ cup (2 oz./65 g) sugar
½ cup (2 oz./65 g) flour

Succès almond meringue
3–4 egg whites (4 oz./120 g)
2 tablespoons (1 oz./25 g) sugar
⅓ cup (2 oz./50 g) confectioners' sugar
1 cup minus 1 tablespoon (2 ½ oz./75 g) ground almonds
2 ½ tablespoons (1 oz./25 g) all-purpose flour

Raspberry jam
4 oz. (125 g) raspberries
⅔ cup (4 oz./125 g) sugar

Vanilla Bavarian cream
2 sheets (4 g) gelatin
½ vanilla bean
½ cup (125 ml) milk
2 egg yolks
Scant ⅓ cup (2 oz./65 g) sugar
¾ cup (200 ml) heavy cream

⅓ cup (80 ml) raspberry brandy
2 oz. (60 g) neutral glaze
Raspberry coulis and raspberries macerated in eau-de-vie for garnish

7-inch (18-cm) dessert ring, measuring 2 inches (5 cm) deep

Raspberry and Vanilla Bavarian Cream Layer Cake ★★

Serves 6
Preparation time: 1 hour 45 minutes
Cooking time: 30 minutes
Chilling time: 2 hours

Prepare the printed sponge.
Whisk the butter with the confectioners' sugar until light and fluffy.
Incorporate the egg white. Pour in all of the flour and mix until smooth. Stir in the pink coloring. On a silicone baking sheet, smooth the paste very thinly. Using an icing comb, make circular movements to remove some of the paste and create a pattern. Alternatively, you can use any sort of stencil to make the pattern, and even openwork fabric.
Place in the freezer while you continue the recipe.

Make the Genoese sponge.
Preheat the oven to 350°F (180°C).
Place the eggs and sugar in a round-bottom mixing bowl and set it over a bain-marie heated to 140°F (60°C). Whip until the mixture reaches the ribbon stage and remove from the heat. Sift the flour and carefully fold in half of it with a flexible spatula. When it is incorporated, fold in the remaining flour, taking care not to deflate the mixture. Do not overmix. Quickly spread it over the patterned printed sponge and smooth it with an offset spatula. Bake for 10 to 15 minutes. The sponge must stay moist and must not color. Slide it onto a rack and let cool.

Make the Succès almond meringue base.
The oven should remain at 350°F (180°C).
Whip the egg whites until they form firm peaks. Stir in the sugar with the whisk until the mixture is firm and shiny. Combine the confectioners' sugar, ground almonds, and flour and, with a flexible spatula, fold them into the meringue, taking care not to deflate the mixture. Spoon into a piping bag and pipe a disk, slightly smaller than the dessert ring, onto a baking sheet (silicone or lined with parchment paper).
Bake for about 10 minutes. The meringue must be dry to the touch and must not color.

Prepare the raspberry jam.
In a medium heavy-bottom saucepan, cook the raspberries and sugar until the temperature reaches 225°F (107°C). Pour into a round mold a little smaller than the dessert ring and freeze.

Make the vanilla Bavarian cream.
Soften the gelatin sheets in a bowl of cold water. Slit the vanilla bean lengthwise and scrape the seeds into the milk. In a saucepan, heat the milk with the vanilla bean and seeds. Beat the egg yolks with the sugar until pale and thick. When the milk is simmering, pour half of it over the egg yolk mixture, beating constantly. Return the mixture to the saucepan and cook, stirring constantly and removing the saucepan from the heat from time to time, until it reaches 185°F (85°C) or coats the back of a spoon. (If the egg yolks are in constant contact with high heat, they may coagulate.)
Squeeze the water from the gelatin sheets and stir into the custard until completely dissolved. Strain through a fine-mesh sieve and cool to about 68°F (20°C).
Whip the cream until it holds soft peaks. Whisk the custard preparation to smooth it. Gradually fold in the whipped cream, working carefully so as not to deflate the mixture.

Assemble the dessert.
Cut a strip of printed sponge just ½ inch (1 cm) shorter than the height of the dessert ring. Stand it inside the ring, joining the two ends without a gap. Cut a circle of the Succès base to fit the bottom of the ring. Place it, softer side upward, in the ring. Moisten it with raspberry brandy. Pour the Bavarian cream halfway up the ring. Carefully place the disk of frozen raspberry jam over the Bavarian cream. Pour in the remaining Bavarian cream and smooth the top with a spatula. Chill until set, about 2 hours. Evenly spread the top with neutral glaze. With a paper decorating cone (see p. 147), pipe a decoration of raspberry coulis. Dot raspberries soaked in liqueur around the edge of the dessert.

Techniques
Genoese sponge >> p. 76
Succès almond meringue >> p. 77
Egg-based Bavarian cream >> p. 97
Stencils and printed sponges >> p. 142

Creamy Peach and Orange Log Dessert ★★

Serves 8
Preparation time: 2 hours/Cooking time: 30 minutes
Freezing time: 3 hours

Prepare the gelled orange layer (can be made a day ahead).
Soften the gelatin in the cold water. Place 1 ½ tablespoons (20 g) sugar in a small heavy-bottom saucepan and heat until it turns a light caramel color. Quickly stir in 1 teaspoon (5 g) butter and the orange juice. Stir in the egg yolk and remaining 1 ¼ tablespoons (15 g) sugar. Cook to 185°F (85°C). Stir in the gelatin sheets (they will have absorbed all the water) until completely dissolved. Cool to 95°F (35°C). Mix in the remaining butter. Pour a thin layer (⅕ in./5-6 mm) into a mold the same length as the Yule log mold. Chill until set, about 30 minutes.

Prepare the Joconde sponge (can be made a day ahead).
Preheat the oven to 350°F (180°C). Line a 12 x 16-inch (30 x 40-cm) baking sheet with a silicone baking mat. Combine the ground almonds and confectioners' sugar and sift in the flour. In the bowl of a stand mixer, beat the whole eggs and 1 egg white with the sifted dry ingredients. Meanwhile, whip the 5 remaining egg whites until they form soft peaks. Add the sugar and whip until incorporated to obtain a French meringue (see p. 176). The meringue should not be too firm. Pour the browned melted butter into the egg mixture. Carefully fold the meringue into the egg mixture. Spread very thinly over the baking sheet. Bake for about 15 minutes, until dry on top, springy to the touch, and very lightly golden.

Make the peach mousse.
Soften the gelatin sheets in a bowl of cold water. Heat one-third of the puréed peaches with the sugar until it is dissolved. Remove from the heat. Squeeze the water from the gelatin sheets and stir into the hot mixture until completely dissolved. Stir in the remaining peach purée to cool the mixture to 68°F-77°F (20°C-25°C). Whip the cream until it holds soft peaks and carefully fold it in with a whisk in several additions.

Make the glaze.
Soften the gelatin in 3 tablespoons (40 ml) cold water. Bring the remaining water and sugar to a boil. Remove from the heat. Stir in the softened gelatin. Add coloring as needed. Cool to 68°F-77°F (20°C-25°C).

Assemble the dish.
Pour about one-quarter of the peach mousse into the log mold. Cut a strip of the gelled orange layer and center it over the peach mousse. Pour in the remaining peach mousse and top with a strip of Joconde sponge. Freeze for at least 3 hours. Set a rack over a baking tray and carefully turn the dessert onto it. Pour the glaze generously over the dessert to cover it completely. Decorate with grapefruit segments, chocolate, and peach quarters.

Ingredients

Gelled orange layer
1 ½ sheets (3 g) gelatin
1 tablespoon (15 ml) cold water
2 ¾ tablespoons (1 ¼ oz./35 g) sugar, divided
2 tablespoons (1 oz./30 g) butter, divided
Scant ⅓ cup (70 ml) orange juice
1-2 egg yolks (1 oz./30 g)

Joconde sponge
1 cup (3 oz./85 g) ground blanched almonds
⅔ cup (3 oz./85 g) confectioners' sugar
2 ½ tablespoons (1 oz./25 g) flour
2 whole eggs plus 6 egg whites, divided
3 ½ tablespoons (1 ½ oz./40 g) sugar
2 tablespoons (1 oz./ 25 g) butter, melted until brown and cooled

Peach mousse
4 sheets (8 g) gelatin
10 oz. (300 g) puréed peaches
¼ cup (2 oz./50 g) sugar
1 ¼ cups (300 ml) heavy cream

Glaze
4 sheets (8 g) gelatin
¾ cup (200 ml) cold water
1 cup (7 oz./200 g) sugar
Pink food coloring

Garnish
1 grapefruit, segmented
Orange chips
1 ½ oz. (40 g) bittersweet chocolate
1 peach, quartered

7-inch (18-cm) Yule log mold

Techniques
Joconde sponge >> p. 69
Fruit mousse >> p. 109
Cutting citrus segments >> p. 130
Fruit chips >> p. 131
Glazing a log-shaped cake and dessert >> p. 148

Ingredients

Jelly roll
3 egg yolks (1 ¾ oz./50 g)
2 whole eggs
¾ cup (5 oz./140 g) sugar, divided
2-3 egg whites (2 ¾ oz./80 g)
⅓ cup (1 ½ oz./40 g) flour
3 tablespoons (1 oz./30 g) cornstarch

Syrup
¼ cup (2 oz./50 g) sugar
3 tablespoons (50 ml) water
1 teaspoon (5 ml) vanilla extract

Butter cream (green and brown)
1 ¼ cups (9 oz./250 g) sugar
Scant ⅓ cup (70 ml) water
4 egg yolks
2 ¼ sticks (9 oz./250 g) butter, softened and diced
2 tablespoons unsweetened cocoa powder
  dissolved in 2 tablespoons milk
Green food coloring

7-inch (18-cm) Yule log mold
A piping bag fitted with a carded basket tip

Yule Log ★ ★

Serves 8
Preparation time: 1 hour 30 minutes
Cooking time: 30 minutes
Chilling time: 2 hours

Prepare the jelly roll (can be made a day ahead).
Preheat the oven to 400°F (200°C). Line a 12 x 16-inch (30 x 40-cm) jelly roll pan with parchment paper. With an electric beater at high speed, whip the egg yolks, whole eggs, and ⅔ cup (4 ½ oz./125 g) sugar until tripled in volume (5-6 minutes). Whip the egg whites with the remaining sugar until they form firm peaks. Fold carefully into the egg and sugar mixture. Sift the flour and cornstarch together and fold in carefully. Immediately spread on the prepared jelly roll pan about ⅕ inch (5 mm) thick. Bake for 6 to 7 minutes, until lightly colored and springy to the touch. Do not let it dry out; it has to be soft enough to roll. Transfer to a cooling rack and cover with a cloth or sheet of parchment paper.

Prepare the syrup.
In a heavy-bottom saucepan, cook the sugar and water to 243°F-250°F (117°C-121°C). Remove from the heat, stir in the vanilla extract, and let cool.

Make the butter cream.
In a stand mixer fitted with a whisk, or with an electric beater, begin beating the egg yolks to a foamy consistency. Gradually pour three-quarters of the syrup over the yolks, beating constantly. Continue until the temperature of the mixture cools to about 85°F (30°C).
At medium speed, gradually add the butter and whip until the mixture reaches a creamy consistency. Set aside two small bowls of butter cream (just enough for the decoration). Of these, leave one bowl plain and color the other green. Stir the cocoa mixture into the large bowl of butter cream.

Assemble and decorate the cake.
Moisten the sponge with the remaining syrup. Spread the sponge with a thin layer of chocolate butter cream and roll up tightly. Trim the ends to use as knots of the tree trunk. Set the log firmly on a tray so that it is stable. Chill for 2 hours.
Spoon the butter cream into a piping bag fitted with a carded basket tip and cover the log completely. Dip a fork into boiling water and run it along the butter cream in wavy lines to imitate the tree bark. Take the green butter cream and use a paper decorating cone to draw some ivy vines. If you want to make leaves, cut the tip of the cone into a V shape. Mask both ends of the log with plain butter cream.

 Techniques
Jelly roll (Swiss roll) >> p. 78
Butter creams >> p. 95
Moistening sponge layers >> p. 133

334

Creamy Pistachio Log Dessert ★ ★ ★

Serves 8
Preparation time: 2 hours/Cooking time: 40 minutes
Freezing time: 3 hours

Prepare the butter cream.
Follow recipe on page 95, incorporating the praline paste after the butter.

Make the jelly roll.
Preheat the oven to 400°F (200°C). Line a 12 x 16 inch (30 x 40-cm) jelly roll pan with parchment paper. With an electric beater at high speed, whip the egg yolks, whole eggs, and ⅔ cup (4 ½ oz./125 g) sugar until tripled in volume (5-6 minutes). Whip the egg whites with the remaining sugar until they form firm peaks. Fold carefully into the egg and sugar mixture. Sift the flour and cornstarch together and fold in carefully. Immediately spread the batter over the prepared jelly roll pan about ⅕ inch (5 mm) thick. Bake for 6 to 7 minutes, until dry to the touch and just browned. Immediately slide onto a cooling rack. When cool, spread with a thin layer of butter cream. Roll tightly and chill.

Prepare the dacquoise.
Preheat the oven to 340°F (170°C). Sift the flour and combine with the confectioners' sugar and hazelnuts. Whip the egg whites until they form soft peaks. Add the granulated sugar and whip briefly until the mixture is shiny but not too firm. With a flexible spatula, carefully fold the dry ingredients into the meringue. Spoon the mixture into a piping bag and pipe a strip on a prepared baking sheet. Bake for 10 minutes, until nicely golden but still soft.

Make the pistachio Bavarian cream.
Soften the gelatin sheets in a bowl of cold water. In a saucepan, heat the milk and pistachio paste. In a bowl, beat the egg yolks and sugar until pale and thick. When the milk mixture begins to simmer, pour half over the egg-sugar mixture. Return it all to the saucepan and cook, stirring constantly and removing the saucepan from the heat from time to time, until it reaches 185°F (85°C). Squeeze the water from the gelatin and stir it into the custard until completely dissolved. Strain through a fine-mesh sieve into a mixing bowl and cover with plastic wrap flush with the surface. Let cool to about 77°F (25°C). Whip the cream until it forms soft peaks. With a whisk, gradually fold the whipped cream into the cooled custard.

Prepare the glaze (this can be made a day ahead and reheated).
Soften the gelatin sheets in the water. Combine the milk, cream, and glucose in a saucepan and bring to a boil. Remove from the heat and stir in the white chocolate and glazing paste. Squeeze the water from the gelatin sheets and stir into the mixture until completely dissolved. Stir in the green coloring. Take about 2 tablespoons of this glaze and incorporate the titanium dioxide, if using. Incorporate into the rest of the glaze. Use at 77°F (25°C).

Assemble and decorate the log.
Half-fill the mold with the Bavarian cream. Center the jelly roll on top. Fill with the Bavarian cream and top with a strip of dacquoise. Freeze for 3 hours. Set a rack over a tray and turn the pistachio log onto it. Pour over the glaze, covering it completely, and garnish with chocolate decorations of your choice.

Ingredients

Butter cream
1 ¼ cups (9 oz./250 g) sugar
Scant ⅓ cup (70 ml) water
4 egg yolks
2 ¼ sticks (9 oz./250 g) butter
2 oz. (50 g) praline paste, softened

Jelly roll
3 egg yolks (1 ¾ oz./50 g)
2 large whole eggs
¾ cup (5 oz./140 g) sugar, divided
2-3 egg whites (2 ¾ oz./80 g)
⅓ cup (1 ½ oz./40 g) flour
3 tablespoons (1 oz./30 g) cornstarch

Dacquoise
2 ½ tablespoons (1 oz./25 g) flour
Scant 1 cup (4 oz./115 g) confectioners' sugar
1 ⅓ cups (4 oz./115 g) ground hazelnuts
4-5 egg whites (5 ½ oz./165 g)
Scant ½ cup (3 oz./85 g) sugar

Pistachio Bavarian cream
4 sheets (8 g) gelatin
1 cup (250 ml) milk
2 oz. (50 g) pistachio paste
4 egg yolks (3 oz./80 g)
⅔ cup (4 ½ oz./125 g) sugar
1 ⅔ cups (400 ml) heavy cream
Green food coloring

Glaze
2 sheets (4 g) gelatin
1 tablespoon plus 1 teaspoon (20 ml) cold water
½ cup (125 ml) milk
⅓ cup (75 ml) heavy cream
1 oz. (25 g) glucose syrup
5 oz. (150 g) white couverture chocolate
5 oz. (150 g) ivory glazing paste
Green food coloring
⅓ oz. (10 g) titanium dioxide (optional)

Garnish
Chocolate decorations (see pp. 182-85)

7-inch (18-cm) Yule log mold

Techniques
Hazelnut dacquoise sponge ›› p. 72
Jelly roll (Swiss roll) ›› p. 78
Butter creams ›› p. 95
Egg-based Bavarian cream ›› p. 97

Ingredients

Ladyfingers
5 eggs, separated
⅔ cup (4 ½ oz./125 g) sugar
¾ cup plus 2 tablespoons (3 ½ oz./100 g) flour
2 ½ tablespoons (1 oz./25 g) cornstarch
Confectioners' sugar for sprinkling

Syrup
½ cup (3 ½ oz./100 g) sugar
Scant ½ cup (100 ml) water
1 teaspoon (5 ml) vanilla extract

Bavarian cream
4 sheets (8 g) gelatin
9 oz. (250 g) mixed strawberry and raspberry
  purée, unsweetened
4 egg yolks (3 oz./80 g)
½ cup (3 ½ oz./100 g) sugar
1 ⅔ cups (400 ml) heavy cream

Decoration
5 oz. (150 g) strawberries, cut into quarters
3 ½ oz. (100 g) raspberries
3 tablespoons (1 oz./25 g) confectioners' sugar

7-inch (16-cm) diameter dessert ring, measuring
  2 inches (5 cm) deep, or a charlotte mold

Strawberry-Raspberry Charlotte ★★

Serves 8
Preparation time: 1 hour
Cooking time: 30 minutes
Chilling time: 2 hours

Prepare the ladyfingers.
Preheat the oven to 400°F (200°C).
Whisk the egg whites with the sugar until firm and shiny. Lightly beat the egg yolks and fold them carefully into the meringue mixture with a flexible spatula, taking care not to deflate it. Sift the flour and cornstarch together and fold in carefully.
Spoon the batter into a piping bag fitted with a plain tip and pipe two 7-inch (16-cm) disks, starting from the center and working in a spiral. Pipe onto prepared baking sheets a strip of eighteen to twenty 2-inch (5-cm) long ladyfinger batons, side by side, to line the dessert circle vertically. Sprinkle lightly with confectioners' sugar, wait 5 minutes, and sprinkle again. Bake for about 10 to 12 minutes, but do not let them color. Transfer to a cooling rack.

Make the syrup.
Bring the sugar and water to a boil. Remove from the heat, let cool, and stir in the vanilla extract.

Prepare the Bavarian cream.
Soften the gelatin sheets in a bowl of cold water. Bring the puréed fruit to a boil. Beat the egg yolks with the sugar until pale and thick. Remove the fruit from the heat and stir in the egg yolk and sugar mixture. Return to the heat until the temperature reaches 185°F (85°C). Remove from the heat, squeeze the water from the gelatin sheets, and stir them in until completely dissolved. Cool to 77°F (25°C). Whip the cream until it holds soft peaks. Carefully fold it into the cooled fruit mixture. The Bavarian cream must now be molded immediately.

Assemble the dish.
Cut the strip of ladyfinger sponge batons to fit the dessert ring. Place one of the ladyfinger disks at the base of the ring and brush it with syrup. Pour the Bavarian cream to halfway up the ring and decorate with some of the cut strawberries and raspberries. Lightly press down the second ladyfinger disk, popping any air bubbles. Moisten it with syrup. Fill the dessert ring with the remaining Bavarian cream and chill for 2 hours, until set. To serve, cover the top with the remaining strawberries and raspberries and dust lightly with confectioners' sugar.

Techniques
Ladyfingers >> p. 73
Egg-based Bavarian cream >> p. 97
Moistening sponge layers >> p. 133
Assembling a charlotte >> p. 145

Glossy Chocolate Layer Cake ★ ★ ★

Serves 8
Preparation time: 2 hours
Cooking time: 40 minutes
Freezing time: 4 hours

Prepare the Sacher sponge.
Preheat the oven to 350°F (180°C). Place the almond paste in a mixing bowl and gradually mix in the egg and egg yolks to soften it. Whip the egg whites until they form soft peaks. Add the sugar and whip until the mixture is firm and shiny. With a flexible spatula, carefully fold the egg whites into the almond paste and egg mixture in several additions. Sift the flour and cocoa powder together and fold in carefully. Stir in the melted butter and cocoa paste until completely incorporated. Butter a pastry ring slightly smaller than the dessert ring and pour or spoon the batter into it. (There will be extra batter that can be baked and frozen for another use. The sponge keeps, well wrapped, for 4 weeks.) Bake for 10 minutes, until dry to the touch but still springy. Transfer carefully to a cooling rack.

Make the gelled coulis.
Line a baking sheet with parchment paper or a silicone baking mat and set a 7-inch (16-cm) tart ring over it (or use a lined tart pan). Combine the sugar and NH pectin. Heat the puréed raspberries, glucose, and invert sugar to 113°F (45°C). Stir in the sugar-pectin mixture. Simmer for 2 minutes. Pour into the prepared tart ring and freeze, flat.

Prepare the shiny chocolate glaze.
In a saucepan, bring the water, heavy cream, sugar, and invert sugar to a boil. Stir in the cocoa powder until completely smooth. Let boil for 2 minutes, stirring frequently. Remove from the heat. Stir the gelatin sheets and any remaining soaking water into the mixture until completely dissolved. Process briefly with an immersion blender. Transfer to a bowl, cover with plastic wrap flush with the surface, and chill. Heat to 80°F-82°F (27°C-28°C) just before using.

Prepare the macarons.
Combine the ground almonds with the confectioners' sugar. Process with a blade knife so that the mixture is as fine and delicate as possible. Stir in half the egg whites. Heat the granulated sugar and water to 250°F (120°C) to make a syrup. Make an Italian meringue (see method p. 177) by pouring the cooked syrup over the remaining egg whites (whipped), continuing to whip until the meringue has cooled completely. It will be smooth and hold many small peaks. Add the red coloring. (It will darken when baked, so do not overcolor.) With a large scraper, combine the two mixtures, which will deflate slightly. Spoon the mixture into a piping bag fitted with a plain tip and pipe small disks onto a silicone baking sheet set on a thick

baking pan, or on two ordinary baking pans. Let stand for 30 minutes until a crust forms; the mixture should not stick to your fingers when touched. Preheat the oven to 310°F (155°C). Bake for 12 minutes; do not let brown.

● Chef's note
It's hard to make small quantities of this recipe. These quantities will yield enough macarons for you to serve on another occasion. When they are cool and dry, carefully store the extra macarons in an airtight container and freeze for up to 4 weeks.

Make the chocolate mousse.
Begin melting the chocolate in a bain-marie. Maintain it at 113°F-122°F (45°C-50°C). In another bain-marie, heat the water, sugar, and egg yolks until the mixture begins to coagulate around the edges. Remove from the bain-marie and whip energetically until completely cooled (*pâte à bombe*, see p. 197). Whip the heavy cream until it holds soft peaks and carefully fold it into the *pâte à bombe*. Take one-third of this mixture and quickly incorporate it into the melted chocolate. Incorporate the chocolate mixture into the *pate à bombe* and whipped cream mixture. Be ready to use quickly, before the chocolate sets.

Assemble the dessert.
This dessert is assembled upside down as it will be turned out. Place the dessert ring on a sheet of food-safe acetate or parchment paper. Half-fill it with chocolate mousse, pressing down gently so that there are no unsightly air bubbles. Set the disk of gelled coulis over it, ensuring that it is horizontal. Spoon in more of the chocolate mousse, leaving just enough room to top it with a disk of Sacher sponge at the level of the rim. Freeze for 4 hours. Turn out of the ring onto a rack. Ensure that the glaze is at 80°F-82°F (27°C-28°C). Pour it over the dessert, covering it evenly. Wipe off any excess with a spatula. Let the glaze drip off for a few minutes and transfer to a serving platter.

Finish and decorate.
Stick the macarons around the side of the cake with a little melted chocolate and decorate as you wish.

Techniques
Chocolate Sacher sponge >> p. 69
Macarons >> p. 79
Chocolate mousse >> p. 106
Shiny chocolate glaze >> p. 116
Fruit coulis >> p. 128
French meringue >> p. 176
Italian meringue >> p. 177
Pâte à bombe >> p. 197

Ingredients

Sacher sponge

7 oz. (200 g) almond paste,
  50 percent almonds
1 extra large egg (2 ½ oz./70 g)
5 egg yolks (3 ½ oz./95 g)
3 egg whites (4 oz./110 g)
Scant ⅓ cup (2 oz./65 g) sugar
½ cup minus 1 tablespoon (2 oz./50 g)
  flour
3 tablespoons (⅔ oz./20 g) unsweetened
  cocoa powder
3 tablespoons (2 oz./50 g) butter, melted
  and cooled
2 oz. (50 g) cocoa paste, melted and cooled

Gelled coulis

2 tablespoons (1 oz./25 g) sugar
¹⁄₁₀ oz. (3 g) pectin NH
7 oz. (200 g) puréed raspberries
1 oz. (25 g) glucose syrup
½ oz. (15 g) invert sugar

Shiny chocolate glaze

Scant ½ cup (100 ml) water
⅓ cup (80 ml) heavy cream
⅓ cup (2 ½ oz./70 g) sugar
3 oz. (85 g) invert sugar
½ cup (2 ½ oz./70 g) unsweetened
  cocoa powder
5 sheets (10 g) gelatin, softened
  in 3 tablespoons (50 ml) water

Macarons

1 ¾ cups (5 oz./150 g) ground almonds
Generous 1 cup (5 oz./150 g)
  confectioners' sugar
½ cup (3 ½ oz./105 g) egg whites, divided
¾ cup (5 oz./150 g) sugar
3 tablespoons (50 ml) water
Red food coloring, preferably powdered

Chocolate mousse

9 oz. (250 g) bittersweet chocolate,
  64 percent cocoa
1 tablespoon (20 ml) water
¼ cup (2 oz./50 g) sugar
2 egg yolks
1 ¾ cups (450 ml) heavy cream

7-inch (16-cm) diameter dessert ring,
  measuring 2 inches (5 cm) deep

Ingredients

Flour-free chocolate sponge

3 eggs, separated
Scant ⅔ cup (4 oz./120 g) sugar
¼ cup (1 oz./30 g) unsweetened
   cocoa powder

Crisp praline layer

1 oz. (25 g) milk couverture chocolate
1 oz. (25 g) cocoa butter
3 oz. (80 g) hazelnut paste
2 oz. (50 g) hazelnut praline
3 oz. (80 g) Gavotte crêpe dentelle cookies,
   crushed (available online)

Chocolate mousse

7 oz. (200 g) bittersweet couverture chocolate,
   64 percent cocoa
1 teaspoon finely grated orange zest
¾ cup (200 ml) cream (30% fat content) or milk
1 cup (250 ml) heavy cream

Chocolate velvet

3 oz. (80 g) bittersweet couverture chocolate,
   64 percent cocoa
3 oz. (80 g) cocoa butter (or clarified butter)
(You can also use store-bought chocolate velvet)

A little melted chocolate for decoration

7-inch (16-cm) diameter dessert ring,
   measuring 2 inches (5 cm) deep (the dessert
   will not come up to the top)

🥄 Techniques

Flour-free chocolate sponge >> p. 71
Chocolate velvet (for spraying) >> p. 119
French meringue >> p. 176
Crunchy praline layer >> p. 190

Crisp and Creamy Layered Chocolate Dessert ★ ★

Serves 8
Preparation time: 1 hour 30 minutes/Cooking time: 30 minutes
Freezing time: 2 hours 30 minutes/Defrosting time: 2 hours
Best made a day ahead

Prepare the flour-free chocolate sponge.

Preheat the oven to 340°F (170°C). Line a 12 x 16-inch (30 x 40-cm) baking sheet with a silicone baking mat. Whip the egg whites until they form soft peaks. Stir in the sugar until the mixture is firm and shiny. Beat the egg yolks well. Carefully fold the egg white mixture into the egg yolks. Sift in the cocoa powder and, with a flexible spatula, stir it in until just combined.
Spread it out on the baking sheet to about ¼ inch (5 mm) and bake for 15 to 20 minutes, until it springs back to the touch; the inside should remain moist. Carefully transfer it to a cooling rack (it is very fragile).

Make the crisp praline layer.

Set a 7-inch (16-cm) diameter tart ring over a lined baking sheet.
Melt the couverture chocolate with the cocoa butter in a bain-marie. The temperature must not exceed 118°F (48°C). Remove from the heat and stir in the hazelnut paste and praline. Gently stir in the crushed dentelle cookies. Pour into the prepared tart ring to a depth of ⅕ inch (5 mm) and freeze.

Prepare the chocolate mousse.

Chop the chocolate. In a saucepan, add the orange zest to the ¾ cup (200 ml) milk or cream, bring to a boil, and simmer for 2 to 3 minutes to infuse. Whip the heavy cream until it holds soft peaks. Strain the liquid with the orange zest through a fine-mesh sieve over the chocolate. Stir until smooth to make a ganache. When the ganache thickens, at about 86°F (30°C), carefully fold in the whipped cream. The mousse must be used immediately before it sets.

Assemble the dessert.

Line a baking sheet with a silicone baking mat or parchment paper and set the dessert ring over it. Cut out a disk of chocolate sponge slightly smaller than the ring and place it at the bottom. Pour in ½ inch (1 cm) of the chocolate mousse. Place the disk of crisp praline over the mousse and fill to ½ inch (1 cm) below the rim with the remaining mousse. (The dessert should be slightly lower, about ½ in./1 cm, than the rim of the dessert ring.) Smooth with an offset spatula and freeze for 2 hours. (The velvety texture is obtained by spraying a frozen surface with the chocolate velvet, see below.)

Finish with the chocolate velvet.

Melt the couverture chocolate with the cocoa butter in a bain-marie. The temperature must not exceed 118°F (48°C). Pour the hot mixture into an electric spray gun, then spray the frozen dessert uniformly. Decorate with chocolate piped from a paper decorating cone. This dessert must be served chilled, not frozen, so refrigerate for about 2 hours.

Chestnut Cream in a Macaron Shell ★

Serves 6
Preparation time: 1 hour
Cooking time: 12 minutes
Drying time: 30 minutes

Make the macaron shell.
Mix the ground almonds together with the confectioners' sugar. Process with a blade knife so that the mixture is as fine and delicate as possible. Stir in half the egg whites. Heat the granulated sugar and water to 250°F (120°C) to make a syrup. Make an Italian meringue (see method p. 177) by whipping the remaining egg whites and then pouring the cooked syrup over them, continuing to whip until the meringue has cooled completely. It will be smooth and hold many small peaks. Add the red coloring. (The color will darken when baked, so do not overcolor.) With a large scraper, combine the two mixtures, which will deflate slightly. Spoon the mixture into a piping bag fitted with a plain tip and pipe small adjacent disks (to make a ring of circles with a hole in the center, see illustration p. 343) onto a silicone baking sheet set on a thick baking pan, or on two ordinary baking pans. Let stand for 30 minutes until a crust forms; the mixture should not stick to your fingers when touched. Preheat the oven to 310°F (155°C).
Bake for 12 minutes; do not let brown.

Prepare the chestnut cream.
In a stand mixer fitted with a paddle, combine the butter, chestnut cream, and rum. Start at low speed and gradually increase to medium. Beat until very smooth, like creamed butter.

Assemble the dish.
Turn a macaron ring onto a rack. Spoon the chestnut cream into a piping bag and pipe little dollops on each rounded part of the ring. Top with another macaron ring and dust with confectioners' sugar.

● **Chef's notes**
Chestnut cream, which is also sometimes called chestnut spread, contains chestnuts, sugar, and vanilla. In addition, some brands include glucose and candied chestnuts.
You can vary this recipe by experimenting with different colorings for the macaron and other flavors for the cream.

Techniques
Macarons >> p. 79
Italian meringue >> p. 177

Ingredients

Macaron shell
1 ¾ cups (5 oz./150 g) ground almonds
Generous 1 cup (5 oz./150 g) confectioners' sugar
½ cup (3 ½ oz./105 g) egg whites, divided
¾ cup (5 oz./150 g) sugar
3 tablespoons (50 ml) water
Pink food coloring, preferably powdered

Chestnut cream
1 ¼ sticks (5 oz./150 g) butter, softened
5 oz. (150 g) chestnut cream (*crème de marron*)
1 ¾ teaspoons (8 g) rum

Confectioners' sugar for dusting

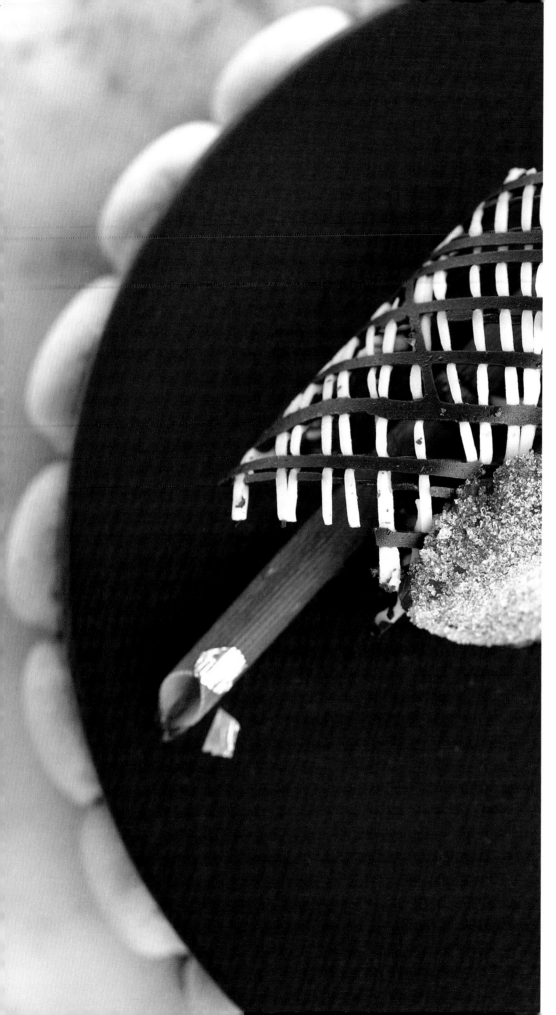

Ingredients

Candied rose petals
1 egg white, extra fresh
1 pinch salt
A few unsprayed rose petals
¾ cup (5 oz./150 g) sugar (refined to ensure
  that there are no blemishes)

Cinnamon-scented coconut pastry
1 stick (4 oz./125 g) salted butter, softened
Scant ½ cup (3 oz./80 g) sugar
⅔ oz. (20 g) invert sugar
½ teaspoon (2 g) salt
1 egg (2 oz./50 g) plus 1 egg yolk (20 g)
1 cup plus 2 tablespoons (5 oz./150 g) flour
1 cup (3 oz./80 g) unsweetened shredded coconut
¼ cup (20 g) ground almonds
¾ teaspoon (3 g) ground cinnamon

Litchi-apple compote
2 sheets (4 g) gelatin
7 oz. (200 g) apples
5 oz. (150 g) litchis
¼ cup (2 oz./50 g) sugar
2 teaspoons (10 ml) litchi liqueur

Rose-scented white chocolate mousse
3 sheets (6 g) gelatin
8 oz. (225 g) white couverture chocolate
1 ¾ cups (450 ml) heavy cream, divided
2 egg yolks
¼ cup (2 oz./50 g) sugar
A few drops of essential rose oil

Macaron cookies
1 ¾ cups (5 oz./150 g) ground almonds
Generous 1 cup (5 oz./150 g) confectioners' sugar
½ cup (3 ½ oz./105 g) egg whites, divided
¾ cup (5 oz./150 g) sugar
3 tablespoons (50 ml) water

Shiny bittersweet chocolate glaze
⅔ cup (150 ml) water
½ cup (130 ml) heavy cream
½ cup (3½ oz./100 g) sugar
4 oz. (125 g) invert sugar
Scant 1 cup (3 ½ oz./100 g) unsweetened
  cocoa powder
7 ½ sheets (15 g) gelatin, softened in
  5 tablespoons (75 ml) water

7-inch (16-cm) diameter dessert ring,
  measuring 2 inches (5 cm) deep

White Chocolate Mousse with Litchi-Apple Compote ★ ★ ★

Serves 8
Preparation time: 2 hours/Chilling time: 2 hours
Freezing time: 4 hours 30 minutes/Resting time: 1 hour
Cooking time: 30 minutes

A day ahead, prepare the candied rose petals.
Lightly beat the egg white with the salt. With a brush, carefully spread the egg white on both sides of the petals, making sure to coat them evenly. Dust on both sides with the sugar and place them on parchment paper. Set carefully on a radiator or in an 85°F (30°C) oven and leave overnight, until dry.

Make the cinnamon-scented coconut pastry.
Cream together the butter, sugar, and invert sugar. Add the salt and beat in the egg and egg yolk. When the mixture is smooth, beat in the dry ingredients until just combined. Knead very lightly with your hands, shape into a disk, cover with plastic wrap, and chill for 20 minutes.

Prepare the litchi-apple compote.
Soften the gelatin sheets in a bowl of cold water. Wash and peel the fruit. Remove the cores from the apples and pit the litchis. Dice all the fruit. Place in a saucepan over low heat and cook gently until softened (about 15 minutes). (If you are using apples with a high water content, such as Granny Smith, make sure you let most of the water evaporate.) Stir in the sugar and remove from the heat. Squeeze the water from the gelatin and stir it in until completely dissolved. Let cool and add the liqueur. Pour into a tart ring slightly smaller than the dessert ring to a depth of ½ inch (1 cm). Freeze for 30 minutes.

Make the rose-scented white chocolate mousse.
Soften the gelatin in a bowl of cold water. Chop the chocolate. In a medium heavy-bottom saucepan, heat ⅓ cup (75 ml) of the heavy cream. Beat the egg yolks with the sugar until pale and thick. When the cream is simmering, pour half of it over the egg yolk and sugar mixture, stirring constantly. Return the mixture to the saucepan and cook, stirring constantly and removing the saucepan from the heat from time to time, until it reaches 185°F (85°C) or coats the back of a spoon. Immediately strain the hot liquid over the chocolate and stir until smooth. Squeeze the water from the gelatin sheets and stir in until completely dissolved. Place in the refrigerator and cool to about 77°F (25°C): the mixture should be just beginning to gel.
Whip the remaining cream until it holds soft peaks and fold it carefully into the custard mixture. Stir in the essential oil. The mousse must now be molded rapidly.

Assemble the dessert.
This dessert is assembled upside down, as it is turned out.
Place the dessert ring on a sheet of food-safe acetate or parchment paper. Half-fill it with chocolate mousse, pressing down gently so that there are no air bubbles. Set the frozen compote layer over it, ensuring that it is horizontal. Pour in the remaining chocolate mousse. Freeze for 4 hours.

Make the macaron cookies.
Combine the ground almonds with the confectioners' sugar. Process with a blade knife so that the mixture is as fine and delicate as possible. Stir in half the egg whites. Heat the granulated sugar and water to 250°F (120°C) to make a syrup. Make an Italian meringue (see method p. 177) by whipping the remaining egg whites and then pouring the cooked syrup over them, continuing to whip until the meringue has cooled completely. It will be smooth and hold many small peaks. With a large scraper, combine the two mixtures, which will deflate slightly. Spoon the mixture into a piping bag fitted with a plain tip and pipe small disks onto a silicone baking sheet set on a thick baking pan, or two ordinary baking pans. Let stand for 30 minutes until a crust forms; the mixture should not stick to your fingers when touched. Preheat the oven to 310°F (155°C). Bake for 12 minutes; do not let brown.

Make the shiny bittersweet chocolate glaze.
Bring the ⅔ cup water, heavy cream, sugar, and invert sugar to a boil. Stir in the cocoa powder until completely smooth. When completely dissolved, simmer for 2 minutes, stirring frequently. Remove from the heat. Stir in the softened gelatin sheets until completely dissolved. Process briefly with an immersion blender. Transfer to a mixing bowl and cover with plastic wrap flush with the surface until needed. Chill if necessary.

Decorate the dessert.
Turn the dessert out of the ring onto a rack set over a dish deep enough to catch any excess glaze. If necessary, heat the glaze to 86°F (30°C). Pour over the dessert, wiping off any excess with a spatula. Let drain for a few minutes and transfer to a serving platter. Decorate with macaron cookies and rose petals.

Techniques
Sweetened short pastry (crumbled) >> p. 18
Macarons >> p. 79
Chocolate mousse >> p. 106
Shiny chocolate glaze >> p. 116
Candied rose petals >> p. 169

Black Forest Cake ★

Serves 8
Preparation time: 1 hour 30 minutes
Cooking time: 25 minutes

Prepare the chocolate Genoese sponge.
Preheat the oven to 350°F (180°C). Butter and flour the cake pan.
Place the eggs and sugar in a round-bottom mixing bowl and set it over a bain-marie heated to 140°F (60°C). Whip until the mixture reaches the ribbon stage, then remove from the heat. Sift the flour and carefully fold in half of it with a flexible spatula. Sift the cocoa powder into the remaining flour and fold in, taking care not to deflate the mixture.
Fill the pan three-quarters to the top with the sponge batter. Bake for 20 to 25 minutes, until it is well risen, springy to the touch, and a cake tester comes out dry. Turn it onto a rack and let cool.

Prepare the syrup.
Bring the water and sugar to a boil. Let cool and add the cherry juice.

Make the Chantilly cream.
Pour the cream into a bowl (chilled, if possible) and add the sugar. Whisk briskly, or at medium speed if using an electric beater, until it holds soft peaks. Add the vanilla extract and whip for a few more seconds until light and airy. Chill immediately.

Assemble and decorate the cake.
Cut the sponge horizontally into three disks. Moisten each one with the syrup. Spoon a ½-inch (1-cm) layer of Chantilly cream on the first disk and dot with cherries. Repeat with another layer of sponge, cream and cherries. Place the third disk on the top and cover completely with Chantilly cream, smoothing it with a spatula. Decorate with more cream using a piping bag fitted with a small star tip. Apply chocolate shavings around the sides and dot the top with cherries.

● **Chef's note**
You can use all sorts of cherries: canned, in kirsch, Amarena, griotte, and Morello.

Techniques
Genoese sponge >> p. 76
Chantilly cream >> p. 94
Moistening sponge layers >> p. 133

Ingredients

Chocolate Genoese sponge
4 eggs
⅔ cup (4 oz./125 g) sugar
¾ cup plus 3 tablespoons (3 ½ oz./110 g) flour
2 tablespoons (15 g) unsweetened cocoa powder
2 teaspoons (10 g) butter and 1 tablespoon (10 g) flour for the cake pan

Syrup
3 tablespoons (50 ml) water
¼ cup (2 oz./50 g) sugar
3 tablespoons (50 ml) cherry juice

Chantilly cream
1 cup (250 ml) heavy cream, well chilled
3 tablespoons (1 ½ oz./35 g) superfine sugar
1 teaspoon (5 ml) vanilla extract

Decoration
4 oz. (120 g) cherries, canned or soaked in eau-de-vie, drained
3 ½ oz. (100 g) chocolate shavings

8-inch (20-cm) round cake pan, measuring 2 inches (5 cm) deep

Ingredients

Genoese sponge
4 eggs
⅔ cup (4 oz./125 g) sugar
1 cup (4 oz./125 g) flour

Mousseline cream
1 vanilla bean
1 cup (250 ml) milk
½ cup (3 ½ oz./100 g) sugar, divided
2 egg yolks
Scant ¼ cup (1 oz./35 g) cornstarch
1 stick plus 1 tablespoon (4 ½ oz./130 g) butter,
    softened, divided

Syrup
½ cup (120 ml) water
Scant ½ cup (3 oz./80 g) sugar
2 tablespoons (30 ml) liqueur (optional)

Marbled almond paste
4 oz. (120 g) almond paste, 50 percent almonds
Red food coloring
2 ½ tablespoons (20 g) confectioners' sugar

10 oz. (300 g) strawberries, washed
    and carefully patted dry

6-inch (15-cm) diameter dessert ring
    measuring 2 inches (5 cm) deep

Techniques
Genoese sponge >> p. 76
Almond paste decorations >> p. 132

Strawberry and Mousseline Cream Layer Cake (*Fraisier*) ★ ★

Serves 6
Preparation time: 1 hour 15 minutes/Cooking time: 35 minutes
Chilling time: 2 hours

Make the Genoese sponge.
Preheat the oven to 350°F (180°C). Line a rimmed 12 x 16-inch (30 x 40-cm) baking sheet with a silicone baking mat or parchment paper.
Place the eggs and sugar in a round bottom mixing bowl and set it over a bain-marie heated to 140°F (60°C). Whip until the mixture reaches the ribbon stage then remove from the heat. Sift the flour and carefully fold in half of it with a flexible spatula. When it is incorporated, fold in the remaining half, taking care not to deflate the mixture.
Pour over the prepared baking sheet to a thickness of no more than ¼ inch (6-7 mm) and even it with a spatula. Bake for 15 minutes. The sponge must stay moist and must not color. Slide onto a rack and let cool.

Prepare the mousseline cream (to be used as soon as possible).
Prepare the mousseline cream following the technique on page 100.

Prepare the syrup for moistening.
Bring the water and sugar to a boil. Let cool and add the liqueur, if using.

Assemble the layer cake.
Line a baking sheet with parchment paper. Set the dessert ring over it. Hull the strawberries and cut them in half lengthwise. Place them around the rim with the flat side against the metal. Cut a disk of Genoese sponge slightly smaller than the ring and place at the base. Moisten it with syrup and spoon out a generous layer of mousseline cream, pressing it gently against the strawberry halves. Dot a few strawberries over the cream and smooth with an offset spatula. Cut out a second disk of sponge to the dimensions of the ring and press it gently over the cream. Moisten it and fill the ring with the remaining mousseline cream. Smooth the top and chill.

Prepare the marbled almond paste.
Knead the almond paste lightly to soften it. Divide it in half and add a few drops of red coloring to one part. Roll each half into a sausage shape, place one over the other, and press down lightly. Cut in half across the center and place one half over the other, doubling the number of stripes. Press down again and repeat, so that each time the number of stripes increases, until the paste is as marbled as you require. Dust the work surface with confectioners' sugar. Keeping the visible stripes facing downward, roll the paste out very finely (to less than ⅛ in./2 mm) to make a disk the size of the cake. Transfer the disk to the top of the cake and press down lightly with the rolling pin to trim the edges.

● **Chef's note**
Use the decoration of your choice, such as a strawberry dipped in neutral glaze.

Black Currant Mousse and Pear Layer Cake ★★

Serves 8
Preparation time: 1 hour 30 minutes
Cooking time: 15 minutes
Chilling time: 2 hours

Make the Succès almond meringue base and center.
Preheat the oven to 350°F (180°C). Whip the egg whites until they form firm peaks. Stir in the sugar with the whisk until the mixture is firm and shiny. Combine the confectioners' sugar, ground almonds, and flour and, with a flexible spatula, fold them into the meringue, taking care not to deflate the mixture. Spoon into a piping bag and pipe out two disks, slightly smaller than the dessert ring, onto a baking sheet (silicone or lined with parchment paper). Bake for about 10 minutes. The meringue must be dry to the touch and must not color.

Prepare the black currant mousse.
Soften the gelatin in a bowl of cold water. Heat one-third of the puréed black currants with the sugar. Remove from the heat. Squeeze the water from the gelatin sheets and stir into the heated black currants until completely dissolved. Add the remaining puréed black currants and cool the mixture to 68°F-77°F (20°C-25°C). Whip the cream until it holds soft peaks and gradually whisk it into the fruit mixture, taking care not to deflate it. It is now ready to be used and must be molded before it sets.

Assemble the dessert.
Set the dessert ring on a lined baking sheet. Place a disk of meringue at the bottom. Pour in 1 inch (2.5 cm) of black currant mousse. Dice the pears. Arrange the dice over the top of the mousse. Gently place the second disk of Succès meringue over it and pour in the remaining mousse. Smooth with an offset spatula. Chill for 2 hours.

Prepare the glaze.
Bring the water and sugar to a boil. Remove from the heat. Stir the softened gelatin sheets into the syrup until dissolved. Divide the syrup in half. Color one half with the red coloring. Cool to about 77°F (25°C). Brush the top with the red glaze, making a marbled pattern, and use a spatula to spread the clear glaze over that. Transfer to a serving platter and carefully remove the dessert ring. Serve chilled.

● **Chef's notes**
Add a decorative touch by drawing a chocolate pattern with a paper decorating cone (see p. 147). You can make this dessert with other fruit like raspberries and apricots.

Techniques
Succès almond meringue >> p. 77
Fruit mousse >> p. 109
Making a paper decorating cone >> p. 147

Ingredients

Succès almond meringue
4 egg whites (4 oz./120 g)
2 tablespoons (1 oz./25 g) sugar
⅓ cup (2 oz./50 g) confectioners' sugar
1 cup minus 1 tablespoon (2 ½ oz./75 g) ground almonds
2 ½ tablespoons (1 oz./25 g) all-purpose flour

Black currant mousse
4 sheets (8 g) gelatin
10 oz. (300 g) puréed black currants
¼ cup (2 oz./50 g) sugar
1 ¼ cups (300 ml) heavy cream

4 oz. (120 g) drained canned pears

Glaze
4 sheets (8 g) gelatin, softened in 3 tablespoons (45 ml) water
⅔ cup (150 ml) water
1 cup (7 oz./200 g) sugar
Red coloring

8-inch (20-cm) diameter dessert ring

Ingredients

Genoese sponge
4 eggs
⅔ cup (4 oz./125 g) sugar
1 cup (4 oz./125 g) flour
Butter and flour for the cake pan

1 cup (3 oz./80 g) sliced almonds for decoration

Coffee butter cream
1 ¼ cups (9 oz./250 g) sugar
Scant ⅓ cup (70 ml) water
4 egg yolks
2 ¼ sticks (9 oz./250 g) butter, softened and diced
2 teaspoons (10 ml) coffee extract

Syrup
3 tablespoons (50 ml) strong espresso (or water)
¼ cup (2 oz./50 g) sugar
1 tablespoon plus 1 teaspoon (20 ml)
  coffee-flavored liqueur

7-inch (18-cm) round cake pan, measuring
  2 inches (5 cm) deep

Techniques
Genoese sponge >> p. 76
Butter creams >> p. 95
Moistening sponge layers >> p. 133
Making a paper decorating cone >> p. 147

Mocha Cake ★★

Serves 8
Preparation time: 1 hour 15 minutes
Cooking time: 30 minutes

Spread the sliced almonds on a baking tray and lightly roast them in the oven at 350°F (180°C) for 6 to 8 minutes. Let cool.

Prepare the Genoese sponge.
Preheat the oven to 350°F (180°C). Butter and lightly flour the cake pan. Place the eggs and sugar in a round-bottom mixing bowl and set it over a bain-marie heated to 140°F (60°C). Whip until the mixture reaches the ribbon stage then remove from the heat. Sift the flour and carefully fold in half of it with a flexible spatula. When it is incorporated, fold in the remaining half, taking care not to deflate the mixture. Do not overmix. Pour the batter to three-quarters of the depth of the pan and bake for 15 to 20 minutes, until a cake tester comes out clean. The sponge must stay moist and must not color. Immediately turn it onto a rack and let cool.

Make the coffee butter cream.
Combine the sugar with the water in a saucepan to make a syrup and cook to 243°F–250°F (117°C–121°C). With an electric beater, whip the egg yolks until foamy. Pour the syrup over the egg yolks, beating constantly. Continue to beat until the mixture cools to about 86°F (30°C). It will become increasingly foamy. At medium speed, incorporate the diced butter. Add the coffee extract. Transfer to a mixing bowl, cover with plastic wrap flush with the surface, and chill if not using immediately.

Make the syrup.
Briefly boil together the espresso and sugar. Let cool and stir in the coffee liqueur.

Assemble and decorate the cake.
Cut the sponge horizontally into three disks with a long serrated knife. Moisten the disks with the syrup. Spread the bottom disk with ½ inch (1 cm) of butter cream. Cover with a disk of sponge and then a layer of butter cream. Top with the third disk and, with a spatula, cover the entire surface of the cake with butter cream, making a thicker layer on the top than around the side. Lightly heat a serrated knife and run it along the top to make stripes or zigzags. Press the sliced almonds around the side. Spoon the remaining butter cream into a piping bag fitted with a small star tip and pipe rosettes around the top. Make finer decorations with a paper decorating cone.

● Did you know?
This cake takes its name from the port of Moka in Yemen, which as early as the seventeenth century was well known for its fine coffee. The cake has been made in Paris since the nineteenth century.

Opéra Coffee and Chocolate Layer Cake ★ ★ ★

Serves 8
Preparation time: 2 hours 15 minutes
Cooking time: 40 minutes
Chilling time: 1 hour

Prepare the Joconde sponge (this can be made a day ahead).
Preheat the oven to 350°F (180°C). Line two 12 x 16-inch (30 x 40-cm) rimmed baking pans. Mix the ground almonds and confectioners' sugar together and sift in the flour. In the bowl of a stand mixer, beat the two eggs with the sifted dry ingredients. Meanwhile, whip the egg whites until they form soft peaks. Add the sugar and whip until incorporated. The meringue should not be too firm. Pour the browned melted butter into the egg mixture. Carefully fold in the meringue. Spread very thinly over the prepared baking pan. Bake for about 15 minutes, until dry on top, springy to the touch, and very lightly golden.

Make the coffee butter cream.
Combine the sugar with the water in a saucepan to make a syrup and cook to 243°F–250°F (117°C–121°C). With an electric beater, whip the egg yolks until foamy. Pour the syrup over the egg yolks, beating constantly. Continue to beat until the mixture cools to about 86°F (30°C). It will become increasingly foamy. At medium speed, incorporate the diced butter. Add the coffee extract. Transfer to a mixing bowl, cover with plastic wrap flush with the surface, and chill if not using rapidly.

Prepare the syrup.
Briefly boil together the water and sugar. Let cool and stir in the coffee extract.

Prepare the bittersweet chocolate ganache.
Melt the chocolate in a bain-marie set over a pot of barely simmering water. Heat the cream and pour it gradually over the melted chocolate, stirring constantly until smooth.

Make the glaze.
Combine all the ingredients in a mixing bowl and heat over a bain-marie to 104°F (40°C). Whisk until smooth.

Assemble and decorate the cake.
Cut the Joconde sponge into rectangles of the desired size of the cake or the size of the dessert frame. Brush one with a thin layer of melted dark chocolate glazing paste. Place it in the dessert frame. Moisten with syrup and pour in a thin layer (about ⅛ in./3 mm) of ganache. Set another layer of sponge over it. Moisten with syrup. Cover with a layer of butter cream slightly thinner than the ganache layer. Place the third layer of sponge on the top and moisten with syrup. Continue layering to the top of the frame. Spread another layer of butter cream over it. Smooth the butter cream with a spatula, adding a little if necessary. Place in the refrigerator for 1 hour. Cover the top with the glaze and smooth. Carefully remove the dessert frame. Fill a paper decorating cone with melted chocolate or any leftover ganache and trace out a decoration on the glaze.

Ingredients

Joconde sponge
1 cup (3 oz./80 g) ground almonds
Scant ⅔ cup (3 oz./80 g) confectioners' sugar
2 ½ tablespoons (1 oz./25 g) flour
2 eggs
5 egg whites
3 ½ tablespoons (1 ½ oz./40 g) sugar
1 tablespoon (20 g) butter, melted until brown and cooled

Coffee butter cream
1 ¼ cups (9 oz./250 g) sugar
Scant ⅓ cup (70 ml) water
4 egg yolks
2 ¼ sticks (9 oz./250 g) butter, softened and diced
2 teaspoons (10 ml) coffee extract

Syrup
¼ cup (60 ml) water
⅓ cup (2 oz./60 g) sugar
1 tablespoon plus 1 teaspoon (20 ml) coffee extract

Bittersweet chocolate ganache
5 oz. (150 g) bittersweet chocolate, 64 percent cocoa
⅔ cup (150 ml) heavy cream

Glaze
4 oz. (125 g) dark chocolate glazing paste (*pâte à glacer brune*, available online)
2 oz. (50 g) bittersweet couverture chocolate
1 tablespoon (12 ml) grapeseed oil

2 oz. (50 g) dark chocolate glazing paste

Special equipment: an adjustable cake frame, or an 8 x 12-in. (20 x 30-cm) dessert frame

Techniques
Joconde sponge >> p. 69
Butter creams >> p. 95
Moistening sponge layers >> p. 133
Making a paper decorating cone >> p. 147
French meringue >> p. 176

Classic pastries

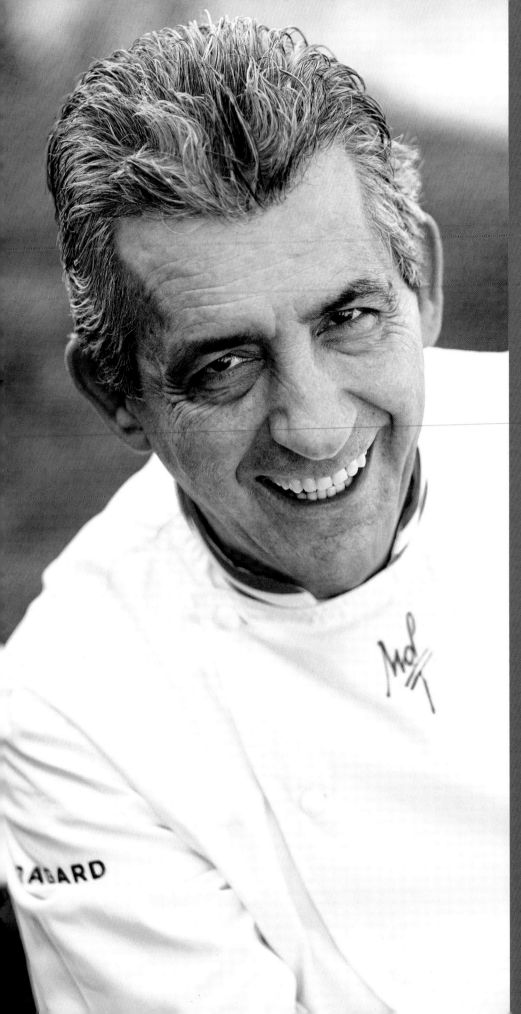

Philippe Urraca

Meilleur Ouvrier de France, pâtisserie

My idea was to revisit a chocolate and
raspberry tartlet, transforming it into a
long, slim shape. In updating this dish,
it was important to keep the balance
between the shortcrust pastry and the
ganache. Whether you serve it as a cake or
plated dessert, my version offers a subtle
harmony of fruit and chocolate.

Choco-Raspberry Tartlets

Serves 10

Preparation time: 1 hour

Cooking time: 20 minutes

Freezing time: 20 minutes

Make the chocolate shortcrust.

Melt the cocoa paste. Combine the butter, confectioners' sugar, and cocoa paste. Add the egg and salt. Combine the flour with the cocoa powder and ground almonds. Incorporate the dry ingredients into the batter. Mix until smooth and chill. Roll the dough very thinly, to less than ⅛ inch (2 mm). Cut into ten rectangles measuring 4 x 1 ¼ inches (11 x 3 cm) and bake at 300°F (150°C) for 12 minutes.

Prepare the chocolate-raspberry ganache.

Melt the bittersweet and milk chocolate together. Bring the puréed raspberries to a boil with the cream and butter. When the mixture is smooth, pour it over the melted chocolate, blend, and add the eau-de-vie. Spread the ganache on a baking sheet; it should be just under ½ inch (10 mm) thick. Place in the freezer to set. Cut it into ten rectangles measuring 4 x 1 inch (10 x 2.5 cm).

Make the chocolate glaze.

Bring the water to a boil with the sugar, cream, and glucose syrup. Pour the mixture into the glazing paste. Melt the chocolate in a bain-marie set over a pot of barely simmering water and incorporate it into the mixture. When the mixture is at 95°F (35°C), it is ready to use.

Assemble the dish.

Coat the ganache with chocolate glaze and place it on the rectangle of shortcrust. Decorate with a raspberry and a piece of edible gold leaf.

Ingredients

Chocolate shortcrust

½ oz. (15 g) cocoa paste

1 ¼ sticks (5 oz./140 g) butter

⅔ cup (3 oz./80 g) confectioners' sugar

1 egg (2 oz./50 g)

¼ teaspoon (1.5 g) salt

2 cups (9 oz./250 g) flour

3 tablespoons (20 g) unsweetened cocoa powder

Generous ⅓ cup (1 oz./30 g) ground almonds

Chocolate-raspberry ganache

6 oz. (165 g) bittersweet chocolate, 70 percent cocoa

4 oz. (115 g) milk chocolate

5 oz. (150 g) puréed raspberries

½ cup (125 ml) heavy cream

1 tablespoon (14 g) butter

1 tablespoon plus 1 teaspoon (20 ml) raspberry eau-de-vie

Chocolate glaze

Scant ½ cup (100 ml) water

½ cup (3 ½ oz./100 g) sugar

1 cup (250 ml) heavy cream

2 ½ tablespoons (2 oz./50 g) glucose syrup

1 lb. (500 g) dark chocolate glazing paste (*pâte à glacer brune*, available online)

3 ½ oz. (100 g) bittersweet couverture chocolate

Decoration

10 raspberries

Edible gold leaf

Ingredients

Dough

½ cup (3 oz./80 g) raisins
3 tablespoons (50 ml) rum
1 cake (0.6 oz./20 g) fresh yeast
1 ¼ cups (300 ml) water, divided
4 cups (1 lb./500 g) flour
2 teaspoons (10 g) salt
2 ½ teaspoons (10 g) sugar
4 eggs, room temperature
1 ¾ sticks (7 oz./200 g) butter

Syrup

1 ¼ cups (9 oz./250 g) sugar
2 cups (500 ml) water
Flavoring of your choice (star anise,
   citrus zest, cinnamon stick, etc.)
2 oz. (60 g) light glaze
3 tablespoons (40 ml) water

Chantilly cream

⅔ cup (150 ml) heavy cream
2 ½ tablespoons (20 g) confectioners' sugar
1 teaspoon vanilla extract or the seeds
   of 1 vanilla bean

7 oz. (200 g) assorted red berries for garnish
Eight individual baba molds or one 10-inch
   (25-cm) baba mold

Techniques

Baba or savarin dough >> p. 41
Chantilly cream >> p. 94
Moistening sponge layers >> p.133

Rum Babas ★★

Serves 8
Preparation time: 2 hours
Cooking time: 25 minutes

A day (or at least 2 hours) ahead, prepare the dough.
Rinse the raisins under cold water and soak them in the rum.
Dilute the yeast in 3 tablespoons (50 ml) tepid water. Sift the flour and make a well in the center. Sprinkle the salt at the outer edge of the flour so that it does not come into direct contact with the yeast. Add the sugar. Lightly beat the eggs. Pour the diluted yeast and eggs into the well.
Mix with a spatula or by hand. Work the dough energetically until it becomes elastic, gradually incorporating the remaining water. You can also use a stand mixer fitted with a dough hook, starting at low speed and then increasing to medium, about 25 minutes altogether.
Stop kneading when the dough no longer sticks to your fingers or the sides of the bowl. It should now be smooth, shiny, and very elastic. Melt the butter until just warm and mix it into the dough. Knead energetically (or at medium to fast speed, 8-10 minutes), again until the butter is thoroughly combined in the dough. Cover with plastic wrap and let rise for 30 to 40 minutes at 77°F-83°F (25°C-30°C), until doubled in volume.
Flatten the dough to expel any air bubbles (punching down).
Drain the raisins and lightly knead them into the dough until just evenly distributed. Butter the molds and half-fill them with the dough, either by hand or with a piping bag. Let rise again until the dough reaches the top of the molds. Preheat the oven to 400°F (200°C) for individual babas and 350°F (180°C) for a large one. (The larger size needs to be baked more slowly.) Bake the individual babas for about 25 minutes, and the large size for up to 40 minutes, until a cake tester comes out dry.
Immediately turn them out onto a cooling rack so that no condensation forms on the crust. Let cool completely.

Make the syrup.
Combine all the ingredients and bring to a boil. Simmer for 2 to 3 minutes, remove from the heat, and let infuse until a thermometer registers about 105°F (40°C). Place the babas in the syrup and use a ladle to drench them with it. To test that they are sufficiently soaked, prick use a long needle, which should slide in without any resistance at all. Set them on a rack to drain and transfer to a plate.
Heat the light glaze with the water and brush the babas.

Prepare the Chantilly cream.
Whip the cream and confectioners' sugar until it forms firm peaks. Stir in the vanilla. Spoon the whipped cream into a piping bag fitted with a star tip and pipe the cream into the center of the babas. Garnish with the fruit.

● Chef's note

You can drench your babas with rum or any other alcoholic beverage when they have been soaked in syrup.

Canelés, a specialty of Bordeaux ★

Serves 8 (2-3 per person)
Preparation time: 30 minutes
Chilling time: at least 12 hours
Cooking time: 1 hour

Combine the flour and sugar in a mixing bowl. Heat the milk and butter to 105°F-120°F (40°C-50°C). Whisk the hot mixture into the dry ingredients until smooth. Whisk in the egg, egg yolks, and rum. Chill, for 12 hours if possible.

Preheat the oven to 400°F (200°C). Grease the *canelé* molds.

Pour the batter into the molds to nine-tenths of the depth. Place in the oven and immediately lower the temperature to 350°F (180°C). Bake for about 1 hour, until the crusts are nicely browned and lightly caramelized. Immediately turn out of the molds.

● **Chef's notes**

Canelés are best prepared a day ahead: the batter rests and the flour absorbs more of the liquid, ensuring that the crumb is moist.

Traditionally, canelés are made in copper molds (these give the best results) that are greased with beeswax.

They travel well and make an excellent snack.

Ingredients
1 cup (4 ½ oz./125 g) flour
1 ¼ cups (9 oz./250 g) sugar
2 cups (500 ml) milk
2 tablespoons (1 oz./25 g) butter
1 egg plus 3 egg yolks
2 tablespoons (30 ml) rum
Butter or beeswax (see Chef's notes)
to grease the molds

Special equipment: *canelé* molds,
copper if possible

Ingredients

⅓ cup (2 oz./50 g) raisins
2 teaspoons (10 ml) brown rum

Pastry cream

1 vanilla bean
1 ¼ cups (300 ml) milk
2 egg yolks
⅓ cup (2 oz./60 g) sugar
3 tablespoons (1 oz./30 g) cornstarch

Choux pastry

4 tablespoons (2 oz./60 g) butter, room temperature
⅔ cup plus 1 tablespoon (3 oz./90 g) all-purpose flour
⅔ cup (150 ml) water
½ teaspoon (2 g) salt
½ teaspoon (2 g) sugar
3 eggs

Puff pastry base

10 oz. (300 g) puff pastry
5 tablespoons (3 oz./80 g) butter
Scant ½ cup (3 oz./80 g) sugar

Confectioners' sugar for dusting

Pastry Cream Turnovers ★

Makes 12 turnovers
Preparation time: 1 hour
Chilling time: 30 minutes
Cooking time: 20 minutes

Soak the raisins in the rum.

Make the pastry cream.
Slit the vanilla bean lengthwise and scrape the seeds into the milk. Pour the milk into a saucepan, add the vanilla bean, and begin heating.
In a mixing bowl, briskly whisk the egg yolks, sugar, and cornstarch until pale and thick. When the milk is simmering, pour half of it over the egg yolk mixture, beating continuously. Return the mixture to the saucepan with the remaining milk and bring to a boil stirring continuously. Let simmer for 2 to 3 minutes, still stirring. Remove vanilla bean. Transfer to a mixing bowl, cover with plastic wrap flush with the surface, and cool rapidly.

Prepare the choux pastry.
Dice the butter. Sift the flour. In a large saucepan, bring the water, salt, sugar, and butter to a boil. When all the butter has melted, remove from the heat and stir in all the flour. Return the saucepan to the heat. With a wooden spoon or spatula, beat briskly to dry out the mixture. Continue until the batter pulls away from the sides of the saucepan. Remove from the heat and let cool to no hotter than 122°F (50°C), to avoid cooking the eggs when they are added. Still using a wooden spoon or spatula, beat in the eggs, one by one, until smooth and shiny.

Assemble the turnover.
Roll the puff pastry to an 8 x 16-inch (20 x 40-cm) rectangle under ⅛ inch (3 mm) thick. Melt the butter and brush it over the puff pastry. Sprinkle with the sugar. Roll the pastry like a jelly roll. The diameter at this stage should be 3 inches (8 cm) and the length 14 inches (35 cm).
Chill for 30 minutes, until firm and cold.
Preheat the oven to 350°F (180°C).
Cut into slices ¾ inch (1.5 cm) thick. Roll each slice into an oval, under ⅛ inch (3 mm) thick. Place the more attractive side facing downward (the top will be garnished).
Drain the raisins. Combine the pastry cream, choux pastry, and drained raisins. On one side, place a dollop of the mixture. Fold over like a turnover. There is no need to seal the sides as the choux pastry swells and prevents the garnish from leaking out. These turnovers are not basted either. Bake for about 20 minutes, until well risen and a nice golden color.
Transfer to a cooling rack and dust with confectioners' sugar.

Techniques
Basic choux pastry >> p. 34
Pastry cream >> p. 99

Apple Turnovers ★

Makes 10 turnovers
Preparation time: 45 minutes
Resting time: 2 hours
Chilling time: 1 hour
Cooking time: 30 minutes

Make the puff pastry.
On a work surface or in a mixing bowl, sift the flour and incorporate the salt. Make a well and pour in the water. Working rapidly with your hands, blend the ingredients together until fully blended. Shape into a disk and chill for 20 minutes.
Ensure that the butter has the same consistency as that of the dough. If not, you may have to bash it (still wrapped) with a rolling pin. Roll the dough into a rough cross shape, leaving the center thicker than the rest. Place the butter between two sheets of parchment paper and soften it more with the rolling pin, at the same time shaping it into a square so that it fits into the center of the dough. Set the butter in the center and fold over each of the four parts of the cross. It will look like the back of an envelope (see p. 25).
Lightly flour the work surface and roll the dough to form a rectangle three times longer than its width. It should be lengthwise in front of you. Fold the upper third downward and then fold the lower third over this to make three layers. Rotate the folded dough a quarter-turn and repeat the procedure, rolling it out to make a rectangle with the same proportions and folding it in three in the same way. Each time, be careful to make neat angles and to roll out evenly and not too thinly, as this would crush the butter-dough structure. Cover well with plastic wrap and chill for 30 minutes. Repeat the procedure: roll out, fold, and make a quarter-turn; roll out, fold, cover with plastic wrap, and chill for 30 minutes. Repeat once more to make the fifth and sixth turns. Once again, wrap and chill for at least 30 minutes.

Prepare the applesauce.
Peel the apples and drizzle them with lemon juice. Dice them and drizzle again with lemon juice. Add your chosen flavoring and stew them gently with a little water, covered, so that the steam helps cook them. Cook until well softened but not reduced to a purée. Stir in the sugar and let cool.

Assemble and bake the turnover.
Roll the dough to a thickness of ⅛ inch (3 mm) and cut ten circles measuring 6 ½ inches (16-17 cm) in diameter. Roll each circle out, flattening the middle to leave the edges thicker, until they are ovals about 8 inches (20 cm) long. Spoon a generous serving of cooled applesauce on one half, brush the rim with the beaten egg, and fold over. Brush with egg and chill for 1 hour. Place the beaten egg in the refrigerator during this time.
Preheat the oven to 340°F (170°C). Brush the turnovers again with the egg wash. With the tip of a small knife, draw a leaf pattern or other design of your choice on the top. Carefully transfer the turnovers to a baking sheet lined with parchment paper. Bake for 30 minutes, until golden brown.
If you wish, brush them with syrup (equal parts sugar and water) while they are still hot.

Ingredients
Puff pastry
1 ⅔ cups (7 oz./200 g) all-purpose flour
Scant 1 teaspoon (4 g) salt
Scant ½ cup (100 ml) water
1 ¼ sticks. (5 oz./150 g) butter
at room temperature

Applesauce
1 lb. (500 g) apples
Juice of 1 lemon
3 ½ tablespoons (1 ½ oz./40 g) sugar
Flavoring, such as vanilla,
cinnamon, or citrus zest

1 egg, lightly beaten
Syrup made with half sugar,
half water (optional)

Techniques
Puff pastry >> p. 24
Stewing fruit >> p. 210

Croquembouche ★ ★ ★

Serves 8
Preparation time: 2 hours 30 minutes
Cooking time: 1 hour

Make the choux pastry and cook the choux balls.
Dice the butter. Sift the flour.
In a large saucepan, bring the water, salt, sugar, and butter to a boil. When all the butter has melted, remove from the heat and stir in all the flour. Return the saucepan to the heat. With a wooden spoon or spatula, beat briskly to dry out the mixture (at this stage, it is known in French as a *panade*). Continue until the batter pulls away from the sides of the saucepan. Remove from the heat and let cool to no hotter than 122°F (50°C), to avoid cooking the eggs when they are added. Transfer to a mixing bowl. Continue working with a wooden spoon or spatula and beat in the eggs, one by one, only adding an egg when the previous one is fully incorporated. The mixture must be smooth and shiny.
Preheat the oven to 400°F (200°C).
Spoon into a piping bag fitted with a plain tip about ⅓ inch (8 mm) wide and pipe about 24 small, regularly shaped balls onto a baking sheet. Brush with a beaten egg. Dip a fork into water and score the top with the tines to ensure that the puffs are evenly shaped. Bake for 15 to 20 minutes, until golden brown and nicely puffed. Lower the heat to 340°F (170°C) and bake for an additional 20 minutes to dry out the choux pastry.

Make the pastry cream.
Slit the vanilla bean lengthwise and scrape the seeds into the milk. Pour the milk into a saucepan, add the vanilla bean, and begin heating. In a mixing bowl, briskly whisk the egg yolks, sugar, and cornstarch until pale and thick. When the milk is simmering, pour half of it over the egg yolk mixture, beating continuously. Return the mixture to the saucepan with the remaining milk and bring to a boil stirring continuously. Let simmer for 2 to 3 minutes, still stirring. Remove from the heat. Remove the vanilla bean. Whip in the butter. Transfer to a mixing bowl, cover with plastic wrap flush with the surface, and immediately place in the refrigerator to chill.

Prepare the nougatine.
Toast the almonds for 8 to 10 minutes in a 350°F (180°C) oven. Meanwhile, in a copper saucepan if you have one, caramelize the sugar and glucose syrup until reddened, about 330°F (165°C). Remove from the heat and stir in the butter and hot almonds. Pour the mixture onto a silicone baking sheet, ensuring it is slightly spread out, and let cool. It must remain pliable.
As soon as it is cool enough to handle, roll it thinly and cut to the desired shapes. You can make a round base to hold the pyramid

of choux pastries. If you wish, you can drape other pieces over a rolling pin or clean, dry bottle, to make curved shapes. Let cool completely and store in an airtight container. (If nougatine comes into contact with moisture, it spoils.)

Make the royal icing.
Make sure the mixing bowl used for the icing is perfectly clean and dry. Sift in the confectioners' sugar. With a spatula or wooden spoon, combine three-quarters of the confectioners' sugar with the egg white. Beat energetically, gradually adding the remaining sugar. Mix in the lemon juice. The icing must be perfectly white. Check the consistency: it should stand in small peaks with tips that hold at the end of the spatula. Add more confectioners' sugar if necessary. Store in an airtight container.

Make the caramel.
Combine all the ingredients and cook over high heat until reddened, about 330°F (165°C). Immediately remove from the heat. It is ready to use. To prevent the caramel from cooling too quickly and hardening, place the saucepan over a dessert ring.

Assemble the croquembouche.
Spoon the well-chilled pastry cream into a piping bag fitted with a plain tip. With a small icing tip, pierce the base of each choux puff. Fill the choux puffs with pastry cream. Dip the top of each choux puff into the caramel and place it, caramel side down, on a silicone baking sheet, making sure that it is flat and that the caramel does not run. Use a little caramel to glue them together in a circle and place them with the caramel facing outward. For the next layer, stagger the choux puffs in relation to the previous layer, and use one less. Continue until all the choux puffs are assembled in a cone shape.
Place on the nougatine base or in a baked shortcrust base.

● **Did you know?**
Antonin Carême (1783–1833) prepared spectacularly constructed desserts such as the croquembouche, traditionally served on grand celebratory occasions.

Techniques
Basic choux pastry >> p. 34
Pastry cream >> p. 99
Sugar decorations >> p. 134
Royal icing >> p. 140
Nougatine >> p. 166

Ingredients

Choux pastry

7 tablespoons (3 ½ oz./100 g) butter, room temperature
1 cup plus 2 tablespoons (5 oz./150 g) all-purpose flour
1 cup (250 ml) water
1 teaspoon (5 g) salt
1 teaspoon (5 g) sugar
5 eggs, plus 1 egg for the egg wash

Pastry cream

1 vanilla bean
2 cups (500 ml) milk
4 egg yolks (3 oz./80 g)
½ cup (3 ½ oz./100 g) sugar
5 tablespoons (1 ½ oz./45 g) cornstarch
5 tablespoons (3 oz./80 g) butter, room temperature, diced

Nougatine

3 ½ oz. (100 g) chopped almonds
¾ cup (5 oz./150 g) sugar
3 ½ oz. (100 g) glucose syrup
2 teaspoons (10 g) butter

Royal icing

¾ cup (3 ½ oz./100 g) confectioners' sugar
1 ½ tablespoons egg white (20 g)
½ teaspoon (2 ml) lemon juice

Caramel

2 ⅔ cups (1 lb. 2 oz./500 g) sugar
3 ½ oz. (100 g) glucose syrup
⅔ cup (150 ml) water

Ingredients

1 ¾ cups (5 oz./150 g) ground almonds
Generous 1 cup (5 oz./150 g)
  confectioners' sugar
Scant ½ cup (3 ½ oz./105 g) egg whites,
  divided
¾ cup (5 oz./150 g) sugar
3 tablespoons (50 ml) water

Flavors or food colorings, preferably
  in powder form

Filling 1

4 oz. (125 g) white chocolate
¼ oz. (8 g) cocoa butter (or 1 ½ teaspoons
  clarified butter)
3 ½ oz. (100 g) puréed apricots
1 ¾ teaspoons (8 ml) heavy cream
A few saffron filaments
2 oz. (50 g) moist dried apricots, very finely diced

Filling 2

1 vanilla bean
3 ½ oz. (100 g) white chocolate
¾ cup (200 ml) heavy cream, divided

Filling 3

1 egg, lightly beaten
⅓ cup (2 oz./60 g) sugar
½ teaspoon (2 g) finely grated lemon zest
2 tablespoons (30 ml) lemon juice
7 tablespoons (3 ½ oz./100 g) butter

Assorted Macarons ★★

Makes 20 filled macarons

Preparation time: 40 minutes/Cooking time: 12 minutes

Macarons require precision. For best results, weigh all your ingredients.

Make the macarons.

Line a heavy baking sheet (or use two baking sheets) with a silicone baking mat. Mix the ground almonds with the confectioners' sugar. Process with a blade knife so that the mixture is as fine and delicate as possible. Stir in half the egg whites until fairly firm. Make an Italian meringue (see p. 177). Cook the sugar and water to 250°F (120°C), keeping an eye on the thermometer. When it reaches 243°F-250°F (117°C-121°C), begin whipping the remaining egg whites in a stand mixer until they hold firm peaks. Gradually pour the cooked syrup (at 250°F/120°C) over the egg whites, still whipping. Continue until the meringue has cooled completely. (It will be smooth and hold many small peaks.) Add the flavors and/or food coloring. With a large scraper, combine the two mixtures, which will deflate slightly. Spoon the mixture into a piping bag fitted with a plain tip and pipe small disks onto the prepared baking sheet. Let stand for 30 minutes until a crust forms; the mixture should not stick to your fingers when touched. Preheat the oven to 310°F (155°C). Bake for 12 minutes; do not let darken. Remove the silicone baking sheet with the macarons from the baking sheet and let cool.

Make the fillings.

1. Melt the white chocolate and cocoa butter in a bain-marie over barely simmering water. Chop the apricots finely. Remove the chocolate mixture from the heat and stir in the remaining ingredients and the apricots. Whisk until smooth and chill.
2. Finely chop the white chocolate. Slit the vanilla bean lengthwise, scrape the seeds into half the cream, and heat the cream. When it comes to a simmer, remove from the heat and add the white chocolate. Whisk until smooth and let cool. Add the remaining cream and carefully whip until the mixture begins to firm and hold small peaks. (Be careful not to go beyond this stage.)
3. Combine the first four ingredients in a bain-marie and heat to 180°F (83°C), stirring from time to time. Let cool to 104°F (40°C) and stir in the butter. Process well and chill.

Assemble the macarons.

Spoon each filling into a piping bag fitted with a small plain tip. Pipe a dollop on the undersides of half the macarons. Lightly top with another macaron.

● **Chef's note**

Macarons will keep for 2 to 3 days in an airtight box in the refrigerator.

 Techniques

Macarons >> p. 79
  Italian meringue >> p. 177

Raspberry Mille-Feuille ★ ★

Serves 8
Preparation time: 2 hours 30 minutes/Chilling time: 2 hours
Cooking time: 30 minutes/Cooling time: 1 hour

Make the puff pastry.
On a work surface or in a mixing bowl, sift the flour and incorporate the salt. Make a well and pour in the water. Working rapidly with your hands, blend the ingredients together until fully blended. Shape into a disk and chill for 20 minutes. Ensure that the butter has the same consistency as that of the dough. If not, you may have to bash it (still wrapped) with a rolling pin. Roll the dough into a rough cross shape, leaving the center thicker than the rest. Place the butter between two sheets of parchment paper and soften it more with the rolling pin, at the same time shaping it into a square so that it fits into the center of the dough. Set the butter in the center and fold over each of the four parts of the cross. It will look like the back of an envelope (see p. 25). Lightly flour the work surface and roll, fold, and chill the dough, following the procedure on page 375. Make six turns in all. Wrap and chill for at least 30 minutes.
Preheat the oven to 350°F (180°C). Roll out to a thickness of just under ⅛ inch (3 mm) and cut into a strip 5 inches (12 cm) wide and the length of the baking sheet. Keep the edges as smooth as possible. Prick the dough at fairly close intervals so that it does not rise too much during baking. Sprinkle with sugar and bake for 30 minutes. If, after 15 minutes, it has begun to rise, flatten it gently by placing a clean, dry baking sheet on it until baked. Bake until a light golden color and watch that the sugar does not darken. Transfer carefully to a cooling rack.

Prepare the Diplomat cream.
Soften the gelatin sheets in a bowl of cold water. Slit the vanilla bean lengthwise and scrape the seeds into the milk. In a heavy-bottom saucepan, heat the milk with the vanilla seeds and bean. Whip the egg yolks, sugar, and flour until the mixture is pale and thick. When the milk is simmering, remove from the heat and gradually pour half over the egg mixture, whisking continuously. Return the mixture to the saucepan and stir continuously until it simmers. Let simmer 2-3 minutes, still stirring. Remove from the heat. Remove the vanilla bean. Squeeze the water from the gelatin sheets and whisk them into the custard cream. Transfer to a mixing bowl, cover with plastic wrap flush with the surface and chill to about 60°F (15°C). Do not leave it too long; it must not set before the whipped cream is incorporated. With an electric beater, whip the heavy cream until it forms firm peaks. Stir the chilled custard cream again and carefully fold in the whipped cream.

Assemble the mille-feuille.
With a serrated knife and using a sawing motion, carefully cut the strips of puff pastry into 1 ¼ x 5-inch (4 x 12-cm) rectangles. Spoon the Diplomat cream into a piping bag fitted with a plain tip and pipe small dollops on the first layer, alternating them with raspberries. Carefully set a second layer of puff pastry over this and repeat the procedure. Top with a third layer of puff pastry and dust with confectioners' sugar.

Ingredients

Puff pastry
1 ⅔ cups (7 oz./200 g) all-purpose flour
Scant 1 teaspoon (4 g) salt
Scant ½ cup (100 ml) water
1 ¼ sticks (5 oz./150 g) butter, room temperature
¼ cup (2 oz./50 g) sugar for sprinkling

Diplomat cream
2 ½ sheets (5 g) gelatin
¼ vanilla bean
1 cup (250 ml) milk
2 egg yolks
Scant ⅓ cup (2 ½ oz./65 g) sugar
3 tablespoons (1 oz./30 g) flour
1 cup (250 ml) heavy cream

8 oz. (250 g) raspberries
Confectioners' sugar for dusting

Techniques
Puff pastry >> p. 24
Diplomat cream >> p. 103

● **Chef's note**
This is best served soon after making to ensure the puff pastry remains crisp in contrast with the creamy filling.

Ingredients

Puff pastry
1 ²⁄₃ cups (7 oz./200 g) all-purpose flour
Scant 1 teaspoon (4 g) salt
Scant ½ cup (100 ml) water
1 ¼ sticks (5 oz./150 g) butter,
   room temperature
¼ cup (2 oz./50 g) sugar for sprinkling

Mousseline cream
½ vanilla bean
1 cup (250 ml) milk
½ cup (3 ½ oz./100 g) sugar, divided
2 egg yolks
Scant ¼ cup (1 oz./35 g) cornstarch
   or custard powder
1 stick plus 1 tablespoon (4 ½ oz./130 g)
   butter, softened, divided

Marbled topping
7 oz. (200 g) white fondant icing
²⁄₃ oz. (20 g) bittersweet chocolate

Mousseline Cream Mille-Feuille ★ ★

Serves 6
Preparation time: 2 hours 30 minutes
Chilling time: 2 hours
Cooking time: 30 minutes
Cooling time: 1 hour

Make the puff pastry.
On a work surface or in a mixing bowl, sift the flour and incorporate the salt. Make a well and pour in the water. Working rapidly with your hands, blend the ingredients together until fully blended. Shape into a disk and chill for 20 minutes. Ensure that the butter has the same consistency as that of the dough. If not, you may have to bash it (still wrapped) with a rolling pin. Roll the dough into a rough cross shape, leaving the center thicker than the rest. Place the butter between two sheets of parchment paper and soften it more with the rolling pin, at the same time shaping it into a square so that it fits into the center of the dough. Set the butter in the center and fold over each of the four parts of the cross. It will look like the back of an envelope (see p. 25). Lightly flour the work surface and roll the dough to form a rectangle three times longer than its width. It should be lengthwise in front of you. Fold the upper third downward and then fold the lower third over this to make three layers.
Rotate the folded dough a quarter-turn and repeat the procedure, rolling it out to make a rectangle with the same proportions and folding it in three in the same way. Each time, be careful to make neat angles and to roll out evenly and not too thinly, as this would crush the butter-dough structure.
Cover well with plastic wrap and chill for 30 minutes.
Repeat the procedure: roll out, fold, and make a quarter-turn; roll out, fold, cover with plastic wrap, and chill for an additional 30 minutes. Repeat once more to make the fifth and sixth turns. Once again, wrap and chill for at least 30 minutes.
Preheat the oven to 350°F (180°C). Roll out to a thickness of just under ⅛ inch (3 mm) and cut three identical rectangles, 4 ¾ inches (12 cm) wide. Keep the edges as smooth as possible. Prick the dough at fairly close intervals so that it does not rise too much during baking. Sprinkle with sugar and bake for about 15 minutes. If, after half the cooking time, it has begun to rise, flatten it gently by placing a clean, dry baking sheet on it until baked. Bake until a light golden color and watch that the sugar does not darken. Transfer carefully to a cooling rack.

Prepare the mousseline cream (preferably just before it is used).
Slit the vanilla bean lengthwise and scrape the seeds into the milk. In a medium heavy-bottom saucepan, heat the milk with the vanilla bean and half the sugar. Beat the egg yolks with the remaining sugar until thick and pale and incorporate the

cornstarch. When the milk is simmering, pour half of it over the egg yolk mixture, stirring constantly. Return the mixture to the saucepan and cook, stirring constantly, until thickened. Remove from the heat and whisk in half the butter. Transfer to a mixing bowl and cover with plastic wrap flush with the surface. Place in the refrigerator until it has cooled to 77°F (25°C). Dice the remaining butter. Transfer the cream mixture to a stand mixer fitted with a paddle beater. Beat at high speed, adding the remaining butter, until the cream expands and becomes airy. Spoon into a bowl and cover with plastic wrap. Use rapidly or store at no cooler than 50°F (10°C).

Assemble the mille-feuille.
With a spatula, spread a ⅓-inch (8-mm) layer of mousseline cream over one rectangle of puff pastry. Work as lightly and quickly as possible so as not to scrape off any of the fragile pastry. Set another strip of puff pastry over the cream and cover with another layer of cream (same depth). Turn the last strip of puff pastry upside down and set it carefully over the mousseline cream so that it is perfectly flat and ready to be marbled.

Apply the marbled topping.
For the most attractive effect, you will need to work fast to make this decoration. Heat the fondant icing to 104°F (40°C), adding a little water if necessary to adjust the consistency, which should be as runny as honey, very shiny, and sticky. Using a bain-marie, melt the chocolate. Make a paper decorating cone (see p. 147), then fill with the chocolate. Pour the white fondant over the puff pastry and smooth it with a stainless steel spatula. You may need to smooth it from one side to another a second time; it should be as even as possible. Immediately draw six to eight parallel lines in chocolate along the length and then, with a toothpick, trace lines at a slight angle, working backward and forward and leaving about 1 ½ inches (4 cm) between them. Let set for a few minutes. Remove any drips of fondant or chocolate.

Cut into portions.
With a sharp, serrated knife, cut portions using a sawing motion. Wipe the knife clean after each cut. Refrigerate until serving time.

Techniques
Puff pastry >> p. 24
Mousseline cream >> p. 100
Fondant icing >> p. 114
Marbling a mille-feuille >> p. 143
Making a paper decorating cone >> p. 147

Paris-Brest ★★

Serves 8
Preparation time: 1 hour
Cooking time: 50 minutes

Make the choux pastry.
Dice the butter. Sift the flour. In a large saucepan, bring the water, salt, sugar, and butter to a boil. When all the butter has melted, remove from the heat and stir in all the flour. Return the saucepan to the heat. With a wooden spoon or spatula, beat briskly to dry out the mixture. Continue until the batter pulls away from the sides of the saucepan. Remove from the heat and let cool to no hotter than 122°F (50°C), to avoid cooking the eggs when they are added. Transfer to a mixing bowl. Continue working with a wooden spoon or spatula and beat in the eggs, one by one, only adding an egg when the previous one is fully incorporated. The mixture must be smooth and shiny.
Spoon the dough into a piping bag fitted with a plain ½-inch (1-cm) tip and on a silicone baking sheet pipe a ring with a diameter of 6 inches (15 cm). Pipe another ring outside this circle, ensuring the two are touching. Pipe a third circle on top of these two, centered over the join of the two rings.
Preheat the oven to 375°F (190°C).
Lightly beat the egg and brush the dough rings, then sprinkle the sliced almonds over the top.
Bake for 25 to 30 minutes, until golden brown and well puffed. Lower the temperature to 340°F (170°C) and leave for 20 minutes with the oven door ajar (with a wooden spoon if necessary) to dry out the pastry. Transfer immediately to a rack so that any remaining moisture can evaporate.

Prepare the mousseline cream.
Soften the praline paste. Slit the vanilla bean lengthwise and scrape the seeds into the milk. Heat the milk in a saucepan with the vanilla bean and half the sugar. Beat the egg yolks with the remaining sugar until thick and pale and incorporate the cornstarch. When the milk is simmering, pour half of it over the egg mixture, stirring constantly. Whisk in the praline paste. Return the mixture to the saucepan and cook, stirring constantly, until thickened. Remove from the heat, remove the vanilla bean, and whisk in half the butter. Transfer to a mixing bowl and cover with plastic wrap flush with the surface. Place in the refrigerator until it has cooled to 77°F (25°C). Dice the remaining butter. Transfer the cream mixture to a stand mixer fitted with a paddle beater. Beat at high speed, adding the remaining butter, until the cream expands and becomes airy and light. It should hold peaks when the whisk is lifted from the bowl. If not for immediate use, cover with plastic wrap, and store (briefly) at a temperature no lower than 50°F (10°C).

Assemble the Paris-Brest.
With a large serrated knife, cut the large ring of choux pastry horizontally at two-thirds of its height. Half-fill the bottom of the ring with mousseline cream, piping in a twisted pattern. Set the top third of the ring on top of the cream and dust lightly with confectioners' sugar.

Ingredients

Choux pastry
7 tablespoons (3 ½ oz./100 g) butter, room temperature
1 cup plus 2 tablespoons (5 oz./150 g) flour
1 cup (250 ml) water
1 teaspoon (5 g) salt
1 teaspoon (5 g) sugar
5 eggs
1 egg for the egg wash
½ cup (1 oz./30 g) lightly roasted sliced almonds

Praline mousseline cream
3 oz. (80 g) praline paste (see recipe p. 160, or store-bought)
½ vanilla bean
1 cup (250 ml) milk
½ cup (3 ½ oz./100 g) sugar, divided
2 egg yolks
Scant ¼ cup (1 oz./35 g) cornstarch or custard powder
1 stick plus 1 tablespoon (1 ½ oz./130 g) butter, softened, divided

Scant ¼ cup (1 oz./30 g) confectioners' sugar for dusting

Techniques
Basic choux pastry >> p. 34
Mousseline cream >> p. 100
Praline paste >> p. 160

Ingredients

Puff pastry
1 ⅔ cups (7 oz./200 g) all-purpose flour
Scant 1 teaspoon (4 g) salt
Scant ½ cup (100 ml) water
1 ¼ sticks (5 oz./150 g) butter,
　room temperature
1 egg for the egg wash

Almond cream
7 tablespoons (3 ½ oz./100 g) butter, softened
½ cup (3 ½ oz./100 g) sugar
2 eggs (3 ½ oz./100 g)
1 cup plus 3 tablespoons (3 ½ oz./100 g)
　ground almonds
1 ½ tablespoons (15 g) cornstarch
1 teaspoon (5 ml) vanilla extract
1 tablespoon (15 ml) rum

Syrup
3 tablespoons (50 ml) water
¼ cup (2 oz./50 g) sugar

Techniques
Puff pastry >> p. 24
Almond cream >> p. 90
Decorating a *pithiviers* >> p. 146

● **Did you know?**
This cake, which takes its name from the town of Pithiviers in central France, has been a well-known specialty since the mid-nineteenth century. This is the classic recipe, but other versions have substituted savory fillings.

Pithiviers Filled with Almond Cream ★ ★

Serves 6
Preparation time: 2 hours 30 minutes/Chilling time: 3 hours
Cooking time: 40 minutes

Make the puff pastry.
On a work surface or in a mixing bowl, sift the flour and incorporate the salt. Make a well and pour in the water. Working rapidly with your hands, blend the ingredients together until fully blended. Shape into a disk and chill for 20 minutes. Ensure that the butter has the same consistency as that of the dough. If not, you may have to bash it (still wrapped) with a rolling pin. Roll the dough into a rough cross shape, leaving the center thicker than the rest. Place the butter between two sheets of parchment paper and soften it more with the rolling pin, at the same time shaping it into a square so that it fits into the center of the dough. Set the butter in the center and fold over each of the four parts of the cross. It will look like the back of an envelope (see p. 25). Lightly flour the work surface and roll the dough to form a rectangle three times longer than its width. It should be lengthwise in front of you. Fold the upper third downward and then fold the lower third over this to make three layers. Rotate the folded dough a quarter-turn and repeat the procedure, rolling it out to make a rectangle with the same proportions and folding it in three in the same way. Each time, be careful to make neat angles and to roll out evenly and not too thinly, as this would crush the butter-dough structure. Cover well with plastic wrap and chill for 30 minutes. Repeat the procedure twice, making six turns in all. Once again, wrap and chill for at least 30 minutes.

Prepare the almond cream.
In a mixing bowl, cream the butter and whisk in the sugar until light. Add the eggs, one by one, whisking until thoroughly combined. Whisk in the ground almonds and then the cornstarch. Stir in the vanilla and rum.

Assemble the *pithiviers*.
Roll the dough to a thickness of ⅛ inch (3 mm). Cut out one scalloped 8-inch (20-cm) disk. Cut out another disk, just slightly larger, diameter about 8 ½ inches (22 cm) to use for the top layer. Transfer the smaller one to a baking sheet lined with parchment paper. Lightly beat the egg and brush the rim of the disk. Spread the almond cream just less than ½ inch (1 cm) thick over the pastry, stopping at about ¾ inch (1.5 cm) from the edge. Carefully set the larger disk over the almond cream. With a small, sharp knife, make shallow, angled incisions at close intervals around the rim to seal the cake. Brush the top with the egg, taking care that none of it runs down the sides (this would prevent the cake from rising evenly). Chill for 30 minutes. Brush the top again with the egg wash. With the tip of a small kitchen knife, draw arcs, starting from the center and taking care not to pierce the puff pastry (see p. 146).
Chill for 1 hour. Preheat the oven to 340°F (170°C).
Bake for 35 to 40 minutes, until puffed up and golden. Prepare a syrup: heat the water with the sugar. As soon as you remove the cake from the oven, brush it with the syrup. As it dries, it will become shiny.

Choux Puff *Religieuses* Filled with Mango Diplomat Cream ★★

Serves 8
Preparation time: 1 hour 45 minutes
Cooking time: 40 minutes

Make the shortcrust topping.
Rub the flour, sugar, and butter together with your fingers until a smooth dough forms. Shape into a disk and place between two sheets of parchment paper. Roll out very thinly (under ⅛ in. or 2 mm). Place in the freezer for 20 minutes.

Make the choux puffs.
Line two baking sheets with silicone baking mats or parchment paper. Make choux pastry following the method on page 386. Preheat the oven to 350°F (180°C). Spoon the batter into a piping bag fitted with a plain tip and pipe eight 1 ¼-inch (4-cm) balls on one baking sheet. On the other, pipe eight smaller balls, about 1 inch (2.5 cm) in diameter. (Once the choux batter has been piped into balls, it can remain at room temperature while you bake the first sheet. It's important, however, not to leave the batter in the bowl.) Cut the shortcrust topping into disks just a little larger than the unbaked balls of choux pastry (both sizes) and set them over the tops. Bake the large choux puffs for 25-30 minutes, until golden and puffed. Reduce the heat to 340°F (170°F), leave the oven door slightly ajar, and bake for an additional 20 minutes to dry out the choux puffs. Transfer immediately to a cooling rack. Increase the temperature to 400°F (200°C) and bake the small choux puffs for 20 minutes, until golden and puffed. Dry them out as for the large ones. Let cool completely.

Prepare the butter cream.
Combine the sugar with the water in a saucepan and cook to 243°F-250°F (117°C-121°C). With an electric beater, whip the egg yolks until foamy. Pour the syrup over the egg yolks, beating constantly. Continue to beat until the mixture cools to about 86°F (30°C). Incorporate the butter at medium speed. Transfer to a mixing bowl, cover with plastic wrap flush with the surface, and chill.

Make the mango Diplomat cream.
Combine the mango and passion fruit juices in a saucepan and heat. Whip the egg yolks, sugar, and flour until the mixture is pale and thick. When the liquid is simmering, gradually pour in half over the egg and sugar mixture, whipping continuously. Return the mixture to the saucepan and stir continuously until it simmers. Let simmer 2-3 minutes, still stirring. Remove from the heat and let cool to room temperature. Whip the cream until it holds soft peaks and fold it carefully into the mixture. Pierce a small hole at the base of each of the choux puffs (use a small icing tip). With a piping bag fitted with a small plain tip, fill the choux puffs.

Prepare the white chocolate squares.
Melt the chocolate in a bain-marie. When the temperature reaches 104°F (40°C), remove from the heat and immediately spread it over a cold surface (a marble slab, if you have one, or tiles, or even a clean mirror). Keep spreading and turning it until it cools to 79°F (26°C). Return it to the bain-marie very briefly until the thermometer registers 82.5°F (28°C). Immediately spread it very thinly on the sheet of transfer paper. As soon as it begins to set, cut it into 2-inch (5-cm) squares.

Assemble the dish.
Heat the fondant to 104°F (40°C). Add the yellow food coloring and adjust the consistency with water, if necessary. It should be as runny as honey, very shiny, and sticky. Dip the choux puffs halfway to the top and wipe off any drops with your finger.
At the top of the large choux puffs, pipe a small dollop of butter cream and glue on a white chocolate square. Place a smaller choux puff on the chocolate square and keep in place by piping small touches of buttercream all around.

Ingredients

Shortcrust topping
¾ cup plus 2 tablespoons
  (3 ½ oz./100 g) flour
½ cup (3 ½ oz./100 g) light brown sugar
7 tablespoons (3 ½ oz./100 g)
  butter, diced

Choux pastry
7 tablespoons (3 ½ oz./100 g) butter,
  room temperature
1 cup plus 2 tablespoons (5 oz./150 g)
  all-purpose flour
1 cup (250 ml) water
1 teaspoon (5 g) salt
1 teaspoon (5 g) sugar
5 eggs
1 egg for the egg wash

Butter cream
¾ cup (4 oz./125 g) sugar
2 tablespoons (35 ml) water
2 egg yolks
1 stick (4 oz./125 g) butter,
  softened and diced

Mango Diplomat cream
1 ⅔ cups (400 ml) mango juice
Scant ½ cup (100 ml) passion fruit juice
4 egg yolks
½ cup (3 ½ oz./100 g) sugar
½ cup (2 oz./60 g) flour
1 cup (250 ml) heavy cream

White chocolate squares
3 ½ oz. (100 g) white chocolate

3 ½ oz. (100 g) fondant icing
Yellow food coloring

Special equipment: 1 sheet transfer
  paper

Techniques
Basic choux pastry ›› p. 34
Choux pastry with crumbled
  topping ›› p. 37
Butter creams ›› p. 95
Diplomat cream ›› p. 103

Ingredients

Macaroons

3 ½ cups (9 oz./250 g) unsweetened
   shredded coconut
1 ¼ cups (9 oz./250 g) sugar
3 eggs, lightly beaten
2 ½ tablespoons (1 oz./25 g) flour

Chocolate sauce

3 ½ oz. (100 g) bittersweet chocolate
½ cup (125 ml) heavy cream (crème fraîche,
   if possible)

A little unsweetened shredded coconut
   for decoration

Coconut Macaroons

Makes 15 macaroons
Preparation time: 20 minutes
Cooking time: 6 minutes

Make the macaroons.
Preheat the oven to 350°F (180°C). Line a baking sheet with parchment paper.
Combine all the ingredients until they form a thick paste.
With your fingers, shape small pyramids. Place them on the prepared baking
sheet. Bake for 5 to 6 minutes, until lightly browned.
Immediately transfer to a cooling rack and let cool.

Prepare the chocolate sauce.
Chop the chocolate. Bring the cream to a boil and pour it over the chocolate
to melt it. After a few minutes, whip the mixture until smooth.
Dip the tips of the macaroons into the chocolate sauce and immediately into
the shredded coconut.

Technique
Chocolate sauces >> p. 120

Gâteau Saint-Honoré ★★

Serves 12
Preparation time: 2 hours 30 minutes
Cooking time: 1 hour 15 minutes

Prepare the puff pastry.
On a work surface or in a mixing bowl, sift the flour and incorporate the salt. Make a well and pour in the water. Working rapidly with your hands, blend the ingredients together until fully blended. Shape into a disk and chill for 20 minutes.
Ensure that the butter has the same consistency as that of the dough. If not, you may have to bash it (still wrapped) with a rolling pin. Roll the dough into a rough cross shape, leaving the center thicker than the rest. Place the butter between two sheets of parchment paper and soften it more with the rolling pin, at the same time shaping it into a square so that it fits into the center of the dough. Set the butter in the center and fold over each of the four parts of the cross. It will look like the back of an envelope (see p. 25). Lightly flour the work surface and roll the dough to form a rectangle three times longer than its width. It should be lengthwise in front of you. Fold the upper third downward and then fold the lower third over this to make three layers. Rotate the folded dough a quarter-turn and repeat the procedure, rolling it out to make a rectangle with the same proportions and folding it in three in the same way.
Each time, be careful to make neat angles and to roll out evenly and not too thinly, as this would crush the butter-dough structure. Cover well with plastic wrap and chill for 30 minutes. Repeat the procedure: roll out, fold, and make a quarter-turn; roll out, fold, cover with plastic wrap, and chill for a an additional 30 minutes. Repeat once more to make the fifth and sixth turns. Once again, wrap and chill for at least 30 minutes. Roll the dough to a thickness of just less than ⅛ inch (3 mm) and cut out two 7-inch (18-cm) disks. Chill for 1 hour.

Make and bake the choux pastry.
Dice the butter. Sift the flour.
In a large saucepan, bring the water, salt, sugar, and butter to a boil. When all the butter has melted, remove from the heat and stir in all the flour. Return the saucepan to the heat. With a wooden spoon or spatula, beat briskly to dry out the mixture. Continue until the batter pulls away from the sides of the saucepan. Remove from the heat and let cool to no hotter than 122°F (50°C), to avoid cooking the eggs when they are added. Transfer to a mixing bowl. Continue working with a wooden spoon or spatula and beat in the eggs, one by one, only adding an egg when the previous one is fully incorporated. The mixture must be smooth and shiny.
Preheat the oven to 375°F (190°C).

Lightly beat the egg for the egg wash and brush the disks of puff pastry. With a piping bag fitted with a small plain tip, pipe a ring of choux pastry around the rims of the disks. Pipe a half-spiral in the center so that the puff pastry doesn't brown too much. Then pipe about twenty-four 1-inch (2.5-cm) choux puffs on a baking sheet to fit around the rim of the cake. (Bake them after the disks.) Bake the disks for 25 to 30 minutes, until the choux pastry is golden brown. Lower the temperature to 340°F (170°C) and leave the oven door slightly ajar (prop open with a wooden spoon, if necessary). Bake for an additional 20 minutes to dry out. Transfer to a cooling rack. Increase the oven temperature to 400°F (200°C) and bake the small choux puffs for about 20 minutes.

Make the Chiboust cream.
Soften the gelatin in a bowl of cold water. Slit the vanilla bean lengthwise and scrape the seeds into the milk. Pour the milk into a saucepan, add the vanilla bean, and begin heating.
In a mixing bowl, briskly whisk the egg yolks, ½ cup (3 ½ oz./100 g) sugar, and flour until pale and thick. When the milk is simmering, pour half of it over the egg yolk mixture, beating continuously. Return the mixture to the saucepan and bring to a boil stirring continuously. Let simmer 2-3 minutes, still stirring. Remove from the heat. Squeeze the water from the gelatin sheets and whisk them into the custard cream until completely dissolved. Make an Italian meringue (see method p. 177) by pouring cooked syrup made from the remaining sugar and the ⅔ cup (160 ml) water over the whipped egg whites, still whipping. Check the temperatures of both mixtures: they should be at about 122°F (50°C). Whisk the pastry cream to ensure it is smooth and fold in the Italian meringue, still hot, taking care not to deflate the mixture. Let cool slightly. Pierce a small hole in the base of each choux puff and pipe in some Chiboust cream.

Make the caramel and assemble the gâteau.
Combine the ingredients in a heavy-bottom saucepan and cook over high, even heat until reddened, about 330°F (165°C). Immediately remove from the heat and use to assemble the cake. To prevent the caramel from cooling too quickly, place the saucepan over a dessert ring. If it does harden, gently re-heat it until it reaches the desired consistency.
Dip the tops and bottoms of the choux puffs in the caramel. Cool on a sheet of parchment paper. Place them, side by side, on the rim of the base, with the flat side upward. Pipe a generous serving of Chiboust cream in the center and place a caramelized choux puff in the middle.

Ingredients

Puff pastry
1 ⅔ cups (7 oz./200 g) all-purpose flour
Scant 1 teaspoon (4 g) salt
Scant ½ cup (100 ml) water
1 ¼ sticks (5 oz./150 g) butter, room
    temperature

Choux pastry
7 tablespoons (3 ½ oz./100 g) butter,
    room temperature
1 cup plus 2 tablespoons (5 oz./150 g)
    all-purpose flour
1 cup (250 ml) water
1 teaspoon (5 g) salt
1 teaspoon (5 g) sugar
5 eggs
1 egg for the egg wash

Chiboust cream
5 sheets (10 g) gelatin
½ vanilla bean
2 cups (500 ml) milk
4 eggs, separated, plus 4 egg whites
3 cups (1 ¼ lb./580 g) sugar, divided
½ cup (2 oz./60 g) flour
⅔ cup (160 ml) water

Caramel
1 ¼ cups (9 oz./250 g) sugar
2 oz. (50 g) glucose syrup
⅓ cup (75 ml) water

Techniques
Puff pastry >> p. 24
Basic choux pastry >> p. 34
Chiboust cream >> p. 104
Italian meringue >> p. 177

● Did you know?
*The Gâteau Saint-Honoré was created
in the mid-nineteenth century at the
Chiboust pastry store at the Palais Royal
in Paris. Later, the Julien brothers, master
pastry makers, gave it the shape and
taste it has today. Saint Honoré is the
patron saint of bakers and millers,
and is celebrated on May 16.*

Loaf cakes and cookies

Yann Brys

Meilleur Ouvrier de France, pâtisserie, and creative director at prestigious pastry store Dalloyau, Paris

The Mont-Blanc, a classic of French pâtisserie, was the inspiration for this recipe. It is a dessert I'm particularly fond of, a reminder of my childhood. I wanted to make a cake that reproduced the flavors and respected the original textures and components. So I worked on making a moist dough, scented with vanilla, to which I added pieces of rum-scented candied chestnuts. I wanted it to be a visual allusion to the traditional Mont-Blanc, with its squiggles of chestnut paste that make it so unique and so delicious. I added delicate disks of meringue to add a little crunch to the tasting experience. The meringues also suggest a snowy mountaintop. Reinterpreting classics of our gastronomic heritage is fun, allowing one to rework basic ingredients and, most of all, to add a personal touch. My adaptation of this recipe to create a cake that can be transported easily while still being as succulent as the original proved an interesting experience for me.

Mont-Blanc Loaf

Makes 1 loaf to serve 6

Preparation time: 1 hour

Cooking time: 40 minutes (plus 4 hours "drying" in the oven)

Make the syrup.

Heat the water and sugar. Stir in the rum.

Prepare the batter.

Preheat the oven to 350°F (175°C). Butter and flour a loaf pan. Beat together the butter, sugar, and honey. Slit the vanilla bean lengthwise and scrape the seeds into the mixture. Beat the eggs and divide in half. Stir one half into the mixture. Sift the flour and baking powder and stir in until just combined. Stir in the remaining eggs. Carefully stir in the chestnut bits, orange zest, and rum. Pour the butter into the prepared loaf pan and bake for 35 to 40 minutes, until a cake tester comes out clean.
Turn out onto a rack, brush with syrup, and cool.

Prepare the chestnut vermicelli.

Heat the water and sugar together and add the rum. Gradually stir this syrup into the chestnut paste. Stir the chestnut cream into the mixture. Spoon into a piping bag fitted with a very fine plain tip and pipe over the top of the loaf to make a bird's nest of vermicelli. Dust with confectioners' sugar.

Make the crisp orange meringue cookies.

Sift the confectioners' sugar into a bowl. Stir in the egg white and orange zest. With a pastry stencil or decorating grill, pipe small shapes. Dry out in a 100°F (40°C) oven for 4 hours. Dot them around the top of the loaf.

Serve at room temperature.

Ingredients

Syrup

3 tablespoons (50 ml) water

3 ½ tablespoons (1 ½ oz./40 g) sugar

1 teaspoon (5 ml) aged rum

Batter

1 stick (4 oz./115 g) finest-quality butter, softened

½ cup plus 1 tablespoon (4 oz./110 g) sugar

Scant 1 tablespoon (15 g) acacia honey

1 vanilla bean

3 eggs

1 cup plus 1 tablespoon (4 ½ oz./135 g) flour

Scant 1 teaspoon (3 g) baking powder

2 ½ oz. (75 g) candied chestnuts, broken into bits

Finely grated zest of ½ orange

1 tablespoon (15 ml) aged rum

Butter and flour for the loaf pan

Chestnut vermicelli

1 tablespoon (15 ml) water

1 heaping tablespoon (15 g) sugar

½ teaspoon (3 ml) aged rum

3 ½ oz. (100 g) chestnut paste

2 oz. (50 g) chestnut cream (*crème de marron*)

Confectioners' sugar for dusting

Crisp orange meringue cookies

⅓ cup (2 oz./50 g) confectioners' sugar

1 ½ teaspoons (7 g) egg white

Finely grated zest of ½ orange

Ingredients

Pistachio sponge

2 eggs

3 egg yolks (1 ¾ oz./50 g)

Scant 1 cup (6 oz./175 g) sugar

1 cup plus 1 tablespoon (5 oz./135 g) flour

½ teaspoon (2 g) baking powder

2 tablespoons (1 oz./30 g) butter

2 ½ oz. (70 g) pistachio paste

3 tablespoons (50 ml) heavy cream

½ teaspoon (2 g) salt

Raspberry fruit jelly

⅕ oz. (6 g) yellow pectin

1 cup plus 2 tablespoons (8 oz./227 g) sugar, divided

9 oz. (250 g) raspberry purée, 10 percent sugar

2 oz. (50 g) glucose syrup

⅙ oz. (5 g) citric acid solution 50/50

Butter cream

⅔ cup (4 ½ oz./125 g) sugar

2 tablespoons (35 ml) water

2 egg yolks

1 stick (4 ½ oz./125 g) butter, diced and softened

1 teaspoon (5 ml) vanilla extract

Special equipment: a 6 x 8-inch (16 x 18-cm) dessert frame

Techniques

Butter creams >> p. 95

Gelled fruit >> p. 156

Pistachio and Raspberry Layer Cake ★ ★

Serves 6

Preparation time: 1 hour 30 minutes

Cooking time: 40 minutes

Chilling time: 1 hour

Prepare the pistachio sponge.

Preheat the oven to 350°F (180°C)

Whisk the eggs, egg yolks, and sugar together to the ribbon stage. Sift the flour and baking powder together and fold into the egg mixture until just combined. In a small saucepan, soften the butter, pistachio paste, heavy cream, and salt. Whisk together and incorporate into the egg and flour mixture. Stop when smooth. Spread over a 12 x 16-inch (30 x 40-cm) baking sheet to a thickness of just under ½ inch (1 cm) and bake for 15 to 20 minutes. It should spring back to the touch. Do not overbake; it should retain its moistness.

Make the raspberry fruit jelly.

Combine the yellow pectin with the 2 tablespoons sugar. Heat the raspberry purée but do not boil. Pour in the pectin-sugar mixture, stir in the remaining sugar and glucose syrup, and heat to 225°F (107°C). Stir in the citric acid and pour onto a silicone baking sheet or baking frame to a thickness of about ¼ inch (5 mm). Let cool and turn onto a chopping board.

Prepare the butter cream.

In a small saucepan or copper pot, cook the sugar and water to 243°F–250°F (117°C–121°C). In the bowl of a stand mixer at medium speed, whip the egg yolks until foamy. Increase the speed to pour the syrup over the egg yolks, whisking continuously, and continue to whisk for a few minutes at medium speed. The mixture will foam as it cools to form a *pate à bombe*. Continue until it reaches 85°F (30°C). Add the butter and whisk until thoroughly combined. Stir in the vanilla. Transfer to a mixing bowl and cover with plastic wrap flush with the surface.

Assemble the layer cake.

Cut the pistachio sponge into rectangles the size of the dessert frame. Place one piece of sponge inside the frame. With an offset spatula, spread a thin layer of butter cream over it. Cut the fruit jelly to the same dimensions and place it over the butter cream. Rinse the knife frequently, dry it well, and rub it with alcohol so that it does not stick to the jelly as you cut. Repeat and top with a layer of sponge. Chill.

● **Chef's note**

This layered cake can be cut into cubes or rectangles. Serve it with custard, or use it, finely sliced, to line a layered dessert, alternating the lines horizontally and vertically for variety.

Financiers ★

Makes 8 *financiers*
Preparation time: 25 minutes
Cooking time: about 10 minutes

Preheat the oven to 340°F (170°C).
Combine the sugar and ground almonds. Lightly beat the egg whites and stir them into the sugar-almond mixture. Fold in the flour. Gradually stir in the butter.
Pour the batter into the molds and bake for about 10 minutes, until lightly browned. They must remain moist, so do not overbake.

● Chef's notes
These financiers are delicious when baked with a few fresh raspberries. You can also flavor the batter with orange zest or pistachio paste. For the pistachio paste option, use 1 tablespoon (20 g) pistachio paste, well softened, and reduce the butter to 7 tablespoons (3 ½ oz./105 g).

Ingredients
¾ cup (5 oz./150 g) sugar
1 cup minus 1 tablespoon (2 ½ oz./75 g) ground almonds
4 egg whites
½ cup (2 oz./60 g) flour
1 stick (4 ½ oz./125 g) butter, melted until browned

Special equipment: 8 *financier* molds or other shallow molds

Ingredients

7 oz. (100 g) pitted prunes
2 tablespoons (30 ml) brown rum
1 cup plus 1 tablespoon (5 oz./140 g) flour
Scant ½ cup (3 oz./80 g) sugar
2 eggs
2 cups (500 ml) warm milk
Butter to grease the pan

9-inch (20-22-cm) baking pan. Traditionally,
   this is made and often served in a deep oval
   4 ½-cup (1-liter) ovenproof dish

Breton Custard Flan with Prunes ★

Serves 6
Preparation time: 30 minutes
Cooking time: 35 minutes

Soak the prunes in the rum for at least 30 minutes.
Preheat the oven to 400°F (200°C).
Combine the flour and sugar in a round-bottom mixing bowl and make a
well in the center. Place the eggs in the well and briskly beat them in with
a whisk. Gradually whisk in the milk.
Generously butter the pan. Spread the prunes over the bottom and cover
with the batter. Bake for at least 35 minutes, until it is set and the top is
lightly browned.
Let cool and turn out of the pan.

Brownies ★

Makes 20 brownies
Preparation time: 40 minutes
Cooking time: 15 minutes

Make and bake the brownies.
Preheat the oven to 340°F (170°C).
Melt the butter and chocolate in a bain-marie. Whisk the eggs and sugar in a mixing bowl until pale and thick. Whisk in the melted butter-chocolate mixture. Sift the flour and mix with the ground almonds. Fold into the batter until just combined. Stir in the vanilla, cinnamon, and chopped nuts.
Pour the batter into individual silicone molds, about 1 inch (2-3 cm) deep. Bake for about 10 minutes, until a cake tester comes out dry.

Prepare the chocolate sauce.
Bring the cream to a boil and pour it over the chopped chocolate. Let stand for a few minutes while the heat melts the chocolate, then stir vigorously until smooth. Place the brownies on serving plates and drizzle with sauce, covering them partly or entirely.

● **Chef's notes**
Use pistachios, hazelnuts, or almonds as alternatives to pecans or walnuts. You can also pour the batter into a large, buttered pan and slice it afterwards.

Techniques
Brownies >> p. 74
Chocolate sauces >> p. 120

Ingredients
Brownie batter
1 stick (4 oz./110 g) butter
2 oz. (60 g) bittersweet chocolate, 70 percent cocoa
2 eggs
½ cup (3 ½ oz./100 g) sugar
½ cup (2 oz./65 g) flour
Generous ⅓ cup (1 oz./30 g) ground almonds
1 teaspoon (5 ml) vanilla extract
1 small pinch ground cinnamon
2 ½ oz. (75 g) walnuts or pecan nuts, chopped

Chocolate sauce
½ cup (125 ml) heavy cream
3 ½ oz. (100 g) bittersweet chocolate, chopped

Ingredients

2 sticks (9 oz./250 g) butter, softened
1 ¼ teaspoons (7 g) salt
Scant 1 cup (6 oz./180 g) sugar, divided
4 eggs, separated, plus 1 egg yolk
⅓ cup (2 ½ oz./70 g) light brown sugar
1 teaspoon (5 ml) vanilla extract
2 cups (9 oz./250 g) flour
¾ teaspoon (3 g) baking powder
1 tablespoon (20 g) pistachio paste
Green food coloring
Finely grated zest of ½ orange
Orange food coloring
2 oz. (50 g) light colored glaze
2 tablespoons (25 ml) water
Candied orange peel or slices and pistachios
  for decoration

10 x 5-inch (25 x 10-cm) loaf pan

Marble Cake ★

Serves 8
Preparation time: 30 minutes
Cooking time: 40 minutes

Preheat the oven to 350°F (180°C). Butter the loaf pan.

Cream the butter with the salt and ¾ cup (5 oz./150 g) sugar.

With a whisk or electric beater, whip the egg yolks, light brown sugar, and vanilla to the ribbon stage.

Whip the egg whites until they hold firm peaks. Gradually stir in the remaining sugar with a whisk until firm and shiny.

With a flexible spatula, fold the egg yolk mixture into the creamed butter. Carefully fold in the meringue. Sift the flour with the baking powder and fold it in.

Divide the batter between two mixing bowls. Soften the pistachio paste and stir it into a bowl with a few drops of green coloring (the quantity depends on the strength). Stir the orange zest and orange coloring into the other bowl. Spoon the two batters into the prepared pan, making sure they are not regularly layered. The baking process will ensure that the marbling is attractive.

Before you put it in the oven, dip a knife into some butter and make a slit along the length of the top of the loaf. This ensures it rises well and forms a nice bump.

Bake for 35 to 40 minutes, until nicely risen and a cake tester comes out dry. Turn out of the pan and let cool. Heat the glaze with water and brush over the top. Decorate with candied orange peel or slices and pistachios.

 Technique
French meringue >> p. 176

Cookies ★

Makes 12 cookies
Preparation time: 30 minutes
Chilling time: 1 hour
Cooking time: 20 minutes

With a whisk, cream the butter and sugar. Whisk in the eggs and egg yolk.
Sift the flour and baking powder, mix together with the ground hazelnuts,
and stir into the mixture. Stir in the chocolate chips and/or nougatine pieces.
Gather the dough together and on a sheet of parchment paper, shape it into a
1 ½-inch (3.5-cm) log. Ensure it is tightly rolled. Chill until firm, about 1 hour.
Preheat the oven to 350°F (180°C).
Cut ½-inch (1-cm) slices and place them on a silicone baking mat, leaving
almost 2 inches (4.5 cm) between them, as they will spread.
Bake for 20 minutes, until golden. Immediately transfer to a cooling rack so
that they don't reabsorb any moisture.

Technique
Cookies >> p. 74

Ingredients
2 sticks (9 oz./250 g) butter, room temperature
Scant ½ cup (3 oz./80 g) brown sugar
2 eggs plus 1 egg yolk
2 ½ cups (10 ½ oz./300 g) flour
1 ½ teaspoons (6 g) baking powder
1 cup plus 3 tablespoons (3 ½ oz./100 g)
ground hazelnuts
13 oz. (350 g) chocolate chips *or*
13 oz. (350 g) nougatine pieces *or*
half chocolate chips, half nougatine pieces

Yoghurt Cake ★

Serves 6
Preparation time: 15 minutes
Cooking time: 30 minutes

Preheat the oven to 340°F (170°C). Butter the baking pan.
Whip the eggs and sugar together until pale and thick. Add the yoghurt and oil and whip to combine. Sift in the flour and baking powder and stir until just combined.
Pour the batter into the pan and bake for about 30 minutes, until golden on top and a cake tester comes out dry.

Ingredients
2 eggs
1 ¼ cups (9 oz./250 g) sugar
⅔ cup (150 ml) yoghurt
¼ cup (60 ml) neutral oil
1 ⅔ cups (7 oz./200 g) flour
1 tablespoon (11 g) baking powder
Butter for the loaf pan

10 x 5-inch (25 x 10-cm) loaf pan
or six individual molds of the shape
of your choice

● **Chef's note**
This cake, so quick and easy to make, is often the first cake children learn to bake in France, and is served for their goûter, their afternoon snack. Spice it up with vanilla, other spices, or citrus zest, and add chopped nuts.

Ingredients

1 ¼ cups (4 ½ oz./125 g) rye flour
1 cup (4 ½ oz./125 g) flour
1 tablespoon plus 1 teaspoon (15 g) baking powder
1 teaspoon gingerbread spice mix (see chef's note)
⅔ cup (150 ml) heavy cream
⅔ cup (9 oz./250 g) honey
2 tablespoons (2 oz./30 g) butter
½ cup (3 ½ oz./100 g) sugar
3 eggs

10 x 5-inch (25 x 10-cm) loaf pan

Spice Loaf Cake

Serves 8
Preparation time: 25 minutes
Cooking time: 45 minutes

Preheat the oven to 340°F (170°C). Butter the loaf pan.
Sift together the rye flour, white flour, baking powder, and spice.
In a bain-marie, warm the cream, honey, butter, and sugar until tepid.
Pour the mixture into the dry ingredients and mix together with an electric beater. Add the eggs one by one, making sure each one is fully incorporated before adding the next one.
Pour into the pan and bake for 35 to 45 minutes, until nicely browned on top and a cake tester comes out dry. Turn onto a cooling rack.

● Chef's notes

Gingerbread spice mix usually includes cinnamon, star anise, nutmeg, ginger, cloves, cardamom, and vanilla in varying amounts and proportions. If you don't have a readymade mix, you can make your own.
Since beekeepers can move their beehives, depending on the season, they can gather different types of honey. Different honeys will affect the flavor of the loaf.

Technique
Gingerbread >> p. 63

Fruit and Candy Cake ★

Serves 4 to 6
Preparation time: 30 minutes
Cooking time: 20 minutes

Make the fruit jelly.
Soften the gelatin sheets in a bowl of cold water. In a small saucepan, bring the fruit juices to a boil and melt the gummy candy in the liquid. Squeeze the water from the gelatin sheets and stir into the fruit juice and jelly mixture until completely dissolved. Pour into the square pan.

Prepare the raisin-sesame cookie base.
Preheat the oven to 350°F (180°C).
Cream the butter with the sugar. Stir in the egg and add the raisins and sesame seeds. Sift the flour and baking powder into the mixture and stir until just combined.
Roll the dough into a rectangle about ¼ inch (5 mm) thick, place on a baking sheet, and bake for 14 to 15 minutes, until lightly colored. Let cool.

Make the Chantilly cream.
Whip the cream until it holds firm peaks. Stir in the sugar and vanilla extract.

Assemble the cakes.
Cut the cookie base into rectangles of about 1 ½ x 4 inches (4 x 10 cm). Cut the fruit jelly into smaller rectangles and center each piece on a cookie base. Fill a piping bag with the Chantilly cream and pipe small dollops of it on top, then decorate with colored candies.

Techniques
Sweetened short pastry (crumbled) >> p. 18
Chantilly cream >> p. 94

Ingredients

Fruit jelly
6 sheets (12 g) gelatin
⅓ cup (75 ml) lemon juice
½ cup (125 ml) pineapple juice
1 ½ oz. (40 g) jelly babies
or other gummy candy

Raisin-sesame cookie base
1 stick (4 oz./125 g) butter, softened
½ cup (3 ½ oz./100 g) sugar
1 egg
Scant ½ cup (2 oz./70 g) raisins
3 tablespoons (1 oz./30 g) sesame seeds, toasted
2 cups (9 oz./250 g) flour
1 teaspoon (5 g) baking powder

Chantilly cream
Scant ½ cup (100 ml) heavy cream
2 tablespoons (15 g) confectioners' sugar
A few drops of vanilla extract

Assorted candies to decorate

8-inch (20-cm) square pan

Lemon Loaf Cake ★

Serves 6

Preparation time: 25 minutes
Cooking time: 40 minutes

Preheat the oven to 350°F (180°C). Butter the loaf pan. If you wish, line it with parchment paper. Whip the eggs, sugar, and salt until thick and pale. Mix in the lemon zest, cream, and rum. Sift in the flour and baking powder and mix briskly to incorporate. Stir in the melted butter.
Bake for 35 to 40 minutes, until nicely browned and a cake tester comes out clean. Immediately turn onto a cooling rack. Let cool completely before cutting.
If using apricot jam or preserves to glaze, heat until melted, strain to remove any lumps of fruit, let cool a little, and glaze the cake using a pastry brush while the glaze is still warm.

● Chef's note

If you wrap this cake in plastic wrap as soon as it cools, it will keep well for several days.

Ingredients

5 eggs
1 cup plus scant 1 cup (12 oz./350 g) sugar
1 teaspoon (5 g) salt
Finely grated zest of 1 lemon
(unsprayed or organic)
⅔ cup (150 ml) heavy cream
2 teaspoons (10 ml) rum
2 ¼ cups (9 oz./275 g) flour
1 ¼ teaspoons (5 g) baking powder
7 tablespoons (3 ½ oz./100 g) butter, melted
Butter for the loaf pan
Apricot jam or preserves to glaze (optional)

10 x 5-inch (25 x 10-cm) loaf pan

Ingredients

1 stick (4 oz./125 g) butter, softened
⅔ cup (4 oz./125 g) sugar
2 large eggs
1 cup (4 ½ oz./125 g) flour
1 ½ teaspoons (6 g) baking powder
1 apple, sliced

6-inch (15-cm) diameter pan with
  removable bottom

Apple Pound Cake ★

Serves 6
Preparation time: 25 minutes
Cooking time: 40 minutes

Preheat the oven to 340°F (170°C). Butter and flour the pan.
Cream the butter with the sugar. Incorporate the eggs. Sift in the flour and baking powder and stir until just combined.
Pour the batter into the cake pan and decorate the top with apple slices.
Bake for about 40 minutes, until a cake tester comes out clean.

Loaf cakes and cookies

Tarts

Manuel Lopez

Artisan candy maker

Most members of the public, even the most enthusiastic foodies, find it hard to differentiate between a candy maker and a chocolatier or a pastry chef. The candy maker makes products whose principal ingredient is sugar. He is both a guardian of know-how—some of which goes back many centuries—and a purveyor of a multitude of feelings connected to our imagination, our nostalgia for our childhood, vacations, and sweet treats. The candy cake I present here is a throwback to French candy-making tradition, with its fruit jellies from the Vaucluse and Auvergne regions and its Montélimar nougat, and to a generic childhood when we were spoiled with marshmallows and candies of all colors and textures. The association here is surprising: I recommend you taste this dessert with your eyes shut. Sweet dreams!

Candy Cake

Serves 10 (makes about 50 good-sized candies)

Preparation time: 1 hour/Cooking time: 40 minutes

Prepare the white nougat.

Preheat the oven to 300°F (150°C). Oil or butter a sheet of parchment paper, or line a confectionery frame with a silicone baking sheet. Spread the almonds and pistachios on a baking sheet and roast for about 20 minutes. Take 1 teaspoon (5 g) of the sugar and set it aside. In a saucepan, place the remaining sugar, glucose syrup, and water and bring to a boil. Let simmer until it registers 293°F (145°C). Meanwhile, begin heating the honey and vanilla in another saucepan. Whip the egg white with a pinch of salt and add the reserved sugar. When the honey registers 250°F (120°C), gradually pour it over the egg white, whisking constantly. Carefully whisk in the syrup. With a flexible spatula, stir in the nuts. Spread the mixture on the prepared sheet and let cool.

Make the raspberry fruit jelly.

Blend the raspberries and heat with the sugar and pectin. When the mixture comes to a boil, add the glucose syrup and continue cooking until the thermometer registers 221°F (105°C). Stir in the lemon juice. Even if you are using a nonstick dish, line it with greased parchment paper. Pour the mixture into a dish: it should be slightly less than ½ inch (1 cm) deep.

Prepare the pistachio marshmallow.

In a saucepan, heat the water, sugar, and half the invert sugar. Soften the gelatin sheets in a bowl of cold water. When the syrup comes to a boil, dip the thermometer into it. At 257°F (125°C), remove from the heat. Squeeze the water from the gelatin sheets and stir them in until completely dissolved. Place the remaining invert sugar in a stand mixer and begin beating at low speed. Slowly pour the syrup down the side of the bowl, increasing the speed until the paste increases in volume and thickens. Reduce the speed and pour in the pistachio (or alternative) flavoring and coloring. Line the bottom of a dish with greased parchment paper and grease the sides. Pour in the marshmallow mixture. Cover with plastic wrap, but do not let it come into contact with the mixture. Let cool.

The next day, assemble the candy cake.

Use a well-sharpened knife for all the cutting, if possible double-handled, and cut cleanly without sawing. Peel the parchment paper from the nougat and cut it into a rectangle of the desired size. Repeat for the raspberry jelly and set it over the nougat. Place the marshmallow on a board and dust it with a mixture of cornstarch and confectioners' sugar to facilitate cutting. Cut a rectangle of marshmallow and place on the cake. Decorate it with leftover trimmings from the three layers and other decoration, as desired. To cut servings—whether slices like a cake, or squares like large candies—pull the knife out cleanly to remove it. You can store the servings for several weeks, wrapped in cellophane paper.

Ingredients

White nougat
3 ½ oz. (100 g) blanched almonds
1 oz. (25 g) shelled pistachios
Generous ⅔ cup (4 ½ oz./130 g) sugar, divided
2 tablespoons (1 ½ oz./40 g) glucose syrup
2 tablespoons (30 ml) water
2 ½ tablespoons (2 oz./50 g) honey
½ teaspoon (3 ml) vanilla extract
1 egg white (1 oz./30 g)
1 pinch salt

Raspberry fruit jelly
14 oz. (400 g) raspberries
2 cups (14 oz./400 g) sugar
⅓ oz. (10 g) yellow pectin
3 tablespoons (2 oz./60 g) glucose syrup
Juice of 1 lemon

Pistachio marshmallow
3 tablespoons (50 ml) water
¾ cup (5 oz./140 g) sugar
4 oz. (110 g) invert sugar, divided
5 sheets (10 g) gelatin
½ teaspoon (3 ml) pistachio flavoring
(or almond or orgeat)
3 drops green coloring
Neutral oil for greasing

To assemble
3 tablespoons (1 oz./30 g) cornstarch
½ cup (2 ½ oz./70 g) confectioners' sugar
Decoration such as violet-flavored sugar (optional)

A day ahead: make the nougat, jelly, and marshmallow layers.

Ingredients

2 tablespoons (30 g) butter, plus some
  for the pan
⅔ cup (3 oz./80 g) flour
4 eggs
⅔ cup (4 oz./125 g) sugar
½ teaspoon (2 g) salt
1 cup (250 ml) milk
3 ½ oz. (100 g) cherries, unpitted, washed,
  and patted dry

6-inch (15-cm) diameter tart pan

Variation:
Mascarpone clafoutis
⅔ cup (3 ½ oz./100 g) cornstarch
1 cup plus 3 tablespoons (3 ½ oz./100 g) ground
  almonds
3 eggs
½ cup (3 ½ oz./100 g) sugar
½ teaspoon (2 g) salt
1 ½ cups (13 oz./375 g) mascarpone
1 ¼ cups (300 ml) milk

Cherry Clafoutis ★

Serves 6
Preparation time: 25 minutes
Cooking time: 30 minutes

Preheat the oven to 350°F (180°C). Generously butter the pan.
Melt the butter and allow to cool a little.
Sift the flour into a mixing bowl and make a well in the center. In another mixing bowl, whip the eggs with the sugar and salt until pale and thick. Pour into the well and stir in gradually until completely incorporated. Whisk in the milk and then the melted butter.
Wash the cherries, then remove the stalks but not the pits. Butter a tart mold and arrange the cherries in it. Pour the batter over the cherries.
Bake for about 30 minutes, until nicely browned on top and a cake tester inserted into the batter comes out clean.

For a more luxurious version, try a mascarpone clafoutis (see list of ingredients for the variation). Follow the method above, but replace the flour with cornstarch and ground almonds, and add mascarpone.

● **Chef's note**
Although it may not be very pleasant to deal with the unpitted cherries, the pits impart a mild taste that improves the flavor of this simple cake, and helps retain the juiciness of the fruit without softening the batter. Traditionally, the stems were carefully snipped off with a pair of scissors, rather than broken off, so that the cherries were not pierced.

Parisian Custard Tart ★

Serves 6
Preparation time: 45 minutes
Chilling time: 40 minutes
Cooking time: 45 minutes

Make the sweet shortcrust pastry.
Butter the tart pan.
Dice the butter. Sift the flour onto the work surface. Working with the tips
of your fingers, rub the butter into the flour. Work quickly until the butter is
absorbed by the flour. The mixture should look like pale sand. This procedure
gives the crust a crumbly texture; it also neutralizes the action of the gluten
in the flour and prevents it from becoming elastic.
Dissolve the sugar and salt in the water. Make a well in the center of the
combined flour and butter and pour the liquid and the egg yolk into it. Work
with the palms of your hands to incorporate the wet ingredients into the dry
ones. Stop as soon as the dough is smooth.
Shape it into a disk and cover in plastic wrap. Chill for 20 minutes to relax
the dough. Roll it into a disk less than ⅛ inch (2-3 mm) thick and transfer
it to the tart pan, ensuring that it is neatly pressed around the rim. Chill for
an additional 20 minutes to firm. (This prevents shrinkage during baking.)

Prepare the custard filling.
In a heavy-bottom saucepan, heat the milk. Whip the egg yolks, sugar, and
cornstarch until the mixture is pale and thick. When the milk is simmering,
gradually pour half over the egg and sugar mixture, whipping continuously.
Return the mixture to the saucepan and stir continuously until it simmers
and thickens. Let cool—you can speed up the process by placing the bowl in
a larger one with ice cubes.

Assemble the flan.
Preheat the oven to 375°F (190°C)
Pour the custard into the tart shell. Bake for 35 minutes, until the flan is
marbled with brown.

Techniques
Shortcrust pastry (sweet version) >> p. 30
Custard flan filling >> p. 105

Ingredients

Sweet shortcrust pastry
5 tablespoons (2 ½ oz./65 g) butter,
room temperature, plus some for the pan
1 cup (4 oz./125 g) flour
2 ½ teaspoons (10 g) sugar
½ teaspoon (3 g) salt
3 tablespoons (40 ml) water
1 egg yolk

Custard
2 cups (500 ml) milk
2 egg yolks
½ cup (3 ½ oz./100 g) sugar
¼ cup (1 ½ oz./40 g) cornstarch

6-inch (15-cm) diameter tart pan

Ingredients

Sweet shortcrust pastry
5 tablespoons (2 ½ oz./65 g) butter,
    room temperature, plus some for the pan
1 cup (4 oz./125 g) flour
2 ½ teaspoons (10 g) sugar
½ teaspoon (3 g) salt
3 tablespoons (40 ml) water
1 egg yolk

Filling
½ cup (125 ml) milk
½ cup (125 ml) heavy cream
2 eggs plus 1 egg yolk
¼ cup (2 oz./50 g) sugar
1 teaspoon (5 ml) vanilla extract
1 tablespoon (15 ml) plum brandy

8 oz. (250 g) plums, preferably greengages,
    but you can use any firm, sweet plum
2 oz. (50 g) raspberries

7-inch (18-cm) tart pan or ring

Alsace-Style Plum Tart ★

Serves 4
Preparation time: 40 minutes
Chilling time: 20 minutes
Cooking time: 25 minutes

Make the sweet shortcrust pastry.
Butter the tart pan.
Dice the butter. Sift the flour onto the work surface. Working with the tips of your fingers, rub the butter into the flour. Work quickly until the butter is absorbed by the flour. The mixture should look like pale sand. This procedure gives the crust a crumbly texture; it also neutralizes the action of the gluten in the flour and prevents it from becoming elastic.
Dissolve the sugar and salt in the water. Make a well in the center of the combined flour and butter and pour the liquid and the egg yolk into it. Work with the palms of your hands to incorporate the wet ingredients into the dry ones. Stop as soon as the dough is smooth.
Shape it into a disk and cover in plastic wrap. Chill for 20 minutes to relax the dough. Roll it into a disk less than ⅛ inch (2-3 mm) thick and transfer it to the tart pan, ensuring that it is neatly pressed around the rim. Chill for an additional 20 minutes to firm. (This prevents shrinkage during baking.)

Prepare the filling.
Lightly beat all the ingredients together without making any bubbles. Strain through a fine-mesh sieve and cover with plastic wrap. Chill until used.

Assemble and bake the tart.
Preheat the oven to 350°F (180°C). Wash the plums and cut them in half lengthwise. Remove the pits. Arrange the plum halves, cut side upward, on the dough. Arrange the raspberries in the center. Cover with the filling and bake for 25 to 30 minutes, until the custard mixture starts to brown lightly in parts. Immediately remove the tart from the pan and cool it on a rack so that it does not reabsorb any moisture.

Techniques
Shortcrust pastry (sweet version) >> p. 30
Baked creams >> p. 92

Pear and Almond Cream Tart ★

Serves 6
Preparation time: 1 hour
Chilling time: 30 minutes, plus a few hours to cool the pears
Cooking time: 40 minutes

Prepare the poached pears (these can be made a day ahead).
Bring the water, sugar, and slit vanilla bean to a boil. Peel the pears and sprinkle them with a little lemon juice. Working from the base, remove the cores (seeds and fibers). Dip the pears in the boiling syrup, carefully placing a round rack weighted down with a heavy object over them to keep them from surfacing. Simmer gently for 10 to 12 minutes. Remove from the heat and let cool completely, for several hours.

Make the sweet shortcrust pastry.
Butter the tart pan.
Dice the butter. Sift the flour onto the work surface. Working with the tips of your fingers, rub the butter into the flour. Work quickly until the butter is absorbed by the flour. The mixture should look like pale sand. This procedure gives the crust a crumbly texture; it also neutralizes the action of the gluten in the flour and prevents it from becoming elastic.
Dissolve the sugar and salt in the water. Make a well in the center of the combined flour and butter and pour the liquid and the egg yolk into it. Work with the palms of your hands to incorporate the wet ingredients into the dry ones. Stop as soon as the dough is smooth.
Shape it into a disk and cover in plastic wrap. Chill for 20 minutes to relax the dough. Roll it into a disk less than ⅛ inch (2 to 3 mm) thick and transfer it to the tart pan, ensuring that it is neatly pressed around the rim. Chill for an additional 20 minutes to firm. (This prevents shrinkage during baking.)

Prepare the almond cream.
In a mixing bowl, cream the butter and whisk in the sugar until light. Add the egg and whisk until combined. Whisk in the ground almonds and cornstarch. Stir in the vanilla and rum.

Assemble and bake the tart.
Preheat the oven to 340°F (170°C). Spread half the almond cream over the tart base. Cut the pears in half and slice them thinly. Arrange them over the almond cream. Carefully spread the remaining almond cream into the spaces. Bake for 30 minutes, until the almond cream has set (a cake tester should not have any traces of dough or almond cream, even though it will be moist) and the top is a nice golden brown. Immediately transfer to a cooling rack. Let cool.
Heat the glaze with the water and brush the top of the tart.

● **Did you know?**
Fasquelle, a pastry chef in Paris, invented this dessert in about 1850. It is called a tarte bourdaloue *in France, after a pastry chef whose shop was located in the rue Bourdaloue in Paris.*

Ingredients

Poached pears
1 ¾ cups (400 ml) water
1 cup (7 oz./200 g) sugar
½ vanilla bean, slit lengthwise
3 pears
Juice of ½ lemon

Sweet shortcrust pastry
1 cup plus 2 tablespoons (5 oz./150 g) flour
5 tablespoons (2 ½ oz./65 g) butter, room temperature, plus some for the pan
2 ½ teaspoons (10 g) sugar
½ teaspoon (3 g) salt
3 tablespoons (40 ml) water
1 egg yolk

Almond cream
3 tablespoons (50 g) butter
¼ cup (2 oz./50 g) sugar
1 egg
Generous ½ cup (2 oz./50 g) ground almonds
1 tablespoon (10 g) cornstarch
1 teaspoon (5 ml) vanilla extract
1 teaspoon (5 ml) rum

3 oz. (80 g) light glaze
3 tablespoons (40 ml) water

8-inch (20-cm) tart pan or ring

Techniques
Shortcrust pastry (sweet version) >> p. 30
Almond cream >> p. 90

Ingredients

Sweetened short pastry
1 stick (4 oz./125 g) butter, softened
2 cups (9 oz./250 g) flour
½ cup (3 ½ oz./100 g) sugar
½ teaspoon (3 g) salt
1 egg

Ganache
1 vanilla bean
⅔ cup (150 ml) heavy cream
5 oz. (150 g) bittersweet chocolate,
  64 percent cocoa
2 tablespoons (1 oz./30 g) butter,
  room temperature, diced

Chocolate mousse
¾ cup (200 ml) heavy cream, divided
3 ½ oz. (100 g) bittersweet chocolate,
  64 percent cocoa
1 tablespoon (20 g) butter, room temperature

Decoration
3 ½ oz. (100 g) chocolate: white,
  bittersweet, and milk

Two 6-inch (15-cm) tart rings

Chocolate Tart
with Chocolate Mousse ★ ★

Serves 8
Preparation time: 1 hour 30 minutes
Chilling time: 30 minutes
Cooking time: 20 minutes

Make the sweetened short pastry.
Dice the butter. Sift the flour onto a work surface or into a mixing bowl. Make a well in the center and place the butter in it. Working with your fingers, quickly crush the butter into the flour until the texture is like sand. For an optimal crumbly texture, stop when just combined. Sprinkle the sugar and salt in and combine. Lightly beat the egg with a fork. Incorporate the egg with a pastry scraper and the palm of one hand. Stop as soon as the dough is smooth: it should not become elastic.
Shape the dough into a thick disk and cover in plastic wrap. Chill for 20 minutes.
Preheat the oven to 320°F (160°C).
On a lightly floured board, roll the dough to a thickness of ⅛ inch (3 mm) and line the two tart rings. Bake blind (see p. 212) for 15 to 20 minutes until golden. Let cool on a rack.

Prepare the ganache.
Slit the vanilla bean lengthwise and scrape the seeds into the cream. Bring the cream to a boil. Chop the chocolate. Pour the hot cream over the chocolate, stir with a spatula until smooth, and incorporate the butter. Let cool and pour into the tart crust, smoothing with an offset spatula.

Make the chocolate mousse.
Bring half the cream to a boil. Chop the chocolate. Pour the hot cream over the chocolate, stir with a spatula until smooth, and incorporate the butter. Whip the remaining cream until it forms soft peaks and, with a flexible spatula, fold it carefully into the melted chocolate.

Finish and decorate the tart.
Spoon the chocolate mousse into a piping bag fitted with a star tip and pipe small rosettes on the ganache. Prepare chocolate decorations of your choice (openwork, frills, striped with two or more colors, etc.).

Techniques
Sweetened short pastry (crumbled) >> p. 18
Chocolate ganache >> p. 186
Baking blind (prebaking) >> p. 212

Tropical Tart ★

Serves 6
Preparation time: 1 hour 20 minutes
Chilling time: 20 minutes
Cooking time: 40 minutes

Make the sweetened short pastry.
Dice the butter. Sift the flour onto a work surface or into a mixing bowl. Make a well in the center and place the butter in it. Working with your fingers, quickly crush the butter into the flour until the texture is like sand. For an optimal crumbly texture, stop when just combined. Sprinkle the sugar and salt in and combine. Lightly beat the egg with a fork. Incorporate the egg with a pastry scraper and the palm of one hand. Stop as soon as the dough is smooth: it should not become elastic.
Shape the dough into a thick disk and cover in plastic wrap. Chill for 20 minutes.

Prepare the creamy coconut filling.
Whip the butter with the sugar until it is light and fluffy. Lightly beat the egg and stir it in. Add the vanilla and rum. Beat in the ground almonds and shredded coconut until light.

Make the garnish.
Slit the vanilla bean lengthwise and scrape out the seeds. Peel and core the pineapple and cut it into ½-inch (1-cm) cubes. Heat the butter in a sauté pan. Begin lightly coloring the pineapple cubes and stir in the vanilla seeds. After a few minutes, sprinkle with sugar and flambé with the rum. Remove from the heat as soon as the pineapple is lightly colored; it must not soften. Let cool.

Assemble and bake the tart.
Preheat the oven to 350°F (180°C).
On a lightly floured board, roll the dough to a thickness of ⅛ inch (3 mm) and line the tart ring. Arrange the pineapple cubes on the shell and cover with the coconut filling. Bake for about 30 minutes, until lightly browned on top. Immediately transfer to a cooling rack. Let cool.
Heat the glaze with the water and brush the top of the tart.

Techniques
Sweetened short pastry (crumbled) >> p. 18
Almond cream >> p. 90

Ingredients

Sweetened short pastry
5 tablespoons (2 ½ oz./75 g) butter, room temperature
1 cup plus 2 tablespoons (5 oz./150 g) flour
⅓ cup (2 oz./60 g) sugar
¼ teaspoon (2 g) salt
1 egg

Creamy coconut filling
3 tablespoons (2 oz./50 g) butter, softened
¼ cup (2 oz./50 g) sugar
1 egg
1 teaspoon (5 ml) vanilla extract
1 teaspoon (5 ml) rum
Generous ⅓ cup (1 oz./30 g) ground almonds
⅓ cup (1 oz./30 g) unsweetened shredded coconut

Garnish
1 vanilla bean
1 pineapple
4 tablespoons (2 oz./60 g) butter
⅓ cup (2 oz./60 g) sugar
3 tablespoons (50 ml) rum

2 oz. (60 g) light glaze
2 tablespoons (30 ml) water

8-inch (20-cm) tart ring

Ingredients

Choose either of two methods to make
this tart: blind bake the pastry shell (see p. 212)
and fill it with cooked lemon cream enriched
with whipped cream (Filling 1),
or bake the pastry and lemon cream
(Filling 2) together. The shortcrust
pastry recipe is identical for both.

Sweetened short pastry

1 stick (4 oz./125 g) butter, softened
2 cups (9 oz./250 g) flour
½ cup (3 ½ oz./100 g) sugar
½ teaspoon (3 g) salt
1 egg

Filling 1

⅔ cup (150 ml) lemon juice
3 tablespoons (50 ml) water
2 eggs (3 ½ oz./100 g) plus 1 large egg yolk
   (¾ oz./20 g)
⅓ cup (2 ½ oz./75 g) sugar
1 ½ tablespoons (15 g) cornstarch
3 tablespoons (2 oz./50 g) butter
Scant ½ cup (115 ml) heavy cream

Filling 2

¾ cup (200 ml) lemon juice
Scant ½ cup (100 ml) water
5 egg yolks (3 oz./90 g)
1 cup (7 oz./200 g) sugar
¼ cup (1 ½ oz./40 g) cornstarch
3 tablespoons (2 oz./50 g) butter
1 teaspoon (5 ml) vanilla extract (optional)

Italian meringue

1 cup (7 oz./200 ml) sugar
¼ cup (60 ml) water
3 egg whites (3 ½ oz./100 g)
1 pinch of salt

Julienned candied lemon zest for decoration

Two 6-inch (15-cm) tart rings

Techniques
Sweetened short pastry (crumbled) >> p. 18
Lemon cream >> p. 105
Italian meringue >> p. 177
Baking blind (prebaking) >> p. 212

Lemon Meringue Tart ★★

Serves 8
Preparation time: 1 hour 30 minutes/Chilling time: 30 minutes
Cooking time: 25 minutes

Prepare the sweetened short pastry.
Follow the method given on page 422.
Shape the dough into a thick disk and cover in plastic wrap. Chill for 20 minutes.
Divide the dough into two pieces and roll them out into disks of ⅛ inch (3-4 mm). Line the two tart rings. If you are using Filling 1, first blind bake the tart shells (see p. 212) at 320°F (160°C) for 15 to 20 minutes, until nicely golden. Transfer to a rack and let cool.

Make Filling 1: cooked lemon cream to fill baked tart shell.
In a heavy-bottom saucepan, bring the lemon juice and water to a boil. Whip the eggs and egg yolk with the sugar until thick and pale. Beat in the cornstarch. When the liquid is simmering, pour it over the egg and sugar mixture, stirring constantly. Return the mixture to the saucepan and cook as you would a pastry cream, stirring constantly and removing the saucepan from the heat from time to time, until it thickens and coats the back of a spoon. Transfer to a bowl to cool and stir in the butter, cover with plastic wrap flush with the surface, and cool. Whip the cream until it holds soft peaks and carefully fold it into the lemon mixture. Pour into the cooled baked tart shells.

Or, prepare Filling 2: lemon cream to bake with the pastry.
In a heavy-bottom saucepan, bring the lemon juice and water to a boil. In a mixing bowl, whip the egg yolks and sugar until pale and thick. Beat in the cornstarch. When the liquid is simmering, pour it over the egg and sugar mixture, stirring constantly. Return the mixture to the saucepan and cook as you would a pastry cream, stirring constantly and removing the saucepan from the heat from time to time, until it thickens and coats the back of a spoon. Stir in the butter, as well as the vanilla, if using. Preheat the oven to 350°F (180°C). Pour the cream into the unbaked tart shell. Bake for 20 minutes, until the lemon cream is set (the top will be dry) and lightly colored.

Make the Italian meringue.
In a heavy-bottom saucepan, heat the sugar and water to make a syrup. When it registers 230°F (110°C), begin beating the egg whites with a pinch of salt in a stand mixer fitted with a whisk. When they hold firm peaks and the syrup has reached 243°F-250°F (117°C-121°C), take the pan off the heat and gradually pour the syrup into the egg whites in a steady stream, whisking continuously and taking care that the hot syrup does not splatter. Continue whisking until the meringue has cooled to about 85°F (30°C). It will be dense, shiny, and form many small peaks.

Assemble and decorate the tart.
When the tart has cooled, spoon the meringue into a piping bag fitted with a star or plain tip and pipe rosettes over the lemon cream. Brown lightly under a salamander or the broiler. Decorate with julienned lemon zest.

Cream Cheese Tartlets ★

Serves 4
Preparation time: 1 hour
Chilling time: 20 minutes
Cooking time: 25 minutes

Make the sweet shortcrust pastry.
Dice the butter. Sift the flour onto a work surface or into a mixing bowl. Make a well in the center and place the butter in it. Working with your fingers, quickly crush the butter into the flour until the texture is like sand. For an optimal crumbly texture, stop when just combined. Dissolve the sugar and salt in the water. Make a well in the center and add the liquid. Lightly beat the egg yolk with a fork. Incorporate the egg with a pastry scraper and the palm of one hand. Stop as soon as the dough is smooth: it should not become elastic.
Shape the dough into a thick disk and cover in plastic wrap. Chill for 20 minutes.
On a lightly floured surface, roll it into six disks less than ⅛ inch (2-3 mm) thick and transfer them to the tart rings, neatly pressing the dough around the rims.

Prepare the cream cheese filling.
In a mixing bowl, combine the *fromage blanc*, zest, egg yolks, custard powder, and cornstarch.
Whip the egg whites until they form firm peaks. Whisk in the sugar until the mixture is firm and shiny. Carefully fold it into the cream cheese mixture and gradually stir in the milk. (The filling will deflate slightly.)

Assemble the tartlets.
Preheat the oven to 340°F (170°C).
Pour the cream cheese filling into the tart shells and bake for 20 to 25 minutes, until set and lightly browned on top.

● **Chef's note**
Fromage blanc (white cheese) is a soft cow's-milk cheese with a high moisture content, popular as a dessert in France with jams and coulis. You can substitute 14 oz. (400 g) cream cheese softened with a scant ½ cup (100 ml) heavy cream, or any other very soft, unsalted cheese.

Techniques
Shortcrust pastry (sweet version) >> p. 30
French meringue >> p. 176

Ingredients

Sweet shortcrust pastry
5 tablespoons (2 ½ oz./65 g) butter, softened
1 cup (4 oz./125 g) flour
2 ½ teaspoons (10 g) sugar
½ teaspoon (3 g) salt
3 tablespoons (40 ml) water
1 egg yolk (20 g)

Cream cheese filling
18 oz. (500 g) *fromage blanc*
or farmer's cheese (see chef's note)
½ teaspoon (2 g) finely grated lemon zest
8 egg yolks (5 oz./150 g)
3 tablespoons (2 oz./50 g) custard powder,
or 3 tablespoons (2 oz./50 g) cornstarch
combined with 1 teaspoon (5 ml) vanilla extract
3 tablespoons (2 oz./50 g) cornstarch
4 egg whites (5 oz./150 g)
¾ cup (5 oz./150 g) sugar
Scant ½ cup (100 ml) milk

Six individual 2 ¾-inch (7-cm) tart rings

Ingredients

Sweetened short pastry
1 stick (4 oz./125 g) butter, softened
2 cups (9 oz./250 g) flour
½ cup (3 ½ oz./100 g) sugar
½ teaspoon (3 g) salt
1 egg

Diplomat cream
1 ½ sheets (3 g) gelatin
¼ vanilla bean
½ cup (125 ml) milk
1 egg yolk
3 tablespoons (1 ¼ oz./35 g) sugar
2 tablespoons (15 g) flour
½ cup (125 ml) heavy cream

12 oz. (350 g) assorted fresh fruit (red currants, plums, apricots, strawberries, black currants, etc.)
3 oz. (80 g) light glaze
3 tablespoons (40 ml) water
8 cape gooseberries for garnish

Eight 3-inch (8-cm) tart rings

Seasonal Fruit Tartlets ★★

Serves 8
Preparation time: 1 hour
Chilling time: 20 minutes
Cooking time: 15 minutes

Make the sweetened short pastry.
Dice the butter. Sift the flour onto a work surface or into a mixing bowl. Make a well in the center and place the butter in it. Working with your fingers, quickly crush the butter into the flour until the texture is like sand. For an optimal crumbly texture, stop when just combined. Sprinkle the sugar and salt in and combine. Lightly beat the egg with a fork. Incorporate the egg with a pastry scraper and the palm of one hand. Stop as soon as the dough is smooth: it should not become elastic.
Shape the dough into a thick disk and cover in plastic wrap. Chill for 20 minutes.
Preheat the oven to 350°F (180°C).
Place the dough on a lightly floured surface and roll into eight disks less than ⅛ inch (2-3 mm) thick. Transfer to the tart rings, pressing the dough neatly around the rims.
Blind bake the shells (see p. 212) for 12 to 15 minutes, until nicely golden.

Prepare the Diplomat cream.
Soften the gelatin sheets in a bowl of cold water.
Slit the vanilla bean lengthwise and scrape the seeds into the milk. In a heavy-bottom saucepan, heat the milk with the vanilla seeds and bean. Whip the egg yolk, sugar, and flour until the mixture is pale and thick. When the milk is simmering, remove from the heat and gradually pour half over the egg mixture, whisking continuously. Return the mixture to the saucepan and stir continuously until it simmers. Let simmer 2-3 minutes, still stirring.
Remove from the heat. Remove the vanilla bean. Squeeze the water from the gelatin sheets and whisk them into the custard cream.
Transfer to a mixing bowl, cover with plastic wrap flush with the surface (this will prevent a skin from forming) and chill to about 60°F (15°C). Do not leave it too long; it must not set before the whipped cream is incorporated. With an electric beater, whip the heavy cream until it forms firm peaks. Stir the chilled custard cream again and carefully fold in the whipped cream with a flexible spatula.

Assemble the tartlets.
Spoon the Diplomat cream three-quarters of the way to the top. Arrange the fruit in a dome over it. Heat the glaze with the water and carefully brush the tops of the tarts. Top with a Cape gooseberry.

Techniques
Sweetened short pastry (crumbled) ›› p. 18
Chantilly cream ›› p. 94
Diplomat cream ›› p. 103
Baking blind (prebaking) ›› p. 212

Apple and Peach Compote Tartlets ★

Serves 4
Preparation time: 1 hour
Chilling time: 20 minutes
Cooking time: 30 minutes

Make the sweet shortcrust pastry.
Dice the butter. Sift the flour onto a work surface. Working with your fingertips, rub the butter into the flour. Work as quickly as possible until the butter is incorporated into the flour; it should look like pale sand. For an optimal crumbly texture, stop when just combined.
Dissolve the sugar and salt in the water. Make a well in the center and pour in the liquid and egg yolk. Still working with your fingers, mix the dry and liquid ingredients. Use the palm of your hand to knead lightly, just until the dough is smooth.
Shape it into a ball, cover with plastic wrap, and chill for 20 minutes.
Butter the tartlet rings. On a lightly floured surface, roll the dough into four disks less than ⅛ inch (2-3 mm) thick and transfer them to the tartlet rings, neatly pressing the dough around the rims.

Prepare the peach compote.
Dip the peaches briefly into boiling water and refresh immediately. Remove the skin, cut into halves to remove the pits, and dice. Cook over low heat until the liquid has evaporated. Stir in the sugar and let cool.

Assemble and bake the tartlets.
Preheat the oven to 350°F (180°C).
Spoon the peach compote into the tart shells. Peel, core, and finely slice the apples. Arrange them over the peach layer, covering it completely. Brush the apple slices very lightly with beaten egg to give them an attractive color. Bake for 15 to 20 minutes, until the edges of the apples are browned. Immediately transfer the tartlets onto a cooling rack and let cool. Heat the glaze with the water and brush the tops.

Techniques
Shortcrust pastry (sweet version) >> p. 30
Stewing fruit >> p. 210
Peeling fruit >> p. 216

Ingredients

Sweet shortcrust pastry
5 tablespoons (2 ½ oz./65 g) butter, softened, plus some for the tartlet rings
1 cup (4 oz./125 g) flour
2 ½ teaspoons (10 g) sugar
½ teaspoon (3 g) salt
3 tablespoons (40 ml) water
1 egg yolk (20 g)

Peach compote
3 peaches
3 ½ tablespoons (1 ½ oz./40 g) sugar

Apple garnish
2 apples
1 egg, beaten
1 ½ oz. (40 g) light glaze
1 tablespoon (20 ml) water

Four 3-inch (8-cm) tartlet rings

Ingredients

Sweet shortcrust pastry
5 tablespoons (2 ½ oz./65 g) butter, softened
1 cup (4 oz./125 g) flour
2 ½ teaspoons (10 g) sugar
½ teaspoon (3 g) salt
3 tablespoons (40 ml) water
1 egg yolk (20 g)

Apples
2 ¾ lb. (1.2 kg) apples
Juice of 1 lemon

Caramel
Scant ⅔ cup (4 oz./120 g) sugar
1 stick (4 oz./120 g) butter, well chilled

9-inch (22-cm) tatin or cake pan

Technique
Shortcrust pastry (sweet version) ›› p. 30

Tarte Tatin ★

Serves 6
Preparation time: 1 hour
Chilling time: 20 minutes
Cooking time: 40 minutes

Make the sweet shortcrust pastry.
Dice the butter. Sift the flour onto a work surface. Working with your fingertips, rub the butter into the flour. Work as quickly as possible until the butter is incorporated into the flour; it should look like pale sand. This procedure gives the crust a crumbly texture; it also neutralizes the action of the gluten in the flour and prevents it from becoming elastic.
Dissolve the sugar and salt in the water. Make a well in the center and pour in the liquid and egg yolk. Still working with your fingers, incorporate the dry ingredients into the liquid.
Use the palm of your hand to knead lightly, just until the dough is smooth. Roll out the dough until it is ⅐ inch (3-4 mm) thick and shape it into a disk about 1 inch (2.5-3 cm) larger than the pan. Cover with plastic wrap and chill for 20 minutes.

Prepare the apples.
Peel and halve the apples. Core them and rub them with lemon juice.

Make the caramel.
Place the sugar in a heavy-bottom saucepan and cook, stirring gently, until it turns a reddish caramel color (330°F/165°C). Immediately pour it into the base of the cake or tatin pan and swirl it around quickly until the base is evenly covered. Dice the butter and dot it over the caramel.

Assemble and bake.
Preheat the oven to 350°F (180°C).
Arrange the apple halves in the mold, standing up and tightly packed. Cover with the dough, tucking it in around the rim.
Bake for about 35 minutes, until the pastry is golden and crisp, and the apples have softened (test with a cake tester). Remove from the oven and immediately turn the tart over onto a platter, taking care not to burn yourself with the caramel.
Should you make the tart ahead of time, you can let it cool in the pan. Reheat it by placing it briefly under the broiler, or use a kitchen torch, and turn out of the pan.

● **Chef's notes**
Traditionally, this upside-down cake is served with crème fraîche or vanilla ice cream. The temperatures and textures complement each other marvelously.

● **Did you know?**
This tart was created in the late nineteenth century by the Tatin sisters in the region of Sologne. Curnonsky, a celebrated gastronomic critic, made it famous in 1926.

Nut and Caramel Tartlets ★

Serves 6
Preparation time: 1 hour
Chilling time: 40 minutes
Cooking time: 30 minutes

Make the sweetened short pastry.
Dice the butter. Sift the flour onto a work surface or into a mixing bowl. Make a well in the center and place the butter in it. Working with your fingers, quickly crush the butter into the flour until the texture is like sand. For an optimal crumbly texture, stop when just combined. Sprinkle the sugar and salt in and combine. Lightly beat the egg with a fork. Incorporate the egg with a pastry scraper and the palm of one hand. Stop as soon as the dough is smooth: it should not become elastic.
Shape the dough into a thick disk and cover in plastic wrap. Chill for 20 minutes.
Preheat the oven to 320°F (160°C). Place the dough on a lightly floured surface and roll into eight disks less than ⅛ inch (2-3 mm) thick. Transfer to the tartlet rings, pressing the dough neatly around the rims.
Blind bake the shells (see p. 212) for 12 to 15 minutes, until nicely golden. Transfer to a rack and let cool.

Prepare the filling.
Roast the nuts, with the exception of the pistachios. Preheat the oven to 350°F (180°C) and spread the nuts evenly on a baking sheet. Bake for 5 to 7 minutes and let cool.
In a small saucepan, heat the cream. In a nonstick pan, melt the sugar, stirring constantly. When it turns a light caramel color, mix in the butter and immediately add the hot cream. Stir until combined and add all the nuts. Remove the nut-caramel mixture from the heat and pour it into the tartlet shells. Let cool.

● **Chef's note**
Getting the caramel just right will ensure your tartlets are delicious. Do not let it darken or it will add a bitter note to the filling.

Techniques
Sweetened short pastry (crumbled) >> p. 18
Baking blind (prebaking) >> p. 212

Ingredients
Sweetened short pastry
5 tablespoons (2 ½ oz./75 g) butter, softened
1 cup plus 2 tablespoons (5 oz./150 g) flour
⅓ cup (2 oz./60 g) sugar
¼ teaspoon (2 g) salt
1 egg

Filling
2 oz. (50 g) pecan nuts
2 oz. (50 g) hazelnuts
2 oz. (50 g) pine nuts
½ cup (120 ml) heavy cream
¾ cup (5 oz./150 g) sugar
2 teaspoons (10 g) butter
2 oz. (50 g) shelled pistachios

Six 3-inch (8-cm) tartlet rings

Iced desserts

David Wesmaël

Meilleur Ouvrier de France, glacerie (ice-cream making)

The vacherin—a traditional iced dessert of meringue, ice cream, sorbet, and Chantilly cream—has been a favorite in France for many generations now. So it was quite a challenge to create a modern take on it that would find favor with a wide public, one that was original and playful, but mainly one that could be easily made at home. It's always difficult to make ice creams and sorbets in the home kitchen without the essential freezing equipment. That's why I have provided simple recipes for fresh fruit sorbets in a granita version that is simply frozen and doesn't require churning. It's the harmony between the pure taste of the fruit and the sweetness of sugar that gives the right quality to the granitas. The different fruits are showcased in a refreshing array of colors and textures: the meringue has crunch, the vanilla-scented Chantilly is soft, and the sorbets are fresh and tangy.

A Contemporary Vacherin with Four Fruit Sorbets

Makes 6 individual desserts
Preparation time: 1 hour
Freezing time: 4 hours
Cooking time: 20 minutes

Ingredients

Swiss meringue
Scant ½ cup (3 ½ oz./100 g) egg whites
1 cup (7 oz./200 g) sugar

Granny Smith granita sorbet
3 Granny Smith apples
1 tablespoon plus 1 teaspoon (20 ml) lemon juice
3 ½ tablespoons (1 ½ oz./42 g) sugar
2 tablespoons (28 ml) water

Apricot granita sorbet
9 oz. (250 g) apricots
¼ cup (2 oz./55 g) sugar
3 tablespoons plus 1 teaspoon (50 ml) water

Raspberry granita sorbet
7 oz. (200 g) fresh raspberries
¼ cup (2 oz./55 g) sugar
4 tablespoons plus 1 teaspoon (65 ml) water

Lemon granita sorbet
About 3 lemons (depending on their juiciness)
⅓ cup (2 ½ oz./75 g) sugar
½ cup (120 ml) water

Chantilly cream
½ vanilla bean
2 cups (500 ml) whipping cream, well chilled
Generous ½ cup (2 ¾ oz./75 g) confectioners' sugar

1 bag multicolored candies

Prepare the Swiss meringue.

Pour the egg whites into a heat-resistant mixing bowl and add the sugar. Set the bowl over a bain-marie and whip until the mixture reaches 104°F (40°C). Pour into the bowl of a stand mixer. Take a freezer bag, and at one corner, cut a 1 ¼-inch (3-cm) opening. Place Scotch tape near the opening so that you can control the flow of the meringue. Spoon the meringue mixture into the bag and, on a silicone baking sheet, pipe twelve fine strips, each 1 ¼ x 7 inches (3 x 18 cm).
Bake at 250°F (120°C) with the oven door slightly ajar for 20 minutes.
Transfer the silicone baking sheet carefully to a rack for the meringue bases to cool.

Make the Granny Smith granita sorbet.

Wash, peel, and core the apples. Process them with the lemon juice; you will need 7 ½ oz. (210 g) of puréed apple.
In a heavy-bottom saucepan, bring the sugar and water to a boil, whisking frequently. Let cool to 84°F (30°C) and pour over the puréed apples. Process together. Pour into an ice tray with 1-inch (2.5-cm) cube compartments and freeze. Reserve until the dessert is assembled.

Make the apricot granita sorbet.

Wash the apricots and cut them in two. Remove the pits. Process them; you will need 7 oz. (195 g) of puréed apricot.
In a heavy-bottom saucepan, bring the sugar and water to a boil, whisking frequently. Let cool to 84°F (30°C) and pour over the puréed apricots. Process together. Pour into an ice tray with 1-inch (2.5-cm) cube compartments and freeze. Reserve until the dessert is assembled.

Make the raspberry granita sorbet.

Wash the raspberries and pat them dry carefully. Process them and strain through a fine-mesh sieve; you will need 6 ⅓ oz. (180 g) of puréed raspberry.
In a heavy-bottom saucepan, bring the sugar and water to a boil, whisking frequently. Let cool to 84°F (30°C) and pour over the puréed raspberries. Process together. Pour into an ice tray with 1-inch (2.5-cm) cube compartments and freeze. Reserve until the dessert is assembled.

Make the lemon granita sorbet.

Wash the lemons and squeeze them. You will need 7 tablespoons (3 ¾ oz./105 g) lemon juice.

In a heavy-bottom saucepan, bring the sugar and water to a boil, whisking frequently. Let cool to 84°F (30°C) and pour over the lemon juice. Process together. Pour into an ice tray with 1-inch (2.5-cm) cube compartments and freeze. Reserve until the dessert is assembled.

Prepare the Chantilly cream.

Slit the vanilla bean lengthways and scrape out the seeds. Pour the whipping cream into a chilled mixing bowl. Add the confectioners' sugar and the vanilla bean seeds. Whip to a firm Chantilly texture. To pipe, use a piping bag or a plastic freezer bag, as described for the Swiss meringue.

Assemble the dish.

Chill the plates in the freezer.

With the bag of Chantilly cream, pipe a small mound in the center of each plate and set a strip of cooled meringue over it. Turn out the cubes of granita sorbet and place them in a straight line over the meringue, alternating the colors and flavors. Pipe small waves of Chantilly cream over the sorbet, making a small up-and-down motion with your hand. Set a second strip of meringue on top and pipe a second layer of Chantilly waves over the top. Scatter small multicolored candies over the Chantilly cream and in the plate to add touches of color to the dessert.

If you wish to assemble the desserts ahead of time, place the cubes of granita sorbet over the meringue and return to the freezer, and simply add the Chantilly cream at the last minute, with, optionally, a fruit coulis.

Iced Yule Log ★ ★ ★

Make all the components with the exception of the chocolate velvet spray and the cigarette paste a day ahead. It is best assembled at least 12 hours before you add the finishing touches so that it is well frozen.

Serves 12
Preparation time: 2 hours 30 minutes
Cooking time: 1 hour
Freezing time: 3 hours
Yule log mold, 10 x 4 ¾ in., depth 4 in. (25 x 12 cm, depth 10 cm)

Prepare the almond sponge.
Preheat the oven to 350°F (180°C). Line a rimmed 12 x 16-inch (30 x 40-cm) baking sheet with a silicone baking mat.
In a stand mixer fitted with the paddle beater, slowly beat the almond paste to soften it, gradually adding the egg whites and the invert sugar. Increase the speed as the mixture becomes more liquid. When it is perfectly smooth, pour in the hot melted butter and continue to beat until incorporated. Spread it out very evenly on the baking sheet and bake for 15 minutes.

Prepare the macarons.
Combine the ground almonds with the confectioners' sugar. Process with a blade knife so that the mixture is as fine and delicate as possible. Stir in half the egg whites. Make an Italian meringue. Cook the sugar and water, keeping an eye on the thermometer. When it reaches 243°F-250°F (117°C-121°C), begin whipping the remaining egg whites in a stand mixer until they hold firm peaks. Gradually pour the cooked syrup (at 250°F/121°C) over the egg whites, still whipping. Continue until the meringue has cooled completely. With a large scraper, gradually combine the two mixtures, which will deflate slightly. The batter should be smooth and shiny. Spoon the mixture into a piping bag fitted with a plain tip and pipe small teardrop shapes onto a silicone baking sheet. Let stand for 30 minutes until a crust forms; the mixture should not stick to your fingers when touched. Preheat the oven to 310°F (155°C).
Bake for 12 minutes; the macarons should not color.

Make the black currant jelly.
Combine the yellow pectin with 1 tablespoon (14 g) sugar. Heat the black currant purée but do not boil. Pour it over the pectin and sugar mixture, add the remaining ½ cup (3 ½ oz./100g) sugar and glucose syrup and heat to 225°F (107°C). Stir in the citric acid and immediately pour onto a rimmed silicone baking sheet or frame, just ⅕ inch (5 mm) thick. When set, turn onto a board sprinkled with sugar and cut into the desired shape. Rinse the knife regularly and dry it with alcohol so that it doesn't stick to the jelly.

Prepare the strawberry sorbet.
Bring the water and sugar to a boil. Pour the syrup into the puréed strawberries and process until smooth. Pour the mixture into an ice-cream maker and follow the manufacturer's instructions. When it is churned, transfer the sorbet to a small, curved mold. Center a strip of the black currant jelly along the length and freeze.

Make the vanilla ice cream.
Slit the vanilla bean in half lengthwise and scrape out the seeds. In a saucepan, heat the milk and cream with the vanilla bean and the seeds. Beat the egg yolks with the sugar until pale and thick. When the milk is simmering, pour half of it over the egg yolk and sugar mixture, whisking constantly. Return the mixture to the saucepan and cook, stirring constantly and removing the saucepan from the heat from time to time, until it reaches 185°F (85°C) or coats the back of a spoon. Do not let it boil. This is a quick and effective method for making a pouring custard. Remove the vanilla bean, cool rapidly, pass through a sieve, and transfer to an ice-cream maker. Process according to the manufacturer's instructions. When it is churned, it can be transferred into the log mold.

Assemble the dish.
Fill the log mold to three-quarters with the vanilla ice cream. Press in the strawberry sorbet and black currant jelly and cover with a strip of almond sponge. Freeze, preferably for 12 hours. Turn out of the mold only when the chocolate velvet spray is ready. On the day of serving, prepare the chocolate velvet and cigarette paste.

Make the chocolate velvet.
In a bain-marie, melt the cocoa butter and couverture chocolate to 122°F (50°C). Pour the mixture into an electric spray gun and spray over the frozen dessert for a velvety effect.
Add a few red currants and strawberries for decoration.

Prepare the cigarette paste.
Preheat the oven to 350°F (180°C). Line a baking sheet with a silicone baking mat. Whisk the butter with the confectioners' sugar until light and fluffy. Incorporate the egg white. Pour in all of the flour and mix until smooth. Add a few drops of vanilla extract. Drop small mounds of paste on the prepared baking sheet and use the back of a spoon to smooth it into very thin disks. Bake for a few minutes, until evenly colored. Immediately pinch the disks to curve them. Use to decorate the iced log.

Techniques

Macarons >> p. 79
Pouring custard (crème anglaise) >> p. 91
Chocolate velvet (for spraying) >> p. 119
Sorbets >> p. 201
Custard-based ice creams >> p. 204

Ingredients

Almond sponge
9 oz. (250 g) almond paste, 70 percent
  almonds, room temperature
3 egg whites (3 ½ oz./100 g)
1 tablespoon plus 1 teaspoon (1 oz./25 g)
  invert sugar
5 tablespoons (2 ½ oz./75 g) butter,
  melted and browned, still hot

Macarons, for decoration
1 cup minus 1 tablespoon (2 ½ oz./75 g)
  ground almonds
Generous ½ cup (2 ⅔ oz./75 g)
  confectioners' sugar
Scant ¼ cup (1 ¾ oz./50 g) egg whites,
  divided
⅓ cup (2 ½ oz./75 g) sugar
5 teaspoons (25 ml) water

Black currant jelly
¹⁄₁₀ oz. (3 g) yellow pectin
Generous ½ cup (4 oz./114 g) sugar,
  divided
4 oz. (125 g) black currant purée,
  10 percent sugar
1 tablespoon plus 1 teaspoon
  (1 oz./25 g) glucose syrup
¹⁄₁₀ oz. (2.5 g) citric acid solution, 50/50

Strawberry sorbet
Scant ½ cup (100 ml) water
1 ¼ cups (9 oz./250 g) sugar
1 lb. 7 oz. (650 g) puréed strawberries

Vanilla ice cream
1 vanilla bean
1 ⅔ cups (400 ml) milk
Scant ½ cup (100 ml) heavy cream
6-7 egg yolks (4 oz./120 g)
½ cup (3 ½ oz./100 g) sugar

Chocolate velvet
5 oz. (150 g) cocoa butter
5 oz. (150 g) bittersweet couverture
  chocolate
Red currants and strawberries
  for decoration (optional)

Cigarette paste
3 tablespoons (2 oz./50 g) butter, softened
⅓ cup (2 oz./50 g) confectioners' sugar
Scant ¼ cup (1 ¾ oz./50 g) egg whites
½ cup minus 1 tablespoon (2 oz./50 g) flour
A few drops of vanilla extract

Iced Layered Coffee Dessert ★ ★

Serves 8
Preparation time: 1 hour 45 minutes
Cooking time: 20 minutes
Freezing time: 3 hours

Make the Genoa loaf cake.
Preheat the oven to 350°F (180°C). Line two rimmed 12 x 16-inch (30 x 40-cm) baking sheets (or at least 9 ½ x 9 ½ in./24 x 24 cm). Make a French meringue: whip the egg whites until they form soft peaks. Add ¼ cup (2 oz./50g) sugar and whip briefly until the mixture is shiny but not too firm. With an electric beater, whip the eggs, egg yolks, and remaining sugar together until the ribbon stage. Sift the cornstarch and confectioners' sugar and combine with the ground almonds. With a flexible spatula, fold the dry ingredients into the egg and sugar mixture. Stir in the melted butter. With a flexible spatula, carefully fold the meringue mixture into the batter. Spread the batter over the prepared baking sheets and bake until golden brown on top, about 15 minutes. This sponge should remain very soft: remove it from the oven while it still springs back to the touch.

Prepare the coffee ice cream.
For a quick, failsafe method of making this ice cream, simply combine all the ingredients in a heavy-bottom saucepan and bring slowly to 185°F (85°C), stirring constantly, just like a pouring custard. Immediately remove from the heat and cool. Pour into an ice-cream maker and process according to the manufacturer's instructions.

Assemble the dish.
Cut two disks of Genoa sponge. Place one disk on a sheet of parchment paper and set the dessert ring over it. Place in the freezer to firm up. Spread coffee ice cream over the sponge layer to about two-thirds of the depth, pressing down hard so that no air bubbles form. Set the second disk of sponge over the ice cream, and fill to the top with ice cream, ensuring that there are no air bubbles. Smooth the top and freeze.

Make the glaze.
Soften the gelatin sheets in the water. Pour the milk, cream, and invert sugar into a heavy-bottom saucepan and bring to a boil. Remove from the heat and stir in the white couverture chocolate, ivory glazing paste, and softened gelatin sheets (they will not need to be squeezed, as they will have absorbed all the water) until completely dissolved. Set aside 2 tablespoons of the mixture and dissolve the titanium dioxide in it, pressing it with a pestle if necessary, or use a spatula on a clean work surface, to ensure it is smooth. Add the rum, if using. Place the frozen dessert on a rack set over a dish deep enough to catch any drip-off. Pour the remaining glaze over quickly, working first to cover the sides. With an offset spatula, carefully smooth the surface. Insert a flat spatula under the cake and work it round to remove the small drops of glaze at the base. Return the dessert to the freezer. Melt the bittersweet chocolate with the reserved 2 tablespoons of glaze and, using a paper decorating cone filled with the molten chocolate, decorate the dessert. Just before serving, add the chocolate-covered coffee beans on and around the cake.

Ingredients

Genoa loaf cake
3 egg whites (3 ½ oz./100g)
Scant 1 ½ cups (10 oz./275 g) sugar, divided
5 eggs plus 3 egg yolks
1 cup minus 2 ½ tablespoons (4 oz./125 g) cornstarch
3 tablespoons (1 oz./25 g) confectioners' sugar
3 ½ cups (10 ½ oz./300 g) ground almonds
1 ½ sticks (6 oz./175 g) butter, melted and cooled to lukewarm

Coffee ice cream
6-7 egg yolks (4 oz./120 g)
½ cup (3 ½ oz./100 g) sugar
1 ⅔ cups (400 ml) milk
Scant ½ cup (100 ml) heavy cream
A few drops of coffee extract (or instant coffee), to taste

Glaze
2 sheets (4 g) gelatin
1 tablespoon plus 1 teaspoon (20 ml) water
½ cup (125 ml) milk
⅓ cup (75 ml) heavy cream
2 tablespoons (1 ½ oz./40 g) invert sugar
4 oz. (125 g) white couverture chocolate
4 oz. (125 g) ivory glazing paste
3 g titanium dioxide (optional)
1 ½ teaspoons (7 ml) rum (optional)

Decoration
2 oz. (60 g) bittersweet chocolate
A small handful of coffee beans coated with bittersweet chocolate

Dessert ring, diameter 8 ½ in. (22 cm), height 1 in. (2.5 cm)

Techniques
Genoa loaf cake >> p. 71
Ivory glaze >> p. 117
Making a paper decorating cone >> p. 147
Glazing a log-shaped cake and dessert >> p. 148
French meringue >> p. 176
Egg-enriched ice creams >> p. 203

Ingredients

Nougatine
2 oz. (50 g) chopped almonds
⅓ cup (2 ½ oz./75 g) sugar
2 ½ tablespoons (2 oz./50 g) glucose syrup
1 teaspoon (5 g) butter

Nougatine ice cream
1 vanilla bean
1 ⅔ cups (400 ml) milk
6-7 egg yolks (4 oz./120 g)
½ cup (3 ½ oz./100 g) sugar
Scant ½ cup (100 ml) heavy cream

Swiss meringue
3 egg whites (3 ½ oz./100 g)
Scant 1 cup (7 oz./200 g) sugar

Progrès sponge
2 egg whites (2 oz./60 g)
¼ cup (1 ¾ oz./50 g) sugar
Scant 1 cup (4 ½ oz./125 g)
  confectioners' sugar
½ cup (1 ¾ oz./50 g) ground almonds
½ cup (1 ¾ oz./50 g) ground hazelnuts

Apricot sorbet
Scant 1 cup (220 ml) water
2 tablespoons (25 ml) lemon juice
⅓ cup (2 ½ oz./70 g) sugar
1 ¾ oz. (50 g) atomized glucose
½ oz. (15 g) invert sugar
⅒ oz. (2 g) SL 64 stabilizer
1 lb. 2 oz. (500 g) apricot pulp

Dessert ring

Techniques
Progrès sponge >> p. 74
Pouring custard (crème anglaise) >> p. 91
Swiss meringue >> p. 176
Sorbets >> p. 201

Nougatine Ice Cream and Apricot Sorbet Layered Dessert ★ ★ ★

Serves 6
Preparation time: 2 hours
Cooking time: 2 hours 20 minutes
Maturing time (for sorbet): 4 hours
Freezing time: 4 hours

Prepare the nougatine.

Preheat the oven to 350°F (180°C). Lightly roast the chopped almonds for 6 minutes. They should still be warm when you stir them into the caramel.

In a heavy-bottom saucepan, copper if possible, heat the sugar and glucose syrup. When the temperature reaches 340°F (170°C) and the caramel is a reddish color, remove from the heat and stir in the butter and chopped nuts.

Pour onto a silicone baking sheet, spread out a little, and let cool. As soon as the nougatine is cool enough to handle (it must still be malleable), roll it as thinly as possible. Cut out a few decorative shapes (drape triangles over a rolling pin, for example) and chop the rest to incorporate into the ice cream.

Make the nougatine ice cream.

Follow the recipe for pouring custard on p. 91 and heat the ingredients to 185°F (85°C). Cool quickly and pour into an ice-cream maker. Follow the manufacturer's instructions to process the ice cream. As soon as it is churned, remove from the ice-cream maker and stir in the nougatine bits. Place in the freezer.

Make a Swiss meringue.

Prepare a bain-marie, heating the water to 125°F-130°F (52°C-55°C).

In a round-bottom mixing bowl, lightly beat the egg whites to liquefy them.

Pour in the sugar and whip energetically, lifting the egg whites high, to incorporate as much air as possible. When the mixture begins to foam, set the bowl over the bain-marie and whisk until the mixture thickens, triples in volume, and becomes shiny. At this stage it should register 113°F (45°C) on a thermometer. Remove from the heat and continue to whisk until the meringue cools to room temperature.

Prepare the Progrès sponge.

Preheat the oven to 250°F (120°C). Line a rimmed 12 x 16-inch (30 x 40-cm) baking sheet with parchment paper.

Lightly beat the egg whites to liquefy them. Then whisk energetically, lifting the whisk high to incorporate as much air as possible, until the egg whites hold soft peaks. Stir in the sugar with the whisk, using a circular movement.

Combine the confectioners' sugar, almonds, and hazelnuts and, with a flexible spatula, carefully fold them into the meringue. Spoon the mixture into a piping bag and pipe spirals to make a base of the desired size (slightly smaller than the dessert ring). Bake for 1 ½ to 2 hours. The meringue must be dry to the touch and must not color.

Make the apricot sorbet.

Combine the water and lemon juice in a saucepan. When the water reaches 77°F (25°C), add the sugar, atomized glucose, invert sugar, and stabilizer. Cook to 185°F (85°C) for 3 minutes to pasteurize. Blend and cool rapidly, and cover with plastic film. Refrigerate for at least 4 hours to allow the flavors to mature. Add the apricot pulp and blend. Process in an ice-cream maker according to the manufacturer's instructions. Pour into a mold just under ½ inch (1 cm) thick, slightly smaller than the dessert ring. Freeze at 0.4°F (-18°C).

Assemble the dish.

Place the disk of Progrès sponge in the dessert ring. Spread a smooth layer of nougatine ice cream over. Center the layer of apricot sorbet over it and fill the dessert ring with nougatine ice cream. Smooth the surface and freeze till firm. Cover with Swiss meringue, decorating as you wish. To finish, dot with curved nougatine triangles and, if wished, a few sautéed, cooled apricot halves.

Aniseed Liqueur and Peanut Ice Cream with Macarons ★ ★

Serves 10
Preparation time: 1 hour 15 minutes
Cooking time: 20 minutes
Maturing time: 12 hours
Freezing time: 4 hours

Make the macaron cookies.
Combine the ground almonds with the confectioners' sugar. Process with a blade knife so that the mixture is as fine and delicate as possible. Stir in half the egg whites.
Prepare an Italian meringue: combine the sugar and water in a saucepan and heat to 243°F-250°F (117°C-121°C). Meanwhile, begin whipping the remaining egg whites in a stand mixer until they hold firm peaks. Gradually pour the cooked syrup over the egg whites, still whipping. Continue until the meringue has cooled completely. With a large scraper, combine the two mixtures, which will deflate slightly. Incorporate any flavorings or colorings at this stage. Spoon the mixture into a piping bag fitted with a plain tip and pipe small disks onto a silicone baking sheet set on a thick baking pan, or two ordinary baking pans. Let stand for 30 minutes until a crust forms; the mixture should not stick to your fingers when touched. Preheat the oven to 310°F (155°C).
Bake for 12 minutes; do not let brown.

Prepare the aniseed liqueur and peanut ice cream.
Place the milk in a saucepan with the cream, vanilla bean and seeds, and egg yolks. Heat to 104°F (40°C). Whisking vigorously, add the milk powder, sugar, glucose, and stabilizer, and increase the temperature to 185°F (85°C), still stirring constantly. Add the liquid pastis extract and cook at 185°F (85°C) for 3 minutes to pasteurize. Remove the vanilla bean, then blend and cool quickly to 39°F (4°C). Cover with plastic wrap and leave to mature for at least 12 hours at 39°F (4°C).
Blend, and then process in an ice-cream maker according to the manufacturer's instructions, adding the aniseed liqueur at the very end, before removing from the machine. Transfer to a plastic tub.
Stir in the chopped roasted peanuts using a spatula to distribute them evenly. Transfer to molds and freeze at 0.4°F (-18°C) before shaping scoops. Serve with the macarons as an accompaniment.

Techniques
Macarons >> p. 79
Italian meringue >> p. 177
Egg-enriched ice creams >> p. 203

Ingredients

Macaron cookies
1 ¾ cups (5 oz./150 g) ground almonds
1 generous cup (5 oz./150 g) confectioners' sugar
½ cup (3 ½ oz./105 g) egg whites, divided
¾ cup (5 oz./150 g) sugar
3 tablespoons (50 ml) water
Flavoring or coloring (optional)

Aniseed liqueur and peanut ice cream
(It is advisable to measure your ingredients using the metric system and to weigh the liquid ingredients)
1036 g whole milk
250 g heavy cream
1 vanilla bean, slit lengthwise
144 g egg yolks
75 g skim milk powder
260 g sugar
80 g atomized glucose
7 g SE 30 emulsified stabilizer
5 g liquid pastis extract
25 g aniseed liqueur, such as Pastis
Roasted peanuts as needed, chopped

Baked Alaska ★★

Serves 8
Preparation time: 1 hour 30 minutes/Cooking time: 15 minutes
Maturing time: 12 hours/Freezing time: 3 hours

Make the vanilla ice cream.
In a saucepan, combine the liquid ingredients (milk, cream, and egg yolks). Slit the vanilla bean in half and scrape out the seeds. Add to the pan and, stirring constantly, heat to 104°F (40°C). Whisking vigorously, add the dry ingredients (milk powder, sugar, glucose, and stabilizer). Pasteurize by heating to 185°F (85°C) and cooking at this temperature for 3 minutes. Blend and let cool for a while, covered with plastic wrap. Leave to chill and mature in the refrigerator for at least 12 hours. Blend, process in an ice-cream maker according to the manufacturer's instructions, transfer to a container, and freeze at 0.4°F (-18°C).

Prepare the Genoese sponge.
Preheat the oven to 350°F (180°C). Place the eggs and sugar in a round-bottom mixing bowl and set it over a bain-marie heated to 140°F (60°C). Whip until the mixture reaches the ribbon stage. Sift the flour and carefully fold in half of it with a flexible spatula. When it is incorporated, fold in the remaining half, taking care not to deflate the mixture. Do not overmix. Pour evenly onto a silicone baking sheet, about ⅛ inch (4-5 mm) thick. Bake for 15 to 20 minutes. The sponge must stay moist and must not color. Slide it onto a rack and let cool.

Make the Italian meringue.
In a heavy-bottom saucepan, heat the sugar and water to form a syrup. When it registers 230°F (110°C), begin beating the egg whites with the salt in a stand mixer fitted with a whisk. When they hold firm peaks and the syrup has reached 243°F-250°F (117°C-121°C), take the pan off the heat and gradually pour the syrup into the egg whites in a steady stream, whisking continuously and taking care that the hot syrup does not splatter. Continue whisking until the meringue has cooled to about 85°F (30°C). It will be dense, shiny, and form many small peaks.

Assemble the dessert.
Cut the Genoese sponge into two 7 x 3-inch (18 x 8-cm) rectangles. On the first rectangle, place a 2 ½-inch (6-cm) thick layer of ice cream to fit exactly over the sponge. Set the second sponge rectangle over the ice cream. Smooth the sides and place in the freezer until firm. With a spatula, cover the entire cake with Italian meringue. Spoon the remaining Italian meringue into a piping bag fitted with a star tip and decorate the surface.

Finish and serve.
Preheat the oven to 450°F (230°C) and place the dessert in there for a few minutes to brown the meringue lightly, keeping a careful eye on it. Alternatively, use a kitchen torch without allowing the flame to come into direct contact with the meringue. In a small saucepan, heat the liqueur to about 105°F (40°C). Carefully set it alight and immediately pour over the Baked Alaska. Sprinkle with the roasted sliced almonds if you wish and serve immediately.

Ingredients

Vanilla ice cream
(It is advisable to measure the ice cream ingredients using the metric system and to weigh the liquid ingredients)
1036 g whole milk
390 g heavy cream
60 g egg yolks
1 vanilla bean
65 g skim milk powder
295 g sugar
50 g atomized glucose
6 g SE 30 emulsified stabilizer

Genoese sponge
4 eggs (7 oz./200 g)
⅔ cup (4 oz./125 g) sugar
1 cup (4 oz./125 g) flour

Italian meringue
1 cup (7 oz./200 g) sugar
¼ cup (60 ml) water
3 egg whites (3 ½ oz./100 g)
1 pinch salt

⅓ cup (80 ml) Grand Marnier, or other orange liqueur to flambé
1 ½ oz. (40 g) roasted sliced almonds (optional) for garnish

Techniques
Genoese sponge >> p. 76
Masking a dessert >> p. 126
Italian meringue >> p. 177
Egg-enriched ice creams >> p. 203

Ingredients

Vanilla ice cream (It is advisable to measure the ice cream ingredients using the metric system and to weigh the liquid ingredients)
518 g whole milk
125 g heavy cream
72 g egg yolks
½ vanilla bean
37 g skim milk powder
130 g sugar
40 g atomized glucose
3.5 g emulsified stabilizer SE 30

Poached fruit
½ vanilla bean
4 firm peaches
2 cups (500 ml) water
1 ¼ cups (9 oz./250 g) sugar

Red currant coulis
4 oz. (125 g) red currants
1 tablespoon (20 ml) water
2 tablespoons (25 g) sugar

Chantilly cream
Scant ½ cup (100 ml) heavy cream, well chilled
2 tablespoons (1 oz./25 g) superfine sugar
½ teaspoon (2.5 ml) vanilla extract

Peach Melba ★★

Serves 8
Preparation time: 1 hour 15 minutes
Cooking time: 25 minutes
Maturing time: 12 hours
Freezing time: 3 hours

Make the vanilla ice cream.
In a saucepan, combine the liquid ingredients (milk, cream, and egg yolks). Slit the vanilla bean in half lengthwise and scrape out the seeds. Add to the pan and, stirring constantly, heat to 104°F (40°C). Whisking vigorously, add the dry ingredients (milk powder, sugar, glucose, and stabilizer). Pasteurize by heating to 185°F (85°C) and cooking at this temperature for 3 minutes. Blend and let cool for a while, covered with plastic wrap. Leave to chill and mature in the refrigerator for at least 12 hours.
Blend, process in an ice-cream maker according to the manufacturer's instructions, transfer to a container, and freeze at 0.4°F (-18°C).

Poach the fruit.
Slit the vanilla bean in half lengthwise and scrape out the seeds. Immerse the peaches for a few seconds in boiling water and remove the skins. Make a syrup with the water and sugar, add the vanilla bean and seeds, bring to a boil and poach the peaches for 6 to 8 minutes. Let cool in the syrup. Cut into halves and remove the pits.

Prepare the red currant coulis.
Pick the red currants off their stems and cook them with the water. Add the sugar and strain through a fine-mesh sieve. Let cool.

Make the Chantilly cream.
In a round-bottom mixing bowl, chilled if possible, pour the cream, sugar, and vanilla extract. Begin by whisking slowly, lifting up the cream to incorporate as much air as possible. When it begins to thicken, increase the speed. Continue until it holds firm peaks when the whip is lifted up.

Assemble the dish.
Place the serving bowls in the freezer until cold. Place a generous scoop of ice cream in each one and top with half a peach. Drizzle with red currant coulis and garnish with dollops of Chantilly cream.

Techniques
Chantilly cream >> p. 94
Fruit coulis >> p. 128
Egg-enriched ice creams >> p. 203
Peeling fruit >> p. 216

Iced desserts

Belle Hélène-Style Pears Poached in Red Wine ★

Serves 4
Preparation time: 1 hour 15 minutes
Cooking time: 12 minutes
Chilling time: 2 hours
Maturing time: 12 hours
Freezing time: 3 hours

Poach the pears.
Slit the vanilla bean lengthwise and scrape the seeds into the red wine. Bring the wine to a boil with the sugar and vanilla seeds and bean. Peel the pears and rub them with lemon juice. Core the pears from the bottom, removing any fibers. Place the pears in the boiling syrup and keep them in place by weighing them down with a weight set over a rack. Let simmer gently for 10 to 12 minutes. Let cool in the syrup for a few hours. Cut in half.

Make the vanilla ice cream.
In a saucepan, combine the liquid ingredients (milk, cream, and egg yolks). Slit the vanilla bean in half lengthwise and scrape out the seeds. Add to the pan and, stirring constantly, heat to 104°F (40°C). Whisking vigorously, add the dry ingredients (milk powder, sugar, glucose, and stabilizer). Pasteurize by heating to 185°F (85°C) and cooking at this temperature for 3 minutes. Blend and let cool for a while, covered with plastic wrap. Leave to chill and mature in the refrigerator for at least 12 hours.
Blend, process in an ice-cream maker according to the manufacturer's instructions, transfer to a container, and freeze at 0.4°F (-18°C).

Make the chocolate sauce.
Chop the chocolate. Bring the cream to a boil. Take off the heat, pour it over the chopped chocolate and let the heat melt it. After a few minutes, stir the mixture until smooth.

Prepare the Chantilly cream.
In a round-bottom mixing bowl, chilled if possible, pour the cream, sugar, and vanilla extract. Begin by whisking slowly, lifting up the cream to incorporate as much air as possible. When it begins to thicken, increase the speed. Continue until it holds firm peaks when the whip is lifted up.

Assemble the dish.
Chill four oval ramekins. Place a scoop of vanilla ice cream in each and place a half-pear over it. With a piping bag fitted with a star tip, pipe little rosettes of Chantilly cream around the edge. Pour the chocolate sauce over and serve immediately.

● Did you know?
This was one of a number of dishes created in Paris around 1864 in honor of Jacques Offenbach's operetta La Belle Hélène. *Savory tributes included sautéed chicken suprêmes Belle-Hélène, served with asparagus croquettes and sliced truffles.*

Ingredients

Poached pears
½ vanilla bean
2 cups (500 ml) red wine
1 ¼ cups (9 oz./250 g) sugar
4 pears
Juice of 1 lemon

Vanilla ice cream
(It is advisable to measure the ice cream ingredients using the metric system and to weigh the liquid ingredients)
518 g whole milk
3125 g heavy cream
72 g egg yolks
½ vanilla bean
7 g skim milk powder
130 g sugar
40 g atomized glucose
3.5 g emulsified stabilizer SE 30

Chocolate sauce
3 ½ oz. (100 g) bittersweet chocolate, 64 percent cocoa
½ cup (125 ml) crème fraîche or heavy cream

Chantilly cream
Scant ½ cup (100 ml) heavy cream, well chilled
1 ½ tablespoons (15 g) superfine sugar
½ teaspoon (2.5 ml) vanilla extract

Ingredients

Choux puffs

7 tablespoons (3 ½ oz./100 g) butter, room temperature
1 cup (4 oz./125 g) flour
1 cup (250 ml) water
1 teaspoon (5 g) salt
1 teaspoon (5 g) sugar
5 eggs
1 egg for the egg wash

Chocolate sauce

3 ½ oz. (100 g) bittersweet chocolate, 64 percent cocoa
½ cup (125 ml) crème fraîche or heavy cream

10 oz. (300 g) vanilla ice cream (see p. 203, or previous recipe p. 454)
A few roasted sliced almonds and a little Chantilly cream (optional)

Profiteroles ★★

Serves 8
Preparation time: 1 hour
Cooking time: 45 minutes

Prepare the choux puffs.

Dice the butter. Sift the flour. In a large saucepan, bring the water, salt, sugar, and butter to a boil. When all the butter has melted, remove from the heat and stir in all the flour. Return the saucepan to the heat. With a wooden spoon or spatula, beat briskly to dry out the mixture. Continue until the batter pulls away from the sides of the saucepan. Remove from the heat and let cool slightly, to 122°F (50°C) or a little less, when you can touch it with your finger. (Any hotter and the eggs that are added will be cooked.)
Transfer to a mixing bowl. Continue working with a wooden spoon or spatula and beat in the eggs, one by one, only adding an egg when the previous one is fully incorporated. The mixture must be smooth and shiny.
Preheat the oven to 400°F (200°C).
Spoon the batter into a piping bag fitted with a plain tip (diameter 8) and pipe twenty-four equally sized balls on a baking sheet. Beat the egg for the egg wash to liquefy it and brush the top of the choux balls with it, then dip a fork into water and score the top with the tines to ensure that the puffs are evenly shaped.
Bake for 25 to 30 minutes, until golden and well puffed. Reduce the heat to 340°F (170°C), leave the oven door slightly ajar, and bake for an additional 20 minutes to dry out the choux puffs. Transfer immediately to a cooling rack.

Make the chocolate sauce.

Chop the chocolate. Bring the cream to a boil. Take off the heat, pour it over the chopped chocolate and let the heat melt it. After a few minutes, stir the mixture until smooth. Keep hot until needed.

Assemble the dessert.

Cut the choux puffs in half horizontally. Fill with a generous scoop of ice cream and set the top back on. Pour over the hot chocolate sauce. If you wish, scatter with a few roasted sliced almonds and dollops of Chantilly cream.

Techniques

Basic choux pastry >> p. 34
Chocolate sauces >> p. 120
Egg-enriched ice creams >> p. 203

Iced Kirsch and Candied Fruit Soufflé ★ ★

Serves 8
Preparation time: 1 hour 15 minutes
Cooking time: 30 minutes
Freezing time: 4 hours

A few hours ahead, soak the candied fruit in the kirsch.

Make the *pâte à bombe.*
Combine the sugar and water and cook to about 250°F (120°C). Beat the egg yolks.
Pour the hot syrup over the egg yolks, beating constantly. Continue beating until the mixture cools completely.

Prepare the Italian meringue.
In a heavy-bottom saucepan, begin cooking the sugar and water. When it registers 230°F (110°C), begin whipping the egg whites in a stand mixer fitted with a whisk. When they hold firm peaks and the syrup registers 243°F-250°F (117°C-121°C), gradually pour the syrup into the egg whites, whisking continuously and taking care that the hot syrup does not splatter. Continue whisking until the meringue has cooled to about 85°F (30°C). It will be dense, shiny, and form many small peaks.

Assemble the soufflé.
Drain the candied fruit, reserving the kirsch. Whip the cream until it holds firm peaks. Add the kirsch to the whipped cream and fold it in. Set aside a little of the Italian meringue to top the soufflés. Fold the Italian meringue into the *pâte à bombe.* Stop when the mixture is smooth. Carefully fold in the whipped cream, and then pour the drained candied fruit into the mixture.
Line the ramekins with food-safe acetate or parchment paper, attaching the ends together with a paper clip or Scotch tape.
Pour in the soufflé mixture and smooth with a spatula.
Freeze for at least 4 hours.
Top with a little meringue mixture and heat with a kitchen torch. Remove the paper and serve immediately.

Techniques
Italian meringue >> p. 177
Pâte à bombe >> p. 197

Ingredients
4 oz. (125 g) candied fruit, diced
⅓ cup (80 ml) kirsch

Pâte à bombe
¾ cup (5 oz./150 g) sugar
3 tablespoons (50 ml) water
10 egg yolks (7 oz./200 g)

Italian meringue
Scant ⅔ cup (4 oz./120 g) sugar
3 tablespoons (40 ml) water
2 egg whites (2 oz./60 g)

3 cups (750 ml) heavy cream

Ingredients

(It is advisable to measure the ingredients for the sorbets using the metric system and to weigh the liquid ingredients)

Pineapple-ginger sorbet

75 g water
80 g sugar
30 g atomized glucose
1.5 g SL 64 stabilizer
300 g pineapple pulp
5 g fresh ginger rhizome, grated

Raspberry sorbet

110 g water
60 g sugar
30 g atomized glucose
1.3 g SL 64 stabilizer
330 g raspberry pulp

Flour-free chocolate sponge

6 egg whites (6 ½ oz./190 g)
1 ¼ cups (8 ½ oz./240 g) sugar
8 egg yolks (5 oz./150 g)
⅔ cup (2 ½ oz./75 g) unsweetened cocoa powder

12 tube-shaped lollipop molds (different diameters)

Iced Pineapple-Raspberry Lollipops ★★

Serves 6
Preparation time: 1 hour/Cooking time: 30 minutes
Maturing time: 4 hours/Freezing time: 4 hours

Prepare the pineapple-ginger sorbet (the day before).
In a saucepan, heat the water to 77°F (25°C) and whisk in the sugar until it is fully dissolved. Whisking vigorously, add the atomized glucose and stabilizer, then heat to 185°F (85°C) and cook at this temperature for 3 minutes to pasteurize, stirring constantly. Blend and let cool for a while, covered with plastic wrap. Allow to chill and mature for at least 4 hours in the refrigerator. Stir in the pineapple pulp and grated ginger and blend well. Process in an ice-cream maker according to the manufacturer's instructions, then mold the sorbets in tube-shaped molds that are closed at one end, measuring 4 inches (10 cm) in length and ¾ inch (2 cm) in diameter, and insert a wooden stick at the open end. Place vertically in the freezer and freeze at 0.4°F (-18°C).

Prepare the raspberry sorbet.
Proceed as for the pineapple-ginger sorbet. In a saucepan, heat the water to 77°F (25°C) and whisk in the sugar until it is fully dissolved. Whisking vigorously, add the atomized glucose and stabilizer, then heat to 185°F (85°C) and cook at this temperature for 3 minutes to pasteurize, stirring constantly. Blend and let cool for a while, covered with plastic wrap. Allow to chill and mature for at least 4 hours in the refrigerator. Stir in the raspberry pulp and blend well. Process in an ice-cream maker according to the manufacturer's instructions. Using a piping bag, fill tube-shaped molds that are closed at one end, measuring 4 inches (10 cm) in length and 1 ¾-2 inches (4-5 cm) in diameter, to a height of one-third of the mold. Remove the frozen pineapple-ginger lollipops from the freezer and unmold. Then insert them into the raspberry sorbet molds, so they are in the center and the raspberry sorbet surrounds the pineapple-ginger sorbet. Place them back in the freezer, stored vertically, for 4 to 5 hours at 0.4°F (-18°C).

Prepare the flour-free chocolate sponge.
Preheat the oven to 340°F (170°C). Line a rimmed 12 x 16-inch (30 x 40-cm) baking sheet with parchment paper. Whip the egg whites until they form soft peaks. Stir in the sugar with the whisk until the mixture is firm and shiny. Beat the egg yolks well. Carefully fold the egg whites into the egg yolks. Sift in the cocoa powder and, with a flexible spatula, stir it in until just combined. Spread the mixture out on 1 or 2 baking sheets to about ¼ inch (5 mm) and bake for 15 to 20 minutes, until it springs back to the touch; the inside should remain moist.

Assemble the dish.
When the sponge has cooled, cut it into rectangles the same size as the lollipops. Set the lollipops squarely in the center and serve.

 Techniques
Flour-free chocolate sponge >> p. 71
Sorbets >> p. 201

Iced Praline Lollipops ★★

Serves 10

Preparation time: 1 hour
Cooking time: 30 minutes
Maturing time: 12 hours
Freezing time: 4 hours

In a saucepan, combine the milk, cream, and egg yolks. Slit the vanilla bean in half lengthwise and scrape out the seeds. Add to the pan and, stirring constantly, heat to 104°F (40°C). Whisking vigorously, add the milk powder, sugar, invert sugar, and stabilizer. Stir in the praline paste. Pasteurize by heating to 185°F (85°C) and cooking at this temperature for 3 minutes. Blend and let cool for a while, covered with plastic wrap. Leave to chill and mature for at least 12 hours in the refrigerator. Blend. Process in an ice-cream maker and immediately pour into silicone lollipop molds. Insert sticks. Freeze for at least 4 hours at 0.4°F (-18°C).

Heat the two glazing pastes separately to 86°F (30°C). Carefully turn the ice creams out of the molds and dip into the glaze, then dip directly into the chopped almonds. Return immediately to the freezer.

Ingredients

(It is advisable to measure the ice cream ingredients using the metric system and to weigh the liquid ingredients)

1036 g whole milk
100 g heavy cream
60 g egg yolks
½ vanilla bean
70 g skim milk powder
80 g sugar
80 g invert sugar
6 g SE 30 emulsified stabilizer
250 g almond-hazelnut praline paste

10 oz. (300 g) brown glazing paste
10 oz. (300 g) white glazing paste
5 oz. (150 g) chopped roasted almonds

Ingredients

3 ½ oz. (100 g) chopped almonds
3 ½ oz. (100 g) chopped hazelnuts
¼ cup (2 oz./55 g) sugar
Scant ⅓ cup (3 ½ oz./100 g) honey
Seeds of ½ vanilla bean
4 egg whites (4 oz./120 g)
2 cups (500 ml) heavy cream, well chilled
3 ½ oz. (100 g) unsalted pistachios
2 oz. (60 g) diced candied orange peel
2 oz. (60 g) diced candied cherries
3 ½ oz. (100 g) nougatine, broken
  into small bits (see recipe p. 166)
Bunches of red currants for garnish
¾ cup (200 ml) raspberry coulis to serve

Techniques
Fruit coulis >> p. 128
Nougatine >> p. 166
Italian meringue >> p. 177

Iced Nougat ★

Serves 8
Preparation time: 40 minutes
Cooking time: 15 minutes
Freezing time: 4 hours

Preheat the oven to 350°F (180°C) and roast the almonds and hazelnuts for 5 to 7 minutes. Let cool.

Prepare an Italian meringue following the procedure on page 177, making a syrup with the sugar, honey, and vanilla seeds. In a stand mixer fitted with a whisk, begin whipping the egg whites. When the syrup registers 250°F (120°C), pour it carefully over the egg whites, whisking continuously. Continue whisking until the meringue has cooled to 85°F (30°C). Whip the cream until it holds firm peaks and carefully fold it into the meringue.

Carefully stir in the nuts, candied fruit, and nougatine bits.

Pour into silicone molds or a loaf pan and immediately place in the freezer for at least 4 hours.

To finish, turn out of the molds, garnish with red currants, and serve with raspberry coulis.

Ingredients

Iced chocolate mousse
1 cup (250 ml) milk
8 egg yolks (5 oz./150 g)
⅔ cup (4 oz./125 g) sugar
Scant ⅓ cup (3 ½ oz./100 g)) invert sugar
Scant ⅓ cup (3 ½ oz./100 g) glucose syrup
13 oz. (375 g) bittersweet chocolate,
   50 percent cocoa, chopped
1 ½ cups (350 ml) heavy cream

Glaze
4 sheets (8 g) gelatin
2 tablespoons plus 2 teaspoons
   (40 ml) water
1 cup (250 ml) milk
⅔ cup (150 ml) heavy cream
2 ½ tablespoons (2 oz./50 g) glucose syrup
10 oz. (300 g) white chocolate
10 oz. (300 g) white glazing paste
Red colorant

Candy-Pink Iced Chocolate Lollipops ★★

Serves 10
Preparation time: 1 hour
Cooking time: 30 minutes
Freezing time: 12 hours

Prepare the iced chocolate mousse.
In a heavy-bottom saucepan, heat the milk. Beat the egg yolks with the granulated sugar until pale and thick. When the milk is simmering, pour half of it over the egg yolk and sugar mixture, stirring constantly. Return the mixture to the saucepan with the rest of the milk and add the invert sugar and glucose syrup. Cook, stirring constantly and removing the saucepan from the heat from time to time, until it reaches 185°F (85°C) or coats the back of a spoon. Strain the custard through a fine-mesh sieve over the chocolate. Stir until smooth and cover with plastic wrap. Chill rapidly to about 68°F (20°C). Whip the cream until it holds soft peaks. Carefully fold it into the cooled chocolate custard. Immediately pour into silicone lollipop molds, insert sticks, and freeze for 3 to 4 hours.

Make the glaze.
Soften the gelatin sheets in the water.
In a heavy-bottom saucepan, bring the milk, cream, and glucose syrup to a boil. Remove from the heat and stir in the gelatin sheets (without draining them) until completely dissolved. Process briefly with an immersion blender. Place the white chocolate and glazing paste in a mixing bowl. Mix in the milk and gelatin mixture. Divide the glaze into three: leave one plain, and color the other two different shades of pink, using the red colorant.

Finish the dish.
Remove the frozen lollipops from the molds and set them over a rack. Coat them in glaze, working as rapidly as possible. If you wish, draw out stripes in different colors.

Useful information and general advice

Ingredients

For all recipes, unless otherwise specified, the following should be noted:
- Butter is unsalted
- Eggs are large (US) or medium (UK)
- Sugar is granulated
- Salt means fine sea salt
- Vanilla extract means pure vanilla extract
- Milk is always whole (full fat), as its higher butterfat content ensures a better taste than if skim milk is used
- Ground almonds are preferably blanched
- Gelatin is used in sheet form
- Cream has a minimum butterfat content of 30–35 percent

Getting started: setting up (*mise en place*)

It's important to read through the recipe carefully before you begin. Decide what can—or needs to be—made ahead, particularly if the recipe has several components. Sometimes elements of a dish require an overnight rest in the refrigerator; others may need time for their flavors to develop. Tart shells must be sufficiently chilled before they are baked.

The ingredients are listed in their order of use; some may have to be prepared ahead of time. Run through the recipe, checking them off. Ensure that you have all the ingredients, as well as the necessary equipment, before you start.

Try to make a habit of what professionals call *mise en place*, putting everything in place before you begin. Measure all your ingredients (see below), and take out all the utensils you will need, to avoid last-minute panics at vital junctures of the cooking process. *Mise en place* considerably reduces stress levels in the kitchen.

Butter, eggs, and milk need to be taken out of the refrigerator and brought to room temperature so that they are more easily incorporated into the preparations; cream, if it is to be whipped, must be well chilled (chilling the bowl helps, too).

Measuring ingredients: the importance of precision

Pastry chefs are like scientists when it comes to precision: every ingredient is accurately weighed. French chefs even weigh liquid ingredients, and in most French home kitchens there is a kitchen scale. All the metric measurements given here have been converted into cups, spoons, and imperial measurements. To avoid awkward amounts, weights have been rounded up or down, usually to the nearest half-ounce, or the nearest quarter, third, or half of a cup. The exceptions are certain recipes for ice creams and sorbets, for which the quantities are extremely precise, making it difficult to convert. It is advisable to measure the ingredients for these recipes using the metric system and to weigh the liquid ingredients.

A set of digital scales should prove a good-value and useful investment; most will give both metric and imperial readings. Do remember, however, that you should use only one system while working on a particular recipe. If you are using cups and spoons, sift dry ingredients after measuring.

Using your oven

All ovens have their individual quirks. If you've had yours for a while, you will know how to fine-tune temperatures and times. As a general rule, set the baking sheet or pan on the center rack. If you're making cookies, rotate the sheets midway so that they color evenly. And always remember that baking times are given as a guideline: you also need to keep a careful eye on them and test your baked goods for doneness. Small pieces can often be baked more quickly at higher temperatures, while larger ones need more time in the oven. Many of the recipes here specify temperatures for both sizes. When baking cakes or cookies, resist the temptation to open the oven door, particularly during the initial stage: this will cause a drop in temperature and alter the way the cake rises. The exception is choux pastry, where an open oven door is needed in its second stage of baking only (see p. 34).

Preparing cake pans

To avoid leaving cake stuck to the pan, it is crucial to prepare your pan properly. It might take a little time, but the effort is worth it. Brush the pan carefully with melted butter, not forgetting the corners. If you're in a hurry, place it briefly in the refrigerator for the butter to set. Sprinkle the pan lightly with flour, just a tiny dusting, and shake and tilt the pan until the entire surface is coated with a thin white film. Turn the pan upside down and rap it to remove the excess. For soufflés, dust the mold with sugar.

If you are making thin sponge layers for a complex dessert, simply cover the rimmed baking pan with a silicone baking mat or sheet of parchment paper. When the sponge layer is baked, transfer it gently to a cooling rack. If you've used parchment paper, place the sponge upside down and carefully peel it off.

If you are baking choux puffs or éclairs, make the task easier by lightly wiping the baking sheet with a thin film of butter. Dip your finger into the flour and shake it just above the spot that will be the center of the round or rectangle to pipe out. Repeat over the entire sheet for even spacing.

Using a pastry or piping bag

It takes some practice to get the hang of using a pastry bag. Chefs simply hold it in one hand and scrape the mixture in with the other. First, fit the tip into the opening. If the batter or icing is very fluid, tuck the plastic into the tip to seal it temporarily.

Initially, you might want to start by fitting your bag into a small water jug (or similar container), folding the overhang round the rim so that it stays in place. If the batter is fairly fluid, simply pour it in, otherwise use a scraper. Filling a pastry bag actually means half-filling it, because you will need to twist it shut and leave sufficient grip to be able to handle it easily. When it is half full, push the mixture down, removing any pockets of air, and twist shut. Pull away the part that is sealing the tip. Use one hand to guide the bag while you push lightly on the batter to begin piping. With more experience, you will be able to do without the jug and simply hold the bag in one hand with the open end folded back around your thumb and forefinger.

Shaping macarons and disks

A purpose-designed silicone baking mat for macarons will help you pipe evenly shaped disks. If you don't have one, simply use a pencil to trace circles on a sheet of parchment paper, turn it upside down, and use it to line your baking sheet. Do the same to make large disks for layered desserts.

Checking when pouring custard, pastry cream, and variations are done

There are two ways of testing to see when a pouring custard (the foundation for many more complex creams) is done. The traditional test is to see whether it coats the back of a spoon. This involves dipping a spoon or heatproof spatula into the saucepan and holding it horizontally. Trace a horizontal line along the middle of it with your finger; if the separation between the two parts holds, the custard is cooked. The second requires checking the temperature, as custard reaches the right texture at 185°F (85°C), when it is pasteurized. If it is not cooled rapidly, it will continue to cook. Transfer it from the saucepan into a bowl set over a larger bowl filled with cold water and ice cubes.

Covering with plastic wrap and storing in airtight containers

We strongly recommend covering cooled pastry cream, as well as its more complex variations, with plastic wrap flush with the surface. The main reason is to prevent a skin from forming; the second is to prevent any odors from permeating it as it cools or waits to be used. Cut a sheet of wrap to the right size and press it lightly over the surface of the cream, removing any air bubbles.

Nuts, with the exception of pistachio nuts, develop their aromas more fully when lightly roasted. Their high oil content means that they should not be overexposed to high temperatures; for the same reason, they should be stored in an airtight container in the refrigerator and used rapidly.

Pouring honey or glucose syrup

Before measuring out honey or glucose syrup, wipe the container (spoon or bowl) very lightly with a touch of neutral oil so that it slips out easily.

Caramelization

There are two ways of making caramel: the wet method, where water and sugar are cooked together, and the dry method, in which sugar is cooked on its own.

Whichever you use, there are a few things to bear in mind. Select the most refined sugar possible (sugar cubes, if you can) to ensure that the sugar is free of the impurities that cause it to recrystallize or burn. In fact, the main concern in caramelizing sugar is preventing recrystallization. Making caramel is a process that will require your undivided attention and a few precautions. It's important for the sugar

to reach the right color: a pale caramel has little taste and a too-dark caramel will be bitter and probably even unusable.

Wet method

1. *Mise en place*: Make sure that all the material is clean. If you're using a copper pan, clean it with salt and vinegar and rinse it well. Otherwise, select an appropriately sized heavy-bottom saucepan. Prepare a bowl of cold water, a pastry brush, a skimming spoon, a candy thermometer, and a bowl of cold water larger than the pan so that you can dip the pan in it to stop the cooking process.

2. Spread the sugar evenly over the bottom of the pan. Pour in the water: you will need one-third of the weight of the sugar.

3. Bring to a boil over low to medium heat. The sugar should not cook too quickly as it will be hard to control the process. If you are using a gas range, ensure that the flames do not lick the sides of the pan.

4. As soon as the syrup begins to boil, skim it regularly. Rinse the thermometer under hot water and place it in the pan, ensuring that it does not touch the bottom. Do not touch the contents of the pan in any other way: this only adds to the risk of recrystallization.

5. Keep the insides of the pan clean. As it cooks, the sugar will splatter onto the sides. Dip the brush in water and wash the grains downward. If you don't do this, they will caramelize and affect the color of your preparation.

6. When the desired temperature is nearly reached (about 9°F–10°F or 5°C below the temperature required), turn the heat down.

7. At the temperature recommended by the recipe, immediately remove from the heat and dip the bottom of the pan into the cold water. Use the cooked sugar immediately.

8. If you accidentally cook the sugar to a higher temperature, add just a little cold water and cook again. Although you can get it back to the right temperature, you will not be able to reverse the color.

Dry method

A dry caramel is faster to make than a wet caramel, but is harder to control.

1. *Mise en place* is essential, with all equipment spotless: a clean heavy-bottom saucepan, a candy thermometer, a heatproof spatula or wooden spoon, and a bowl of cold water larger than the pan.

2. Spread the sugar evenly over the bottom of the saucepan.

3. Place over low to medium heat. The sugar should not cook too quickly. The edges and bottom are the first to liquefy and brown. With the spatula, push the liquefied sugar toward the center. The crucial point is reached when all the sugar starts to color: do not leave it unwatched as the cooking process accelerates at this point.

4. If the caramel begins to look lumpy, lower the heat and stir to melt those unwanted chunks. If they don't dissolve, they can be strained out later.

5. As soon as it has reached the color or temperature specified in the recipe, reduce the heat to low and add the liquid or butter. Immediately stir until smooth and proceed according to the recipe.

If you do not have a thermometer, refer to the test for caramel on page 237.

If you overcook the sugar, or if it recrystallizes, it is easier simply to start the process again.

Using gelatin sheets

Pastry chefs generally use gelatin in the form of transparent sheets, weighing precisely 2 grams, to ensure that certain creamy preparations hold their shape. Gelatin sheets are simple to use and dissolve better than powder, which can leave residual granules.

In this book, there are two methods for preparing gelatin sheets. One method specifies an exact quantity of water to use, while the other (more frequent) gives the instruction to "soften the gelatin sheets in a bowl of cold water."

Gelatin sheets absorb precisely five times their weight in water, and no more. For certain preparations, such as gelled fruit, it is important not to incorporate any excess water. For these recipes, therefore, we give an exact volume of water, sometimes specifying a certain number of tablespoons plus one or two teaspoons. If you follow these directions, the gelatin absorbs all the water and does not require squeezing. No unwanted liquid will be incorporated into the preparation. Depending on the recipe, it can be lightly heated to dissolve or directly incorporated into a warm mixture and stirred until dissolved

For preparations such as Bavarian creams, simply place the gelatin sheets in a bowl of cold water until they soften. This will take no more than 10 minutes. When they are rubbery, remove them from the bowl and squeeze out as much water as possible with your hands. Place them in the warm liquid or preparation and stir until you can no longer see any traces. Be careful not to let it boil at this stage. After that, simply follow the directions in the recipe for setting times.

Certain highly acidic fruits, such as kiwi and pineapple, as well as papaya, contain an enzyme that breaks down the protein molecules in gelatin and prevents it from setting. To avoid this problem, cook the fruit beforehand. Canned fruit can be used directly, as the pasteurization process neutralizes the enzyme.

Bear in mind that gelatin is an animal product; agar-agar, a substitute made from seaweed, may be used, but follow directions carefully for the quantities needed.

Cooking with chocolate

Recipes generally specify the percentage of cocoa solids. This indicates the amount of cocoa butter contained in the chocolate. Since cocoa butter, a fat, acts as a firming agent, not only does it affect the final texture of your preparation, it also determines how much cream is required.

If you don't have the exact type mentioned, use a chocolate with a percentage that is as close as possible. Of course, you shouldn't use milk chocolate and bittersweet interchangeably. For important advice on using chocolate, see page 181.

Using fleur de sel

Usually from Guérande, Brittany, fleur de sel is hand-harvested from the salt marshes of the Atlantic. It is a delicate, flaky salt taken from the surface, where it floats, not touching the coarser gray salt below. It is not used for cooking but for subtle seasoning, usually at the last minute. It is excellent with chocolate and caramel. If you don't have fleur de sel, substitute as delicate a flaky salt as possible.

Using and making vanilla sugar

Small sachets of vanilla sugar are found in practically every French home kitchen. If you can't get it online, it is easy to make. Recycle a used vanilla bean (see p. 195) by rinsing it and drying it thoroughly. Place it in a jar, cover with sugar, and seal. After about 1 week, you will have a delightfully fragrant sugar. Other substitutes include 1 teaspoon of pure vanilla extract with 1 tablespoon of sugar or the seeds of a vanilla bean.

Equipment

A **pastry brush** is useful for egg washes and moistening sponge layers. The **heavy-bottom pans** recommended in many of the recipes have the advantage of absorbing and distributing heat from the stovetop far more evenly than those with thin bases. This reduces the risk of burning and uneven cooking. Heavy-bottom pans are essential for cooking sugar and dairy produce, but you will be able to use them for all your other cooking, not just for caramels and pastry cream.

If you do not have a **bain-marie**, also known as a **double boiler**, make your own hot water bath by setting a heatproof bowl over a larger pan of simmering water, ensuring that the base of the bowl is not in direct contact with the base of the pan. Fragile ingredients such as chocolate should not come into direct contact with heat.

Whisks: a balloon whisk is best used to whip egg whites and cream, while a longer whisk is useful for stirring preparations, particularly in saucepans.

Egg whites and cream are most efficiently whipped in a **round-bottom bowl**, whether you are using a whisk or an electric beater.

A **flexible spatula** is the best utensil for folding flour into batters. These spatulas are available in rubber and silicone, and some are heat-resistant. Professionals use them as a hygienic alternative to the wooden spoon.

Tart and tartlet rings make it very easy to unmold tarts and serve them attractively, and are not as tricky to use as they may initially appear. An excellent alternative are tart pans with removable bottoms.

If you're making jams and jellies, **copper pots** give the best results. Not only does copper diffuse heat more evenly than other metals, but the copper oxide facilitates the solidification of pectin, the setting agent, whether it is added or occurs naturally in your fruit.

Dessert rings, higher than tart rings, help you assemble complex desserts and ensure that their shape remains neat.

Glossary of techniques and terms

A - B

abaisser

French term meaning to roll out pastry with a rolling pin or in a laminator, to the required thickness.

bain-marie

A utensil, also known as a double boiler or a hot water bath, which consists of an outer container to hold water and an inner container in which the ingredients to be heated or cooked are placed. The hot water may either be simmering or at a slightly lower temperature, depending on the recipe.

baking blind

A technique used for pastry shells that either require longer cooking times than their fillings, or are to be filled with an uncooked garnish. The pastry is pricked all over and left to rest, then lined with parchment paper weighted with dried beans or pie weights to ensure the base doesn't rise. The paper and weights are removed before the end of the cooking time so that the pastry can turn an even, golden color.

beurre manié

A mixture of softened butter and flour used as a thickening agent in liquids. It is added in small pieces and beaten in thoroughly.

beurre noisette

A browned butter, made by heating the butter gently. The milk proteins and sugar in the whey caramelize, giving the butter its distinctive hazelnut (*noisette* in French) aroma. From the moment it bubbles, it requires careful attention, just like caramel. It must be removed from the heat as soon as it becomes deep brown in color.

beurre pommade

Softened butter, brought to room temperature, which is whipped or beaten until creamy.

To melt butter, simply place it in a small saucepan over medium heat. Remove as soon as it is liquid.

blanching

An ingredient is blanched by plunging it into boiling water briefly, then removing and draining it, or refreshing it in ice water before draining. The technique can be used to remove bitterness; citrus peel needs to be blanched several times.

boiling

Heating a liquid until it reaches "boiling point," which for water occurs at 212°F (100°C) and for certain oils and fats can be 400°F (200°C).

C

candying (crystallizing)

This is a method of preservation using sugar syrup. The fruit is blanched and drained before being placed in increasingly concentrated sugar syrup solutions over a period of time. Any water in the fruit is gradually replaced by the syrup and the fruit is thus preserved.

caramelizing (see p. 467 for full explanation)

Heating sugar—either with water (wet method) or on its own (dry method)—until it turns brown and liquefies into caramel.

clarifying

To clarify butter it needs to be melted slowly in a heavy-bottom saucepan so that the water content can evaporate. The milk solids will sink to the bottom. When the foam stops rising to the top, remove the saucepan from the heat and skim. Strain it through a fine-mesh sieve into a heat-resistant container, ensuring that any solids remain behind. You will be left with the butterfat, which keeps for several weeks in the refrigerator.

Clarified butter can be used as a substitute for cocoa butter in certain recipes but it has other uses. Without the milk solids, clarified butter has a higher "smoke point" (350°F/180°C), thereby facilitating cooking. Note that when "clarified butter" is listed as an ingredient, the weight in grams is given after clarification, i.e. with about 20–25 percent of its volume removed.

coating

Applying a covering of chocolate, icing, or other ingredient to improve the appearance of a dish.

See also "coating the back of a spoon," p. 467.

cocoa butter

The fat that is naturally present in the cocoa bean. Cocoa butter can be added when couverture chocolate is made. It is a solid fat that acts as a hardener in certain preparations.

compote

A dessert of fresh or dried fruit in a sugar syrup.

coulis

A fruit coulis is a thick sauce made from raw or cooked fruit that is puréed with sugar and used to accompany hot or cold dessert dishes.

creaming

Combining sugar with a solid fat, usually butter. The mixture should increase in volume and become paler in color.

D

deglazing

Liquid is poured into a pan after its contents have been emptied to aid the removal of any congealed solids from the bottom of the pan, by scraping and stirring to combine them with the liquid. The liquid is worked over a high heat and brought to a simmer. It results in a flavorful sauce or base for a sauce.

détrempe

A French term that designates the flour and water paste that is a base for pastry dough, before the butter is added to make puff pastry, croissant dough, and so on.

dicing

Cutting an ingredient into small cubes. Fruit and vegetables are often diced; butter can also be diced.

drying out

A technique used when cooking choux pastry. The dough is cooked initially at a higher temperature to ensure it rises quickly and forms a crust; the temperature is then lowered and the oven door opened to evacuate any remaining moisture from the pastry.

E

emulsifying

Combining two liquids that normally don't mix, such as water and oil, to create an emulsion.

en papillote

This is a method of cooking in baking parchment or aluminum foil to preserve all the juices. *Papillote* also describes the wrapping around some candies or chocolate.

F

flambéing

Involves pouring an alcoholic beverage (often cognac or liqueur) over a food and then setting a flame to it. The process intensifies the flavor of the dish and is often recommended when the juices in a pan are required to make a sauce. It is also a rather spectacular way to serve certain desserts.

To flambé, warm the liqueur in a deep dish, pour it over the hot food, then ignite, using a long match set to the edge of the dish holding the food. Allow to cook until all the flames have burned out, and do not lean over the dish.

For the recipes in this book, only the liqueur for the Baked Alaska (p. 450) needs prior warming, to no more than about 104°F (40°C).

folding in

This is a technique used to incorporate whipped cream or egg whites into other preparations, and dry ingredients into thicker batters. The aim in both cases is to retain a light, airy texture. You may need to incorporate the ingredients in several additions, particularly if there is a significant difference in textures. For the whipped cream or egg whites into which you have carefully incorporated air bubbles, use either a flexible spatula or a whisk. Start in the center and rotate the mixing bowl as you draw the utensil outward and then back to the center. Do not press against the sides of the bowl. For dry ingredients, a flexible spatula works efficiently and the movement is the same. In both cases, it's essential to stop as soon as the mixture is smooth and has reached a uniform color. If you overmix, you will deflate the whipped cream or egg whites, or toughen the texture of your batter.

fondant

A paste made from a sugar syrup mixture that is kneaded as it cools to make a smooth paste. It can be used to make candies or heated to make a pouring fondant that can be used as an icing.

G

garnishing

Finishing a dish with one or several accompaniments; these can range from a simple scattering of nuts to more elaborate combinations. A garnish is designed to add a visual embellishment or contrast, and usually to contribute flavor as well.

glazing

In pâtisserie, glazing means covering the top (and in some cases, the sides) of a tart with a fondant icing, water icing, chocolate, sugar syrup, fruit glaze, etc. Some pastries (such as the *galette des rois*) may be glazed by dusting with confectioners' sugar or basting with sugar syrup as soon as they are removed from the oven.

gratin

A crust, usually made up of breadcrumbs and egg or breadcrumbs and grated cheese, which protects the food beneath and forms a tasty, crusty layer when broiled or browned in the oven.

I - K

infusing

To infuse a liquid is to steep an aromatic ingredient in it until the flavor is imparted to the liquid. Hot cream is commonly infused to create a base for desserts; wine and milk can also be infused with herbs, spices, and citrus zest. Depending on the texture and size of the aromatic ingredient, the liquid may need to be strained before use.

kneading

A technique used for working dough, either by hand or using a mixer fitted with a dough hook. It develops the gluten in the flour, which acts as a binding agent and captures the gases created by the yeast. Manual kneading requires pressing, folding, and turning using both hands, and then pushing away from the body. When a dough is well kneaded it will be smooth and elastic.

L

laminator
A machine for rolling pasta or pastry dough.

lining
To line a tart ring with dough, as a base for a tart, pie, etc. When the dough is rolled out, transfer it from the work surface by draping it over the rolling pin. Center it over the prepared tart ring or pan. Unroll it and press it in gently so that it fits snugly. Press the dough into the sides and trim it by rolling the rolling pin in one movement from one side to another; the excess dough will be neatly cut off.

M

macerating
Softening or soaking raw or dried foods (fruits, for example) using a liquid such as liqueur, sugar syrup, or brandy. This process imparts flavor and is the method used to produce cordials and liqueurs (see p. 215).

making a well
Professionals often pour their flour in a ring on a work surface and pour the liquid ingredients into the center (the "well") to be gradually incorporated. You can do the same in a mixing bowl, making a hollow with a spoon in the center. Simply pour in the liquid ingredients and beat them in gradually.

marbling
A technique used to create an attractive and professional finish on a cake or a dessert or as a background for a plated dessert (see p. 125).

masking
To cover evenly with a cream, couverture chocolate glaze, almond paste, jam, or other ingredient to "mask" any blemishes (see p. 126).

mise en place (see p. 466 for full explanation)
Setting up equipment and preparing ingredients (measuring, cleaning, chopping, etc.) before beginning a recipe.

moistening
A technique that adds flavor to sponge layers. A syrup or fruit juice is dabbed lightly onto the sponge using a brush (see p. 133).

P

pastillage
This is a confectionery paste that is used to decorate cakes. It is made of confectioners' sugar mixed with water and gelatin, then kneaded. Coloring is sometimes added before it is rolled to the desired shape and dried out thoroughly (see p. 139).

pâte à bombe
A whisked preparation of eggs and sugar that is used as the base for buttercream and mousse recipes.

pâte à foncer
"Lining" pastry, or plain tart crust. This can be made in sweet or savory versions, depending on the recipe.

pâte brisée
Shortcrust pastry, used as the basis for a range of tarts, flans, and pies.

pâte fermentée
A fermented starter dough that is allowed to ferment for a period before being added to the main dough mix, imparting extra flavor.

pâtisserie
This term from French describes the baked goods themselves, the place where they are sold, and the offerings produced by the pâtissier (pastry chef), whose output also includes a wide range of desserts.

piping (see p. 466 for full explanation)
Using a pastry or piping bag that can be fitted with various tips to pipe out evenly sized and shaped portions of batter or icing.

poaching
Cooking by heating in a simmering liquid. Fruit is poached in sugar syrup, and other desserts, such as mousses, are produced using a poaching method in the oven, with the dishes placed in a baking pan half-filled with water.

Q - R

quenelle
In dessert terms, a serving of ice cream or sorbet shaped into an oval or egg shape using spoons is referred to as a quenelle.

resting (chilling)
It is vital for pastry doughs or batters to "rest" in the refrigerator when being prepared. It allows the gluten to relax so the dough doesn't become too elastic, and chilled dough with reduced elasticity is much easier to roll out.

ribbon stage
When eggs or egg yolks and sugar are beaten together sufficiently well, whether in a mixing bowl or over a bain-marie, the mixture reaches the ribbon stage. This means that it is so thick that when it is lifted with a spatula or the beaters, it flows slowly downward, making folds like a ribbon.

rising (proving)
The term used to describe a yeast dough swelling with the activity of the yeast.

rolling out

Flattening dough with a rolling pin to the desired thickness. To roll out dough, use as little flour as possible to prevent the dough from sticking to the work surface. Scatter it from between your fingertips, as if you were sowing seeds. If you dust the surface too heavily, some of the flour will inevitably be incorporated into the dough and change the texture. Keep turning the dough so that it does not stick after pressure is applied.

rubbing in

Combining flour with fat using the fingertips, as in the first stage of producing a pastry dough. The texture should resemble sand. The remaining ingredients are added to this base.

S

sifting (sieving)

Putting powdered ingredients through a sieve to remove any lumps, as well as to aerate and combine certain ingredients. Flour should be sifted with baking powder so that the raising agent is well distributed. Unsweetened cocoa powder tends to form lumps and should always be sifted before it is used.

softening

Butter, depending on its fat content and the temperature in your kitchen, needs time to soften. No hard and fast rules for time can be given, but try not to use butter straight from the refrigerator if your recipe calls for butter at room temperature. To speed up the process, dice it and leave in a warm place, but don't let it melt.

sponge base (*biscuit*)

This forms the base for many classic desserts. It uses flour, eggs, and sugar as its basic ingredients. French cakes and desserts often comprise numerous sponge layers that are always very thin. When ready for baking the batter is spread out thinly on baking sheets and cut to the desired shape when cooked and cooled, rather than being baked as a cake that rises high and is then cut horizontally.

T · V · W · Z

tempering

The process of heating and cooling chocolate to make it ready for use for dipping, undercoating, and coating (see p. 182).

viennoiserie

The French word refers to specific bakery offerings —not usually bread, but richer doughs or puff pastries, including croissants, brioches, fruit buns, etc. They are often eaten for breakfast in France. The term sometimes encompasses some of the more elaborate breads as well.

whisking (whipping)

Beating ingredients, such as cream or egg whites, with a whisk until they are light, to incorporate air bubbles into them.

zest

Citrus zest (also called rind) refers only to the colored outer part of the skin, the most flavorful part of the outer layer. Citrus peel includes the peel, the bitter white pith, and sometimes a little of the flesh. It must be prepared with a suitably sharp knife. When a recipe calls for finely grated zest, be careful to stop zesting as soon as you see the white pith. You can juice the fruit for another (or the same) recipe.

Index

Video sequences (QR codes)

The video sequences show professionals at work and therefore the quantities, cooking times, and other specifics may vary slightly from the recipes in the book, which have been adapted for use in the home. In addition, the sequences show the key steps but do not necessarily include all the details of the recipes in the book. When putting techniques into practice or making recipes, follow the precise indications given in the book.

Acknowledgments

The authors wish to thank the many partners and suppliers who made this book possible:

• **Bordier:** butter for the table and cooking (www.lebeurrebordier.com)
• **Bragard:** chefs' clothing (www.bragard.fr)
• **CNGF:** Confédération nationale des Glaciers de France (www.lemondedudessert.fr)
• **Cointreau:** liqueurs for pastry (www.cointreau.fr)
• **Didier Stéphan's web site:** professional demonstrations of pastry and ice-cream making (www.sucreglace.com)
• **Ducros:** spices (www.ducros.fr)
• **Ercuis:** tableware (www.ercuis.com)
• **Eurolam:** knives (www.eurolam-thiers.com)
• **GH diffusion:** food packaging (gh-diffusion.com)
• **Lactalis:** dairy products (www.lactalis.fr)
• **Louaisil:** fresh fruit and vegetables
• **Lycée hôtelier Sainte-Thérèse, La Guerche-de-Bretagne** (www.lyceehotelier.com)
• **Méchinaud:** aromatic herbs and vegetables for restaurants (www.mechinaud-saveurs.com)
• **Panaget:** wooden workstations (www.panaget.com)
• **Raison:** hard cider and apple juice (www.loicraison.fr)
• **Raynaud:** Limoges porcelain (www.raynaud.fr)
• **Ricard:** alcoholic beverages (www.ricard.fr)
• **Silikomart:** silicone molds and baking mats (www.silikomart.com)
• **Sojasun:** soy-based products (www.sojasun.com)
• **Super U:** groceries (www.superu-laguerchedebretagne.com)
• **Transgourmet:** supplies for pastry making (www.transgourmet.fr)
• **Triballat:** dairy products (www.triballat.fr)
• **Vahiné:** nuts and candied fruit, baking aids (www.vahine.fr)